Cultural Commons and Urban Dynamics

Emanuela Macrì · Valeria Morea ·
Michele Trimarchi
Editors

Cultural Commons and Urban Dynamics

A Multidisciplinary Perspective

Springer

Editors
Emanuela Macrì
Magna Graecia University
Catanzaro, Italy

Valeria Morea
Erasmus University Rotterdam
Rotterdam, The Netherlands

Michele Trimarchi
Magna Graecia University
Catanzaro, Italy

ISBN 978-3-030-54417-1 ISBN 978-3-030-54418-8 (eBook)
https://doi.org/10.1007/978-3-030-54418-8

This Springer imprint is published by the registered company Springer Nature Switzerland AG
The registered company address is: Gewerbestrasse 11, 6330 Cham, Switzerland

Acknowledgements

This volume has been made possible thanks to the joint effort and trust of many people and institutions. Its source is the international project Innovate Heritage whose founders Caterina Benincasa and Elliat Graney-Saucke supported and diffused the conference "Cultural Commons and Urban Dynamics. A New Economic Paradigm for a Complex Social Map", held in Catanzaro on 11 and 12 October 2019 and funded by the University of Catanzaro "Magna Graecia", whose Chancellor is Professor Giovanni Battista De Sarro, and the Department of Laws, Economics and Sociology, whose Director is Professor Geremia Romano. Our sincere gratitude also extends to the members of the scientific committee Caterina Benincasa, Lia Fassari, Emma Galli, Manfred Holler, Arjo Klamer, Martina Löw and Danila Longo for their methodological and critical contributions; to the Journal of Public Finance and Public Choice and the European Journal of Creative Processes in Cities and Landscapes for the support; and to the artist Ruxandra Lupu who involved the participants in a thrilling creative game whose outcomes unfortunately cannot be incorporated in a book. Last but not least, we are grateful to the reviewers who accepted to read the chapters of this book offering the authors insightful remarks and suggestions.

Introduction: Urban Transition in a Multiple Perspective

In October 2019 a group of economists, sociologists, urban planners, political scientists and artists met in Catanzaro, Italy, to discuss the complex issues arising from a magmatic period when the relationship between society, space and time is radically changing. Nobody could imagine that unexpected events would have emphasised, dramatised and accelerated the need for further interpretations aimed at anticipating the possible shape of the cultural, social and economic paradigm of the next years. Such a need was already emerging from the decline of the industrial society.

In the last 30 years accumulation and technology, variously combined with their predictable outcome of new inequalities and conflicts, have developed around the city as the hub where personal, social, cultural and professional flows have been converging, overcrowding residential areas, relocating offices and institutions, intensifying the friction between centre and periphery, and at the same time among the various patches of multicultural communities. The centrality of these urban hubs has also exerted a powerful influence upon cultural heritage and international tourism, hence redrawing the balance of costs and benefits for the urban communities.

Paradoxically, maybe predictably, metropolitan congestion had elicited a reaction: a growing number of professionals, creative artists and families inverted the route and went back to smaller, smoother places where time is not so rigid, space allows them a more relaxed life, and work is possible, thanks to technology. From digital nomads consulting in marketing for big companies and living in seaside villages, to 'boomerangs' settling in provincial towns and working for metropolitan customers, the need for a more relaxed dimension is spreading throughout the world. The emergency caused by the virus is intensifying such processes that can be interpreted as the most evident symptom of the passage between the late-industrial paradigm and the emerging economic and social structure. At the same time, it is amplifying conflicts, frictions and inequalities generated by the magmatic patchwork of different social groups that share congested spaces and peak times in the metropolitan fabric.

Thus, within such a radical change, the urban community is being modified, also due to the emersion of new skills and competences whose dynamics and fertilisation will lead to reshaping the productive sector, the labour market and the social urgencies. Within such a rapid change, the specialisation rush is leaving space to unstructured hybridisations, within the need to combine technical features and humanistic approaches for a new cultural value chain, aimed at crafting the evolving identity of contemporary society. A multidisciplinary approach is then needed in order for the arising complex issues and their delicate implications to be interpreted and dealt with.

This book collects the views and discussions of many scholars active in different areas that share the question mark whereby the conference on Cultural Commons and Urban Dynamics was shaped, in the awareness that an intensive discussion among academics, professionals and artists on shared concerns would be beneficial in pushing the boundaries of each discipline. We believe that a good book ends with more questions than answers. Thus, we tried to approach the contributions in a way that instigates further dialogue within and between disciplines. An intriguing agenda for future research emerges from the investigations collected in this volume. The aim is to offer a wider scope for interpretation of each involved discipline, whose conventional knowledge seems to be less eloquent in interpreting the emerging phenomena.

The book is organised in four parts. The contributions are grouped based on a combination of methodological approaches and objects of analysis. The value of cultural commons in the urban fabric is focused upon in the first part of the book, where the scope and variety of commons are discussed (Galli and Garzarelli) from Hardin's tragedy to more optimistic and constructive theories. Commons are more pervasive, and their analysis may prove insightful in order for us to interpret complex interactions. Their analysis can prove useful for the design of policies (Borchi), the balance of powers in the urban fabric (Holler and Rupp), the extraction of value from cultural heritage (Bertacchini), the infrastructural choices in the arts system (Sabatini) and the evolution of public art as a driver for shared practices (Morea).

The second part explores the versatile value chain expressed by the city. The fertile network of connections and interactions crossing its infrastructure is a unique source of creativity (Dalfovo), faces delicate issues of material and symbolic accessibility (Errante), and deals with digital tools able to encourage new protocols of co-operation (Dalla Chiesa). In such a respect, the shape of cities generates a common view able to respond to the urgency of shaping multiple identities (Fassari), and can inspire innovative projects aimed at fertilising new functions and unexpected cultural exchanges (Longo, Boeri, Roversi and Orlandi).

The variety of cultural commons, and their crucial value for the urban communities, are reflected in many cases, whose heterogeneous sources, features and impact make any attempts at drawing a model quite difficult and possibly contradictory. In such a respect, cultural commons can arise from shared values in a network of interactions (Antonucci), the preservation of past identity, rites and beliefs in a changing environment (Macrì), the ongoing interactions among different cultural groups (Migone), the struggle—and the eventual frictions—aimed at a diffused acknowledgement of rights (Garcia and Schuck), the ambiguity of institutional dynamics among the legal framework, the municipal action and the urban community (Lenna, Randazzo and Trimarchi).

What happens out there? Cultural commons are older than formal rules: as many ancient experiences show, the city is a collective enterprise (Frascarelli). They prove a fertile cauldron for emerging ferments in the arts system, extracting new values from creativity (Oliana), and at the same time can give eloquent visibility to digital protest, overcoming rules crafted for analogic fractures (Clay). Cities have many stories to tell, and their complex identity can be offered to voyagers inclined to explore them (Bollati and Collina). More than words, images can give us a clear perception of urban dynamics, thanks to the eloquence of a graphic novel (Arboleda and Jankiewicz).

The book combines different views and examines various experiences, starting from the growing literature on commons and focusing upon the specific features of cultural commons, whose value chain stems from the joint dynamics of material infrastructures and shared social practices, within the effective synergy between the analogic and the digital dimensions. The likely direction of our close future will represent a clear change in personal and professional lives, as well as in social, productive and commercial exchanges. In such a framework, commons are mainly cultural, since they refer to the search for shared identity, common motivation, active practices and possibly semantic permeability with respect to the whole urban community.

The exploration of commons will exert a strong impact on our relationship with a more inclusive and friendly space, as well as with a less demanding and rigid time. The benefits of the multidisciplinary approach adopted in the 2019 conference and incorporated in this book invite readers to widen the scope of their cultural route, also in the light of the growing need for a more versatile society in which the myth of competition will gradually give space to shared practices and common challenges.

Emanuela Macrì
Valeria Morea
Michele Trimarchi

Contents

Urban Commons as a Response to Institutional Constraints

From Goods to Orders and Rules of Governance: A Preliminary Exploration . . . 3
Emma Galli and Giampaolo Garzarelli

Towards a Policy for the Cultural Commons . . . 11
Alice Borchi

Urban Heritage as Cultural Capital, District, and Commons: An Economic Perspective . . . 25
Enrico E. Bertacchini

Power in Networks and the Urban Space . . . 37
Manfred J. Holler and Florian Rupp

Commoning the Stage: The Complex Semantics of the Theatre Commons . . . 53
Francesca Sabatini

Public Art Today. How Public Art Sheds Light on the Future of the Theory of Commons . . . 79
Valeria Morea

Art and the City: Dialogues Between Space and Community

The Rocking Cradle of Creativity. Tales of Inertia and Frictions, Cultural and Urban Transformations, Creative Actions . . . 95
Mariangela Dalfovo

Public Space: Mapping the Physical, Social and Cultural Accessibility for the Creation of Urban Commons . . . 113
Lidia Errante

Enhancing Human and Urban Capital: A Value-Oriented Approach . . . 141
Danila Longo, Andrea Boeri, Rossella Roversi, and Serena Orlandi

The Social Aesthetics of Cultural Commons 163
Letteria G. Fassari

From Digitalisation to Crowdfunding Platforms: Fomenting the Cultural Commons 173
Carolina Dalla Chiesa

Experiences of Commons Between Antagonisms and Strategies

From Urban Commons to Commoning as Social Practice 189
Federica Antonucci

Cultural Commons and Historical Identity: The Experience of the Arbëreshë Community in Southern Italy 205
Emanuela Macrì

Migrant Cultures. Contributions of NGOs and Community-Based Organizations to Safeguarding Intangible Cultural Heritage in Santiago, Chile 221
Pascuala Migone

Feminist Movements in the City: New Strategies of Commons in Latin American Context 241
Carolina Gallo Garcia and Elena de Oliveira Schuck

Can Social Fractures Affect the Legal Framework?Towards an Institutional Craftsmanship 255
Verena Lenna, Roberto Randazzo, and Michele Trimarchi

A New Urban Agenda: Interpretation and Action

At the Fringe of Human Freedom: The Concept of Space and Time Within Urban Settlements and Among Nomads in Antiquity 281
Raffaella Frascarelli

Over There: The Mediterranean Surface and the Archetype of the Island as Contemporary Paradigms for Accessing Cultural Commons 297
Novella Oliana

The Design for a Welcoming City: Urban Space and Visitor Flow 309
Ilaria Bollati and Luisa Collina

The Vicissitudes of Digital Dissent 323
Arthur Clay

Berlin, a Repurposed Ruin, and Constant Change as the Fixed Condition: A Photo-Comic 341
Pablo Arboleda and Pawel Jankiewicz

Editors and Contributors

About the Editors

Emanuela Macrì, Ph.D. is post-doc Research Fellow at the Department of Laws, Economics and Sociology of the "Magna Graecia" University of Catanzaro (Italy) where she also teaches Political Economy and Cultural Economics. She holds a Doctor Europaeus Ph.D. in Health Economics and Management at the "Magna Graecia" University. Her research interests lie in the fields of cultural economics and management with a focus on the impact of culture on health and education.

Valeria Morea, Ph.D. is Lecturer and Course Coordinator at Erasmus School of History, Culture and Communication, Department of Arts and Culture, Rotterdam. She teaches Cultural Economics, Economic Geography of Creativity and Urban Development, and Cultural Management and Marketing. Her research explores art in public spaces, the theory of commons and the relationship between the arts and urban well-being.

Michele Trimarchi, Ph.D. is Professor of Public Economics at "Magna Graecia" University of Catanzaro and teaches Cultural Economics at the University of Bologna. He is member of the editorial board of Creative Industries Journal and of the international council of the Creative Industries Federation. His research focuses on cultural economics and policy, strategies of the arts organisations, and contemporary art.

Contributors

Federica Antonucci Department of Architecture and Territory, Mediterranea University, Reggio Calabria, Italy

Pablo Arboleda School of Geographical and Earth Sciences, University of Glasgow, Glasgow, UK

Enrico E. Bertacchini Department of Economics and Statistics "Cognetti de Martiis", University of Turin, Turin, Italy

Andrea Boeri Department of Architecture, University of Bologna, Bologna, Italy

Ilaria Bollati Department of Design, Politecnico di Milano, Milan, Italy

Alice Borchi Faculty of Arts, Humanities and Cultures, University of Leeds, Leeds, UK

Arthur Clay Virtuale Switzerland, Basel, Switzerland;
'Digital Art Weeks' International, Zurich, Switzerland

Luisa Collina Department of Design, Politecnico di Milano, Milan, Italy

Mariangela Dalfovo Trento, Italy

Carolina Dalla Chiesa Erasmus School of History, Culture and Communication, Rotterdam, The Netherlands

Lidia Errante Department of Architecture and Territory, Mediterranea University, Reggio Calabria, Italy

Letteria G. Fassari Department of Social Sciences and Economics, Sapienza Università di Roma, Rome, Italy

Raffaella Frascarelli Nomas Foundation, Rome, Italy;
Research Unit's Laboratory Sociological Aesthetics, Department of Sociology of Cultural Processes and Sociology of Contemporary Cultures-DiSSE, Faculty of Political, Sociological and Communication Sciences, Sapienza Università di Roma, Rome, Italy

Emma Galli Department of Social Sciences and Economics, Sapienza Università di Roma, Rome, Italy

Carolina Gallo Garcia State University of Campinas (UNICAMP), Campinas, Brazil

Giampaolo Garzarelli Department of Social Sciences and Economics, Sapienza Università di Roma, Rome, Italy;
IPEG, SEF, University of the Witwatersrand, Johannesburg, South Africa

Manfred J. Holler University of Hamburg, Hamburg, Germany;
CCR-Munich, Munich, Germany

Pawel Jankiewicz Independent Writer, Berlin, Germany

Verena Lenna IUAV, Venice, Italy;
KU Leuven, Belgium

Danila Longo Department of Architecture, University of Bologna, Bologna, Italy

Emanuela Macrì Department of Laws, Economics and Sociology, Magna Graecia University, Catanzaro, Italy

Pascuala Migone Santiago, Chile

Valeria Morea Erasmus School of History, Culture and Communication, Rotterdam, The Netherlands

Novella Oliana Department of Visual Arts, Aix Marseille Université, Marseille, France

Elena de Oliveira Schuck Brazilian Center of Analysis and Planning (CEBRAP), São Paulo, Brazil

Serena Orlandi Department of Architecture, University of Bologna, Bologna, Italy

Roberto Randazzo Lawyer in Rome, Barrister at the Supreme Court, Rome, Italy

Rossella Roversi Department of Architecture, University of Bologna, Bologna, Italy

Florian Rupp CCR-Munich, Munich, Germany;
Technical University Munich, Munich, Germany

Francesca Sabatini Department of Architecture and Territory, Mediterranea University, Reggio Calabria, Italy

Michele Trimarchi Department of Laws, Economics and Sociology, Magna Graecia University, Catanzaro, Italy

Urban Commons as a Response to Institutional Constraints

From Goods to Orders and Rules of Governance: A Preliminary Exploration

Emma Galli and Giampaolo Garzarelli

Abstract

The purpose of this work is to bring into more explicit contact the theory of commons as developed by Elinor Ostrom and collaborators with the theory of order as developed by Friedrich A. von Hayek. We do so by shifting emphasis from analyzing different types of goods in terms of their intrinsic properties, to goods being analyzed in terms of how the intrinsic properties lead to extrinsic consequences in terms of different governance solutions. Our preliminary considerations suggest that Ostrom and Hayek are complementary when it comes to considering governance solutions. Ostrom's rules for the management of the commons complement Hayek's distinction between orders with abstract and specific rules. Governance is about differences in kinds of rules as much as it is about degrees of rules.

1 The Spectrum of Goods

We are mainly accustomed to defining—and comparing—different types of goods in terms of their intrinsic economic properties. A private good is rival (consumption of one unit of the good by an individual precludes the consumption of the same unit by another individual) and excludable (the person who does not pay a good cannot consume it). A public good is instead defined by the polar opposite intrinsic

E. Galli · G. Garzarelli (✉)
Department of Social Sciences and Economics, Sapienza Università di Roma, Rome, Italy
e-mail: giampaolo.garzarelli@gmail.com

E. Galli
e-mail: emma.galli@uniroma1.it

G. Garzarelli
IPEG, SEF, University of the Witwatersrand, Johannesburg, South Africa

E. Macrì et al. (eds.), *Cultural Commons and Urban Dynamics*,
https://doi.org/10.1007/978-3-030-54418-8_1

properties, namely, non-rivalry and non-excludability. Over the years, other goods have been defined along intermediate lines. Thus, a club (or quasi-public) good is non-rival (up to congestion), but excludable; and a commons (or an open-access) good is rival but non-excludable. Figure 1 shows the standard taxonomy of these goods according to their intrinsic economic properties.

Most of the discipline of public finance effectively verges on how the intrinsic properties of different goods create problems for standard welfare reasoning, leading to so-called market failure and, by difference, to direct government intervention. One needs to simply recall the Samuelsonian statement that, given the negative incentive that a public good engenders for preference revelation, there is the impossibility "of a decentralized spontaneous solution" for the supply of public goods (Samuelson 1954, p. 388). Tiebout (1956), of course, provocatively (Fischel 2001) proved Samuelson wrong with the well-known notion of spontaneous consumer–voter sorting—later dubbed *voting with the feet*. The implications of Tiebout's provocation for the theoretical study of federalism are history.

More generally, Tiebout contains, albeit less explicitly, a lesson of another nature—on method. Tiebout did not present a market failure argument; what he did, if somewhat implicitly, is to perform comparative institutional analysis. He compared the costs and benefits of the ballot to those of a decentralized public sector in terms of learning about public good preferences. In other words, we see a shift in emphasis from analyzing different types of goods in terms of their intrinsic properties, to goods being analyzed in terms of how the intrinsic properties lead to extrinsic consequences in terms of different governance solutions (Garzarelli 2004).

If Tiebout is implicitly a vanguard application of comparative institutional analysis to see if public goods can be supplied through decentralization, Buchanan's theory of clubs (1965) is the first work to consider goods and their different intrinsic properties in terms of an explicit governance solution. The optimal club equilibrium from Buchanan's model in fact is "defined in the process of its emergence" (Buchanan 1982), namely, it endogenously yields both optimal number of club members and optimal level of club good (non-rival and exclusive).

	Rival	Nonrival
Exclusive	Private good	Club or quasipublic good
Nonexclusive	Commons or open access good	Public good

Fig. 1 A standard taxonomy of goods

The same can be said about governance when commons are involved, though the approach is not as theoretically driven, but more of a mixture of fieldwork and theory. Hardin's allegory of a pasture open to all (1968, p. 1244) is proposed to understand how a case of institutional failure occurs. As a rational agent, each "herdsman will try to keep as many cattle as possible on the commons … to maximize his gain … Each man is locked into a system that compels him to increase his herd without limit—in a world that is limited. Ruin is the destination toward which all men rush, each pursuing his own best interest in a society that believes in the freedom of the commons. Freedom in the commons brings ruin to all." As Frischmann (2013, p. 215) emphasizes, Hardin's tragedy illustrates "a rather standard economics problem of interdependence, which involves issues of collective goods or external effects." Hardin (1968) pointed out that the tragedy of the commons was occurring because of a lack of an extrinsic governance solution considering the intrinsic properties of an open-access good. He basically asked for the development of an institutional solution about how to govern goods that are rival and nonexclusive. In his view, commons governance requires either public intervention, which abolishes private autonomy to reduce the over-exploitation of the resource, i.e., the state, or the establishment and enforcement of property and exclusion rights, i.e., the market. In other words, government regulation and privatization are considered alternative ways to solve the problem of resource allocation limiting the use, and guaranteeing the sustainability, of the good.

As Frischmann et al. (2019, p. 218) recall, going through the reactions to Hardin's view (1968), "Elinor Ostrom and other social scientists challenged the frame set by Hardin by asking two foundational sets of questions: First, how well does the tragedy of the commons allegory describe reality? Is it a useful theory for making predictions about real-world behavior of individuals sharing common-pool resources? Does it describe a normal or exceptional situation? Does it provide a useful basis for choosing or designing regulatory solutions? Second, does the binary choice between government command-and-control regulation and private property-enabled markets reflect the full range of options?" (see also Frischmann 2013, p. 390).

2 Governing the Commons

Ostrom (and collaborators) showed that common goods also have an endogenous solution: there are different governance solutions that solve different problems tied to different types of rival and nonexclusive goods. Alternatively stated, not all common goods have identical governance solutions, but the important matter is that the solutions are neither pure market nor pure state, which is the same conclusion one reaches in club theory. The governance world is not in black and white, but in shades of gray.

So, the work of Buchanan (1965) and Ostrom (e.g., 1998) and, less directly, of Tiebout (1956) can be seen as entailing a shift from the polar governance categories of market and state to more nuanced categories of governance. Governance trade-offs are no longer either-or choices, but, like goods, occur along a spectrum. This means that there is a broader interest not just in the intrinsic economic properties of different goods but also in the extrinsic feasible governance categories linked to different goods.

We believe that more attention ought to be given to different goods vis-à-vis their governance structures. In this respect, Hayek provides a useful perspective by thinking about feasible, alternative governance structures—what he called social orders—in terms of abstract and specific rules. Different governance is defined in terms of rules; however, the original issue of reasoning according to polar extremes that one finds in the taxonomy of goods, one finds in Hayek's theory of governance. Our interest is to see how reasoning according to a different good, namely, the commons, can offer insights about orders that are not just polar extremes but operate at different degrees of abstraction.

3 Social Orders and Types of Rules

Hayek (2013) long ago pointed out that it is possible to conceive different social orders in terms of different types of rules. A market is governed by rules that are abstract. Abstract rules are not directed toward any specific end. Rather they are about conveying a general mode of acting sensibly under specific situations that we cannot fully predict and act upon through traditional economic reasoning (maximization subject to constraints). Anticipating many (e.g., Smith 2003; Gigerenzer 2014), Hayek basically asserts that the way to deal with the complexity of everyday choices is by means of rules that do not deal with concrete scenarios. In his words, abstract "concepts are a means to cope with the complexity of the concrete which our mind is not fully capable of mastering … We never act, and could never act, in full consideration of all the facts of a particular situation, but always by singling out as relevant only some aspects of it" (Hayek 2013, p. 29). In this sense, the market is the quintessential abstract-rule governance: it coordinates behavior spontaneously through relative prices as the need emerges. Each time, coordination is an outcome of idiosyncratic adjustment processes, not a predefined static optimization.

When rules are not abstract but specific (or concrete), we have direction toward a specific end. This marks the passage from spontaneity (market order) to design in governance (a planned order that is an organization). Order is "a state of affairs in which a multiplicity of elements of various kinds are so related to each other that we may learn from our acquaintance with some spatial or temporal part of the whole to form correct expectations concerning the rest, or at least expectations which have a good chance of proving correct" (Hayek 2013, p. 37, original emphasis). Organization is instead a type of social order that is directed toward an end (Hayek 2013, pp. 36, 41). Therefore, the rules of an organization are more specific than those of an order; they are less abstract, dependent on purpose, and more concrete. They are designed to pursue an end. A paradigmatic Hayekian illustration of designed governance is the state that ought to supply public goods at efficient cost. One can easily think of other illustrations of designed governance (multinational, bureau, department of defense, etc.).

So Hayek gives us broad institutional categories to think about governance alternatives: abstract rules pertain to spontaneous governance and specific rules to planned governance. This taxonomy served Hayek's purpose well, as he was engaged in the defense of freedom against social planning. Social planning (specific rules) suppresses spontaneity (abstract rules), meaning that it stifles the ability to adapt to unforeseen circumstances and individual initiative, such as entrepreneurship, which cannot but lead to misery. For its purpose of demonstrating the weakness of central planning, the taxonomy is, as constructed, a powerful and fully valid one.

At the same time, note that there is no in between. The choice is at polar extremes; we either have one or the other type of governance. In other words, a spontaneous order reflects the highest degree of abstraction, while the planned order (organization) the highest degree of specificity. Yet already in 1945, we know, for example, that in the planned governance of a Prisoner of War camp, design does not fully eradicate spontaneity: economic relations, such as trading, remained (Radford 1945). Similar cases are documented more recently for US prisons (Skarbeck 2014). Rules can plan governance, but not fully, some spontaneous relations still emerge. In theoretical terms, this entails that Hayek lacks a full spectrum of rules (Whitman 2009).

4 Tailored Governance Systems Within General Principles

In *Governing the Commons*: *The Evolution of Institutions for Collective Action* (1990), Ostrom describes a variety of tangible, *sui generis* situations where a community can self-organize by implementing an efficient governance system of common resources without resorting to either government (regulation) or privatization (market). Using the framework of game theory, Ostrom argues that under certain conditions the users of a common resource can avoid the tragedy and limit the overuse and free-riding pointed out by Hardin (1968). She accordingly develops a series of "design principles" that are aimed to capture the interests of both the individuals and the community. That is to say that she points to principles that guarantee the preservation rather than depletion (viz., the tragedy) of the resource. The principles, which can be maintained through successive generations of users, are the following (e.g., Ostrom 1990, p. 90):

1. Boundaries: clear definition of the boundaries of the resource and of the group of users;

2. Rules: search of a balance between the appropriation of resources for consumption and those used to guarantee the provision, i.e., the demand and supply equilibrium;
3. Participation: use of decision-making methods that guarantee the democratic participation of the community in defining and modifying the operational rules, when needed;
4. Monitoring: control of the resource users' conduct vis-à-vis the rules;
5. Sanctioning: definition of a system of gradual sanctions with respect to the violation of the operational rules whose aim is to elicit conformity;
6. Conflict resolution: design of easy and low-cost mechanisms for conflict resolution among users and users and officials;
7. Autonomy: recognition of the right of self-determination for the community which is not challenged by an external authority;
8. Nested enterprises (for a commons good that is part of a larger system): preferably, design of a polycentric organization in multiple layers to manage appropriation, provision, enforcement, conflict resolution, and governance activities.

These principles are abstract, even though based on factual situations; and empirical evidence supports their validity (Cox et al. 2010). The reasoning they embody seems to be abductive: the research process starts with empirical observations that cannot be explained by the existing range of theories, and so there is a search for the "best" explanation among many alternatives (e.g., Bryman and Bell 2015). Abductive reasoning is characterized by lack of completeness, which may concern either the empirical evidence or the theoretical explanation or both, and shows potential heuristic value from intuition. The intuitive gap-filling implicit in abduction resonates with Hayek's notion of abstract rules.

Ostrom's work does not provide a theoretical solution to the tragedy of commons; rather, it proposes a general method, which is the search for the most efficient (relatively speaking) governance solutions in light of the "particular circumstances of time and place" (Hayek 1945, p. 521)—that is, the specific, concrete characteristics of the resource and the needs of the community. In this search of the solution, the autonomies of both the individual and the community become intertwined in a continuous, pragmatic search for the most adequate governance solution. And this is based on a second-generation paradigm of rationality, according to which individuals are "complex, fallible learners who seek to do as well as they can, given the constraints that they face and who are able to learn heuristics, norms, rules, and how to craft rules to improve achieved outcomes" (Ostrom 1998, p. 9). This is also in line with Hayek's notion of abstract rules.

Therefore, each case has its own specificity and the tragedy of the commons can be avoided through a tailored governance solution for the community which uses the resource (Ostrom 1990, 1994). In different terms, each commons governance develops its own rules within the framework of Ostrom's general principles, implying that a commons good is an intermediate category of good whose governance relies on *sui generis* rules. This means that we can envision a bottom-up approach of sorts, where the design principles become unique in terms of time and place, reflecting an intermediate, rather than polar (market or state governance?), degree of abstraction. Through the creation of a tailored governance system, the commons become an order of intermediate abstraction (like, after all, a club). Many commons orders are therefore possible. Recent works have started to focus on which sets of principles are more relevant, or are more easily implemented, depending on the context (Baggio et al. 2016; Schlager 2016; Villamayor-Tomas et al. 2019).

5 Concluding Remarks

How can Ostrom and Hayek be complementary? In order to explain different orders, including organizations, the absolute concepts of abstraction versus concreteness are limited. While Hayek formulates a well-defined theory of social orders even though he does not apply it to solve governance problems in general, Ostrom pragmatically proposes a method to solve the problem of intermediate cases resorting to *sui generis* rules, which are contained within a spectrum whose extremes are order (i.e., the market) and organization (such as, most notably, the state).

We need degrees of abstraction rather than absolute concepts or reasoning by extreme. The need is not just conceptual (Whitman 2009), but also empirical. For the governance of most types of goods actually lies at the interstices between spontaneity and design. We do not just have either-or trade-offs in kinds of governance, but also trade-offs in degrees of governance (Garzarelli 2006).

References

Baggio, J. A., Barnett, A. J., Perez-Ibarra, I., Brady, U., Ratajczyk, E., Rollins, N. D., Rubiños, C., et al. (2016). Explaining Success and failure in the commons: The configural nature of Ostrom's Institutional Design Principles. *International Journal of the Commons, 10*(2), 417–439.

Bryman A., & Bell, E. (2015). *Business research methods* (4th ed.). Oxford: Oxford University Press.

Buchanan, J. M. (1965). An economic theory of clubs. *Economica, 32*(125), 1–14.

Buchanan, J. M. (1982). *Order defined in the process of its emergence*. Available at: https://www.econlib.org/library/Essays/LtrLbrty/bryRF.html?chapter_num=1#book-reader. Last access on May 10, 2020.

Cox, M., Arnold, G., & Villamayor-Tomas, S. (2010). A review of design principles for community-based natural resource management. *Ecology and Society, 15*(4), Article 38.

Fischel, W. A. (2001). Municipal corporations, homeowners and the benefit view of the property tax. In W. E. Oates (ed.), *Property taxation and local government finance: Essays in honor of C. Lowell Harriss* (pp. 33–77). Cambridge, MA: Lincoln Institute of Land Policy.

Frischmann, B. M. (2013). Two enduring lessons from Elinor Ostrom. *Journal of Institutional Economics, 9*(4), 387–406.

Frischmann, B. M., Marciano, A., & Ramello, G. B. (2019). Retrospectives. Tragedy of the commons after 50 years. *Journal of Economic Perspectives, 33*(4), 211–228.

Garzarelli, G. (2004). Old and new theories of fiscal federalism, organizational design problems, and Tiebout. *Journal of Public Finance and Public Choice, 22*(1–2), 91–104.

Garzarelli, G. (2006). Cognition, incentives and public governance: Laboratory federalism from the organizational viewpoint. *Public Finance Review, 34*(3), 235–257.

Gigerenzer, G. (2014). *Risk Savvy: How to make good decisions*. New York: Viking.

Hardin, G. (1968). The tragedy of commons. *Science, 162*(3859), 1243–1248.

Ostrom, E. (1990). *Governing the commons: The evolution of institutions for collective action*. Cambridge, UK: Cambridge University Press.

Ostrom, E. (1994). *Neither market nor state: Governance of common-pool resources in the twenty-first century*. Washington, DC: International Food Policy Research Institute.

Ostrom, E. (1998). A behavioral approach to the rational choice theory of collective action: Presidential Address, American Political Science Association, 1997. *American Political Science Review, 92*(1), 1–22.

Radford, R. A. (1945). The economic organization of a P.O.W. Camp. *Economica, 12*(48), 189–201.

Schlager, E. (2016). Introducing the importance of context, scale, and interdependencies in understanding and applying Ostrom's design principles for successful governance of the commons. *International Journal of the Commons, 10*(2), 405–416.

Smith, V. (2003). Constructivist and ecological rationality in economics. *American Economic Review, 93*(3), 465–508.

Samuelson, P. A. (1954). The pure theory of public expenditure. *Review of Economics and Statistics, 36*(4), 387–389.

Skarbeck, D. (2014). *The social order of the underworld. How prison gangs govern the American Penal System*. New York: Oxford University Press.

Tiebout, C. M. (1956). A pure theory of local expenditures. *Journal of Political Economy, 64*(5), 416–424.

Villamayor-Tomas, S., Thiel, A., Amblard, L., Zikos, D., & Blanco, E. (2019). Diagnosing the role of the state for local collective action: Types of action situations and policy instruments. *Environmental Science & Policy, 97*, 44–57.

Hayek, F. A. von (1945). The use of knowledge in society. *American Economic Review, 35*(4), 519–530.

Hayek, F. A. von (2013). *Law, legislation and liberty. A new statement of the liberal principles of justice and political economy*. London: Routledge (First published in three books in 1973, 1976, 1979).

Whitman, D. G. (2009). The rules of abstraction. *Review of Austrian Economics, 22*(1), 21–41.

Towards a Policy for the Cultural Commons

Alice Borchi

Abstract

The chapter aims to explore the relationship between cultural policy-makers, activist organisations and their users. In an international landscape where the cultural sector is facing different challenges in terms of funding, access and participation, this paper seeks to find possible pathways to innovation in citizen-led initiatives. Furthermore, it investigates the concept of cultural commons, its practical applications and the kind of policy infrastructure that makes them possible. In order to do so, it will analyse existing policies on the commons available in Italy and will identify further directions towards the legal recognition of cultural commons.

The term 'cultural commons' presents several different definitions and applications. In this chapter, we will examine some of these interpretations, analyse how they are applied on a policy level and identify further pathways for the development of commons-based practices in urban cultural policy. For this purpose, we need to analyse the origin of the discourse on the commons and its contemporary evolution. Ostrom (1990) argues that Garrett Hardin's analysis of "Tragedy of the Commons" (1968), which asserted that humans' economic rationality and individualism prevents them from creating successful strategies for the management of common-pool resources, fails to include many important cultural and behavioural aspects. Indeed, her theoretical framework for the analysis of common-pool resources includes a variety of factors, including the ability of those who use the resource to acknowledge the benefit they can have from the pursuit of the common good and collaborate to design a shared set of rules. According to Ostrom, a group of appropriators is able to manage a common-pool resource in a complex and uncertain environment

A. Borchi (✉)
Faculty of Arts, Humanities and Cultures, University of Leeds, Leeds, UK
e-mail: A.Borchi@leeds.ac.uk

E. Macrì et al. (eds.), *Cultural Commons and Urban Dynamics*,
https://doi.org/10.1007/978-3-030-54418-8_2

(hence the contingency of the commitment) if a series of rules is set. As explained by the author, a group of people sharing a common-pool resource

can be expected to make contingent commitments to follow rules that:

- define a set of appropriators who are authorized to use a Common Pool Resource (design principle 1),
- relate to the specific attributes of the CPR[1] and the community of appropriators using the CPR (design principle 2),
- are designed, at least in part, by local appropriators (design principle 3),
- are monitored by individuals accountable to local appropriators (design principle 4) (…).

When individuals are presented with rules meeting these criteria, a safe, advantageous, and credible commitment can be made. The commitment is to follow the rules so long as (1) most similarly situated individuals adopt the same commitment and (2) the long-term expected net benefits to be achieved by this strategy are greater than the long-term expected net benefits for individuals following short-term, dominant strategies (1990, p. 185).

This set of principles, which was originally applied by Ostrom to natural common-pool resources, can be applied to other forms of management of shared properties and also to practices of co-production. In particular, the term 'commons' has gained a particular relevance in the field of knowledge sharing (Hess and Ostrom 2007). Over the last 20 years, knowledge has become one of the most important economic resources, as it provides the basis for technological and scientific innovation. The role of knowledge in the contemporary economic scenario is so important as to characterise it as a 'knowledge-driven economy'. This term describes:

> (…) an economy in which the generation and the exploitation of knowledge have come to play the predominant part in the creation of wealth. It is not simply about pushing back the frontiers of knowledge; it is also about the more effective use and exploitation of all types of knowledge in all manner of economic activity. (Coates and Warwick 1999, p. 12)

In a knowledge-driven economy, knowledge is not only intrinsically valuable, nor it is only an instrument to improve technology and find more efficient ways to produce goods and make profits; instead, it represents a source of profit per se. Lyotard foresaw this transformation in 1985 and described this process of commodification of knowledge as follows: "Knowledge is and will be produced in order to be sold, it is and will be consumed in order to be valorised in a new production: in both cases, the goal is exchange" (1984, p. 4). Exchange, therefore, is what pushes knowledge forward. Starting from the assumption that in a neoliberal age, the value of every commodity is determined by its exchange value, one can see how knowledge represents a highly profitable source of wealth. As ideas are not physical objects and IT allows them to be reproduced and shared with no geographical

[1]Common-pool resource.

boundaries, the opportunities for exchange are limitless, and the global marketization of knowledge is highly remunerative.

From this concept, some further understanding of knowledge-driven online commons has been advanced, especially for the sphere of creative intellectual property. The Creative Commons license can be seen as the most notable case of regulating this kind of practice, as it allows the use of intellectual property in a flexible way, according to the author's preferences (Creative Commons 2020). This not only encourages co-creative approaches to the generation of online intellectual property but, most importantly, places the authority on the subject directly in the hands of creators. At this stage, however, with the exception of regulations such as the Creative Commons and Open Access licenses, few legal systems offer an official recognition of the concept of commons; property regimes are still fundamentally divided between public and private. For the purposes of this chapter, we will focus on the Italian legal system, which provides some useful examples of how we can understand the commons both as a property regime and as a set of rights.

Italian jurist Stefano Rodotà's definition of commons highlights the interconnectedness of the commons and fundamental human rights; according to the author, the commons can be understood as "the goods functionally necessary for making effective the person's fundamental rights and the fulfilment of her/his personality" (2013, p. 4). However, the sphere of fundamental rights encompasses both the individual and the collective spheres. The relational nature of the commons, according to the author, can foster civic engagement and a sense of community:

> In this sense, [the commons] are a truly "heritage of the humanity" and all interested person must be legitimized to intervene in order to make effective and to protect them. In the very nature of these goods there is the sharing of responsibilities among different actors, the effectiveness of equality, the building up of social relationships instead of selfish separation. (2013, p. 4)

In the Italian context, the design of a law on the commons started with the Rodotà commission for a modification of the laws of the Civil Code on public property. The commission was established by the Ministry of Justice in 2007 and was led by Stefano Rodotà; in 2003, however, scholars Sabino Cassese, Antonio Gambaro, Ugo Mattei and Edoardo Reviglio had already submitted a memorandum recommending the Ministry of Economy and Finance to form a commission to reform the jurisdiction of public assets (Ministero della Giustizia 2007). Over the years, the proposal was subject to several changes, but the key point, that is, the distinction between public property, private property and commons, remained intact. The rationale of the law is to design a new category of property regime—the commons—that is to be understood as a form of "diffuse property" that involves both private and public bodies (Ministero della Giustizia 2008). According to the proposal, natural resources such as rivers and mountains fall into this category, but also heritage, archaeological sites and cultural assets, as they all are things that are functional to the expression of fundamental rights and to the free development of people (idem). This proposal, however, never became a law and was never discussed by the Italian parliament.

The concept of commons as a third category of property that is neither public nor private is not the only one that has been debated in Italian academia. Marella states that the legal concept of commons is not to be understood as a third form of property, but rather as a bundle of rights (2017). The commons, therefore, can be placed in a continuum between private and public properties; the rights connected to the common, such as access and management, can be "disarticulated from ownership" and transferred to other people (idem, p. 83). According to the author, "collective rights of access to those publicly or privately owned resources that are functional to the fulfillment of an individuals' fundamental rights can be grounded on the social function norm" (idem, p. 75); this concept is perfectly in line with the key tenets outlined by Rodotà; the commons are indeed essential to the personal realisation of individuals and to their fundamental rights as a collective. However, as noted by Marella, the legal concept of the commons as a bundle of rights, in various degrees, has been applied exclusively by local governments in the Italian context; on the national level, the Italian Constitution promotes citizen-led initiatives but does not offer a framework for transferring bundles of rights as the one defined in recent local regulations (idem, pp. 80–81). The city of Bologna was a pioneer in this field and created a regulation that allows forms of collaboration between the city council and the citizens for safeguarding tangible, intangible and digital commons (Comune di Bologna 2014). This policy was eventually adopted by several other Italian cities but was never scaled up to a national level.

Therefore, it is clear that the concept of commons is multifaceted, as it encompasses natural and human-made resources (tangible and intangible resources, including knowledge and cultural assets) and, even in the same legal context, there are multiple interpretations of it. From a legal perspective, we can make a distinction between 'commons as property' and 'commons as a bundle of rights'. In the context of Italian legislation, we can see examples of both of these concepts: the Rodotà commission attempted to introduce the first concept as a national policy, but did not succeed; the latter, instead, is now the key principle of a regulation that has been adopted by several Italian cities. Having explored the concept of commons, its evolution and its legal applications, it is now necessary to map the different understandings of 'cultural commons'. Analysing different definitions and uses of the term is necessary to understand its relationship to different areas of cultural policy and its political value.

According to Santagata et al., "Cultural Commons refer to cultures located in time and space—either physical or virtual—and shared and expressed by a community" (2011, p. 1). This definition includes both tangible and intangible forms of culture; it is also relevant to note that it includes forms of cultural production that have an important impact on the economy of a community, such as the brand of Barolo wine (idem, p. 2), not only on its cultural life. Like natural common-pool resources, they are shared systems of collective action, but with an important difference: natural common-pool resources are characterised by exhaustion problems due to limited carrying capacity (Hardin 1968; Ostrom 1990), whereas cultural commons are non-rival in consumption. Bowers provides an alternative definition of the cultural commons, stating that they "include activities, knowledge, skills, and patterns of mutual support that do not rely on a monetized economy" (2009, p. 197); this definition places the cultural commons in the realm of informal economy, with a lesser focus on their material and relevance for the sustenance of the community of appropriators.

Other definitions, based on intellectual property theory, have been formulated by Christen (2005), Halbert (2005), Madison et al. (2010) and Solum (2010). These definitions focus on the cultural commons as knowledge and intellectual property-driven commons, with a strong emphasis on digital forms of commons. The generation, protection and exploitation of intellectual property are a very important aspect of cultural policy, especially for what concerns the development of the creative and cultural industries; this is even more relevant in the digital context. However, this chapter will not focus on this aspect of the cultural commons, as it would require a much broader space and an in-depth analysis of international intellectual property policies; instead, it will focus on the more material aspects of this concept and on its intellectual relevance for the field of cultural policy. For this purpose, this chapter will use Santagata et al.'s (2011) definition of commons for its inclusivity and for its attention to the material aspect, not in its tangible quality but in its vital role in the sustenance of communities of appropriators. To further clarify the relationship between the cultural commons and cultural policy, we will analyse heritage and occupied cultural spaces. These two areas present radically different characteristics, but they also share some very similar concerns in relation to issues of access, management and exploitation.

The concept of cultural heritage, in its tangible and intangible forms, can be understood as a form of commons. Indeed, as explained by Marta Botta (in Ramos 2016, pp. 26–31), heritage and heritage sites constitute a commons, as they are embodiments of a shared past that can be enjoyed by all citizens. Regardless of heritage's property regime, its cultural and social value makes it important for a large number of people; for this reason, it is necessary to regulate its access and management in an inclusive way. Indeed, as analysed by Bruncevic, the safeguard of heritage presents interesting social dilemmas in terms of access, sustainability and exploitation (2014, pp. 50–51); for this reason, we can think of heritage as a common-pool resource characterised by a complex system of values. Using the commons as a conceptual framework poses an interesting opportunity for cultural policy, as it would allow a reconceptualization of heritage, not as a country's exploitable resource (Borchi 2019), but rather as something that has collective value beyond its monetization, and as such needs a collective effort to be preserved and accessed.

The idea of heritage is not limited to the sphere of culture, but it also includes nature, as stated by the UNESCO *Convention Concerning the Protection of the World Cultural and Natural Heritage* (1972). For the purpose of this chapter, it is interesting to analyse the interconnectedness of these two aspects in the context of landscape, to be understood as the interplay of natural and human-made elements. The concept of landscape appears in the Italian Constitution as one of the elements that the State is in charge of preserving for the sake of the common good. Salvatore Settis analyses the relationship between humans and nature from a legal perspective interpreting the concept of landscape as a commons (2012). The author describes how the Italian Constitution takes into account the preservation of the natural environment, which is considered a common property of the whole nation. Moreover, as underlined by Settis, the *Code of Cultural Heritage and Landscape* associates heritage sites to the landscape, making a strong connection between natural assets and man-built works of art and architectural excellence. The concept of landscape can also be intended as 'environment' or 'territory', as these terms belong to the same discourse on the interaction between natural resources and human land modification. Settis (ibid.) argues that the landscape is, indeed, the most neglected part of the national commons: years of poor urban planning, illegal constructions, pollution, bad management of rural areas and deforestation have radically changed the Italian landscape. It is therefore not only the use of natural resources that needs to be regulated, but also how humans intervene in these resources, in order to prevent private interests from damaging something that belongs to everyone. Indeed, as stated by Mitchell, law plays a very important role in the evolution of landscape, both physically and theoretically; landscape also reflects the shortcomings of legal systems, and the inequality and injustice of societies (2003). In the Italian context, we can see the preservation of landscape as the core of WWF's campaign "Riutilizziamo l'Italia[2]", which aims to reconvert abandoned urban and rural spaces into areas that can be enjoyed by the whole community, a sort of modern-day commons that can oppose the enclosures dictated by urban sprawl and speculation (WWF 2020).

The preoccupation with urban abandonment and new enclosures is also central to the occupation of occupied spaces that took place in Italy between 2011 and 2014. In order to understand how these spaces represented, and still represent, a form of commons, as well as the symbolic relevance of the act of occupation, it is necessary to analyse the tradition of occupation in Italian social movements. The act of occupying a place is a highly symbolic gesture that carries many different meanings: it is an act of protest, but it also has an element of performance and narrative content. The #OccupyWallStreet movement that was born in New York in 2011 as a form of protest against financial greed and corruption brought about a new interest in the forms of protest that were once associated with the French movement of 1968. Italy's history of occupation is strongly connected to the history of self-managed social centres; the term chosen to define these *centri sociali*[3] is not 'squats', as the term used in English usually defines occupation for social housing purposes only. Italy's *centri sociali*, like squats, are spaces that offer shelter to the occupiers, but they are aimed at the organisation of political activities and are themselves a form of protest against governmental powers. The occupied buildings are often former factories, as they offer the necessary room to organise assemblies, shows and concerts. They are typically located in industrial areas where the youth population is more likely to face problems such as poverty and lack of

[2]English translation: "Let's re-utilize Italy".
[3]English translation: "social centres".

cultural provision, therefore more in need of a space to experience creative, cultural and political activities.

The experiences of *centri sociali* are very important to understand the nature of occupied cultural places, as they embody the tradition of Italian political activism and present many common features with the organisations born inside occupied cultural spaces between 2011 and 2014. Researching occupied spaces in Italy entails researching grand narratives, to use Lyotard's vocabulary, of the Italian radical left. *Centri sociali* represent an important alternative to the alienation, commodification and conformation of neoliberalised life in Italy. Indeed, the collective of Italian writers, Wu Ming (2002) describes *centri sociali* as the most important resource of the resistance to the second Berlusconi government (2001–2005); in a state where most media were controlled by one person (who was also the country's Prime Minister), spaces where people could gather, talk and disseminate ideas with a clear leftist agenda were crucial. A significant change in the way people use *centri sociali* has been described by Angelo Mastrandrea (2016) in an article about Milan's Leoncavallo, one of the oldest *centri sociali* in Italy. First, some centres sought, and obtained, a legal status. This change can be seen as a necessary step for many organisations; as their role in the cultural and social life of the city became more important and recognised, it was necessary for them to seek public funding. Their illegal status made it impossible for them to obtain any form of official financial support. For example, Leoncavallo, despite being officially recognised by the Region of Lombardy as a cultural association, is still threatened to be forcibly evacuated, because the activists are occupying a building that is private property of the Cabassi family (idem).

Another significant change lies in the way people engage with *centri sociali.* In 1970s, they were mainly a place where activists could organ their activities; several generations over the decades have taken part in the occupations, each of them with different political focuses (from partisans to anti-prohibitionists). According to the activist interviewed in Mastrandea's article, external pressures are limiting people's participation in activism; they are more focused on finding a job or on sustaining themselves between freelancing and short-term contracts. This trend is noticeable in the rise of the creation of co-working spaces, workshops and artisanal laboratories in *centri sociali*. Other initiatives, such as communal gardens and kitchens, provide a significant help for those people who struggle with poverty. Over the years, *centri sociali* also developed a particular attention to migrants and refugees, offering help and support. *Centri sociali*, therefore, started moving their focus from being sites of political activism to include practices of shared production and consumption based on collective processes. In this sense, we can see them as a form of social commoning that not only has a radical political meaning, but also a very important practical role in the everyday life of their communities of appropriators.

In the last 5 years, Italy saw the rise of a number of occupied spaces that share some of the key features of a *centro sociale*, as they are conceived as a space of contestation of the current system and provide a home for the occupants as well, but are radically different in their organisation and mission. These buildings have a symbolic meaning per se, as their former use was cultural, which is the case of *teatri occupati*, occupied theatres all over Italy. At the root of these occupations, there is not only a political and social project but, most importantly, the dissatisfaction and the concern of a group of professionals who work in the field of theatre and culture. The occupation of a building, therefore, is not only an act of contestation, but also an occasion to do what the Italian professionals of the cultural sector felt denied—working. The economic crisis and the subsequent cuts to the arts inevitably provoked a sense of exclusion from the job market and a feeling of helplessness among young cultural professionals, especially in theatre and performance. Theatre professionals were not only looking for a space for aesthetic experimentation, but for the contestation of a system that did not acknowledge the dignity of their work and their right to receive a fair pay. This is coherent with the evolution of other occupied spaces, such as *centri sociali*, that combine activism with daily collective activities, such as knowledge-sharing workshops. We can understand these practices as a form of pre-figurative politics that was and still is at the root of a variety of activists practice, from anarchism to the #Occupy movement (Raekstad 2018).

This kind of artistic practice, intertwined with public engagement and an underlying idea of social justice, eventually found its political counterpart in the theories of the commons. In practice, this meant that these organisations used a shared system of governance based on round tables and collective assemblies; adopted a participatory approach in their artistic work, in some cases blurring the lines between artist, activist, occupant and participant; and tried to keep their work as accessible as possible by using a pay-what-you-want approach or very low ticket prices (Bailey and Mattei 2013; Froment 2016; Borchi 2018). Several occupied spaces eventually joined the "Municipality of Commons" (Municipio dei Beni Comuni), a network that brings together several different associations involved in the cause of the commons. The Municipality of the Commons runs campaigns for the legal recognition of the commons in Italian law and for other causes associated with the common good of the nation. However, one of the key characteristics of these spaces was their dual nature as both sites of protest and resistance *and* as sites of cultural production. In this sense, we can understand occupied cultural spaces as anti-capitalist commons (Caffentzis and Federici 2014).

Caffentzis and Federici provide a detailed analysis of the anti-capitalist commons. First, they should be produced, not given (2014, p. 101). Indeed, the occupations were not mere symbolic acts but were able to produce a system of shared spaces and practices through a relational process. Other systems of resource-sharing in the urban context have appropriated the language of the commons, but without developing a community-oriented relational approach. For example, co-working spaces have become indispensable to freelance and precarious workers, especially from the creative sector, as many young professionals cannot afford a personal office. These organisations seem to have some of the communitarian spirits of the commons and to value collaboration over individualism, but they also share the same objectives of efficiency, innovation and brand culture typical of the neoliberal discourse. Access to the commons, as stated by the authors, is not merely a matter of usage of a resource, but is focused on shared governance:

"Equal access to the means of (re)production and egalitarian decision making must be the foundation of the commons" (idem, p. 102). In the context of the cultural commons, this means blurring the categories of managers, audiences, artists and producers. This process was facilitated in occupied cultural spaces through deliberative practices such as public assemblies and round tables that involved the people at the centre of the occupation, participants and audiences.

The work of the activist also began an important dialogue on participatory governance in Italian culture, in particular on the local level. In a country where public cultural institutions are strongly centralised and often seen as a tourist attraction, rather than a resource for the community, this is an important step forward. Furthermore, Federici and Caffentzis clarify that "commons must guarantee the reproduction of our lives. Exclusive reliance on 'immaterial' commons, like the internet, will not do (2014, p. 101)". Indeed, it is necessary to think of a kind of cultural commons that, if mismanaged, can have limited carrying capacity due to overconsumption. A tradition, a poem or a play can continue to exist no matter how many people consume them; perhaps, it is the contrary: the more people enjoy them over time, the longer they can survive. However, the infrastructure that makes it possible to have them—spaces, instruments, working practices—can instead become insufficient if their use is not regulated. This does not mean that tangible forms of cultural commons are fated to overconsumption and extinction, but they can be preserved if they are managed appropriately.

Having analysed the different understandings of the concept of cultural commons, we can ask: how can we approach their legal recognition within the framework of cultural policy? What key philosophical tenets should underly policies on the cultural commons? And lastly, how can we reconcile the radical, anti-capitalist nature of the commons with their legalisation?

The cultural commons and the shared governance systems that manage them can be seen as an important framework for achieving cultural democracy. As stated by Rodotà, the commons are intertwined with human's fundamental rights, both as individuals and as a collective, and with democracy (2013). Following this thread, it is evident that the cultural commons, their legitimacy and their fruition, cannot be alienated from the sphere of cultural democracy. Gross and Wilson define cultural democracy as "*a sustained but evolving system of governance for substantive cultural freedom*" (2020, p. 12). The authors focus on the notion of "cultural opportunity", its ecological nature and its interconnectedness with different cultural resources (in Gross 2019, p. 2). As stated by Hadley and Belfiore (2018), cultural democracy cannot be achieved without questioning the system of power that lies as the basis for cultural value. In order to do so, it is necessary to re-think about the purpose of cultural policy and the way it functions.

Jancovich and Bianchini (2013) state that cultural policy currently follows "the deficit model", which attributes the problems related to cultural participation to the individual. The creative commons remove the focus on the individual and are based instead on the collective—not only to be intended as the collective enjoyment of the arts, or passive participation, but rather as the collective construction of cultural value. The creation and management of the cultural commons ensure a grassroots approach that enables citizens to determine their own engagement, without a focus on "excellence"—that is, a distinction between high and low forms of culture. Indeed, following Sennett's idea of "disorder" (1970), we can understand the commons as a site where people with different backgrounds can interact and collectively produce culture; this can bring about co-productive processes between professional and non-professional artists, with a strong focus on process rather than product.

The idea of cultural democracy, however, is not neutral; Hadley highlights the importance of the history of this term and its political nature, stressing its relationship with other forms of democracy and its revolutionary essence (2018, p. 53). Institutionalising the concept of cultural democracy might eventually hinder its efficacy and be used as an instrument to reinforce cultural elites.

The threat of depoliticization is also very relevant to the concept of cultural commons, which is indeed a very political one. As indicated by Caffentzis and Federici (2014), the language of the commons has been co-opted by capitalism to legitimise privatisation and dispossession; for this reason, they consider the anti-capitalist nature of the commons to define them as autonomous spaces outside of capitalism. One of the key characteristics of the commons identified by Caffentzis and Federici (idem) is the fact that they are the product of a relational process; for this reason, the authors stress the importance of 'commoning', focusing on the practice that lies at the basis of the commons rather than on the resources themselves. However, as stated earlier, central to Federici and Caffentzis's argument is the material dimension of the commons (2014, p. 101). The materiality of the cultural commons is an essential part to understand their position in the field of cultural production: the practices and the work connected to the reproduction and maintenance of the cultural commons should not be a self-contained exercise, but allow for the livelihood of artists in their cultural environment. Thinking of the commons as something that relies merely on voluntary work, as stated by Bianchi, de-politicise their meaning and excludes people who cannot afford to volunteer in their free time (2018, p. 297). Following Marella's definition of the commons as a bundle of rights (2017), we can now analyse its possible applications on the sphere of the cultural commons and on occupied cultural spaces in particular.

Occupied cultural spaces offer a perfect, yet controversial, example of cultural commons. We can understand them as a resource that is used by a group of appropriators for a social purpose; however, the materiality of this resource can support the appropriators' livelihood. The process of occupation of the cultural spaces is important on two levels: on the symbolic level, it represents an example of pre-figurative politics and the filling of a space that has been left empty by cultural policy; on the practical level, it represents the action of appropriation of a resource by a community that sets a system of shared rules for itself.

The example of L'Asilo (Naples) provides an interesting example of how occupied spaces can successfully reclaim a bundle of rights in relation to their management and access. As stated earlier, this process was possible due to a local regulation modelled after the one implemented by the City of Bologna in 2014.

These local regulations provide a starting point for the development of cultural commons; the issue with this situation, though, is that it relies on individual local governments rather than on a shared national approach. Secondly, as analysed by Bianchi (2018), it challenges the political nature of the commons by reducing them to "volunteering" initiatives that can possibly contribute to austerity measures, not as a radical form of cultural production that challenges neoliberalism.

Another application of the concept of commons that is particularly relevant for the field of cultural policy, as stated earlier, is landscape. The safeguard of union of cultural and natural heritage, and the governance processes that lie at its basis, sets out some new goals for the sphere of cultural policy. The preservation of landscape is a collective responsibility that involves private and public actors beyond the area of culture and the arts and, most importantly, beyond the short-termism of cultural policy. In this context, it is useful to use the concept of 'futurability', thus defined by Tatsuyoshi Saijo: "A person exhibits futurability when this person experiences an increase in happiness as a result of deciding and acting to forego current benefits as long as it enriches future generations" (2018, p. 5). Futurability expands the sphere of shared governance beyond existing generations and prompts a shift in the way people think about the management of shared resources. This should be a key principle in the management of the commons, and of landscape in particular. Landscape is the fragile result of human and natural elements that represent different values and resources; balancing these elements needs long-term vision and a deep understanding of their preservation needs.

The relationship between cultural policy and the cultural commons, therefore, begs two questions. The first is: what cultural policies are needed for the legal recognition and sustainability of the cultural commons?

The first step concerns the legal recognition of the commons in general, not only from a cultural perspective. In the Italian context, the Rodotà proposal on the legal recognition of the commons represented an important first attempt at introducing this concept in the legal system. However, the proposal, whose core was the understanding of the commons as a third form of property beyond public and private, never became a law. The sphere of local policy was more successful by proposing the idea of commons as a bundle of rights in the area of citizen-led initiatives (Marella 2017); recognising citizens' right to preserve and manage urban commons was a fundamental step forward to introduce systems of shared governance in the legal system. Nevertheless, the Collaborative Governance of the Commons model adopted by these regulations, presents some limitations, according to Bianchi, because it excludes antagonistic participatory claims; furthermore, due to its voluntary nature, it is targeted at participants with social capital and free time and does not value the cost of labour; lastly, the administration still holds decision-making power (Bianchi 2018, p. 298). As a result, the concept of commons becomes depoliticised. For this reason, a cultural policy for the commons needs a legal definition of this term that does not only focus on resources and their management and upkeeping, but also on their access and distribution within communities and how these can be achieved through democratic processes. In the context of cultural policy, the safeguard of the cultural commons should not be conceived as an inexpensive way to delegate the upkeep of heritage and cultural sites to volunteers but rather as a way to multiply cultural opportunities (Gross 2019) and to foster spaces that allow people to participate in culture in an independent, bottom-up way. Furthermore, artists and cultural practitioners should be allowed to develop cultural commons that can "guarantee the reproduction of their lives" (Caffenztis and Federici 2014, p. 101) and not exploit their knowledge and skills.

The other question that we need to investigate is: in what ways can the concept of cultural commons affect the sphere of cultural policy-making?

If cultural policy needs to shift from the 'deficit model' towards an approach aimed at ensuring cultural democracy (Jancovich and Bianchini 2013; Hadley and Belfiore 2018), the relational, co-productive nature of the commons can help us understanding possible pathways to participatory approaches to cultural governance. Cultural participation should be understood as a fundamental right and, as such, cultural policy should enable people to enjoy it on their own terms. The commons blur the boundaries between audience and artists, producers and consumers, and as such enable people to create and share cultural opportunities and to share and consume culture as a community, in their own terms. The shared systems of governance that lie at the basis of the cultural commons can be useful to think about forms of cultural participation beyond consultation and tokenism and open up pathways to the co-production of cultural policy.

Secondly, the concept of landscape as a commons can inspire cultural policy to reflect critically on the impact of culture and human-made resource on nature, and its long-term effects. Furthermore, culture has been defined as 'the fourth pillar' of sustainability (Hawkes 2001); indeed, culture plays an important role in the way in which people experience the world, and express and transmit their values. In a time of climate emergency, it is necessary that cultural policy re-assesses its role in fostering sustainable practices and behaviours. In this scenario, the concept of 'futurability' (Saijo 2018) can be particularly useful in thinking about how we intend to hand down our cultural and natural heritage to future generations.

In summary, the commons can provide a useful framework for cultural policy to deliver cultural democracy not only to living generations, but also to future ones. The shared system of governance that characterises the commons can empower citizens in creating and enjoying their own cultural opportunities, thus multiplying cultural values. In practice, this presents several challenges; taking the Italian context as an example, the lack of a national law on the commons hinders the possibility of scaling up local initiatives. On the other hand, current regulations on the safeguard of the commons tend to remove its political connotation, positioning citizen-led initiatives as "volunteering" and not as a radical act of re-appropriation of common resources. In this scenario, the evolution of policy is vital to ensure the sustainability of the cultural commons in the long run. Further research is needed to understand how it is possible to reconcile the radical nature of the commons and the needs of cultural policy. This is indeed a major challenge, but it can be very productive to understand how to re-think the future of cultural participation.

References

Bailey, S., & Mattei, U. (2013). Social movements as constituent power: The Italian struggle for the commons. *Indiana Journal of Global Legal Studies, 20*(2), Article 14.

Bianchi, I. (2018). The post-political meaning of the concept of commons: the regulation of the urban commons in Bologna. *Space and Polity, 22*(3), 287–306. https://doi.org/10.1080/13562576.2018.1505492.

Borchi, A. (2018). Culture as commons: theoretical challenges and empirical evidence from occupied cultural spaces in Italy. *Cultural Trends, 27*(1), 33–45. https://doi.org/10.1080/09548963.2018.1415410.

Botta, M. (2016). Heritage and city commons. In J. M. Ramos (Ed.), *The city as commons: A policy reader* (pp. 26–31). Melbourne, Commons Transition Coalition, (e-Book).

Borchi, A. (2019). Oil, gold, stones: Cultural value in Italian cultural policy. *Arts and the Market, 9*(1), 2–15. https://doi.org/10.1108/AAM-01-2019-0005.

Bruncevic, M. (2014). Fixing the shadows – Access to art and the legal concept of the cultural commons. Thesis for Doctor of Laws, University of Gothenburg, Gothenburg. Available at: https://gupea.ub.gu.se/handle/2077/35600.

Caffentzis, G., & Federici, S. (2014). Commons against and beyond capitalism. *Community Development Journal, 49*(suppl_1), i92–i105. https://doi.org/10.1093/cdj/bsu006.

Christen, K. (2005). Gone digital: aboriginal remix and the cultural commons. *International Journal of Cultural Property, 12*(3), 315–345. https://doi.org/10.1017/S0940739105050186.

Coates, D., & Warwick, K. (1999). The knowledge driven economy: Analysis and background. *The Economics of the Knowledge Driven Economy*, London, 27/01, available at http://citeseerx.ist.psu.edu/viewdoc/download?doi=10.1.1.123.9374&rep=rep1&type=pdf#page=11. Accessed February 15, 2020.

Comune di Bologna. (2014). *Regolamento sulla collaborazione tra cittadini e amministrazione per la cura e la rigenerazione dei beni comuni urbani.* Retrieved from http://www.comune.bologna.it/sites/default/files/documenti/REGOLAMENTO%20BENI%20COMUNI.pdf.

Creative Commons. (2020). *Licenses*. Available at https://creativecommons.org/licenses/.

Froment, P. (2016). Lieux culturels et informalité politique à Naples: une approche par les pouvoirs multisitués. *L'Espace Politique, 29*(2). https://doi.org/10.4000/espacepolitique.3916.

Gross, J. (2019). Practices of hope: care, narrative and cultural democracy. *International Journal of Cultural Policy*, 1–15. https://doi.org/10.1080/10286632.2019.1702032.

Gross, J., & Wilson, N. (2020). Cultural democracy: an ecological and capabilities approach. *International Journal of Cultural Policy, 26*(3), 328–343. https://doi.org/10.1080/10286632.2018.1538363.

Hadley, S. (2018). Towards cultural democracy: Promoting cultural capabilities for everyone. *Cultural Trends, 27*(1), 52–55. https://doi.org/10.1080/09548963.2018.1415417.

Hadley, S., & Belfiore, E. (2018). Cultural democracy and cultural policy. *Cultural Trends, 27*(3), 218–223. https://doi.org/10.1080/09548963.2018.1474009.

Halbert, D. J. (2005). *Resisting intellectual property*. London: Routledge.

Hardin, G. (1968). The tragedy of the commons. *Science, 162*(3859), 1243–1248.

Hawkes, J. (2001). *The fourth pillar of sustainability: Culture's essential role in public planning* (p. 2001). Melbourne: Common Ground P/L.

Hess, C., & Ostrom, E. (2007). *Understanding knowledge as a commons*. London: The MIT Press.

Jancovich, L., & Bianchini, F. (2013). Problematising participation. *Cultural Trends, 22*(2), 63–66. https://doi.org/10.1080/09548963.2013.783158.

Lyotard, J.-F. (1984). *The postmodern condition: A report on knowledge*. Manchester: Manchester University Press.

Madison, M. J., Frischmann, B. M., & Strandburg, K. J. (2010). Constructing commons in the cultural environment. *Cornell Law Review, 95*(4), 657–710. https://doi.org/10.31228/osf.io/76g93.

Marella, M. R. (2017). The commons as a legal concept. *Law and Critique, 28*, 61–86. https://doi.org/10.1007/s10978-016-9193-0.
Mastrandrea, A. (2016). Il Leoncavallo di Milano affronta i suoi primi quarant'anni, Internazionale, 19/03. Available at https://www.internazionale.it/reportage/2016/03/19/centro-sociale-leoncavallo-quarant-anni. Accessed 02/08/2020.
Ministero della Giustizia. (2007). *Commissione Rodotà - per la modifica delle norme del codice civile in materia di beni pubblici – Relazione*. Available at https://www.giustizia.it/giustizia/it/mg_1_12_1.wp?contentId=SPS47617. Accessed March 10, 2020.
Ministero della Giustizia. (2008). *Relazione di accompagnamento al Disegno di legge delega*. Available at https://www.giustizia.it/data/multimedia/2430.pdf. Accessed May 05, 2020.
Mitchell, D. (2003). Cultural landscapes: Just landscapes or landscapes of justice? *Progress in Human Geography, 27*(6), 787–796. https://doi.org/10.1191/0309132503ph464pr.
Ostrom, O. (1990/2012). *Governing the commons*. Cambridge University Press [eBook], Cambridge.
Raekstad, P. (2018). Revolutionary practice and prefigurative politics: A clarification and Defense. *Constellations, 2018*(25), 359–372. https://doi.org/10.1111/1467-8675.12319.
Rodotá S. (2013). Constituting the commons in the context of state, law and politics. In Keynote at the *Economics and the Commons Conference, Berlin*, May 22–24, 2013. Retrieved 30 November, 2013, from http://boellblog.org/wp-content/uploads/2013/10/ECC-Rodota-keynote.pdf.
Saijo, T. (2018). Future design: Bequeathing sustainable natural environments and sustainable societies to future generations. In No SDES-2018-4, Working Papers, Kochi University of Technology, School of Economics and Management. https://EconPapers.repec.org/RePEc:kch:wpaper:sdes-2018-4.
Santagata, W., Bertacchini, E., Bravo, G., & Marrelli, M. (2011). Cultural commons and cultural communities. Paper presented to *Sustaining Commons: Sustaining Our Future, the Thirteenth Biennial Conference of the International Association for the Study of the Commons*, Hyderabad, India. Retrieved from http://hdl.handle.net/10535/7359.
Sennett, R. (1970). *The uses of disorder: Personal identity and city life*. London: Allen Lane.
Settis, S. (2012). *Paesaggio costituzione cemento*. Turin: Einaudi.
Solum, L. B. (2010). Questioning cultural commons. *Cornell Law Review, 95*(4), 817–838.
Wu Ming. (2002). Why not show off about the best things? Retrieved from https://www.wumingfoundation.com/english/giap/giapdigest18.html. Accessed May 04, 2020.
WWF. (2020). Riutilizziamo l'Italia. Available at https://www.wwf.it/il_pianeta/impatti_ambientali/suolo/riutilizziamo_litalia/. Accessed 03/08/2020.

Urban Heritage as Cultural Capital, District, and Commons: An Economic Perspective

Enrico E. Bertacchini

Abstract

This chapter aims at providing an economic perspective to the challenges characterizing integrated conservation and management approaches to urban heritage. Drawing from the cultural economist's toolkit, this contribution introduces the notion of heritage commons to extend and critically re-examine two established notions that have been often used to frame the nexus between cultural heritage and local development at the urban level, namely that of cultural capital and cultural districts.

1 Introduction

With globalization and urbanization, development and tourism pressures are posing major challenges to cities all over the world featuring historic cores and distinctive cultural atmosphere. Mass tourism to major cultural destinations in urban areas risks to deplete the collective values and cultural practices traditionally shared by local communities. Similarly, in many metropolitan areas of developing and emerging countries the preservation of the cultural values of both tangible and intangible heritage is often deemed to hinder new development opportunities.

Amid these threats and concerns, in the last decades scholars and international organizations have increasingly emphasized the role of heritage as a lever for local development and urban regeneration (Greffe 2011; Licciardi and Amirtahmasebi 2012). According to this view, historic buildings and cities represent an asset:

E. E. Bertacchini (✉)
Department of Economics and Statistics "Cognetti de Martiis",
University of Turin, Turin, Italy
e-mail: enrico.bertacchini@unito.it

E. Macrì et al. (eds.), *Cultural Commons and Urban Dynamics*,
https://doi.org/10.1007/978-3-030-54418-8_3

resources embedding and potentially producing value, when properly and efficiently managed. By attracting visitors, entrepreneurs and businesses in search of distinctive places, enhancement of urban heritage can generate economic impact in the form of real estate appreciation, job creation and income growth in the activities related to heritage services.

The attempts for integrating cultural heritage conservation in the process of urban development have often sought to safeguard the character and identity of the historic city as expressed by local culture and heritage. Identity and local character can become part of a city's competitive edge, but are increasingly under threat or destroyed by globalizing processes of urban development. Heritage and local culture may thus become key determinants for the positioning of cities in the global scenario as well as of the quality of life and the well-being of local communities.

With this perspective, in urban conservation and heritage policy circles a new paradigm is increasingly emerging that sets emphasis on integrated approaches to the conservation and management of urban heritage. One of the clearest illustrations is the UNESCO Historic Urban Landscape Recommendation (UNESCO 2011). The concept of Historic Urban Landscape (HUL) has its origins in the problem of governing development in the surroundings of historic buildings or historic urban areas, and it draws its formulation from the broader definition of cultural landscape, considered as the visible features of an area including both its physical structures, the spatial organization and living human elements (Bandarin and Van der Oers 2012). In particular, the Historic Urban Landscape approach goes beyond the traditional concept of historic city as a bundle of heritage goods, tackling the wider question of the management of heritage resources in relation with social and economic dynamics. It is based on the recognition and identification of a layering and interconnection of natural and cultural, tangible and intangible values present in urban contexts (Taylor 2016). It aims at managing the development of historic cities while contributing to the well-being of communities and to the conservation of historic urban areas and their cultural heritage, while ensuring economic and social diversity and residential functions. Yet, while integrated heritage conservation and management approaches emphasize the role of heritage assets and the cultural atmosphere as potential drivers for sustainable development, such an outcome is neither straightforward nor systematic. For instance, sustainable development processes imply the proper coordination between stakeholders and to solve collective action dilemmas characterizing the collective good, multipurpose, and multi-attribute nature of cultural heritage.

This chapter aims at providing an economic perspective to the challenges characterizing integrated conservation and management approaches to urban heritage. Firstly, drawing from the cultural economist's toolkit, this contribution critically re-examines two established notions that have been often used to frame the nexus between cultural heritage and local development at the urban level, namely that of cultural capital and cultural districts. Secondly, it proposes the notion of commons as a new economic category useful for grasping the complexity of urban heritage under the lens of integrated approaches to heritage conservation.

2 Urban Heritage as Cultural Capital

From an economic viewpoint, cultural heritage such as monuments, museums, and historic buildings may be considered as a form of cultural capital, which is an asset that embodies both economic and cultural values (Throsby 2001).

As a physical asset, it embodies economic values because it gives rise to a flow of services over time, and may equally deteriorate (and hence depreciate) if the property is not maintained.

However, as far as its cultural component is concerned, the same physical asset includes also cultural value, some intrinsic or assigned quality that stands apart from the property's financial worth and reflects some evaluation of its significance, for historical, religious, spiritual, symbolic, and identity reasons. Also in this case, being heritage a social construct defined by the community of reference, the stock of cultural value embodied in the heritage goods may equally deteriorate or disappear if not properly conserved, maintained, and transmitted through generations.

The interplay between economic and cultural values challenges standard techniques of economic valuation, which generally drive investment and market exchange decisions (Rizzo and Throsby 2006; Rizzo and Mignosa 2013).

Cultural heritage has direct economic value, in the form of its real estate value or the benefits accruing to tenants or tourists who visit it as a cultural site, that may be captured in the prices and financial valuation given in standard market transactions. However, unlike other standard economic goods, cultural heritage may also generate non-market and non-use benefits, given the component of collective use and significance expressed by its cultural recognition (Navrud and Ready 2002). Non-use values may relate to the asset's existence value (people value the existence of the heritage item even though they may not consume its services directly themselves), its option value (people wish to preserve the option that they or others might consume the asset's services at some future time), and its bequest value (people may wish to bequeath the asset to future generations). Non-use values may also arise as beneficial externalities to individuals who do not directly and willingly use heritage assets for instrumental purpose, but, for example, might enjoy the visual representation and atmosphere living in or passing by areas endowed of heritage assets. Besides such categorical distinctions, as a form of external effect, what is important to notice is that none of the non-use values can be easily captured through pricing mechanisms and in market transactions.

As a result, cultural heritage, even that privately owned, is considered from an economic viewpoint as a form of public good. It generates non-rival and often hardly excludable benefits to a wider group of subjects (i.e., local community, tourists, tourist service providers) that do not directly pay for its preservation and maintenance. In such circumstances, economic theory suggests that there is a risk of sub-optimal provision of investments in heritage preservation as far as proper funding and governance mechanisms are devised to cope with the heritage public good dilemma. This argument has provided also the basic economic justification for public sector intervention and fiscal incentives policies to support cultural heritage preservation.

With this perspective, the recognition of heritage as a form of cultural capital owning public and collective good characteristics leads to some key implications for the management and revitalization of urban historic centers.

The Cost and Collective Action Problem of Historic Centers' Preservation
While it has been recognized that cultural heritage sites pose public good dilemmas that lead to the risk of underinvestment for their preservation, the challenge to safeguard the distinctive traits of historic city centers and guarantee their sustainable long-term management is even more worsened by the generally high fragmentation of ownership of heritage that leads to a context of decentralized and uncoordinated decisions related to the benefits and cost of heritage preservation.

Being heritage buildings a form of real estate property, individual owners of buildings with architectural and historic value generally bear four categories of costs related to heritage conservation: (1) the cost of the heritage regulatory systems; (2) the incrementally greater cost for repair and maintenance ofheritage buildings; (3) the cost of compromises to contemporary use and enjoyment; and (4) the opportunity costs for foregone development opportunities (Productivity Commission 2006). By contrast, the financial return from restoring and preserving historic landmarks and buildings with architectural and cultural value may be perceived by individual owners lower than other alternative development opportunities in the same area. This is mainly due to the potential functional obsolescence of the building or the difficulty in monetizing non-market and public good benefits that accrue indirectly to other beneficiaries (i.e., the enjoyment from aesthetic improvements of the building by the local community).

The Value of Uniqueness and the Sense of Place
Being heritage complexes, made up of historic landmarks and buildings with architectural and cultural value, the cultural capital of historic city cores conveys a unique cultural atmosphere and sense of place (Licciardi and Amirtahmasebi 2012). Such idiosyncratic character is the result of the accumulated forms of cultural expressions that coalesce into the productive milieu, the styles of buildings, and the associated social fabric. Investing in heritage preservation in historic city cores thus means to enhance a resource that is hardly substitutable across space and increasingly worth in the global competition among cities. Firstly, because it helps fostering the image and attractiveness of a city for both tourism and businesses' locational choices. Secondly, because it reinforces the identity and social cohesion of the local community in relation with the place.

One of the major challenges in acknowledging the benefits arising from the distinctive cultural character of historic city centers is that they mostly belong to the category of non-market and public good values as a peculiar feature of cultural heritage goods. As a result, a central issue in heritage economics is the question of identifying the precise dimensions of economic and cultural values that give historic city cores their distinctive character.

Interestingly, much of the methodology developed for assessing environmental benefits has been directly used for the evaluation of the economic benefits stemming from urban heritage preservation (Pagiola 1996; Navrud and Ready 2002).

While most research of this type has focused on the economic valuation of individual historic monuments and archeological sites, only few works have addressed the welfare effects of preserving and enhancing urban heritage complexes. Some seminal works date back to the 90s and are studies conducted in the context of projects funded by World Bank to restore Fez Medina in Morocco and the historic core of the Croatian city of Split (Pagiola 1999; World Bank 1999). Other more recent applications have been undertaken for the city of Valdivia in Chile (Báez and Herrero 2012), Skopje in Macedonia, Tbilisi in Georgia (Throsby 2016), or Port Louis in Mauritius (Bertacchini and Sultan 2020).

The findings of these studies tend to confirm the existence of non-market or unexploited direct use values that are often overlooked by decision-makers and can provide useful guidance to better evaluate the economic relevance of maintaining the distinctive cultural and architectural character of historic city centers.

Sustainability of Urban Heritage
Considering heritage as cultural capital has also a clear parallel with the interpretation of natural environment and ecosystems as natural capital (Throsby 1999; Rizzo and Throsby 2006). Both cultural and natural capital have been inherited from the past, will deteriorate or degrade if not maintained, and impose on the present generation a duty to care for the assets involved so they can be handed down to future generations. This suggests that sustainability principles, such as intergenerational equity, precautionary principle or the recognition of the value of diversity, should be extended also to any analysis of the long-term management of cultural capital, including heritage in urban historic cores (Throsby 2016). One of the key elements for a sustainable approach to historic city centers is the precautionary principle that argues for a risk-averse stance in decision-making when irreversible consequences are possible, such as that of demolishing decaying buildings with architectural and cultural value. In fact, after a building with architectural value has been demolished and a bigger and more modern structure has taken its place, going back in time may not be an option anymore. This is why, in a context of irreversible investments, it is sensible to protect a greater number of buildings with architectural value than would be optimal if there were certainty on how the area will evolve (Rama 2012).

Yet, while sustainability principles provide a theoretical ground for conserving cultural heritage in urban areas, from a social welfare viewpoint they provide little guidance on the level and extent of heritage protection that would be optimal in operational terms. This is because, unlike natural resources and ecosystem services, preferences and attitudes over cultural values expressed or produced by heritage assets are more difficult to be quantified or objectively measured. Moreover, cultural investments to enhance cultural capital may not only be directed toward conservation of existing heritage, but also to new and contemporary artworks and cultural goods.

3 The Role of Cultural Districts in Historic City Cores

While the conservation of heritage aims at preserving or recovering the distinctive physical traits of historic city cores, the cultural and economic values of the heritage assets may be only fully magnified by renovating and revitalizing their significance and adapting their functional uses to the changed or evolving economic and social conditions. Linking heritage conservation with its revitalization thus means to integrate the broader cultural resources of a place as a productive factor into the local economy by leveraging on the intangible heritage and the local system of cultural and creative activities directly or indirectly linked to the heritage of the place. This would allow the buildings to be occupied and utilized for economic uses, which renders the structures and consequently the area competitive with the rest of the city.

To trigger such culture-led development processes, most of the research on this field has paid attention to the role of cultural clusters, districts, or quarters (Santagata 2006; Cooke and Lazzeretti 2008; Evans 2009; Sacco et al. 2013; Marques and Richards 2014). In most cases, all these terms refer to phenomena that share some specific features:

- a spatial concentration of cultural and heritage resources, or culture-related activities in specific areas of cities
- economic specialization that allows the cultural system to utilize both the levers of exogenous growth (with markets outside the territory in question) and endogenous growth (the production factors being specific to the particular territory)
- a system of economic and institutional actors who, between them, have developed a dense network relationship within a particular territory
- small, localized firms and cultural organizations operating in complementary aspects of cultural and artistic markets
- generation of positive spillovers and externalities between the actors of the district that allow them continuously to fine-tune their know-how and their knowledge
- capacity to produce strong symbolic meanings and enhance the identification or reputation of the place at the local and international level.

What is noteworthy to stress here is that the cultural district perspective builds on that of cultural capital by putting emphasis on the entrepreneurial and organizational dimension of the production of cultural heritage-related goods and services. The unit of observation is not the cultural assets forming the stock of cultural capital or generating flows of economic services, but cultural firms, organizations, and professionals which use cultural capital as an input in the productive process. As a result, the key question this approach often seeks to answer is how economic and cultural actors are able to leverage on the cultural capital of a place through an industrial and creative atmosphere and drive local economic development. The first answer comes from a broader conceptualization of cultural heritage (and capital as well), closer to the anthropological perspective of material heritage. Besides the most traditional organizations stewarding official heritage, such as artworks, collections, monuments, and antiquities, under the cultural district approach heritage can take the form of more intangible expressions embedded in creative industries, such as craftsmanship, tastes, and traditional productive know-how and skills (Barrère 2013).

More importantly, the cultural district approach underlines the necessity of collective action among cultural actors to make heritage a driver for local development. While cultural districts and quarters may emerge spontaneously—with firms and cultural organizations exploiting agglomeration economies that spur co-location and the formation of networks of collaboration—in most of the cases, local cultural systems are only "potential" cultural districts. Having a relatively high concentration of cultural activities or heritage assets in a city is not a sufficient condition to activate a district logic. What is necessary is a proactive vision and attitude of the local actors toward the common goal of creating an enhanced image of the cultural and heritage potential of the local system.

In a cultural district, there is a continuous tension between competition and cooperation. Every museum or cultural firm competes against each other to attract visitors, tourists, or to sell their products in local and international markets, but at the same time they need to directly or indirectly cooperate and collaborate to guarantee that the quality and reputation of the overall heritage-related goods of the district is maintained. With this perspective, the link between cultural districts and local development occurs through increasing the awareness of the local cultural actors to behave and operate as a collective and integrated system. In this case, institutions (such as collective marks or standards) and territorial marketing policies play a crucial role to trigger such district logic by enabling a common image of the local cultural system and favoring the cooperation and alignment of incentives by individual actors.

4 Urban Heritage as Commons

Popularized by Elinor Ostrom's pioneering work on natural resource community-based management systems (Ostrom 1990), the term "commons" has been traditionally used in economic analysis to define physical resources which are subject to overuse and appropriation dilemmas (common-pool resources), as well as property and governance regimes over resources that are owned in common or entail collective action. More recently, a growing recognition has emerged that important types of humanly constructed shared resources, such as information, knowledge, infrastructures, or urbanscapes could be appreciated and analyzed as new forms of commons, often subject to enclosure (Hess and Ostrom 2007; Hess 2008).

As heritage and cultural expressions can be generally conceived as social constructs that require some degree of human interaction and transmission in order to be produced and used, no wonder scholars have started looking at them under this new perspective. Crucially, it is possible to identify two main reasons that are leading to the paradigm shift in the heritage discourse toward a commons perspective. Firstly, research on the commons partly originated from a critic to traditional approaches on either state or private property arrangements as the only solutions for the sustainable use of collective resources. Likewise, the debate around heritage has often paid attention only to public authorities for heritage conservation and management or the private tourism sector as the main channel for generating economic opportunities based on heritage. Conversely, today there is a greater recognition of the role of local communities in heritage conservation approaches as well as main targets of the heritage-based sustainable development strategies (Varine 2002; Gould 2018).

In particular, Gould (2017) discusses how commons' self-governance mechanisms might apply to the management of archeological resources, so as to empower the local communities.

Secondly, while cultural heritage has been usually treated in distinct categories depending on its physical and immaterial attributes, recent years have seen a growing awareness of the interplay between tangible, intangible, and material components. This aspect has profound implication also in the way cultural heritage as a specific typology of economic good can be analyzed and interpreted. With this respect, Bertacchini et al. (2012) have proposed a new research agenda which tries to define the domain of cultural commons to study cultural expressions, in both tangible and intangible forms, as shared resources by a community that involves some type of social dilemmas to sustain them.

Dilemmas in Urban Heritage Commons Considering urban heritage as a commons brings some relevant analytical implications for managing heritage in a sustainable way and to enhance local and equitable development. For example, by focusing on the "community" dimension, the commons perspective helps defining a framework to interpret the attributes of the community and the structure of interactions of the actors who share and use the heritage resource. Urban heritage, in the complexity arising from the coexistence and interaction of the built environment, landscape, social fabric, and cultural atmosphere, can be seen as a multi-attribute and multiuse resource which is indeed enjoyed and managed by a community of diverse actors and stakeholders that operate at different scale (i.e., international, national, local) and may express divergent interests in the type of uses of the resource (scientific, leisure, political, livelihood, etc.).

More importantly, the commons perspective allows eliciting and systematizes in a comprehensive framework the various social dilemmas that hinder the role of heritage as a potential sustainable development activator at the local level.

As a physical resource, the urban cultural heritage suffers from the familiar social dilemmas identified in the commons' literature for common-pool resources or public goods, namely appropriation or provision problems.

Appropriation problems generally arise with the overuse, rent dissipation of the resource. This is quite evident in the congestion effects generated by tourism dynamics, where excessive development of tourism demand at cultural sites threatens the sustainable conservation of heritage (Zhang 2012).

Similarly, several different factors might hinder an effective and sustainable conservation of urban heritage, representing a dilemma in the provision of a collective good. For example, the unequal distribution of benefits and cost arising from heritage conservation and rehabilitation projects can lead to conflicts between urban stakeholders reducing the involvement and cooperation by local residents. With this respect, community-based urban heritage rehabilitation approaches can be seen as commons-like social dilemmas. To ensure the sustainable management and development of cultural heritage, the incentives for conservation and use of the shared resources must be aligned between all the stakeholders. If an unbalance exists in the appropriation of benefits deriving from the valorization of urban heritage as well as in the costs deriving from conservation policies incurred by the different actors, the risk is to have no alignment in the incentives for properly conserving heritage and obtaining long-term sustainable development.

Alternatively, the conservation and rehabilitation of urban heritage can be flawed by conflicts among different city governmental and public entities involved in the conservation and management of urban heritage or actors might have different views on the optimal level of conservation to be provided, mainly due to the different geographic scale of the public good that heritage conservation should provide (e.g., for historic city centers included in UNESCO World Heritage List).

The above appropriation and provision problems tend to stem from the tangible component of cultural heritage and impact the integrity of the physical attributes of heritage assets in a way no different from the dilemmas affecting the governance of natural resources. Yet, urban heritage as a commons is subject to other type of social dilemmas and conflicts arising over the definition, use, and appropriation of its cultural values. It is possible to classify the following types of dilemmas over cultural values.

- *Heritage substitution* (cultural vs. economic value): a given productive use of the heritage asset would conflict with the preservation of the cultural values, or of the attribute exhibiting cultural values. The tension between the potential economic return from the new production use and the maintenance of cultural value (which often involves costs for its conservation) leads to a replacement or loss of the cultural value in which the asset is demolished or partially transformed. This dilemma, that falls within the sphere of values, is often associated or confused with the appropriation and provision problems that underlie the physical characteristics of the cultural heritage.

- *Heritage commodification (Disneyfication):* when the attribute of a heritage asset with cultural significance is used as an input to market goods and services, the economic value of the resource increases and the larger demand expressed by individuals outside the local and traditional community risks to dilute or transform the cultural meaning associated with the heritage.
- *Heritagization (Patrimonialization*): this type of dilemma entails a conflict over the definition or appropriation of heritage values between public authorities, commercial actors, and the local community (Gravari-Barbas and Renard 2010). For instance, the risk of degradation of traditional cultural practices as cultural commons depends not only on the loss of the cultural traits by members of the community, but also on the exhaustion or loss of access to urban amenities and tangible heritage assets upon which the traditional cultural expressions are based. As a result, too strict conservation approaches to the physical component of urban heritage may hinder other heritage values that are more likely the expression of local traditional practices.

5 Conclusion

This chapter has provided an economic perspective to the definition of integrated approaches to the conservation and management of the urban cultural heritage. The analysis suggests that the concept of cultural commons, recently introduced in the economic debate, might extend the main interpretative models of cultural capital and cultural district that had been proposed to analyze the trajectories of heritage-based local development, especially in urban context. The concept of cultural capital and that of cultural district share the recognition of the role of cultural resources within production processes to promote local development. However, they place emphasis on distinct issues and dynamics concerning the conservation and management of cultural heritage, which are instead referable to the cultural commons perspective.

Like that of the cultural capital, the idea of cultural commons highlights the opportunity of analyzing heritage in terms of tangible and intangible dimensions as well as sustainability principles. However, looking more directly at the characteristics and behavior of the community, the cultural commons perspective sheds light on the complex social dynamics that lead in the conservation and use of heritage to the interplay between its tangible and intangible components. Further, with regard to the tensions arising in the sustainable management of cultural heritage, the cultural commons approach suggests that they are not limited to the problem of finding a balance between economic and cultural values, but also on the misalignment of incentives and the potential opportunistic behavior of different types of stakeholders.

Finally, besides the concept of cultural capital, cultural commons extends the intellectual framework based on the notion of cultural district. The latter, taking an entrepreneurial and organizational perspective on how to use heritage as an input for production processes, highlighted the collective action problem in coordinating local cultural institutions and firms in the development of heritage-based goods and services. Crucially, the cultural commons extends the collective action problem originally identified in the cultural district model to a wider array of social dilemmas involving the management and conservation of heritage and addresses on a broader perspective the issue of governing the multifaceted dimensions of heritage as a shared resource.

References

Bandarin, F., & Van der Oers, R. (2012). *The historic urban landscape: managing heritage in an urban century*. New York: Wiley.

Báez, A., & Herrero, L. C. (2012). Using contingent valuation and cost-benefit analysis to design a policy for restoring cultural heritage. *Journal of Cultural Heritage, 13*(3), 235–245.

Barrère, C. (2013). Heritage as a basis for creativity in creative industries: the case of taste industries. *Mind and Society, 12*, 167–176.

Bertacchini, E. E., Bravo, G., Marrelli, M., & Santagata W. (Eds.). (2012). Cultural commons: A new perspective on the production and evolution of cultures. Cheltenham: Edward Elgar Publishing.

Bertacchini, E., & Sultan, R. (2020). Valuing urban cultural heritage in African countries: A contingent valuation study of historic buildings in Port Louis, Mauritius. *Journal of African Economies, 29*(2), 192–213.

Cooke, P. N., & Lazzeretti, L. (Eds.). (2008). *Creative cities, cultural clusters and local economic development*. Cheltenham: Edward Elgar Publishing.

Evans, G. (2009). From cultural quarters to creative clusters–creative spaces in the new city economy. In *The sustainability and development of cultural quarters: International perspectives. Institute of Urban History, Stockholm, 3259*.

Greffe, X. (2011). Creativity: The strategic role of cultural landscapes. *Sustainable City and Creativity: Promoting Creative Urban Initiatives, 199*.

Gould, P. G. (2017). Considerations on governing heritage as a commons resource. In *Collision or collaboration* (pp. 171–187). Springer, Cham.

Gould, P. G. (2018). *Empowering communities through archaeology and heritage: The role of local governance in economic development*. London: Bloomsbury Publishing.

Gravari-Barbas, M., & Renard, C. (2010). Une patrimonialisation sans appropriation? Le cas de l'architecture de la reconstruction au Havre. Norois. *Environnement, aménagement, société, 217*, 57–73.

Hess, C. (2008). *Mapping the new commons*. Paper presented at International Association for the Study of the Commons. Cheltenham, UK: University of Gloucestershire.

Hess, C., & Ostrom, E. (Eds.). (2007). *Understanding knowledge as a commons: From theory to practice*. Cambridge, MA: MIT Press.

Licciardi, G., & Amirtahmasebi, R. (Eds.). (2012). *The economics of uniqueness: Investing in historic city cores and cultural heritage assets for sustainable development*. The World Bank.

Marques, L. & Richards, G. (Eds.). (2014). *Creative districts around the world*. Breda: CELTH/NHTV. URL: http://creativedistricts.imem.nl/.

Navrud, S., & Ready, R. C. (Eds.). (2002). *Valuing cultural heritage: Applying environmental valuation techniques to historic buildings, monuments and artifacts*. Cheltenham: Edward Elgar Publishing.

Ostrom, E. (1990). *Governing the commons: The evolution of institutions for collective action*. Cambridge: Cambridge University Press.

Pagiola, S. (1996). *Economic analysis of investments in cultural heritage: Insights from environmental economics*. Washington, DC: World Bank.
Pagiola, S. (1999). Valuing the benefits of investments in cultural heritage: The historic core of split. Washington, DC: World Bank.
Productivity Commission. (2006). Conservation of Australia's historic heritage places, Report No. 37, Canberra.
Rama, M. (2012). heritage investing in the sense of place: Economics of urban upgrading projects with a cultural dimension. In G. Licciardi & R. Amirtahmasebi (Eds.), *The economics of uniqueness: Investing in historic city cores and cultural heritage assets for sustainable development*. World Bank Publications.
Rizzo, I., & Mignosa, A. (Eds.). (2013). *Handbook on the economics of cultural heritage*. Cheltenham: Edward Elgar Publishing.
Rizzo, I., & Throsby, D. (2006). Cultural heritage: Economic analysis and public policy. *Handbook of the Economics of Art and Culture, 1*, 983–1016.
Sacco, P. L., Ferilli, G., Blessi, G. T., & Nuccio, M. (2013). Culture as an engine of local development processes: System-wide cultural districts I: Theory. *Growth and Change, 44*(4), 555–570.
Santagata, W. (2006). Cultural districts and their role indeveloped and developing countries. *Handbook of the Economics of Art and Culture, 1*, 1101–1119.
Taylor, K. (2016). The HISTORIC URBAN LANDSCAPE paradigm and cities as cultural landscapes. Challenging orthodoxy in urban conservation. *Landscape Research, 41*(4), 471–480.
Throsby, D. (1999). Cultural capital. *Journal of cultural economics, 23*(1–2), 3–12.
Throsby D. (2001). *Economics and culture*. Cambridge: Cambridge University Press.
Throsby, D. (2016). Investment in urban heritage conservation in developing countries: Concepts, methods and data. *City, Culture and Society, 7*(2), 81–86.
UNESCO. (2011). *UNESCO Recommendation on the Historic Urban Landscape*. Paris: UNESCO.
Varine, H. D. (2002). *Les racines du futur: le patrimoine au service du développement local*.
World Bank. (1999). *Case study: Rehabilitation of the Fez Medina*. Washington, DC: World Bank.
Zhang, Y. (2012). Heritage as cultural commons: Towards an institutional approach of self governance. *Cultural Commons*, 153–177.

Power in Networks and the Urban Space

Manfred J. Holler and Florian Rupp

Abstract

The urban space paper is introduced by a brief "report" on the founding of Rome by Romulus; he traced a furrow and thereby defined the urban space. The core of the paper, however, defines the urban space by the dimension of collective decision-making expressed in the form of voting games. It offers a power index analysis of the relationship between the agents of a network—applying the Public Good Index (PGI) and the Public Value (PV)—reinterprets previous work by Holler and Rupp (Power in networks: A PGI analysis of Krackhardt's Kite Network. Transactions on computational collective intelligence. Springer, Heidelberg, 2019), and presents new numerical results and gives alternative interpretations. The results confirm our expectations: an increase of links and thereby connectedness tends to increase the power of an agent. The message for policymaking in the urban space is evident. This motivated us to discuss the question of why we should be interested in evaluating the power distribution within a network. Here, our focus is on the accountability of the agents—and the Smart City concept.

M. J. Holler (✉)
University of Hamburg, Hamburg, Germany
e-mail: Manfred.Holler@uni-hamburg.de
URL: http://www.ccr-munich.de

M. J. Holler · F. Rupp
CCR-Munich, Munich, Germany
e-mail: florian.rupp@ccr-munich.de
URL: http://www.ccr-munich.de

F. Rupp
Technical University Munich, Munich, Germany

E. Macrì et al. (eds.), *Cultural Commons and Urban Dynamics*,
https://doi.org/10.1007/978-3-030-54418-8_4

1 Defining the Urban Space

Rome was founded on the 21st of April 753 BC.[1] The foundation of a city was a religious act. The choice of the site was left to the decision of the gods. Romulus, the founder, being a Latin, and therefore a neighbor to the Etruscans, asked the gods to reveal their will by the flight of birds. The Palatine was chosen. Next Romulus "dug a small trench, of a circular form, and threw into it a clod of earth, which he brought from the city of Alba. Then each of his companions…following his example, threw in a little earth, which he had brought from the country from which he had come" …"A man could not quit his dwelling-place without taking with him his soil and his ancestors" (Fustel de Coulange 2006 [1864]), p.136). The filled-up trench became the location of an altar carrying the holy fire of the city.

Having accomplished this ceremony, Romulus used a copper plowshare to trace a furrow which marked the border of the new city. This was executed as a religious act as well. As a consequence, the enclosure was inviolable—and represented a perfect definition of urban space in its sacred-legal and physical dimension. Of course, there were interruptions in this furrow so that men could enter and leave the city. Romulus had raised the plow and carried it over, thereby determining the gates of the city.[2]

To leap over the furrow was a sacrilege. Romulus' brother Remus committed this sacrilege "and paid for it with his life" (Fustel de Coulange 2006 [1864]), p. 137). An alternative interpretation is that he was offered to the gods as a human sacrifice. Machiavelli suggests another interpretation. Given the example of Romulus, "it might be concluded that the citizens, according to the example of their prince, might, from ambition and the desire to rule, destroy those who attempt to oppose their authority" (Machiavelli 1882, p. 120). "…we must assume, as a general rule, that it never or rarely happens that a republic or monarchy is well constituted, or its old institutions entirely reformed, unless it is done by only one individual; it is even necessary that he whose mind has conceived such a constitution should be alone in carrying it into effect. A sagacious legislator of a republic, therefore, whose object is to promote the public good, and not his private interests, and who prefers his country to his own successors, should concentrate all authority in himself; and a wise mind will never censure anyone for having employed any extraordinary means for the purpose of establishing a kingdom or constituting a republic" (Machiavelli 1882, p. 120).[3]

There is the issue of decision-making in founding a city and keep it running. History of Ancient Greece tells us that this was not always accomplished by a single decision-maker, a tyrant or king, but quite often by a collectivity. "…small groups,

[1]This date is given in Fustel de Coulange (2006 [1864]: 138). The following account derives from this text.

[2]These intervals of carrying the plow were called *portae* (Fustel de Coulange 2006 [1864]: 138).

[3]Holler and Marciano (2010) discussed Machiavelli's "possibility hypothesis" with reference to Arrow's notorious "impossibility theorem" which says that, given a set of quite reasonable condition, we cannot exclude that an aggregation of individual preference fails and we cannot derive a social welfare function—unless we accept that it is dictatorial (see Arrow (1963[1951]).

which, having been long-established, were finally joined together in larger ones. Several families formed the phratry, tribe, city, were, moreover, societies exactly similar to each other, which were formed one after the other by a series of federations. …when the different groups became thus associated, none of them lost its individuality, or independence" (Fustel de Coulange 2006 [1864]), p. 127). Again, the urban space was defined by a sacred act. "The tribes that united to form a city never failed to light a sacred fire, and to adopt a common religion" (Fustel de Coulange 2006 [1864]), p. 127).

Within this sacred space, the groups formed networks, and, in general, the position within such a network decided on the impact the various groups had on the decision-making of the city. Classical Athens developed a rather sophisticated apparatus of collective decision-making to balance the interest of specific groups and individuals and to match them with traditional norms and social standards. Its most important institutions were the Assembly, the Council, and the Courts. The Assembly was made of all male citizens who voted on new laws and on whether or not to go to war. The Council consisted of 500 members who did the day-to-day work of the government. Seats in the Council were determined by a lottery of all male citizens. The Court consisted of juries of 201 people for private lawsuits and 501 people for public lawsuits. Decisions were made by voting.

There was a lot of voting prescribed for the governmental institutions of Classical Athens. The urban space was defined by citizenship and participation in collective decision-making, thus extending the concept of citizen as persons who live within the physical boundaries of a city to persons who live within the political, legal, and cultural boundaries of a society.

When it comes to decision-making in the urban space, we see that the basic setting did not change so much—although, today, the religious dimension is far less prominent than it was in ancient Rome or Athens. But even today, a German bishop city has quite a different aura and sometimes the bishop has still a voice even when it comes to decisions that seem exclusively relevant for the city. Gigantic cathedrals, walled castles, splendid palaces, and picturesque parks visualize that, in the past, bishops were a major agent in defining and shaping the urban space. Some of these constructions still belong to the church and must be looked after, partly rebuilt and, now and then, extended.

Bishops are of course not the only ones who had and still have a particular impact on the city's decision-making due to their positions in an underlying network—and, of course, it should be of interest to know who has the power, and how much of it—for those who govern and for those who are governed. There are various tools to evaluate the power of an agent in a network that is meant to capture an important dimension of the urban space. Section 2 briefly discusses centrality measures and the relationship between power and centrality. Section 3 introduces two power measures: Public Good Index and Public Value. Section 4 offers a linear model illustrating the application of the Public Good Index to networks. In Sections 5 and 6, Public Good Index and Public Value are applied to voting games which represent Krackhardt's kite network and a variation of it. In the concluding Section 7, we briefly discuss the question of why we should be interested in evaluating the power distribution within a network—with a reference to responsibility and the Smart City concept for applications.

The focus of the paper is to demonstrate the application of power index analysis examining the relationships of the agents within a network. Thereby, we reinterpret earlier work by Holler and Rupp (2019),[4] present new numerical results, and give alternative interpretations.

2 Power and Centrality

In his seminal paper, Krackhardt (1990) analyzed the kite network in Fig. 1 with respect to three centrality measures: the *degree centrality*, i.e., a vertex is important/powerful the more neighbors it has; *closeness centrality* which captures the shortest paths to other vertices; and the *betweenness centrality*, which expresses the control over information passing between other vertices because of the vertex's position in a network. Somewhat surprising, these concepts picked three different vertices as "winners".[5] The kite structure of Fig. 1 represents the smallest network Krackhardt (1990, p. 351) has "found in which the centrality based on each of the three measures reveals different actors as the most central in the network." Later, examples of smaller networks showing divergent centrality measures were proposed (see, e.g., Brandes and Hildenbrand 2014).

Of course, in Fig. 1, only vertices that are directly or indirectly connected (by links) can communicate with each other—and work together. If the network represents an urban space and we are interested inasmuch as the various agents contribute to the common good produced by this network, then the divergent measures raise the question of which centrality measure to use. However, it is obvious, even from the title of his article, that Krackhardt is interested in the power of the agents forming a network, and the centrality measures are mere proxies—or shall we call them approximations. In this paper, we chose a more direct approach applying power measures, i.e., the Public Good Index (PGI) and the Power Value (PV), to express the power of an agent in a network. We apply these measures to Krackhardt's kite network assuming that the output of the network is a (pure) public good such that non-rivalry in consumption and non-excludability hold. The power focuses on the impact an agent has on the outcome of the kite network: what public good to produce and how much of it. To keep the model simple, we assume that decisions are made by majority voting and that each vertex (i.e., agent) has one vote only. Of course, the second assumption could be modified if the resources of the agents vary. Differences can be taken care of by an unequal distribution of voting weights. Such differentiation is quite likely if the network represents an urban

[4]Figures 1 and 2, the introduction to the Public Good Index and Public Value, etc., are borrowed from Holler and Rupp (2019).

[5]Vertex D has the highest degree centrality, H and I rate highest with respect to betweenness centrality, and F and G have, on the average, the shortest path distance to the other vertices (closeness centrality).

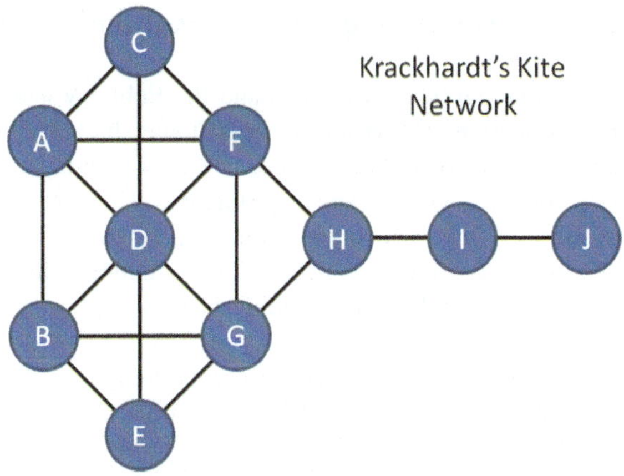

Fig. 1 Krackhardt's kite network

space. Moreover, within the context of the model, we can vary the majority rule as well—for instance, reflecting differences in the demand for resources. Therefore, the more general theory of weighted voting applies.

Krackhardt (1990, p. 349) offers two dimensions of power: the ability to get things done despite resistance and the ability to influence through personal magnetism (charisma). Standard power measures (like the PGI) ignore the second dimension; they focus on modeling Max Weber's definition of power: "In general, we understand by 'power' the chance of a man or of a number of men to realize their own will in a communal action even against the resistance of others who are participating in the action" (Weber 1948[1924], p. 180).

In experimental studies of centrality, it seems quite common to equalize centrality with power. However, in general, these studies are based on noncooperative settings (see, e.g., van Leeuwen et al. 2019)—i.e., binding agreements to form coalitions are excluded—and can handle only small numbers of players. The following analysis assumes that players can agree on forming coalitions and their agreements are binding: it is work in cooperative game theory. This concurs with the assumption that the output of a network is a public good. The vertices of the network are the decision nodes; they represent the players of a corresponding cooperative game. The links define the potential relationships between the players, i.e., what coalition they can form—on what (network) outcomes they can agree. The Public Good Index and the Public Value are the solution concepts to the corresponding cooperative games defined by the network structure u and the decision rule d. Here u summarizes the nodes and the links between the nodes (see, e.g., Figure 1) and d represents how the decision is made and the corresponding outcome. Readers who are familiar with the Public Good Index and the Public Value can skip the next section.

3 The Public Good Index (PGI) and the Public Value (PV)

The Public Good Index (PGI) and the Public Value (PV) refer to Minimum Winning Coalitions (MWCs), i.e., coalitions which are just large enough to produce a particular outcome. For instance, if C is a winning coalition then it is minimal if C_i is a losing coalition, i.e., any member i leaving coalition C turns the winning coalition C into a losing coalition C_i. (C and C_i are set of players of the corresponding cooperative game.) If C is a winning coalition and C_i is a losing coalition then i is essential for the winning of C, i.e., player i is critical; i is a swing player; i has power.[6]

The PGI is a vector that represents the numbers of MWCs which have vertices i for an element. For a particular vertex i this number is c_i. The numbers c_i get standardized such that the "shares" of all vertices add up to one. Thus, $h_i(u, d)$, the PGI of i given a particular network structure u and a decision rule d, is

$$h_i(u,d) = \frac{c_i}{c} = \mathrm{PGI}_i(\Gamma) \quad \text{with network } \Gamma \text{ and } \sum_{i=1}^{n} c_i = c \tag{1}$$

Here, c_i is a function of u and d. In the case of a collective decision problem d is the decision rule, e.g., a majority quorum.

Note that, because of public good assumption, there is "no splitting up of a cake" and no bargaining over shares as in Myerson (1977) and the contributions that build on it.[7] Of course, there are networks that produce (private) goods that invite sharing, but, in this study, we focus on collective decision-making over public goods. It is assumed that each winning coalition represents a particular public good—a specific result for the urban space, e.g., an enlargement of the public traffic system or improvement of the school system. This is part of the story which motivated the application of the PGI.

The PGI has been introduced in Holler (1982) and axiomatized in Holler and Packel (1983).[8] However, as Holler and Li (1995) demonstrated, by looking at the shares only, relevant information can be lost. Therefore, we will also present the non-standardized numbers, i.e., the Public Value (PV): the PV of i is identical with the number of MWCs which have i as a member. Thus, the PV of i, given a particular net structure u and outcome rule d, is

[6]The swing players define the power for the indices of Shapley–Shubik, Penrose–Banzhaf–Coleman, Johnston, and Deegan–Packel. These measures vary in what coalitions are to be considered and how the coalition surplus is *distributed* among their members.

[7]Myerson (1977) presents a bargaining model for networks that connects the (fair) bargaining outcome and the corresponding Shapley value.

[8]For a recent discussion of the PGI, see Holler (2019). Note there are more than ten power indices, but there is only one measure that is serious about measuring the impact of a player in producing a *public good*, i.e., the PGI.

$$p_i(u, d) = c_i = PV_i(\Gamma) \quad \text{with network } \Gamma \text{ and } \sum_{i=1}^{n} c_i = c \tag{2}$$

Again, c_i is a function of the network structure u and the decision rule d. Holler and Li (1995) give an axiomatization of PV.

4 The Linear Model

In order to illustrate the application of the PGI to networks, we will discuss a toy example which demonstrates that you do not need to have resources to have some power when you are connected. Fragnelli (2012) offers a simple example that demonstrates the power of a link.[9] The decision body is given by the weighted voting game v* = (*51*; 35, 30, 25, 10), i.e., the decision rule and vote distribution are d = 51 and w^* = (35, 30, 25, 10), respectively. Note that player 4, having a weight $w_4{}^*$ = 10, is a *dummy* in v^*; player 4 is not *critical* for the winning of any coalition. The set of MWCs is {{1,2},{1,3},{2,3}}. The corresponding power distribution, measured by the PGI, therefore is

$$h(v*) = \left(\frac{1}{3}, \frac{1}{3}, \frac{1}{3}, \frac{0}{3}\right).$$

The voting weights can be interpreted as proxies for the resources an agent can invest into the production of a network good. Solon divided Athens' citizenship into four property classes. Belonging to a given class does not constitute a "right" describing what you can get from your community, but an expectation which the community had of a particular member, i.e., what he can contribute.

Let us introduce a linear network structure, $G°$: (1)–(2)–(3)…(4), to the weighted voting game v^* = (51; 35, 30, 25, 10), with player 4 being unconnected. The set of MWCs is {{1,2},{2,3}}. The corresponding power distribution therefore is

$$h(v_{G^\circ}) = \left(\frac{1}{4}, \frac{2}{4}, \frac{1}{4}, \frac{0}{4}\right).$$

Player 2's dominating power is the result of centrality as the voting weights of players 1, 2, and 3 are equal. The impact of the network positions on the power distribution is even more obvious when we change the network structure to G': (1)–(4)–(2)–(3). The set of MWCs and the values of the PGI are {{1,4,2},{2,3}} and

[9]However, Fragnelli (2012) applies the Banzhaf index to measure power which takes into account *all* winning coalitions. It is not obvious that this index expresses the impact of a decision-maker in the case of a public good. (See Holler 1982, 2019).

$$h(v^\circ) = \left(\frac{1}{5}, \frac{2}{5}, \frac{1}{5}, \frac{1}{5}\right).$$

The example demonstrates that we do not need resources if we are well connected. This looks like a good message to the have-nots. However, many people are well connected only because of their resources. It seems this holds especially for the urban space—of course, not today, but in ancient times.

5 Power in Krackhardt's Kite Network

In order to apply the PGI and the PV to analyze Krackhardt's kite network, we define a voting game $v = (6; 1, 1, 1, 1, 1, 1, 1, 1, 1, 1)$ that has the absolute majority $d = 6$ as a quorum. Of course, this is a very rough approximation because, in general, (a) the weights of the agents in an urban decision problem are not identical and (b), even more drastically, there is no voting. However, quite often voting is just a shorthand of the underlying bargaining process. The quorum $d = 6$ represents the number of votes—perhaps the volume of contributions needed—to accomplish the project. A winning coalition is a set of *at least* six players. Thus, a minimum winning coalition in the network game is a set of six players who are connected. There are 70 minimum winning coalitions which are satisfying the connectivity requirement implied by the network Γ. It should be noted that without the matching constraints implicit to the network, there are 210 minimum winning coalitions for the game $v = (6; 1, 1, 1, 1, 1, 1, 1, 1, 1, 1)$.

To investigate the impact of the vertices I and J on the PGI-power of H, we consider the number of minimum winning coalitions—and calculate the corresponding PGIs—(a) in the complete graph Γ with vertices A to J, (b) those that are present in the subgraph Γ_1 with vertices A to I (without vertex J), and (c) those that are present in the subgraph Γ_2 with vertices A to H (without vertices I and J). These subgraphs have the same edges as the complete graph otherwise. Table 1 gives the PV values, i.e., number c_i of minimum winning coalitions to which a vertex i belongs in these three graphs, as well as the corresponding values of the PGI (rounded to four decimals). Note that we did not reduce the quorum in the case of Γ_1 and Γ_2 in order to "isolate" effects of changes in the network structure.[10]

Table 2 summarizes the corresponding rankings of the vertices defined by their PGI values. This table shows that nodes F and G are relatively strong while D which somehow forms the center of the kite (without tail) is relatively week. This is somewhat surprising, and not really obvious. However, it is obvious that H is the most powerful node when I gets connected. Perhaps it is somewhat surprising that

[10]In general, parliaments and city councils do not change their majority rules if links between parties altered, and, in the extreme, a party became unconnected to any other like going from Γ and Γ_1.

Table 1 Voting game with all decision-makers having the same individual weight 1 and a decision rule $d = 6$ and network structures Γ (Krackhardt's kite), Γ_1, and Γ_2

i	A	B	C	D	E	F	G	H	I	J
$PV_i(\Gamma_2)$	20	20	20	20	20	21	21	20		
$PGI_i(\Gamma_2)$	0.1234	0.1234	0.1234	0.1234	0.1234	0.1296	0.1296	0.1234		
$PV_i(\Gamma_1)$	34	34	32	36	32	39	39	46	17	
$PGI_i(\Gamma_1)$	0.1069	0.1069	0.1006	0.1132	0.1006	0.1226	0.1226	0.1446	0.0817	
$PV_i(\Gamma)$	40	40	36	45	36	50	50	63	43	17
$PGI_i(\Gamma)$	0.0952	0.0952	0.0857	0.1071	0.0857	0.1190	0.1190	0.1500	0.1023	0.0404

Table 2 Ranking of PGI values in accordance with Table 1 (Decision rule $d = 6$ and network structures Γ (Krackhardt's kite), Γ_1, and Γ_2.)

$PGI_i(\Gamma_2)$	F = G > A = B = C = D = E = H
$PGI_i(\Gamma_1)$	H > F = G > D > A = B > C = E > I
$PGI_i(\Gamma)$	H > F = G > D > I > A = B > C = E > J

the power of I increases quite substantially, overtaking A, B, C, and E, when J enters.

Next, we study the voting game $v = (7; 1, 1, 1, 1, 1, 1, 1, 1, 1, 1)$, again given Krackhardt's kite structure. The quorum of $d = 7$ reflects a 2/3 majority: this is a decision rule which is often relevant in changing a constitution or the voting rule itself. It seems relevant if the network requires a strong support, e.g., because contributions to the network produce could be substantial or because the network produce is substantial and production cannot afford major resistance or freeriding.

The number of minimum winning coalitions decreases to 52 as there is, of course, a smaller potential for MWCs as in the case of $d = 6$. Since in the case of the network Γ_2, seven out of eight agents are needed to form an MWC; the position in the network—i.e., connectedness, closeness, and centrality—do not matter much, actually, nothing at all. Therefore, all nodes have the same degree of power. Tables 3 and 4 confirm that node H is the strongest agent in the case of networks Γ_1 and Γ. Somewhat surprising is the career of node I. It is the weakest player in case of the network Γ_1 but metamorphs into the second strongest when J joins as well and network Γ forms (see Table 4).

6 The Impact of the Network Structure: The D-Modified Kite

We have seen that changes in the set of links have substantial consequences for the power distribution. Of course, cutting the links of I, and I and J with node H is substantial for these vertices because they have no alternative: they are no longer

Table 3 Voting game with all decision-makers having the same individual weight 1 and a decision rule $d = 7$ and network structures Γ (Krackhardt's kite), Γ_1, and Γ_2

i	A	B	C	D	E	F	G	H	I	J
$PV_i(\Gamma_2)$	7	7	7	7	7	7	7	7		
$PGI_i(\Gamma_2)$	0.1250	0.1250	0.1250	0.1250	0.1250	0.1250	0.1250	0.1250		
$PV_i(\Gamma_1)$	21	21	21	21	21	22	22	27	20	
$PGI_i(\Gamma_1)$	0.1071	0.1071	0.1071	0.1071	0.1071	0.1122	0.1122	0.1377	0.1020	
$PV_i(\Gamma)$	35	35	33	37	33	40	40	53	46	26
$PGI_i(\Gamma)$	0.0925	0.0925	0.0873	0.0978	0.0873	0.1058	0.1058	0.1402	0.1216	0.0687

Table 4 Ranking of PGI values in accordance with Table 3 (Decision rule $d = 7$ and network structures Γ (Krackhardt's kite), Γ_1, and Γ_2.)

$PGI_i(\Gamma_2)$	A = B = C = D = E = F = G = H
$PGI_i(\Gamma_1)$	H > F = G > A = B = C = D = E > I
$PGI_i(\Gamma)$	H > I > F = G > D > A = B > C = E > J

connected and therefore are no longer candidates for a (minimum) winning coalition within a network. As a consequence, they are powerless; they cannot have any impact on the outcome of the network despite the fact that they have the same voting weight as the other players.

Of course, isolating a node in a network is a rather extreme, however often experienced, structural change in a network. It seems straightforward to analyze the effects of a possibly less substantial modification in the network structure. We assume a D-modified kite network, where the two links C–D and D–E of Krackhardt's kite are erased (see Fig. 2.) Correspondingly, we label the modified network structures by Γ°, Γ_{1°, and Γ_{2°. Again, to investigate the impact of the vertices I and J, we define the voting game $v = (6; 1, 1, 1, 1, 1, 1, 1, 1, 1, 1)$ and count the minimum winning coalitions in the complete graph Γ° with vertices A to J, those that are present in the subgraph Γ_{1° with vertices A to I (without vertex J), and those that are present in the subgraph Γ_{2° with vertices A to H (without vertices I and J). Again, these subgraphs have the same edges as the complete graph otherwise (see Fig. 2 for an illustration).

There is not very much variation in power within the network Γ_{2°, however, nodes F and G are the strongest. When I enters, node H takes over the lead, however, leaving I at the end of the power chain. This is quite similar to the result we derived for the case of the graph Γ_1 when the links of Krackhardt's kite applied. The result is quite different in the cases of Γ°. Compared to the results for Γ, the node's I power career in case of Γ° is more modest when J enters the network Γ_1 to form Γ°.

Tables 7 and 8 list the results of the voting game $v = (7; 1, 1, 1, 1, 1, 1, 1, 1, 1, 1)$ in case of the D-modified kite network. A comparison of the last lines of Tables 6 and 8 reveals that in the D-modified kite the power of I increases

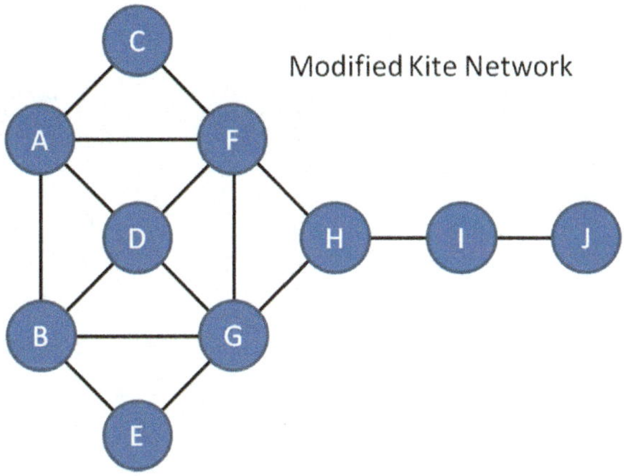

Fig. 2 D-modified kite network

substantially if the decision rule is augmented from $d = 6$ to $d = 7$ and agent J gets connected. There is a strong echo effect of J entering. Comparing Tables 4 and 8 suggests that the career of I is not depending on whether D is directly connected to C and E, or not (Table 5).

But does D's power suffer from cutting the direct links with C and E? Comparing Tables 1 and 5 shows that D loses power. This also holds for comparing 3 and 7, i.e., when a decision rule $d = 7$ instead of $d = 6$ applies if I and J enter. In this case, D could be motivated to keep I and J separated from the network if D is no longer directly linked to C and E. Tables 2 and 6 tell us that the power ranking of D decreases in comparison with A and B when B's links with C and E are cut. (Note in both settings the power of A and B are equal.) A comparison of Tables 4 and 8 suggests that the power ranking of D is even more vulnerable to an entry of J if D is not directly linked to C and E.

The results confirm our expectations: an increase of links and thereby connectedness tends to increase the power of an agent. Hereby links need to be seen in terms of pivotal positions between different groups of agents who allow that agents can contribute (as, e.g., player H). Hence, it is not only the direct neighborhood that counts for power (as in degree centrality) but rather a certain environment with a maximal radius of d-1. Here d represents the quorum of the corresponding voting game.[11] The message for policymaking in the urban space is evident. We do not further discuss the tables above but leave the interpretation to the reader—as we do

[11]In order to form a winning coalition, i needs to be connected to at least $d - 1$ vertices (such that they form a connected subgraph). The required $d - 1$ many nodes can be on any side of i in the network such that the winning coalitions i belong to a circle/sphere with maximal radius $d - 1$. Here, the notion of a radius is in terms of graph neighborhoods: if i has a high enough degree it may be the case that the coalition is formed by direct neighbors of i only, i.e., i is connected to each of the members of its coalition by minimal paths of length 1. In this sense, the worst case that can occur, maximizing the distance, is that actually a $d - 1$ neighbor has to be a member of the coalition. (The shortest path between i and this vertex has length $d - 1$).

Table 5 Voting game with all decision-makers having the same individual weight 1 and a decision rule $d = 6$ and network structures Γ° (D-modified Krackhardt's kite), $\Gamma_{1^{\circ}}$, and $\Gamma_{2^{\circ}}$

i	A	B	C	D	E	F	G	H	I	J
$PV_i(\Gamma_{2^{\circ}})$	19	19	18	18	18	20	20	18		
$PGI_i(\Gamma_{2^{\circ}})$	0.1266	0.1266	0.1200	0.1200	0.1200	0.1333	0.1333	0.1200		
$PV_i(\Gamma_{1^{\circ}})$	32	32	27	30	27	36	36	40	22	
$PGI_i(\Gamma_{1^{\circ}})$	0.1134	0.1134	0.0957	0.1063	0.0957	0.1276	0.1276	0.1418	0.0780	
$PV_i(\Gamma^{\circ})$	38	38	30	37	30	46	46	55	37	15
$PGI_i(\Gamma^{\circ})$	0.1021	0.1021	0.0806	0.0994	0.0806	0.1236	0.1236	0.1478	0.0994	0.0403

Table 6 Ranking of PGI values in accordance with Table 5. (Decision rule $d = 6$ and network structures $\Gamma°$ (D-modified Krackhardt's kite), $\Gamma_{1°}$, and $\Gamma_{2°}$.)

$PGI_i(\Gamma_{2°})$	F = G > A = B > C = D = E = E
$PGI_i(\Gamma_{1°})$	H > F = G > A = B > D > C = E > I
$PGI_i(\Gamma°)$	H > F = G > A = B > D = I > C = E > J

not want to exhaust our readers by exhausting the subject.[12] Our intention was to demonstrate the method of the power index analysis applied to networks—suggesting an additional tool for analyzing urban space when appropriate.

7 Responsibility and the Smart City

After the exercise of calculating PGI and PV and analyzing the result, we may ask ourselves why we should do this exercise—why should we be interested in the distribution of power in networks; why should we measure power. Most obviously, we might be interested in the design of a decision body for a network in order to implement a particular power distribution which supports the decision which we are aiming for, or blocks a choice which we do not want to see materialized, or takes care that the decision body satisfies a norm of fairness. Perhaps, we would like to be able to assign responsibility in order to make network agents accountable for what they decide or for what they could prevent. Accountability could be an issue of fairness but also a key to improving decision-making, e.g., to collect more information, to arrange for more competence, and to do better thinking. Analyzing the power structure could be a helpful tool to improve thinking.[13]

There is another field of applying power index analysis of networks in the urban space: the Smart City. The core of this concept is the comprehensive usage of information technology for managing the city. In the introduction to their forthcoming report *Considerations in the design and implementation of Smart Cities systems*, Orłowski et al. (2019) write that the acceptance of the Smart City vision "is a long-term process in which municipal decision-makers, city residents and civic organizations work out a compromise, which is often the result of merit-based decisions by the authorities but can also result from political decisions, on which the residents only have an indirect influence. Such a complex city system, seen from the perspective of the authorities, city residents and organizations, and taking into account many decision-making processes which are hard to control and analyze, represents a complex environment for the implementation of information technology supporting city management processes."

[12]In his *Picture of Dorian Gray*, Oscar Wilde characterized a Radical member of Parliament by the by now notorious quote: "Like all people who try to exhaust a subject, he exhausted his listeners."
[13]For a more intensive discussion of the relationship of power and responsibility, see Holler (2007).

Table 7 Voting game with all decision-makers having the same individual weight 1 and a decision rule $d = 7$ and network structures $\Gamma°$ (D-modified Krackhardt's kite), $\Gamma_{1°}$, and $\Gamma_{2°}$

i	A	B	C	D	E	F	G	H	I	J
$PV_i(\Gamma_{2°})$	7	7	7	7	7	7	7	7		
$PGI_i(\Gamma_{2°})$	0.1250	0.1250	0.1250	0.1250	0.1250	0.1250	0.1250	0.1250		
$PV_i(\Gamma_{1°})$	20	20	19	19	19	21	21	25	18	
$PGI_i(\Gamma_{1°})$	0.1098	0.1098	0.1043	0.1043	0.1043	0.1153	0.1153	0.1373	0.0989	
$PV_i(\Gamma°)$	33	33	28	31	28	37	37	47	40	22
$PGI_i(\Gamma°)$	0.0982	0.0982	0.0833	0.0922	0.0833	0.1101	0.1101	0.1398	0.1190	0.0654

Table 8 Ranking of PGI values in accordance with Table 7 (Decision rule $d = 7$ and network structures $\Gamma°$ ((D-modified Krackhardt's kite), $\Gamma_{1°}$, and $\Gamma_{2°}$.)

$PGI_i(\Gamma_{2°})$	A = B = C = D = E = F = G = H
$PGI_i(\Gamma_{1°})$	H > F = G > A = B > C = D = E > I
$PGI_i(\Gamma°)$	H > I > F = G > A = B > D > C = E > J

The power index analysis could turn out to be a helpful tool to solve some of these problems—and propose a solution to the responsibility problem inherent in the Smart City concept. Citizens may feel alienated if nobody is accountable of what they experience in their neighborhood. A city of alienated citizens is a challenging result for an urban space.

Acknowledgements The authors would like to thank Barbara Klose-Ullmann for the helpful comments.

References

Arrow, K. J. (1963 [1951]). *Social choice and individual value* (2nd ed.). New York: Wiley.

Brandes, U., & Hildenbrand, J. (2014). Smallest graphs with distinct Singleton Centers. *Network Science, 2,* 416–418.

Fragnelli, V. (2012). A note on communication structures. *Homo Oeconomicus,* 29, 163–171. Republished in Holler, M. J., & Nurmi, H. (Eds.). (2013). *Power, voting, and voting power: 30 years after* (pp. 467-473). Heidelberg: Springer.

Fustel de Coulange, N. D. (2006 [1864]). *The ancient city: A study of religion, laws, and institutions of Greece and Rome* (Orig.: *La cité antique*, Paris 1864), Mineola, NY: Dover Publications.

Holler, M. J. (1982). Forming coalitions and measuring voting power. *Political Studies, 30,* 262–271.

Holler, M. J. (2007). Freedom of choice, power, and the responsibility of decision makers. In J.-M. Josselin & A. Marciano (Eds.), *Democracy, freedom and coercion: A law and economics approach* (pp. 22–45). Cheltenham: Edward Elgar.

Holler, M. J. (2019). The story of the poor public good index. In N. T. Nguyen, R. Kowalzyk, J. Mercik, & A. Motylska-Kruzma (Eds), *Transactions on computational collective intelligence* (Vol. 34, pp. 171–179). Heidelberg: Springer.

Holler, M. J., & Li, X. (1995). From public good index to public value: An axiomatic approach and generalization. *Control and Cybernetics, 24,* 257–270.

Holler, M. J., & Marciano, A. (2010). Machiavelli's possibility hypothesis. *AUCO Czech Economic Review, 4,* 18–31.

Holler, M. J., & Packel, E. W. (1983). Power, luck, and the right index. *Journal of Economics (Zeitschrift für Nationalökonomie), 43,* 21–29.

Holler, M. J. & Rupp, F. (2019). Power in networks: A PGI analysis of Krackhardt's Kite Network. In N. T. Nguyen, R. Kowalzyk, J. Mercik & A. Motylska-Kruzma (Eds), *Transactions on computational collective intelligence* (Vol. 34, pp. 21–34). Heidelberg: Springer.

Krackhardt, D. (1990). Assessing the political landscape: Structure, cognition, and power in organizations. *Administrative Science Quarterly, 35,* 342–369.

Machiavelli, N. (1882). Discourses on the first ten books of Titus Livius. In: *The Historical, Political, and Diplomatic Writings of Niccolò Machiavelli* (Trans. from the Italian by Christian E. Detmold, Boston: James R. Osgood and Co.).

Myerson, R. B. (1977). Graphs and cooperation in games. *Mathematics of Operations Research, 2,* 225–229.

Orłowski, C., Sitek, T., Ziółkowski, A., Kapłański, P., Orłowski, A. & Pokrzywnicki, W. (2019). Introduction. In C.Orłowski, T. Sitek, A. Ziółkowski, P., Kapłański, A. Orłowski & W. Pokrzywnicki (Eds), *Considerations in the design and implementation of Smart Cities systems.* Gdańsk, Poland: CAS IBM Center for Advanced Studies.

Van Leewen, B., Ramalingam, A., Arjona, D. R., & Schram, A. (2019). Centrality and cooperation in networks. *Experimental Economics, 16,* 178–196.

Weber, M. (1948[1924]). Class, status and party. In H. H. Gerth & C. Wright Mills (Eds.), *Essays from Max Weber.* London: Routledge and Kegan Paul.

Commoning the Stage: The Complex Semantics of the Theatre Commons

Francesca Sabatini

Abstract

The paper investigates the present role of theatre in society; in particular, it seeks to identify theatre as a peculiar, complex commons, with a precise spatial, relational and cultural syntax outlined in the first section with relevant examples. The stratification of meanings, archetypes and formats of such commons and the cultural value it has generated in different times and for different societies are described in the second section. Theatre is analysed through the commons analytical framework in the third section, identifying its characteristics of a semantic commons. The policy and strategic implications of the conceptualisation of theatre as a commons are expressed in the fourth section: in particular, its features of publicity and togetherness testify for its power to catalyse powerful instances such as the right to the city and the claim for the resurgence of the public sphere. Examples of policies and practices from the international context are provided that illustrate the emerging map of actions going towards such objectives.

1 Performance, Space, People: The Intertwined Dimensions of the Theatrical Experience

> let us return to the principle [...] Let us take as a model humanity's simple actions, those that occur before our eyes every day. How, for example, does one assemble around a charlatan on a public square in order to hear him? People bunch together and form a circle around him. (Ledoux in Schwarte 2012: 161)

F. Sabatini (✉)
Department of Architecture and Territory, Mediterranean University, Reggio Calabria, Italy
e-mail: francesca.sabatini@unirc.it

E. Macrì et al. (eds.), *Cultural Commons and Urban Dynamics*,
https://doi.org/10.1007/978-3-030-54418-8_5

This statement was not boldly pronounced at the press conference of a contemporary participative performance, nor is it a quote from a 1970s theatre director willing to unchain the binomial association between performance and theatre. In fact, and quite surprisingly, it was written more than 250 years ago by Claude-Nicolas Ledoux, in a letter of 1775 stating his intention to reform the theatrical space and experience.

Ledoux was contributing to a lively and abundant debate within the Enlightenment movement, whose repercussions will be evident until decades after the French Revolution, concerning the role of theatre in society. This theatre *querelle*, in its turn, is all but a circumstantiated moment in time, but rather one of the endless reformative efforts which constellate the history of Western theatre—reforms which testify for the social, cultural and political relevance of theatre in different societies.

Ledoux's statement, within such framework, might be interpreted as a seductive eulogy to the flexibility of the theatrical infrastructure, and the need to restore the purity of the audience–performance relationship: but the matter is actually more complicated than this. He emphasises, in fact, a peculiar aspect of the theatrical practice, that is its spatial characteristics, while hinting at how the spatial articulation of a performance is generated almost by the tension between the audience curiously gathering around the performance, the actors or performers, and what happens in between (the performance itself).

Both the relevance of theatre as a social and political infrastructure and its ability to define a performance space through human relations and interactions testify for its social, cultural and political potential in different times, including our own. In a time that is reacting to the shrinking of public sphere, where political rights are claimed through the struggle for public space, theatrical practices and the performing arts might be able to provide new means of elaborating the political reality and to offer an exhaustive cultural infrastructure for urban complexity.

1.1 Theatre as Space

Almost two hundred years after Ledoux, Max Hermann wrote that *performing arts are spatial arts* (Roselt 2012: 302). He alluded to the impossibility of thinking about performance as separate from the space of performance; but also, and more specifically, he was referring to the copresence of actors and audience in the space and time of the performance, and the subsequent coproduction of the performance by both.

His analysis, however, only accounts for the dramaturgic spatiality (physical and relational), while leaving out a third corollary of the spatiality of theatre: its organisation within the urban and social environment, to which it is so tightly interconnected. The way these three dimensions have been dealt with, the way their boundaries have been stretched and their uses contested characterise theatre's role within a society and its epoch.

1.1.1 Physical Space and Theatrical Architecture

The first dimension, the physical and architectural, pertains to the building, or better, to the space in which both the audience and the stage are located. Adapting theatrical buildings and structures has never just been a matter of taste of the time: in many cases, reforming theatre has been mostly about exiting the conventional spaces of theatre architecture. A mutual influence has occurred in different times between performance and the stage; the former has been subject to the constraints and the structure of the latter; reversely, as performance evolved in its expressive forms, the stage was transformed in its shape, size and position with respect to the audience.

Examples of how theatrical architecture and spaces have been altered according to the specific meaning that was attributed to theatre constellate the millennial history of theatre. Eighteenth century Germany experienced an epistemic revolution through the Enlightenment, which produced the aspiration at a National, morally reforming theatre practice; such reform, in the intentions of its supporters, was to be pursued by displacing performances from the small halls where they were performed, an inheritance of the supposedly loose courtly morals, and holding them in large open spaces.

Twentieth century Arab theatre was sternly pivoted on the rejection of Western theatrical practices and their respective space; therefore, artists would perform in the open air and have the audience gather around them in a circle called *halqa*, thus forming a human amphitheatre which opposed the frontal fruition of Western theatrical architecture.

The contemporary New York based theatre project 'Shakespeare in the Park', taking place in different Manhattan public parks, stretches to the limits the notion of 'performance space', as it stages Shakespeare plays in varying locations changing from one act to the other; the audience is invited to follow the performers around the *impromptu* stages.

1.1.2 Audience and Performance

The articulation of the notion of relational space in theatre is twofold: on the one hand it concerns the distinction between an audience space and a performance space. Questioning the uses of this relational space, the equilibrium and balances within it, has always been on top of the priority list of both theatre administrators and directors in modern times.

Voltaire's *Dissertation on Ancient Tragedy* (1748), for instance, aspired at collocating the audience in a new, separate space, since in eighteenth century France the audience would simply sit on the stage, as close to the performers as it could possibly get, in more recent times. Today, with the institutionalisation of theatre as a form of entertainment, a fracture is created between the performance and its audience. And yet, Voltaire's proposition is being questioned once more by emerging ways of organising the performance space: Vick's *Stiffelio* at Teatro Regio (Parma 2017)[1] had the spectators standing in the parterre, while singers

[1]Folletto (2017).

invaded their space to perform among and interact with the audience. Regardless of the varying degrees of separation (ranging from the neat separation advocated by Voltaire or the sophisticated merging of Vick's play), as a matter of fact the audience coproduces the performance.

In 2018, for example, the director Pippo Delbono staged a controversially personal version of *La Cavalleria Rusticana* at Opera di Roma; his frequent monologues, held among the audience, interrupted the performance, and were in their turn interrupted by the outbursts of discontent from the part of many spectators, creating an unexpected tension.[2] In *La fille du regiment* (Teatro Comunale, Bologna, 2018; directed by Emilio Sagi)[3] the names of the ball's guests were changed into the names of local streets and nearby towns, causing the audience to overreact in exhilaration. In 2006 Wolker Lösch's adaptation of Peter Weiss' "*Marat, Sade*" enacted a sort of proscription list onstage, enumerating the names of the richest men in Germany and causing the audience to participate violently and powerfully to the performance (Wihstutz 2012: 214–215).

1.1.3 The Theatre's Relational Space

Spatial reforms, in which most theatrical transformations have been inscribed, have always been concerned with the transformation of the architectural space, whether it was the institution of private *tribunalia* in the Hellenistic era, marking the first class distinction in classical theatre, or Voltaire's aspiration of an ordered perceptive *apartheid* between the audience and the performance. As it has been noted, however,

> a circular theatre does not necessarily produce a democratic disposition, and a semicircular terraced structure does not necessarily evoke a feeling of equality. The actual effect of these and other constructions [...] lies in the various encounters between the monumental and the ephemeral, processes of building and the uses of architectural space, performances and intrigues. (Schwarte 2012: 162)

This latter articulation of relational space hinted to by Schwarte is perhaps more subtle and intangible, but crucial to the essence of theatre itself. Following David Harvey's economy of public space, it could be said that the stage–audience space mostly carries a relational value: in Harvey's words, a space where *there is no such thing as space outside of the processes that define it* (Harvey 2004: 4)—that is, the space of performance only exists because of the performance itself; in such case, space and time are strictly interrelated, since time, interactions and relations are the actual conditions under which the separation between stage and audience comes into being. The grammar of this relationship does not just articulate the stage–audience spatiality: it is a necessary precondition for the artistic creation itself. As simple as it may seem, without an audience there is no performance, and without this relational moment there is no theatre.

The three dimensions of this relationship refer not only to the way the theatrical space is built and structured, and the way theatre dynamics relate to it, they also describe the way the theatrical space is used by the audience—a usage which has

[2]Ricci (2018).
[3]De Matteis (2018).

varied largely in time. Francesco Reggiani, who in 2018 was still the head of the Historical Archive of Teatro dell'Opera di Roma, came up with a thrilling hypotyposis to describe this restless equilibrium:

> Imagine you're in a pub. People are sitting on bar stools drinking and talking loudly to each other; at their backs, a tv screen is hanged on a wall displaying some sports match. All of a sudden the speaker from the tv raises his voice in an outburst of enthusiasm, announcing the scoring of a point, and it is only now that the gentlemen, who had not paid attention to the tv until that time, turn to the screen and follow the action. This is more or less what an opera theatre looked like in the XVIII century: people talked, gambled, ate, and only when they recognised the beginning of a popular opera aria they would turn to the stage and listen to it in delight.[4]

The blatantly informal atmosphere described by Reggiani's vivid example in the past rings more than a bell: it is but one of the innumerable historical testimonies of how attitudes within theatres and towards theatrical practices have varied in time. Above all, it illustrates how the contemporary fruition of theatre, framed in a rigid behavioural grid, has remained anchored to a paradigm enforced in a somewhat late theatrical era: the audience–performance relational dimension, as well as the system of social relations occurring within the theatrical space, used to be appallingly different from what it is today: more fluid and informal, it has allowed theatre to be the space of interactions and encounter, more than reducing it to a mystical aesthetic ascension. This example should not be looked at nostalgically: it rather raises questions on formats and experiences, and on how biased and static our perception of relations and interactions is with respect to theatrical practices.

To attribute the vastness and richness of the theatrical experience to a list of chronologically ordered playwrights, then, would mean to do very little justice to all the tangible factors which have contributed for thousands of years to building what can be defined the theatrical commons. While being at the core of the theatre commons, in fact, the dramaturgic dimension is but one aspect of what seems to be a much more complex commons, relational, spatial and dramaturgic, which has crossed genres, historical eras and societies as an organic and coherent syntax regardless of the way it has been differently articulated.

The spatial dimension in particular, relational as well as physical and urban, has given shape to a social and cultural infrastructure whose modalities of enactment prove crucial in contemporary debate on society, the urban space, politics and economics: as will be seen shortly, theatre as a manifestation of and within the public sphere; theatre as a collective social practice; the occupation of theatrical spaces as acts of commoning, play today a role of special political relevance, as opposed to an understanding of theatre as "cultural industry", or as a mere form of entertainment.

1.1.4 Theatre's Embeddedness Within the Urban Fabric

The third spatial dimension omitted by Hermann's reflection is the urban one, which connects theatre to the surrounding social and urban environment. Theatres,

[4] Francesco Reggiani was interviewed by the author on July 31, 2018.

just like many other forms of art, have always been used either to represent and embody power, or to question and criticise it. In eighteenth and nineteenth centuries Paris, for instance, the 1er arrondissement was the protagonist of a lively clustering of theatres, whereas at the end of the nineteenth century this centripetal organisation began to be questioned, as was the case with Antoine's *ThéâtreLibre*, polemically located in the popular Place Pigalle (Carlson 2012: 40).

Even today, as urban regeneration dictates the rule for city planning, the positioning of a theatre (as that of cultural venues in general) still holds precise political connotations—in Paris, again, the reformative frenzy of the 1970s led to the building of theatres in peripheries in order to reinforce the cultural infrastructure of disadvantaged areas; still in 2005, in the peripheral neighbourhood of Tor Bella Monaca, a theatre was erected that was expected to represent an attraction pole for the Roman population in the area. Tor Bella Monaca is still perceived as largely abandoned and unsafe, regardless of the regeneration intervention, and the theatre has not attracted the external visitors whose curiosity it was supposed to arise.[5]

Of analogous strategic weakness is the architectural experiment of Elbphilharmonie in the Hannover pier. The rigid structures and hierarchies of conventional theatrical architecture were simply transferred from the centre to a new, regenerated part of the city which, however daring, failed to shake the stern foundations of institutional rules: quite the reverse, it stands as a cathedral in the desert, fascinatingly towering on the Elbe river. It has been transformed into the new symbol of the city, following the strategy of a "generic city boosterism" (McKinnie 2012: 85) rather than representing an actual attempt to de-format performance spaces in the urban fabric.

The conflict between physically structuring, actually living and coactively regulating the theatrical space is probably stronger than that of any other cultural venue: theatre as a social infrastructure manifested mechanisms of inclusion and exclusion. Athenian citizens could partake to theatrical events, while the metics could not, therefore implying a very intricate relationship between political identity and theatrical practices.

The political and social significance of theatres is so explicit as to have required, in modern times, the use of a specific police force to regulate mores and behaviours within it: in 1797, the theatre police in Austria would try and suppress clapping and eating within theatres in order to "enforce a new contemplative approach to aesthetic perception among the audience" (Wihstutz 2012: 21). It was more than an extemporaneous decision by a particularly stern authority, as it would change the modalities of theatrical experience, and, consequently, its format and its very function within the social fabric, shifting from social rite embedded in urban routines to isolated temple of beauty.

[5]During a workshop conducted in 2019 and 2020 by SITDA, the Italian Society of Architectural Technology, Tor Bella Monaca was chosen as the core topic; a series of unstructured interviews conducted throughout the workshop demonstrated the poor results of the regeneration interventions, and how the area is still perceived as largely abandoned and unsafe—regardless of the presence of the theatre.

1.2 The Dramaturgic Commons

In addition to the common spatial traits of theatrical practices a second commonality can be identified: the metro-linguistic component. Differently from the spatial syntax of theatre, the dramaturgic commonality does not pertain to the socioeconomic discourse as much as to the strictly humanistic one; and yet, when considering theatrical dynamics, and specifically those dynamics that are shared and collective, considerations over dramaturgy are called for.

It is impossible to waive from the formulaic aspects of dramaturgy, to the high codification of signs and languages which characterises the specificity of every theatrical form of expression on a global scale, from opera dramaturgy to singing in kabuki theatre. The stratification of theatrical dramaturgy in both content and form is the result of centennial processes involving playwrights, stage directors, actors, composers and the innumerable different declinations that these roles have assumed in different societies; languages, formats, dramaturgic conventions, idiomatic expressions, formulaic gestures have all been codified and absorbed into different theatre forms (Dahlhaus 2002). The syntax metaphor will once more serve its purpose: regardless of the specific codified languages and gestures, every theatrical form has developed a shared code.

Common cognitive traits seem to underlie the theatrical practice. The dramaturgic syntax, then, could be identified as the cognitive framework for both theatrical production and theatrical experience. In fact, signs, symbols, archetypes and tropes serve as the shared knowledge basis for the production and reproduction of artistic forms, and for the shared recognition of a conventional language on the part of both the audience and the performers: the articulated gestural lexicon of nō Japanese theatre, the melodic and metrical articulation of Greek classical plays and the sophisticated codified syllabus of love of the 1700s *marivaudage* represented a shared common ground for theatrical production and communication within the society which generated (and benefitted from) a specific theatrical practice.

2 History of Theory, History of Practice

2.1 Political Rite, Religious Ceremony, Club Good: A Short Chronicle of the Cultural Values of Theatre

In theatre, then, both the gestural language and the verbal one are codified into tropes and conventions which are shared by the performers as well as by the audience, thus constituting a cultural dramaturgic commons.

Yet, it is characterised not only by a common pool of archetypes and contents ranging from themes to characters, but also and especially by a shared spatial and relational language: this complex commonality lies in formats and infrastructures, in codified languages and in signifiers, shaping a collective social, political and cultural experience. The fact that the commons is transversal, however, does not mean it is universal; its cultural value, consequently, is by no means intrinsic, but has changed according to the different uses and formats adopted by different societies. The focus of the following examples will be primarily drawing from European societies.

The Dionysian Festivals, inscribed in a religious rite dedicated to the homonymous god, had neither a merely artistic nor a merely religious role in the life of the city, but rather represented a moment for shaping the civic identity of the citizens, a time of aggregation and of identity building through the production of shared archetypes (Baldry 1971). The fact that theatres were located in strategic positions exemplifies the relevance attributed to theatrical practices: the *agora*, at the meeting point between temples and the crucial nodes of political life. As it has been noted,

> theatres in ancient Greece had greater capacity than there were people in the city. It opened the way for the broader public to take part in key social events and therefore represented an opportunity to experience radical equality. (Schwarte 2012: 154)

Theatre gave voice to the Greek Weltanschauung in the particular form of its relationship with the other, this other being personified by ostracised women, outcasts, enemies—it is not by chance that the most ancient piece of Greek theatre which has survived up to the present day is a tragic account of the battle of Salamis, narrated by the defeated ones, the Persians (Wihstutz 2012: 222). And yet, theatrical representation of the others, the mythopoetic function of theatre and its power to craft political imagination was not a universal instance: only a restricted and rule-bound community could benefit from the theatrical infrastructure; Greek citizenship marked a very precise boundary.[6]

In the middle ages, with the political and public life being heavily impacted by the pervasive presence of religion, miracle and mystery plays took place in public squares in front of religious buildings; itinerant theatre companies, *jongleurs* and storytellers would draw from the most diverse written and oral traditions of religious tales to craft languages and modalities which were at a time transversal to the entirety of religious Europe, and hyper-local, due to the instances of the isolated communities of villages and rising cities.

Rather than being a mere *mimesis* of reality, theatrical expressions of the medieval society came in the form of allegories, whose evocative power enforced the feudal and religious system of the time[7]. Theatre gathered communities around the most important social infrastructure of the time: the church, while theatrical language served as a moral code and a warning accompanying peasants in their everyday life.

---

[6]For an introduction to Greek theatre and citizenship, see Barker (2008), *Tragedy and citizenship: conflict, reconciliation and democracy from Haemon to Hegel*, New York: State University of New York Press; Cartledge (1997).

[7]The Editors of the Encyclopaedia Britannica, Miracle Play, *Encyclopaedia Britannica*, 6th February, 2019, https://www.britannica.com/art/miracle-play, Accessed 30th April, 2020.

The Editors of the Encyclopaedia Britannica, Miracle Play, *Encyclopaedia Britannica*, 30th April, 2018, https://www.britannica.com/art/mystery-play, Accessed 30th April, 2020.

The religious and political dimensions underlying the cultural value of theatre were progressively overcome by the social relevance acquired by the performing arts in a world of rigidly structured social classes. From the sixteenth century onward, in fact, the theatrical experience became a dominant element in the infrastructure of interactions as shaped by social classes and their respective economic attributes; courtly society in central Europe, commissioning, patronising and benefitting from the arts, built the identity of its upper classes around the cultural world, expressed in the form of *salons* and, of course, theatre. A sophisticated society generated a form of entertainment which was just as sophisticated as itself,[8] from the baroquely intrigued love plays to the elegant adaptations of Greek tragedies. The fruition of such culture was private and exclusive: theatre had become a club good.

In the complicated castle of social rules there was, however, room for evasion: it was theatre (again) in the form of theatrical representations of reality such as carnivals and festivals, which allowed for the creation of a temporary heterotopias (Primavesi 2012: 205), the state of exception of a society overwhelmed by conventional practices.

In the years before and after the French revolution, theatre was more than entertainment enforcing the social and cultural power of the ruling class: as the revolution was coming into being, theatres started to overcrowd *boulevards* in France and, later on, the streets of European cities, producing narratives on the recent events and, more meaningfully, influencing political perceptions, political formats and political narratives: theatre, the pre-eminent cultural and social infrastructure of the Revolution, represented the apex and the crafter of the emerging public sphere, and as such it produced a massive impact on the rise of modern politics.[9]

The rule of the bourgeoisie in nineteenth century marked the apex of the theatrical golden era: opera theatre became the preferred form of entertainment, as the middle class gathered around a space of recognition and visibility for the ultimate acknowledgement of its power relationship in the social environment (Bianconi & Pestelli 2003). The archetypes of theatre had already, by then, crystallised in highly recognisable and reproducible forms. Such forms either indulged or criticised bourgeois respectability, or, like most operas by Giuseppe Verdi, enacted a political conflict which served as an allegory of contemporary events.

Regardless of genres and topics, theatrical forms at the time embodied the swansong of a political life which had long ceded its role in the public sphere to social power relationship. The bourgeois revolution had brought a new way of experiencing theatre in the urban fabric: theatres became huge temples of power, widened their capacity and welcomed paying visitors; exclusion and inclusion were determined by economic status. Modern theatre was born.

---

[8]For a more detailed account see Craveri (2001).

[9]The impact of theatrical practices and language on the formation of the modern political sphere is well documented by Sorba (2015).

2.2 The Commons Analytical Framework

It is only by a thorough analysis embedding social, cultural and economic history that considerations over the theatrical commons and its cultural value can be drawn. The cultural value of such commons resulted, historically, from the deep interconnection between a common pool of dramaturgic archetypes; from its strategic position within the urban grid, which evoked the centrality of theatrical practices in the city life; from the complex social interactions which were absorbed by and occurred within the theatrical space, and which in their turn created the necessary preconditions for its urban centrality (be it on the main public square or in the national theatre).

The analytical lens of commons theory help clarify how many of the attributes of theatrical practices are traceable to the features of a commons. Such lens spans from Ostrom's first theorisation of common-pool resources and their common management (1990) to the most recent developments of commons theory (Bollier and Helfrich 2012; Stavrides 2016; Euler 2018): while the former helps, in fact, analyse the physical attributes of commons resources, the latter contribute to understanding the relational systems that are subtended to the management of such resources, something which aptly fits the theatrical case.

Theatre is not a natural resource, but a cultural one; as such, even though it is characterised by a spatial dimension, irreducible and pivotal, it does not share some attributes of natural, physical resources that are usually featured in a commons (such as depletability). Similarly, some of the institutional design principles pointed out by Ostrom cannot be applied to the case of theatres (for example, providing "accessible, low-cost means for dispute resolution"—Ostrom 1990: 100).

On the other hand, theatre cannot be reduced to a cultural resource *tout court*: in the case of cultural commons as identified by Santagata et al. (2011), cultural commons are characterised by space, culture and community. The spatial dimension of cultural commons as it has been theorised is used mostly to refer to the degrees of cohesion and spatial density of communities producing the cultural commons; in this respect, 'space' can either refer to a physical dimension (a region in which a cultural good is produced with shared techniques, and symbolic meanings are communally attributed to it) or to a virtual one (the Academic community is sparse throughout the globe and still shares bound rules and mutual recognition).

Quite the reverse, in the case of the theatrical commons, space accounts for the irreducible physical, social and political dimension of theatrical practices: first of all they not only necessarily *happen* in space, but they *create* the space, a space which is at a time relational and relative to the performance; and second, their political and social relevance lies in the way in which theatre as a cultural infrastructure represents a significant dimension of the public sphere.

For what concerns the other dimension of the cultural commons, "community", another distinction must be made. In the cultural commons analytical framework drafted by Santagata, the community dimension identifies those that produce and benefit from the commons; outside of this category, the cultural commons framework makes a distinction between free riders (those who take advantage of the cultural resource without actively contributing to its maintenance and to the production of new knowledge) and users, who, without contributing directly to the resource, have access rights to it.

The relationship between the dramaturgic commons onstage and the audience is too complex to be comprised in this dichotomy, as the audience does not directly produce the performance, but cannot be considered a user who merely benefits from the resource. The audience rather fits right in between the category of users and that of community, as the audience need not to produce the resource through explicit participative modalities (as has been seen in 1.1.2, its copresence is the necessary precondition for the production of the performance); moreover, the codification of the dramaturgic commons resource, with its tropes, its topic features and its recurring verbal and gestural language, is tacitly accepted and shared by the whole of the theatre community. This aspect will be inspected more in detail in the section dedicated to the relational system of the theatre commons.

It is therefore necessary to move across the multi-disciplinary analytical framework of the commons (the physical, the cultural and the urban) in order to comprise the nature of the theatre commons.

2.2.1 Theatre as a Common-Pool Resource

The first institutional design principle identified by Ostrom in her analysis of common-pool resources is that of clearly defined boundaries, meaning the community that have access to the resource and maintains it. Historically, this has meant determining the exclusion or inclusion of certain social groups in the fruition of theatre; for instance, metics were excluded from representations in Greece, while the belonging to specific social classes determined the inclusion in courtly theatrical practices throughout the seventeenth century (Sorba 2001).

In contemporary society, the way theatre is managed can hardly be said to have commons-like features, since the management of theatres and of theatrical practices is delegated to institutions, which regulate access with pricing and with more subtle relational and behavioural norms.[10] However, if we look not at theatrical institutions but at theatrical practices per se, that is at the simple act of performing and attending theatre, inclusion and exclusion can be said to depend on participation. Participation, in this context, is intended in a broad sense: the audience coproduces the performance by attending to it, sharing its dramaturgy, complying with the performance space (see Sect. 1.1.2).

The second dimension, the congruence between rules and local conditions, is frequently missing from the contemporary picture, as has been seen especially in the contemporary culture-led experiments of urban regeneration involving theatre (Sect. 1.1.4): yet the *genius loci* of theatrical practices, that is the adaptability with

[10]Not much literature exists in academia regarding behavioural norms of exclusion in theatres; yet, more generally, more subtle and indirect forms of exclusion from the public space and the public sphere, which can relate to theatre as long as it is a publicly accessible space, can be found in Carmona (2010), Fraser, N. (1995), *Culture, politics and the public sphere: towards a postmodern conception*, in in Nicholson, L. & Seidman, S. (1995), *Social postmodernism: beyond identity politics*, 287–312, Cambridge: Cambridge University Press.

which spatial and semantic criteria of theatrical organisation has referred to different contexts (from the circular *halqa* to the flexible mobility of Shakespeare in the Park) has always been a constitutive element of the theatrical commons. In the case of theatrical practices the common rules can also refer to the common semantics that underlie the different place-based theatrical expressions, and which determine both rules of appropriation and provision of the theatrical resource. As McAuley, quoting Clifford Geertz, put it, "What enables us to talk about them [different forms of artistic expression] usefully together is that they all inscribe a communal sensibility, present locally to locals a local turn of mind" (Geerts in McAuley 2012: 110).

The third institutional principle would imply that collective-choice arrangements contribute to modifying the rules of use of the theatrical commons. This, however, is today largely made impossible by the top-down management modalities of theatre: behavioural norms within the theatrical space have been somehow institutionalised and imposed (the theatre police in Vienna is but a punctual example of a long history of "behavioural enclosure"). Only more inclusive and participative theatrical practices allow for the flexible adaptation according to the actions of communities, but they remain isolated examples (be them performances which are enriched by the audience's unpredictable reactions or inclusive theatrical projects such as the Mahogany Opera Group, which coproduces opera with and for students and amateurs in unexpected locations).

Monitoring, sanctions and conflict-resolution mechanisms refer to how to comply with free riding. The problem of free riding in theatre can be seen from a twofold perspective: the first is the strictly cultural dimension (the artistic production), and the second is free riding associated with participation. The first dimension relates to the notion of free riding as it pertains to the cultural commons; in the theatrical case this coincides with the theatrical stock of dramaturgy, with plots, language, archetypes. Santagata et al. make a distinction between "core" and "peripheral" communities in the commons (Santagata et al. 2011: 8), the former contributing to the increase of value of the collective good, the latter observing opportunistic behaviour and replicating, without increasing, the production of the resource—a theatrical example could be the performances of Vivaldi in Venice, of Verdi in Rome and of Mozart in Vienna by musical ensembles that specifically target tourists.

On the other hand, free riding with respect to the theatre commons can refer to participation on behalf of the audience; since the boundaries of the commons are defined by participation, it could be said that free riding is associated with a lack of audience involvement in the performance. Nevertheless, participation in the case of theatre can (and, perhaps, should) be intended in a broad sense, because otherwise simply attending the performance without directly contributing to what is happening onstage might be considered an act of free riding, thus giving pre-eminence to those theatrical forms that are oriented towards societal goals. Participation to theatre should rather be intended as the act of "being an audience member", or, as Walmsley puts, it, the audiency (Walmsley 2018): the emotional or imaginative participation of the audience is by no means less relevant than acts of coproduction.

In this respect Hughes, following Ridout (2013), identifies the figure of the 'passionate amateur', "who makes and attends theatre as an act of love" (Hughes 2017: 80). For this reason, keeping the notion of participation broad and identifying opportunistic behaviour on the sole production side seems to be an appropriate framework for inspecting participation and free riding in theatrical practices.

2.2.2 Theatre as a Commoning Practice

Investigating the notion of free riding and of participation in the previous section brings up the core characteristics of the theatre commons: that of being together of 'being in common'—that is, of commoning. This has somehow been overshadowed in the past by the goods-based definition of the commons analysis. A new emphasis has been given to the social and relational aspects of the commons by Euler, for whom "commons is the social form of (tangible and/or intangible) matter that is determined by commoning. Hence, a matter only becomes a commons if people predominantly relate to it by commoning and if, therewith, the social form is determined by these very practices" (Euler 2018: 12).

Theatrical practices present a strong relational component, and seem to aptly relate to this definition: the audience–performance relation is a constitutive dimension of both the theatrical performance per se and the performance space. The fact that theatre cannot happen without a community attending the moment in which it is being performed, and the fact that the community which attends the performance participates directly (though with different degrees of involvement) to the production and the increase of the theatrical resource, testify for the commons-like nature of theatrical practices.

Theatre seems to be quite fitting in the scholarly discourse on the commons which has emphasised the social and relational dimension of commoning. Euler (2018), following Benkler (2006), has placed an emphasis on the notion of *togetherness*, which aptly describes the involvement of the audience in the theatrical creation. In this respect, participation to the theatre commons recalls Mattei's view of the common as a condition of *being* together, rather than *having* together (Mattei 2011: 27). The fact that the theatrical commons consists of a system of relations rather than merely being a matter of ownership is aligned with Roggero's view, according to which it is necessary to "relocate the question of the commons from one centred on property to one focused on relations of production" (Roggero 2010: 6).

In addition to the dimension of *togetherness* that is subtended to the theatrical commons and its modes of production and fruition, Arendt has pointed out another crucial characteristic of the theatrical commons, that is, its eminently *public* dimension. In her work *The Human Condition* (1958) she asserts that the public sphere is the conditions "where people are *with* others and neither *for* nor *against* them—that is, in sheer human togetherness" (Arendt 1998: 180; emphasis added). What is more, she associates the condition of publicity to theatre, as she recalls the affinity between action (the aspect of human condition which articulates the public sphere) and theatre:

> theatre is the political art par excellence; only there is the political sphere of human life transposed into art. By the same token, it is the only art whose sole subject is man in his relationship to others. (Arendt 1998: 188)

These aspects of *publicity* and *togetherness* seem, therefore, to be at the core of the value production process of theatrical practices as a commons. The present modalities of management and fruition of theatre however, still anchored in the mechanical reproduction of archetypical forms and in the fruition schemes of the bourgeois nineteenth century, do not acknowledge for the complexity of the theatrical experience, nor do they reveal its nature as a commons.

2.3 Deconstruction and Definition of a Complex Commons

2.3.1 The Theatrical Syntax

The picture which has just emerged of theatre is at a time plain and complex. Just like Ledoux would have liked us to do, "let us take as a model humanity's simple actions" (Ledoux in Schwarte 2012: 161), and untangle the complex characteristics of the theatre commons.

The analysis in the previous section has demonstrated that theatre has the characteristics of a complex commons, which requires multiple analytical frameworks in order to be fully comprised: it is a physical, or better a spatial resource in which inclusion and exclusion are, today, determined by participation, and which has historically been bound to specific communities. But theatre is not only a common-pool resource, physically and theatrically construed by the copresence of audience and actors, dramaturgically constituted by the archetypes and codes of a stratified common language; it is also a relational resource, an act of commoning where value is created by the act of being together, and which enact a manifestation of the participants' public life.

Once the nature of theatre as a commons has been disentangled, what remains to be examined is what type of commons it is exactly, and what its peculiarity is within the commons framework.

The three dimensions of theatre spatiality are characterised by a significantly coherent grammar—more precisely, a syntax of the theatrical space. In language, the syntax is a common set of rules by which different syntagms can be articulated in many different fashions, and still respond to the same reference framework. Similarly, the stage–audience relationship, the space and architecture which contains such relationship, and the interaction of theatre with the wider urban scale have been articulated into an innumerable set of variables by different societies in different times.

And yet, the constant recombination of spatial and dramaturgic interactions, and the pushing forward of theatrical boundaries, has always occurred within the logics of the theatrical syntax. The simple elements which constitute such syntax's set of rules, and the common ground for these evolutions, are the stage–audience relational space, the physical and architectural dimension, a wider social and political interaction with the urban fabric and the evolution of dramaturgic codes and languages.

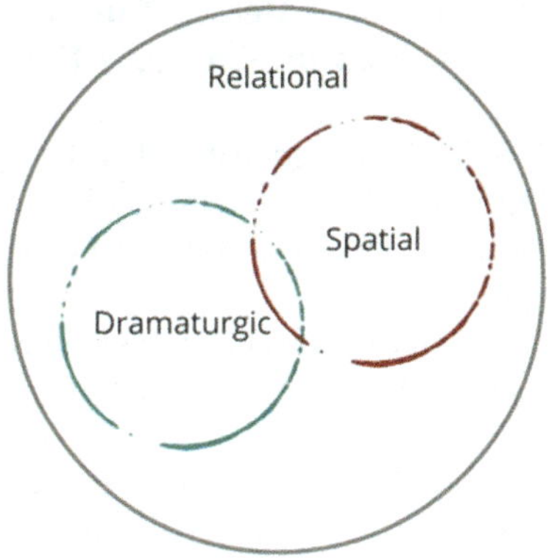

Fig. 1 A conceptual articulation of the dimensions of the theatre commons, which qualifies as semantic commons

The physical and spatial dramaturgic components of such commons are both inscribed in the wider relational dimension of theatre, the act of commoning which underlies on the one hand the creation of a coherent dramaturgic code shared by the audience and the actors and on the other of theatre as a relational space. It is precisely the syntax in which this theatrical manifestations are articulated (regardless of their different time-space dependent qualities) that is at the core of the theatrical commons: theatre is a semantic commons (Fig. 1).

2.3.2 Words Matter

Rather than merely being a taxonomical cavil, understanding the commons nature of theatre matters. It matters first because it helps understand how it generates value and how the theatrical resource is sustained over time (i.e. through knowledge and through relations); second (and consequently) because understanding *who* shapes the resource and *what* the resource actually consists of, in order to be able to properly valorise such resource, and to generate such value sustainably.

Considering theatre for its commons-like features means to attribute proper relevance to its characteristics of publicity and togetherness. This, in turn, would result in a significant switch in policy discourse: theatre, often relegated to the mere dimension of entertainment or uncritically replicated as a part of cultural heritage to be replicated at whatever costs, faces the risk of decay and depletion. Understanding the relational value of theatre implies the craft of new tools and strategies for participation and accessibility, elaborate funding criteria that are more aligned with the value-generating potential of theatre, disentangle the relationship between theatrical space and theatrical architecture by promoting innovating theatrical experiences, and eventually rethink the modes of cultural fruition in the urban space.

What is left of such cultural value today? How are we administering such heritage and how are we generating its actual cultural value today, provided that we generate it at all?

2.4 Theatre Versus Cinema: New Competitors and New Needs in Scholarly Discourse

It is hardly questionable that the relevance of theatres in the contemporary social life is way below the threshold of mere survival. After the apex came decline: the theatrical and musical production ceased to be linked with social occasion and with episodic composition as early as the beginning of the nineteenth century, when Romanticism laid the foundations for the cult of individual genius and for the replication of what would become canon and repertory in the twentieth century (Hauser 1951).

Theatre started to experience a significant drain of creative inputs (Velde 2015): in the twentieth century for the first time, a line was drawn between repertory and new productions. Very little was left, at that point, of the rampant world of impresarios, the energetic production and composition processes and the massive audience attendance rates of theatrical spaces on the part of a wide array of social actors; when addressed in public policy discourse, it is now common to address its issues from the perspective of a form of intangible heritage, whose supposedly intrinsic value allow for its preservation as a merit good. Theatre is no longer a social practice: it has become a part of a doubtfully meritorious cultural heritage.

The fact that the progressive decline of theatre as a social, cultural and political infrastructure, as a space of encounter and of cultural fruition, coincided with the rise of a new, technologically advanced form of entertainment, has led many to interpret such decline solely in the light of economic rationales and theories. Many factors, in fact, have been blamed for the decline of the performing arts, from the flattening democratisation of the theatrical experience on behalf of the film industry (Horkheimer and Adorno 1944), to the incapability of the theatrical economy to recover from sunk cost and production expenses, making the cinematic economies of scale much more advantageous (Baumol and Bowen 1966), to the inability of theatres of coping with the 'marginal revolution' (Throsby 2001), which had on the contrary allowed cinema to add additional consumers at almost no extra cost (Bakker 2012).

2.5 Public Life and Theatrical Practices: Missing Links and Emerging Opportunities

The attention of most scholars was thus caught by the immense cinematic shift of the entertainment industry which characterised the past century; a more radical revolution, however, was occurring in another domain: the social one, and in particular the contraction of the public sphere to the advantage of the private one.

Arendt (1951) was among the first to point out how the necessary precondition for the establishment of a totalitarian regime was citizens' alienation: the vanquishing and the diminishing of the public sphere allowed for and additionally resulted from the rise of a totalitarian State. Totalitarianisms, which pervaded the political experience of the twentieth century marked a most traumatic and radical change in the public–private balance, and set the basis for further exasperation of the public–private divide.

Sennett (1977) brilliantly compared Roman history to the contemporary drifts of social transformations to further clarify such shift: with the rise of the Roman Empire (when the infrastructures of politics became nothing but formal simulacra of Republican institutions), the public and political life of Roman citizens was deprived of its effectiveness; commitment to public good was dramatically drained, as the private sphere absorbed larger and larger portions of individual life. Similarly, as transnational, globalised capital (Sassen 2013) and the commodification of public goods (Carmona 2010; Harvey 2012; Low and Smith 2013) contribute to the shrinking of public spaces in the city, the spaces and practices of public life, together with the responsibilities and benefits that they implied, have reached their lowest level in modern times.

The evolution—or, better, the involution of the social sphere did not only dramatically affect political forms; it is evident in the religious experience, which in the Western world has turned intimate and individualistic whereas it had represented a pre-eminent rationale of social organisation for centuries. Weber's precocious intuition of the ties between public life, religion as an articulation of the latter and the economic infrastructure proves more actual than ever.

Similarly, the contraction of the public sphere concurred to the decline of art forms with an eminent social dimension (such as the performing arts). Curiously enough, however, the syntax and semantics of theatre survived the agony of the theatrical medium, while shifting to other forms of entertainment, namely TV shows such as talk shows and sit-coms. Both have borrowed the theatrical format in assuming the presence of spectators: the former always features an audience which, through emotional reactions, makes the performance vivid and somehow participated, even though onscreen. The latter alternates jokes and puns with recorded laughter, evoking the presence of a live and immediate emotional response to the show.

The cognitive genomes of theatre were transposed, almost unchanged, into other forms of expressions; theatre however was deprived of its role of social and cultural infrastructure, while the value that it produced as a shared practice was dramatically diminished.

3 From Institutions to Actions: A New Focus on Cultural Value and Public Relevance in Policy Discourse for the Performing Arts

Theatre, thus, has now lost its social role as a cultural infrastructure articulating the public dimension. From a policy perspective, what is left of theatre today is a curious artistic hybrid, halfway through a heritage institution and a cultural industry: difficult to frame, and therefore to fund. The policy focus, as with most forms of heritage, is on preservation of theatrical practices and canons, and above all on the institutional entities which operate in this sense.

As archetypes freeze and heritage preservation approaches harden the evaluative criteria for public funding; as the audience finds responses to its cultural claims answered by an individually customised form of entertainment (such as Netflix); as the social life and the structure of the city evolve around new paradigms, leaving theatres lagging behind in pompous temples of beauty, rightful questions arise over the legitimacy of public support to a cultural good whose characteristics are those of a club good, rather than of a public one. Questions arise over the new role of theatre in contemporary society, if it has any.

How can theatre produce a cultural value that is sustainable for the future, and for whom can it produce such value? Is the problem with theatre intrinsic, then, so that its semantics and its archetypes prove out-dated and fail to grasp the complexity of reality? Or is it rather a structural problem, imputable to stern policy regulation, to uneven distribution of the cultural offer (including the theatrical one) in the urban fabric, and to an overall "missing the point" of the actual cultural value of the theatrical commons?

3.1 Theatre and Politics: Power, Engagement and the Political Imagination

Theatre as a space for the creation of political imagination and of social cohesion, for the expression of ancestral dilemmas as well as for the arena for contemporary public debates, proves able to embody contemporary urban, political, social and economic claims of rapidly evolving communities; the public sphere is claiming back its role through struggles for the right to the city (first coined by Lefebvre (1968), and summoned in recent times by Harvey (2012), and specifically by Kruger (2012), and Hughes (2017), who both related it to theatrical practices).

The theatrical commons, with its unique features of cultural infrastructure, has a role to play in this struggle—especially as urban movements and theatrical dynamics share a significant portion of their semantics: Lewis Mumford's depicted the city as "*the stage of social drama*" (Mumford 1937: 82), while movements all over the world use theatre and performance as a powerful medium of communication to raise awareness and involve communities: from re-enactments of dramatic political moments on the streets of Chicago (Kanouse 2008; Levitt 2018), performed as a form of protest to the present economic system; to Extinction Rebellion's[11] and Opéra Pagaï's[12] playful and clever provocations on climate change; to the contemporary and most popular form of public and political demonstrations, flash mobs, share the spatial and relational characteristics of theatrical semantics

[11] Julia, 2019

[12] Opéra Pagaï, https://www.operapagai.com/, accessed Sept. 7th, 2019.

(Ventura 2019)[13]—and activate the mechanisms of gathering echoed in Ledoux's evocative statement.

Theatre, politics and the urban struggle for the reappropriation of the public sphere intertwine in the controversial cases of occupied cultural spaces. Between 2011 and 2014, in Rome, Teatro Valle was occupied and collectively managed after the theatre was closed and left to decay. The number of analogous experiences, from Asilo Filangieri in Naples to Empros Theatre in Athens, testify the will of communities to reappropriate the theatrical experience beyond the physical and managerial boundaries imposed by the institutionalisation of theatrical practices.

The spontaneous resurgence of theatrical activities is pivotal to social interactions in the urban space and to the collective generation and experience of creativity. The spontaneous resurgence of theatrical communities is not, in fact, the simple manifestation of a creative effort, but a demonstration of how theatre, as a social and political activity, is inscribed in the public sphere. The relationship between commoning practices and space is particularly fascinating and complex in the case of an art whose core trait lies in the creation of a relational space (a space, again, in which *there is no such thing as space outside of the processes that define it* —see Sect. 1.1.3). In the words of Hughes, the "theatricalisation of the social world" provides "resilient means of interrupting the smooth processing of commons resources into capital" (Hughes 2017).[14]

However, as noted by Borchi (2018) and Mattei (2011), a precise legal framework allowing for the straightforward identification of commons and cultural commons is still missing in most countries. Among the rules pointed out by the first theoriser of the commons, Elinor Ostrom, for an effective management of the commons is the recognition of the commons from the part of an external authority, as the necessary precondition for avoiding enclosure and the enforcement of exogenous rules.

As a consequence, the absence of a clear regulation concerning the use and management of occupied spaces has insofar led to the end of such collective experiences. The political agenda for culture, and for the performing arts in particular, need to reconsider hierarchies and degrees of stakeholder involvement in order to provide a more flexible and proactive legal framework not only for such "unconventional" management modes, but more generally for hybrid ownership modalities. However, while an institutionalisation of the commons research and legal framework might provide stability and legitimacy to courageous and fertile experiments, a balance is to be found between such instance and the need to keep the framework flexible and adaptable to the different context in which the commons are created (Ostrom 1990), while never losing sight of the radical political significance of the struggle for the commons (Mattei 2011).

[13]The affinities between flash mobs and theatrical semantics testify the liveliness and the present relevance of theatrical dynamics; and yet, concerns arise over the "theatricalisation" of politics, which has turned from powerful instance of dissent into a harmless act of *mimesis*. See Ventura (2019).

[14]Hughes (2017).

3.2 Policies and Practices: A Reflection on Formats, Funding and the Generation of Cultural Value

The odd idiosyncrasy between the failed policy attempts to reanimate theatre and the animated stream of theatrical commons characteristics from one expressive means to the other is perhaps the hint to both the problem and the solution to the long-debated performing arts dilemma.

The fact that theatre is mostly identified with the institutions which enact it, rather than with the *simple human actions* emphasised by Ledoux, has generated a centripetal structure for funding and public support. The particular attention attributed to the institutional setting is not to be underestimated: as has been said by Balestra and Malaguti (2000) on policymaking in Italy (something which can be extended to most civil law countries), emphasis is never placed on projects, but on institutional subjects.

This has immense consequences on the way theatre is valued and, consequently, supported and managed. When analysed through the lens of cultural commons, in fact, theatre appears to be experiencing all the social dilemmas that are typical of the commons. The strong barriers to entry of new cultural inputs, as well as the rigid hierarchic structures which regulate the "public life of theatres", testify for a dramatic enclosure of the theatrical commons, where the policy emphasis is placed exclusively on the financial survival of institutions, and hardly ever on developing projects or impacting the modes of theatrical production and consumption. In spite of the preservation frenzy which affects theatrical institutions, the rigidly enclosed formats of a most social forms of entertainment are now facing a serious threat of sustainability: that of the uncertainty of transmission.

When referring to the dramatic underuse of scientific resources due to excessive intellectual property rights regulation, Michael Heller used the ironic and yet evocative expression *tragedy of the anticommons* (Heller 1998). It is almost needless to say that this epitome perfectly adapts to the theatrical situation: while the cultural offer of theatres barricades itself behind the quest for a self-declared artistic excellence, other forms of entertainment are able to generate cultural products that are entirely tailored on their customers' preferences. The Netflix example might be of a radical sort, but it illustrates how vital it is for cultural institutions to understand the cultural itineraries of their audiences.

As advocated by David Throsby, "it is not necessary to postulate intrinsic or absolute worth in order to establish an existence for cultural value independently of economic value" (Throsby 2001: 32). Quite the reverse, the value of the performing arts can be better assessed according to the definition provided by Charles Taylor of "irreducibly social good" (Taylor 1995), which "contain some elements of benefit that cannot be ultimately attributed to some individual" (ivi). What has made theatrical expression so powerful and transversal until the present day is its prominent ability to adapt to the social and urban fabrics developing around it, and to generate social capital by inducing aggregation and allowing for different nuances of coproduction and audience participation.

3.2.1 De-formatting Content

The collective, common-like nature of the complex theatre commons has generated cultural value throughout the ages and in different social ambiances not just through the artistic quality of its artistic product—i.e. the performance. The constant production of creative inputs, rooted in the vast theatrical knowledge commons; the production of material supplies (ranging from sceneries to costumes to musical instruments), and of critical interactions with the audience, are all fundamental components of the value chain of the performing arts. Such value chain accounts for the fact that the generation of cultural value, particularly in such a stratified, collective and participative form of art, lies in processes, rather than (solely) in outcomes.

Therefore theatre, as a complex commons consisting of a relational and spatial as well as a cultural dimension calls for a holistic approach, addressing both its formats and its contents. The only possible way of ensuring a sustainable use of the theatrical commons is by challenging its formats, rather than replicating its archetypes. Policymaking related to the arts still reflects a manufacturing approach (Trimarchi 2014), following an input-output scheme while assigning rainfall funds according to the merit good argument that is prevailing in the cultural discourse. The anxious efforts put in the uncritical reproduction of meaningless and formal theatrical stereotypes complete a most desolating picture.

Sound policy design for the performing arts, as a consequence, passes from the acknowledgement of this complexity, and the subsequent articulation of a public support which should not just be provided according to qualitative criteria over the reproduction of cultural heritage, or to specific institutions due to their supposedly renowned artistic excellence. However necessary, public support causes a governance problem in that it provides an incentive for theatres not to dialogue with their surrounding environment (Klamer 1996). Especially when it is structured according to a heritage perspective, in which theatres represent the temple of cultural ascension, and the audience is an entity in need for initiation.

Criteria for funding are most conventionally oriented towards the artistic quality of the end product, assigning funds according to the organisational capacity of theatres, while incentives are provided with an emphasis on corollary activities, from the renting of the theatrical spaces to the ability of attracting private funds and donations. This however only bypasses the core problem: the preservation of a fragile and static repertory and support to day-to-day operations for financial survival have shifted the attention from the process of value creation.

The Italian case presents, in this respect, several criticalities: the State fund for the performing arts, in the evaluation for the assignments of rainfall funds to theatres, is focused on numeric indicators such as the dimension of the orchestra, while educational activities see their points halved in the evaluation. The paradox of a public policy exclusively centred on direct impacts and economic indicators culminates in the evaluation of free social-oriented events, which equals zero precisely because it does not produce income for the theatre: public support is missing where it would be needed the most (Sabatini and Trimarchi 2019).

The scenario is by no means more comforting in other countries: French public policies for the performing are both highly centripetal (being absorbed by the Parisian scenario) and centred on the evaluation of artistic criteria rather than of strategic choices (Négrier 2017). The recent debate on cultural policy in the UK has focused extensively on issues related to centralisation and a paternalistic attitude within the criteria of artistic excellence (Gross and Wilson 2018),[15] while emphasis has been recently placed on the jeopardization of public support and, subsequently, community engagement at a National level in the Country (Hadley 2018).

Understanding theatre as a semantic commons in which cultural value lies in creative and social processes, and is generated through a shared, complex semantics, might provide new insights for better policy design for the performing arts. The elements which future policy ought to include feature a cleverer production and use of shared spaces; the generation of social interactions and involvement; the production of a common language, able to address the complexity of the contemporary audience while relating to a century-old common.

3.2.2 Reappropriating Spaces

Shaping theatrical formats is not just a policy and managerial matter, however. Spaces are to be challenged in order to unchain the binomial association between theatres and their fruition—which, as the historical outline has demonstrated, is a modern mystification: the theatrical shape is commonly associated with its most recent drift, the nineteenth century bourgeois structure, located in the productive centre, and rigidly articulated in its stage–audience relationship.

From open air festivals to street artists, from reused buildings to ancient theatres, the spaces of theatre have been as diverse and multiple as the communities they were used by. Whenever space is being supposedly questioned in present times, however, this appears to happen in a flash-mob fashion, an ephemeral experiment claiming to untangle new relationships with society. These experiments, however, still fail to generate critical mass and long-term benefits on both sides, the theatre's and the audience's. This is the case with the Easter eggs at Fiumicino Airport organised by Opera di Roma, in which besides a temporary surprise effect in passers-by very little is done in terms of actual audience engagement in the theatre's everyday activities.

On the other hand, some theatres have begun to question the binomial association between theatrical practices and venues, by either integrating their offer with hybrid productions, or by displacing such productions in unconventional venues; the former is the case of Opéra de Lyon's contemporary music festival, featuring techno music performances as well as children music workshops, challenge conventionally operating venues; the latter is Teatro Massimo in Palermo, which runs a year-long project in the disadvantaged neighbourhood of Danisinni, where

[15]Specifically, the debate on the so called "deficit model", which places an emphasis on artistic outcomes rather than on the democratisation and accessibility of the cultural modes of production and consumption. For an exhaustive account see Gross and Wilson (2018). For an account on the uses of the deficit model in the performing arts policy framework see Walmsley (2018).

cooperation is fostered between the orchestra and the local inhabitants for the production of new operas.

The aforementioned example of Shakespeare in the Park (see Sect. 1.1.1) pushes the spatial challenges of theatre even further for a variety of reasons which involve both form and content of theatrical practices: from the viewpoint of dramaturgy, the audience's participation, while not coinciding strictly with coproduction, is a strong component of the play's development: with the scenes being set in different parts of the Park, the actors directly address the audience and invite them to physically follow them in various locations, disentangling the relationship between both performance space and audience. From the viewpoint of formats, plays are performed in public, open spaces, where price barriers are simply tore down by the gratuity of the performance, create an overtly accessible and informal setting, which in turns triggers familiarity and proximity between audience and performers. What is more, the choice to perform Shakespeare, which can be considered a form of "high" theatre, shows an effort towards the accessibility of cultural heritage to new audiences.

These formats give voice to the contemporary pressures to the disarticulation of spaces and functions in the urban grid while challenging the semantics of physical spaces. In this respect, institutional attention and recognition should be bestowed to sustainable projects with the potential to generate long-term involvement and to mobilise local resources, overcoming the focus group approach of audience development strategy and the income-genre dualism of contemporary audience studies and their demographic indicators.

Performance language is the third component of the theatre commons which still fails to reach appropriate institutional attention. The heritage-oriented focus on theatre tends to privilege conventional formats which however do not grasp the multiplicity and diversity of audience itineraries and the complexity of their cumulative tastes. Theatre is, perhaps, the medium *par excellence* able to combine different expressive forms, but has ceased to integrate them in its body of knowledge with its recent enclosure. However unsystematic, a map can be drawn of theatrical experiments integrating bravely different and contemporary forms of art, ranging widely from comics to fashion, and yet cross-sector partnerships are poorly fostered and searched for. An encouraging example is that of *La FabriqueOpéra*, which involves professionals from diverse fields to generate cross-medium theatrical experiences while remaining true to the artistic quality of performances.

In the words of Frederic Wake-Walker, artistic director of the participative project *Mahogany Opera Group*,

> If you peel away the glossy trappings, theatre not only grapples with the fundamental human need to sing, dance, ritualise and tell stories but also, through its ability to draw together different cultures and genres, is able to express most relevantly our multi-media, multi-cultural existence today.[16]

[16]The Mahogany Opera Group, *Stretching the boundaries of what opera can be and who it is for*, https://www.mahoganyopera.co.uk/about-us/, accessed Sept. 8th, 2019.

In conclusion, the complexity of the semantic commons of theatre, in its articulated spatial, relational and linguistic commonality, proves able to address the complex needs of a complex society, redesigning appropriative strategies of the public sphere and drawing individuals together in social encounters and practices; this, however, is only possible as long as it is not exclusively identified with the institutions which perform it, the physical structures which have hosted it in the past two centuries, and the artistic forms in which it has been attempted to frame it.

Bibliography

Arendt, H. (1996). *The origins of totalitarianism*. San Diego: Harvest Books–Harcourt (1st ed. 1951).

Arendt, H. (1998). *The human condition*. Chicago: The University of Chicago Press (1st ed. 1958).

Bakker, G. (2012). How motion pictures industrialised entertainment. *The Journal of Economic History, 72*(4), 1036–1063.

Baldry, H. C. (1971). *The Greek tragic theatre*. London: Chatto&Windus.

Balestra, C., & Malaguti, A. (2000). *Organizzare Musica: Legislazione, produzione, distribuzione, gestione nel sistema italiano*. Milano: Franco Angeli.

Baumol, J. W., & Bowen, G. (1966). *Performing arts, the economic dilemma: a study of problems common to theatre, opera, music and dance*. New York: Twentieth Century Fund.

Bianconi, L., & Pestelli, G., (Eds). (2003). *The history of Italian Opera: Opera in theory and practice, image and myth*, vol. 2: *Systems*. Chicago: The University of Chicago Press.

Borchi, A. (2018). Culture as commons: Theoretical challenges and empirical evidence from occupied public spaces in Italy. *Cultural Trends, 27*(1), 33–45.

Carlson, M. (2012). The theatre *ici*, 40–46. In E. Fischer-Lichte & B. Wihstutz (Eds.), *Performance and the politics of space: Theatre and topology* (pp. 40–46). London: Routledge.

Carmona, M. (2010). Contemporary public space: Critique and classification, Part One: Critique. *Journal of Urban Design, 15*(1), 123–148.

Cartledge, P. (1997). "Deep plays": Theatre as process in Greek civil life. In P. E. Easterling (Ed.), *Cambridge companion to Greek theatre*. Cambridge: Cambridge University Press.

Craveri, B. (2001). *La civiltà della conversazione* (pp. 332–348). Milano: Adelphi.

Dahlhaus, C. (2002). *Drammaturgia dell'opera italiana* (trans. L. Bianconi). Milano: EDT.

Euler, J. (2018). Conceptualizing the commons: Moving beyond the goods-based definition by introducing the social practices of commoning as vital determinant. *Ecological Economy, 143*, 10–16.

Fraser, N. (1995). Politics, culture and the modern sphere: Toward a postmodern conception. In L. Nicholson & S. Seidman (Eds.), *Social postmodernism: Beyond identity politics* (pp. 287–312). Cambridge: Cambridge University Press.

Gross, J., & Wilson, N. (2018). Cultural democracy: An ecological and capabilities approach. *International journal of cultural policy, 26*(3), 328–343.

Hadley, S. (2018). Towards cultural democracy: Promoting cultural capabilities for everyone. *Cultural trends, 27*(1), 52–55.

Harvey, D. (2004). Space as a key-word. Presented at *Marx and philosophy*, May 24th 2004. London: Institute of Education.

Harvey, D. (2012). *Rebel cities: From the right to the city to the urban revolution*. London: Verso Books.

Hauser, A. (2003). *Storia sociale dell'arte* (Trans. by Bovero A). Torino: Einaudi (1st ed. 1951).

Heller, M. A. (1998). The tragedy of the anticommons: Property in the transition from marx to markets. *Harvard Law Review, 111*(3), 622–688.

Horkheimer, M., & Adorno, T. (1966). *Dialettica dell'illuminismo* (trans. by R. Solmi). Torino: Einaudi (1st ed. 1944).

Hughes, J. (2017). Notes on a theatre commons: Common Wealth's The Deal Versus the People (2015). *Research in Drama Education: The Journal of Applied Theatre and Performance, 22* (1), 76–91.

Kanouse, S. (2008). Performing haymarket. *ACME: An International Journal for Critical Geographies, 7*, 1, 69–87.

Klamer, A. (Ed.). (1996). *The value of culture. On the relationship between economics and arts.* Amsterdam: Amsterdam University Press.

Kruger, L. (2012). What time is this place? Continuity, conflict, and the right to the city. In: E. Fischer-Lichte & B. Wihstutz (Eds.), *Performance and the politics of space: Theatre and topology* (pp. 61–84). London: Routledge.

Low, S., & Smith, N. (Eds.). (2013) *The politics of public space*, London: Routledge.

Lefebvre, H. (2009). *Le droit à la ville*. Paris: Economica (1st ed. 1968).

Mattei, U. (2011). *Beni comuni. Un manifesto*. Bari: Edizioni Laterza.

McKinnie, M. (2012). Performing like a city: London's South Bank and the cultural politics of Urban Governance. In E. Fischer-Lichte & B. Wihstutz (Eds.), *Performance and the politics of space: Theatre and topology* (pp. 85–101). London: Routledge.

Mumford, L. (1937). What is a city? *Architectural records, 82.*

Négrier, E. (2017). *Performing arts and policies in France*. Hal Archives Ouvertes. https://hal.archives-ouvertes.fr/hal-01442237/document.

Ostrom, E. (1990). *Governing the commons: The evolution of institutions for collective action.* Cambridge: Cambridge University Press.

Primavesi, P. (2012). Heterotopias of the public sphere: theatre and festivals around 1800. In E. Fischer-Lichte & B. Wihstutz (Eds.), *Performance and the politics of space: Theatre and topology* (pp. 196–213). London: Routledge.

Roggero, G. (2010). Five theses on the commons. *Rethinking Marxism, 22,* 3.

Roselt, J. (2012). Changes through rapprochement. Spatial practices in contemporary performances (Trans. by M. Breslin & S.I. Jain). In E. Fischer-Lichte & B. Wihstutz (Eds.), *Performance and the politics of space: Theatre and topology* (pp. 309–321). London: Routledge.

Sabatini, F., & Trimarchi, M. (2019). Regulating the stage: Storms, wrecks and lifebelts in the Italian experience. *Journal of Mediterranean Studies, 5*(2), 105–120.

Santagata, W., Bertacchini, E., Bravo, G., & Marrelli, M. (2011). *Cultural commons and cultural communities*. Paper presented at Sustaining Commons: Sustaining Our Future, the Thirteenth Biennial Conference of the International Association for the Study of the Commons, Hyderabad, India, 10–14 September 2011. http://hdl.handle.net/10535/7359.

Sassen, S. (2013). When the center no longer holds: Cities as frontier zones. *Cities, 34,* 67–70.

Schwarte, L. (2012). Equality in theatre architecture: Voltaire's private theatre. In E. Fischer-Lichte & B. Wihstutz (Eds.), *Performance and the politics of space: Theatre and topology* (pp. 151–166). London: Routledge.

Sorba, C. (2015). *Il melodramma della nazione: politica e risentimenti nell'età del Rinascimento.* Bari: Laterza.

Sennett, R. (1977). *The fall of Public Man*. New York: Alfred A. Knopf Inc.

Stavrides, S. (2016). *Common space. The city as Commons*. Zed Books: London.

Taylor, C. (1995). *Philosophical arguments*. Harvard: Harvard University Press.

Throsby, D. (2001). *Economics and culture*. Cambridge: Cambridge University Press.

Velde, F. R. (2015). The economic history of Opera. *European Historical Economics Society.* http://www.ehes.org/ehes2015/papers/Velde.pdf.

Ventura, R. A. (2019). *La guerra di tutti. Populismo, terrore e crisi della società liberale*. Roma: Minimum Fax.

Walmsley, B. (2018). A plea for audiences: from active spectatorship to enactive audiency. In L. Bonet & E. Négrier (Eds.), *Breaking the Fourth Wall: Proactive audiences in the performing arts* (pp. 196–209). Elverum: Kunnskapsverket.
Wihstutz, B. (2012). Introduction. In E. Fischer-Lichte & B. Wihstutz (Eds.), *Performance and the politics of space: Theatre and topology* (pp. 15–28). London: Routledge.

Sitography

De Matteis, P. (2018). La fille du régiment al Teatro Comunale di Bologna firmata Emilio Sagi. *Amadeus Magazine*, November 17, 2018. https://amadeusmagazine.it/rubrica-news/la-fille-du-regiment-al-teatro-comunale-di-bologna-firmata-emilio-sagi/, Accessed April 25th, 2020.
Folletto, A. (2017). Graham Vick, rivoluzionario 'Stiffelio': Voglio che il pubblico sia palco e attore insieme. *la Repubblica*, August 9, 2017. https://www.repubblica.it/spettacoli/teatro-danza/2017/08/09/news/graham_vick_stiffelio_-172594818/. Accessed May 5, 2020.
Julia, *Creative Rebellion: Arts and Culture Highlights from International Rebellion London*, October 21, 2019. https://rebellion.earth/2019/10/21/creative-rebellion-arts-and-culture-highlights-from-international-rebellion-london/. Accessed March 3, 2020.
Levitt, A. (2018). Remembering Haymarket affair and the city's attempt to forget it. *Chicago Reader*, January 5, 2018. https://www.chicagoreader.com/Bleader/archives/2018/05/01/remembering-the-haymarket-affair-and-the-citys-attempts-to-forget-it. Accessed March 3, 2020.
Opéra Pagaï. https://www.operapagai.com/. Accessed September 7, 2019.
Ricci, S. (2018). Applausi e contestazioni a scena aperta: la regia di Pippo Delbono ha diviso il pubblico del Teatro dell'Opera di Roma, regalando un dittico verista a dir poco contraddittorio. *Operalibera*, April 5, 2018. http://www.operalibera.net/joomla/recensioni/spettacoli1/1727-cavalleria-rusticana-pagliacci-teatro-opera-roma-2018. Accessed April 30, 2020.
The Editors of the Encyclopaedia Britannica, Miracle Play, *Encyclopaedia Britannica*, February 6, 2019, https://www.britannica.com/art/miracle-play. Accessed April 30, 2020.
The Editors of the Encyclopaedia Britannica, Miracle Play, *Encyclopaedia Britannica*, April 30, 2018, https://www.britannica.com/art/mystery-play. Accessed April 30, 2020.
The Mahogany Opera Group. *Stretching the boundaries of what opera can be and who it is for.* https://www.mahoganyopera.co.uk/about-us/. Accessed September 8, 2019.
Trimarchi, M. (2014). *From ivory towers to the urban texture.* Innovate Heritage, June 8, 2014. https://www.youtube.com/watch?v=JcfrDFIjXjw. Accessed October, 2019.

Public Art Today. How Public Art Sheds Light on the Future of the Theory of Commons

Valeria Morea

Abstract

Public art and common goods, although belonging to apparently distant realms of inquiry, share a long history and, inevitably, an evolving meaning. This chapter investigates the evolution of the practice of public art with the objective to obtain a viable understanding of how the value of public art is produced today. With a focus on the future of public art, this chapter investigates three public art cases. The results of the qualitative analysis of these public art experiences are interpreted from an institutional economics perspective. The combination of public art and the theory of commons sheds light on what seems to be the most important attributes of common goods in the current debate, that is the social practices that constitute the act of making the commons.

1 Introduction: What is Public Art Today?

The 'commons' is an ancient term that dates back to about eight centuries ago with Magna Carta and the Charter of Forests and indicates something 'out there', where the common men could find a way to make a living, in contrast with the rampant practice of enclosures perpetrated by royal and aristocratic families over time (Standing 2019). The commons is a resourceful space, with no enclosure yet exposed to the behaviours of differently interested users.

In such a potentially free and open space, also art can be found. Many 'out there' can be found in today's multilayered society: the urban setting has placed out the rural areas and the forests, and the digital space challenges the physical one. With

V. Morea (✉)
Erasmus School of History, Culture and Communication, Rotterdam, The Netherlands
e-mail: morea@eshcc.eur.nl

E. Macrì et al. (eds.), *Cultural Commons and Urban Dynamics*,
https://doi.org/10.1007/978-3-030-54418-8_6

this respect, the commons is a concept that is older than both private and public goods. Hence, it seems worthwhile to explore it further in order to understand how commons will look like in the future. Standing (2019) discusses public art as a commons, mainly referring to spontaneous, non-institutional and to some extent subversive artistic practices in public places such as street art and graffiti art. It is, in fact, after being released in the commons that some art becomes commodified and turned into a private good, being Banksy the epitome of such a phenomenon. However, a look on the way public art works today shows some differences with the type of public art we have get used to throughout the centuries.

This chapter argues that today's public art is more similar to the ancestral artistic endeavours than ever and that this makes it feasible to adopt an institutional economics perspective that takes into consideration the commons as something 'out there' that lets individuals play a central role in the realisation of their values. In an attempt to understand the way public art works, this chapter endeavours to apply the theory of commons to public art and, in doing so, it aims to go beyond the mere categorisation of art practices in terms of static characteristics. Instead, dynamic effects are possible to take into consideration when looking at the process that constitutes the life of public art.

2 A Glimpse of Public Art in History

In the beginning, there was public art. In 1940, at Lascaux in France, what is considered the very first artwork in history was discovered (Gombrich 1950). What is even more interesting is that those mural paintings that date back to the Palaeolithic Age, are in facts the earliest example of an art that is public (Standing 2019). In some respects, one could say that public art is even older than non-public art. Or, contentiously, that there is no such thing as public art at all.

With no urge to solve such a dispute, a note certainly worth reading is that over a time as long as humanity, public art has covered different roles in history. Hein maintains that "strictly speaking, no art is 'private'" (Hein 1996, p. 1), mainly because the dichotomy private versus public has changed meanings over time, and with it, the idea that the artist is autonomous. This was hardly the case before the Renaissance, for example, when the artists were not asked to express their artistic or aesthetic vision: "The celebrated treasures of Greece and Rome, as well as the Christian works of the Middle Ages and the age of the fresco that succeeded them, do not exalt the private vision of individual artists so much as they bespeak the shared values and convictions of cultural communities, and are accordingly to be found in those edifices and open places where people regularly gather to commemorate those same values and convictions" (ibidem, p. 2).

The values of the private and the public have evolved over time and so autonomy of (artistic) expression. The public realm was much more central in ancient Greeks and Romans' lives, as well as during the Middle Ages than today. During those times, when art was generally financed by patrons and the boundaries between public and private were not understood as we would today, fora, statuaries, altars or equestrian statues were genuinely public. They were "a visual form, an anthem, or a text" that expressed "its deepest values or unify a coherent social group", something that today "has become a relic of romantic history" (ivi).

Beyond a distinction between private and public inspired by Habermas and Arendt's philosophy (Deutsche 1992; Zebracki 2013; Krause Knight and Senie 2016), art, over time, has been used as a tool of affirmation, of control and authority. Secular and religious powers have exerted consensus and authority using art. Facades, sidewalks and arcades were built and decorated by private affluent families seeking affirmation (Romano 2007). Obelisks collected from 'uncivilised' or conquered cultures were arranged in wide-open public spaces to be symbols of Western colonial power (Hein 1996).

Civic and national powers have, especially in the nineteenth and twentieth centuries, expressed themselves using monuments, in a style that has been defined 'propaganda' public art (Appleton 2006). Art was used as a means to convey political messages from democracies to totalitarian states. The nature of such art is inherently public. Examples of art as propaganda are statues, monuments, architecture at large and even landscape. In Monteverde (Rome), one can find a social housing complex whose buildings shape a fascist lettering. Similarly, Monte Pietralata near the city of Urbino has been shaped to portrait Mussolini's profile. An Italian law states that the 2% of public investments in buildings should be allotted to the public art project. As a result, during Fascism, some artists have felt the pressure of pleasing the regimen with their art when financed within this law (Margozzi 2001).

Both democracies and totalitarian states have used art to express secular powers, and by the same token, revolutions have underpinned the destruction of such art to express a counterfactual or opposite message, as it is the case of, on the one hand, Mexican muralism, and on the other hand, the popular manifestation of revolutionary forces symbolised by the fall of totalitarian symbols of power such as Saddam Hussein in Iraq (Arnoldi 2016). Moreover, religious powers have fostered the arts throughout all history. Since, or even before, the donation of Sutri, the Papacy has played the role of a secular state, one whose public expenditure in the arts would probably make modern countries blush.

The idea that public art is something else than just art is a relatively recent one. Spatiality has been challenged by some, who have questioned whether art needs in fact a public space to be public. So, while the search for the ultimate definition of public art still has to end, Cartiere and Willis have identified some key attributes of public art. Art is public when, alternatively: (1) sits in a publicly accessible space; (2) is of public interest with respect to the contents; (3) is used or maintained by a community, making the case for the creation of a public place; or (4) is publicly funded (Cartiere and Willis 2008).

Hence, it is possible to identify that what is peculiar in this context is that some types of artistic expressions exert a special interest that has social resonance. Concepts of place, communities, public interest, public funds deal necessarily with the public realm. This type of art is public art. New genre public art (Lacy 1995) is considered to be a milestone in the history of public art. Such a new trend has put shared values at the core of the artistic practice and, in doing so, the idea of public art has been pushed further. This highly community-oriented way of making public art may bear the downside of creating a new enclosure that is comparable to the concept of 'third place' as theorised by Oldenburg and Brisset (1982). New genre public art entails project based on activism, participation and social engagement, where co-creation and directedness become a key element of a modern approach to public art (Lacy 1995). In addition to that, the banner of public art has been also fed by non-institutionalised forms of art in public space, such as graffiti and street art (Bengtsen 2013). These relatively new expressions have acquired importance and have evolved in a way that has challenged its subversive essence.

3 Three Cases of Today's (and Tomorrow's) Public Art

Today's institutional public art, at least in western societies, has come to a turning point. People do not receive one unilateral message, as it could have been the case with monuments. They negotiate and produce meanings that directly contribute to the value of the artwork. Moreover, the artworks are relevant insofar as they take part in the urban fabric.

Three cases have been investigated to highlight the key elements of today's public art functioning. With the objective of understanding the role that public art plays in the contemporary local context, the experiences selected are relatively recent, being installed between 2008 and 2018, and little to no previous research has been carried about them. The artworks belong to European capital or second cities, so that a certain degree of homogeneity of context could be achieved. Each of the cases, selected because exemplary (Farquhar 2012), teaches a specific lesson that highlights how public art becomes part of the urban fabric in today's social life of cities. The investigation is based on snowball, unstructured interviews and non-participant observations (Bryman 2012) carried out between spring and autumn 2019. The eight interviewees are persons who hold a stake in the project of installation of the artworks or in the location of installation; they are two museum employees, a civil servant, two activists, two artists and a real estate developer. The information acquired has then been triangulated to secondary data available on websites and newspapers.

(i) **Controversy in Rotterdam: Santa Claus**

Among the symbols of the industrial Rotterdam is a 5 metres tall bronze sculpture that portraits a gnome holding something similar to a Christmas tree. The statue, commissioned to American artist Paul McCarthy by the municipality of Rotterdam in the early 2000s, under the advice of Sculpture International, has brought controversy since the first maquette was unveiled. The statue is, in fact, the depiction of a gnome that looks like a Santa Claus holding a giant sex toy. The composition symbolises the contemporary consumerist system, idiosyncratic of the spirit of Christmas' rush to shopping, that tricks and captures society inescapably.

The issue with the sculpture arose when its very explicit shape was unveiled. It seemed that nobody wanted Santa Claus to be placed anywhere in town. Finally, it was decided that the museum Boijmans Van Beuningen would host it in its courtyard. This decision was somehow a failure: the artwork was commissioned to be exposed in a public space of the city. The courtyard of the museum is accessible only to ticket payers. However, the tall gnome was fated to stay there for a short period. In fact, at that time some ferment was occurring in Nieuwe Binnenweg, a neighbourhood not far from the museum, where a newly established organisation of local shopkeepers was trying to revitalise the area. The spokespersons of the organisation saw in Santa Claus an opportunity. Their goal was to make their neighbourhood thrive, both socially and economically. They lobbied with several formal and informal actions to get the statue placed in their area. Their argument was twofold: on the one hand, they saw the opportunity of a new sculpture as a tool of urban regeneration, that would bring spillover to the surrounding economy, and hence help make the community stronger. On the other hand, the message brought by Santa Claus was one against multinational corporation and globalisation of tastes, consumption and production. Instead, Nieuwe Binnenweg's local economy was, and still is, composed of small and family business: somehow they could embrace the same ideals of Santa Claus and certainly they felt not threatened by them.

For three years, the shopkeepers association carried out several actions aimed at co-opting Santa Claus in their desired location. They organised campaigns in the shop windows, street festivals and other guerrilla actions. They used actively public space as a resource to spread their cause and convince other people to support it. In 2008, after three years of negotiations, the shopkeepers managed to bring the statue in Eendrachtsplein.

Santa Claus is now a 'must-see' of the city of Rotterdam. Locally, since the beginning of the bottom-up endeavour of revitalisation, Nieuwe Binnenweg has developed significantly and it is counted as the hippest area of the city today, with real estate pricing rising and a clearly visible hipster-mania going on. On a wider scale, the statue has not just symbolised the development and consequent gentrification of the neighbourhood, Santa Claus has become idiosyncratic of the spirit of the whole city: sardonic, pragmatic, future-oriented.

(ii) **Urban Design in Barcelona: Carmela**

In San Pere, right next to the Palau de la Musica Catalana, lies the iron sculpture of a face. It is Carmela, a common name for an ideal Mediterranean beauty. It first has appeared in 2016, as a part of a four-pieces exhibition of the Catalan artist Jaume Plensa, hosted by Palau de la Musica. The exhibition was meant to stay no more than four months but when the deadline was approaching, some started a campaign to keep the statue there for a longer time. A petition was launched online by a resident of the area. The main argument was a very simple yet sufficient one: the statue had been able to change the space into an agreeable, pleasant, worthy to stop in place.

The local authorities underpinned the initiative and soon an agreement was achieved between the municipality of Barcelona and the artist. The statue is now on long term loan; the owner of the statue, the artist, does not get a compensation but the municipality must take financially care of the maintenance. The impact is visible on the narrow local dimension of the intersection where Carmela is.

Thanks to Carmela, now Placa de Luis Millet has acquired a dignity of its own. It is now worthwhile for both tourists and locals to spend time here. The space works differently, better, on at least two levels. On the one hand, Carmela is an element of urban design. In particular, its base is used as a bench and interacts with the existing benches next to it. People 'use' Carmela to have a break and sit down. Eventually, the rounded shape of the bench is also conducive of social interactions. This leads to a second level of impact. The aesthetic attributes of Carmela work as a real device for engagement in the space.

Carmela has a very peculiar figure. In fact, its three-dimensional shape has been adapted from the scan of a photograph. The outcome is a very accentuated 3D effect, in which the shape of the face strongly depends on the point of view. This feature makes Carmela highly interactive. People are curious about its forms and get surprised to see how the image builds when walking around it. As a result, the space is not an intersection anymore, yet it is not just a nice spot to have a break. It is actually interesting to stay here. The new place, as Carmela enables it, entails now necessary, optional, and purposively social activities (Gehl 1971), that can be observed in public space.

(iii) Representation in Copenhagen: I am Queen Mary

In March 2018, the prototype of a tall statue of an unknown queen has been unveiled in Larsens Plads, Copenhagen's waterfront, just on the way to the unmissable Little Mermaid. The statue depicts Queen Mary, a former slave from the Virgin Islands, who, in 1879, triggered a revolt in the Danish colony to fight for fair treatment of former slaves workers, uprising that eventually led to the liberation of the Virgin Islands from Denmark.

The news from all over the globe have titled the appearance of Queen Mary as Denmark's first statue of a black woman, implying that the statue was a national project. Instead, this public artwork was an initiative of the two artists Jeannette Ehlers and La Vaughn Belle; the lack of public support explains the fact that the statute is currently a prototype. The project originated from the artists' dissatisfaction for the lack of public discourse around Demark's colonial past. Ironically, their thoughts were confirmed by the public bodies' renitence to support their proposal for a monument about Queen Mary.

Nonetheless, the artist duo managed to find the support of SMK, thanks to its curator Henrik Holm. The museum is a rich collection of cast copies of sculpture from the whole western history of civilisation. But the most crucial fact is that the collection is hosted in the former warehouse where the goods imported from the colonies were first stocked. Also, here is where Queen Mary, imprisoned after the infamous "fireburn" was brought before being imprisoned in Christianshavn's prison. It is in front of this building that I am Queen Mary lies and its collocation in such a meaningful place was possible thanks to the artists' alliance with SMK's curator, who fought to obtain the concession for the sculpture to be installed here.

The presence of Queen Mary has substantiated the discourse about colonisation, lurking in the public realm. While the space has not drastically changed, the statue has changed various patterns of the use of the city. After a couple of demonstrations held by far right-wing deniers against the installation of Queen Mary, the statue has entered tour guides and it has become the gathering point of minority groups such as Black Lives Matter Denmark, that feel now finally represented thanks to a work of art that so explicitly tackles issues that are so relevant—not just—to them.

4 Discussion: An Institutional Economics Perspective on Public Art

Public art has evolved over the centuries. Although the social element has always been central in public art, from graffiti in caves to giant mirroring beans in the metropolis, today's art in public space has gained a new aspect, not just social, rather relational. In fact, what seems to be peculiar of the last decades' public art is that its functioning implies interaction with its recipients, either free or forced-riders.

The value of today's public art is not entirely the message, rather the conversation. Four main areas of impact can be looked at in order to interpret the selected cases. They are the type of the initiative, the intrinsic features for the artwork, the use of the space and the image acquired. These areas entail the virtual trajectory of an artwork in public space that is influenced by the way meanings evolve within them.

The **type of initiative** is the beginning of the artwork. Street art has, traditionally, a marked bottom-up initiative, whereas an equestrian bronze is the most sublime form of top-down initiative. The four cases belong to mixed styles of initiative and nonetheless the ways they have been proposed and promoted still exert a cascade of impacts on the lives of the artworks.

The **intrinsic features** of an artwork are connected to its artistic qualities, such as the style, the genre, the specific meanings, and the messages conveyed, or even the technical features chosen. Most of the times these features are intertwined. Richard Serra's Tilted Arc encountered problems mainly due to its intrinsic features, namely the cumbersome size of the arc and the artistic intention that this choice carried, that is to change the space and consequently draw attention to the atmosphere of the square (Balfe and Wyszomirski 1986; Kelly 1996).

The **use of the space** can be a consequence of the other areas of interpretation of a public artwork. In the famous case of Tilted Arc, the intrinsic features of the piece had huge consequences on the use of the space that was considered unbearable by its users, so that eventually the piece had to be removed. On a general note, it can be safely stated that the ambition of public art is to change the use of the surrounding space. Even in the turbulent case of Tilted Arc, Richard Serra said that the artwork meant to change the space and its removal is in fact a proof of the impact of that (Kelly 1996).

However, the life of today's public art is not limited to influencing its surroundings. Instead, a prominent role is played by those surroundings that, on different extents yet inevitably, do change the artwork. The **image of the artwork** is to be meant as the latest 'result' of the public art project and the negotiation of its meanings. Seldom the result is to be considered definitive, being the social life of public spaces evolutionary in nature. An abstract object of art could pass unnoticed without acquiring a particularly large resonance, as it is the case of Søren Georg Jensen's abstract piece close to I am Queen Mary[1]. The image of artwork can depend or influence the use of the space, it can be reflected by the nickname and can eventually have a positive or negative impact on the urban fabric and the local economy.

Each of the public art experiences investigated sheds light on how public art functions today. The cases can be analysed based on the four aforementioned areas. The installation of each artwork begins with a project initiative and gradually entails the intrinsic features of the piece. Only once the recipients of the artwork enter the discussion, that is, when the artworks are put on public display, the negotiations of meanings begins, with implications on the image acquired and the use of the space where the artwork sits (Senie 1992).

Santa Claus was commissioned by the municipality of Rotterdam advised by the public art organisation of the city. The original intention was to enrich the collection of public artworks of the city with a strikingly controversial piece. However, a strong push back was given to this first intention by the public opinion. Nonetheless, the group of shopkeepers subverted the original initiative and, along with it, the intrinsic features of the artwork. A negotiated public artwork has resulted after Santa Claus was installed in Eendtrachtsplein. The outcry was not so smoothly put down, as observed by Zebracki (2012), and it took some time before the statue was adopted by the surroundings. Eventually, such an adoption resulted in an increased importance of Santa Claus in terms of image. It is now regarded as a symbol of the city, due to its allusive intrinsic feature, but also because its installation coincided with the beginning of a gentrification process of the whole area. This resulted in changes in the way the space is now used. Pedestrian flows are redrawn around the statue, that is, included in touristic tours but also used as a

[1]On the same location of I am Queen Mary, an abstract, untitled marble sculpture by Danish artist Søren Georg Jensen sits since 1979.

reference point by many. What has started as a great controversy seems to have turned into a clever adoption of the polemic Santa Claus by first, a group of interest, then a local community and eventually the whole city and its touristic patterns.

In Barcelona, Carmela was introduced to a space that was no more than a stalemate. Here, the intriguing intrinsic feature of the statue favours a playful experience for passers-by, resulting in a mutated use of the space. Now, with Carmela, the intersection is not a deadlock anymore. People are surprised and engaged by the statue, and they end up staying more time in the space. Comparatively to Santa Claus, the relationship between the areas in interpretation is inverted, insofar the initiative is the result of a visible impact of the installation, initially meant to be temporary, on the space. In fact, the local community of neighbours started a petition for the statue to remain after the end of the exhibition of which it was a part because they could see the difference in the space. It can be concluded that Carmela has been an intelligent operation of urban design carried out by a visual artist.

Unlike the significant impact that Carmela has had on the use of the space, I am Queen Mary has impacted more prominently other areas. In fact, while Larsens Plads has not changed much in terms of pedestrian flows, the statue has had a grand impact on the public realm at large. The initiative that has led to Queen Mary's installation originates from the artists' intention to bring the topic of colonisation in the public realm. In order to do that, they have used public space as a means to diffuse their message, conveyed by the intrinsic feature of Queen Mary and what she represents. The lack of institutional support did not prevent a public discourse about Denmark's colonial past to be triggered. The image of the statue is possibly the most impacted of the areas of interpretation, and it goes together with the intrinsic feature of it. Queen Mary has literally done what the lettering of the informative sign promises, she speaks to many resistance movements and claims a space to challenge the historical narrative.

The three experiences of public art scrutinised offer an understanding of the way art in public space works today. Unlike the art as propaganda, beautification and regeneration (Appleton 2006), today's public art depends heavily on the continuous exchange and negotiation of meanings among the art, its surroundings and the individuals, users, taxpayers, free- and forced-riders. A further question arises after this investigation. How to interpret the process of meaning and values creation, simply put the functioning, of public art in a way that is comprehensive of the contribution of all the actors of the process and at the same time applicable in practice?

A possible answer is found in the theoretical framework of institutional economics and the adoption of the framework of the commons. From the experiences considered, it can be noted that the value of public art is generated socially. Art in public space triggers conversations and shared practices (Klamer 2017), of which the artwork is no more than an important participant. Carmela in Barcelona has activated a space that is now convivial, sociability is favoured yet not univocally provided by the statue. Similarly, Queen Mary in Copenhagen, has been used as a means to substantiate a public discourse that, as a conversation, is constantly nurtured and challenged by the participants. Moreover, people are aware of their relative power to start a conversation and to benefit from an existing one, as it was the case of Santa Claus in Rotterdam.

These evidences allow for an interpretation grounded in the theory of commons as made popular by Elinor Ostrom (1990), and the Institutional Analysis and Development framework, but also in light of the developments of the theory that have embraced intangibility and non-rivalry as essential attributes of cultural commons (Ostrom and Hess 2007; Bertacchini et al. 2012). This is possible because of the infrastructural features of public art, as emerged from the experiences analysed.

Drawing from Frischmann (2012), an infrastructural resource: "(1) may be consumed nonrivalrousely for some appreciable range of demand. (2) Social demand for the resource is driven primarily by downstream productive activities that require the resource as an input. (3) The resource may be used as an input into a wide range of goods and services, which may include private goods, public goods and social goods" (Frischmann 2012, 61).

In other terms, the demand for art in public space derives from the activities, the practices and the negotiation of meanings that the installation of an artwork implies. Public art is, at least to some extent, an input. In the case of Santa Claus, it has worked as an input for the development of the community and the local economy. In Barcelona, Carmela has turned a space into a place, and this was the driver of the collective action aimed at keeping the statue there.

This, hence implies that an infrastructure is a shared resource. And the other side of the coin of the potential non-rivalry is that the users contribute to the resource. As Frischmann puts it: "Users determine what to do with the capabilities that infrastructure(s) provide. Genericness [i.e. the fact that they can be used as an input to different downstream outputs] implies a range of capabilities, options, opportunities, choices, freedoms" (Frischmann 2012, 65). This is the case of what happens with public artworks, whose functioning depends on the genericness of the activities of its recipients, that are the city's users. In fact, "Users choose their activities; they can choose to experiment, to innovate, to roam freely (…) Ultimately, the value of an infrastructure resource is realised by producers and consumers of these outputs" (Frischmann 2012, 65). As a consequence, if these aspects are leveraged, the opportunity of maximisation of the externalities is taken.

Art, when put in a public space, becomes part of the built environment. This characteristic makes it comparable to Frischmann's environmental infrastructures. In fact, following the dynamics of infrastructural resources, the urban fabric absorbs the artwork, that becomes an urban node (Sennett 2018). However, the role that public art plays in the environmental context in which it is posed does not only deal with tangible attributes of the urban experience. While Carmela, in Barcelona, has become an urban node on a predominantly physical level, I am Queen Mary, in Copenhagen, triggers a discourse about colonialism that mainly happens elsewhere, on newspapers or social media and Santa Claus, in Rotterdam, has been holistically adopted as a symbol of the city. Nonetheless, in both cases, art "stops you, makes you think and perhaps represents something that you feel or believe" (Appleton 2006, 68). This means that art in public space, playing the role of an urban node, works as an intellectual infrastructure,[2] defined as a cultural environment that deals with information, community making and socialisation (Frischmann 2012). These types of infrastructure are particular because a distinction between inputs and outputs is hardly possible: it takes an idea to create new ideas.

Hence, acknowledging public art's character of mixed infrastructure seems to be useful to understand today's public art functioning and, as a consequence, the way it can be governed. In fact, the value of public art is generated within the process of its 'consumption'. The commission or the installation of an artwork in public space is no more than just the beginning of its life. As all other goods, also artworks have a biography (Kopytoff 1986).

This process can be interpreted as a common resource. The actors of the commons at hand, based on the Institutional Analysis and Development framework (Ostrom 1990; Hess and Ostrom 2003 and Hess 2007, 2008, 2012), are: (1) the providers, in this case, the artists, the government, the art institutions whose role is to provide the conditions for the resource to exist through external arrangements; (3) the producers, who *make* the commons and *are* the citizens, the tourists and the city users at large; and finally (4) the consumers, who, in fact, as in the case of intellectual infrastructures and cultural commons, are difficult to distinguish from the producers, and sometimes, they may coincide. These roles relate to each other with a strong relation of interdependence, that can be explained in-depth only within the framework of collective resources.

Differently than the traditional commons and some of the urban commons, a cultural aspect here is central. In fact, the resource does not come from the land or natural or built environment as it is the case of the traditional or urban commons. Nonetheless, the tangible element of the artworks displayed in a physical, openly accessible space is not to overlook. At the same time, the life of public art depends on what happens around the artwork, and its value is produced and consumed, and hence constantly negotiated and changed by the 'commoners'.

Such an aspect is of interest for the scholarship on the commons. Although urban phenomena are an integral part of the theorisation of commons, they have often been studied as 'enclaves' (Stavrides 2014), hub, districts, or clusters (Bertacchini and Santagata 2012; Bertacchini et al. 2012). At the same time, the most essential element responsible for what could be called a 'comedy' of the commons, viz. the seminal 'tragedy' of the commons as foreseen by Hardin (1968), is the social aspect of the commons, what Harvey (2014) has identified as an expression of the act of 'commoning'. The element of sociation is increasingly recognised as the most important feature of common resources (Euler 2018), and yet a conceptualisation of it lurks.

5 Conclusions: The Importance of Social Practices

Public art works as an urban node and belongs to its urban fabric. It is part of the built environment and has a character of infrastructure. As a consequence, public art today is no more—and not in a reductive way—than one element of a bigger system

[2]Examples of intellectual infrastructures are: basic research, ideas, languages (Frischmann 2012).

where individuals find a vast range of good reason to benefit from the experience of the space. The demand for public art and its appreciation are derived from the range of capabilities and possibilities that enable and from which it is also shaped. At the same time, it seems that the same behaviours of people contribute to others' experiences. This process is to be interpreted as a matter of interdependence and such a delicate balance of dynamics follows the process of collective resources.

Indeed more than the essence of a certain good, it is the way the good is treated, i.e. governed, that makes a good a commons. It could be implied that it is possible to enhance the value of the common resource if treated appropriately. Thus, it seems important to acknowledge that today's experiences of public art work in a way that follows the patterns of commons resource. More importantly, combining public art to the commons sheds light on the most crucial feature of the current perspectives on commons, as founded on social practices that connect with the urban experience at large. Since Lascaux graffiti, public art has been meant to be a commons.

Today's public art, and most likely tomorrow's too, shows such a disposition towards collective practices much more than in the past, even in semi-institutional artworks as the ones investigated in this research. It seems crucial to recognise that public art generates a collective resource, in order to do justice to the value of the artwork and to re-evaluate, especially viz. the current trends in commodification and endangerment of the commons (Borch et al. 2016; Pratt 2017; Standing and Guy 2019), the importance of people in public spaces, as contributors and not just consumers.

References

Appleton, J. (2006). Who owns public art?. In M. Mirza (Ed.), *Culture vultures. Is arts policy damaging the arts*?.

Arnoldi, M. J. (2016). Locating history in concrete and bronze: Civic monuments in bamako, mali. In K. Knight & H. F. Senie (Eds.), *A Companion to Public Art*. Wiley Blackwell.

Balfe, J. H., & Wyszomirski, M. J. (1986). Public art and public policy. *Journal of Arts Management and Law, 15*(4), 5–29. https://doi.org/10.1080/07335113.1986.9942166.

Bengtsen, P. (2013). Beyond the public art machine: A critical examination of street art as public art. *Konsthistorisk Tidskrift/Journal of Art History, 82*(2), 63–80.

Bertacchini, E., & Santagata, W. (Eds.). (2012). Atmosfera Creativa. Un modello di sviluppo sostenibile per il Piemonte fondato su cultura e creatività. Bologna: Il Mulino.

Bertacchini, E., Bravo, G., Marrelli, M., & Santagata, W. (2012). In *Cultural commons. A new perspective on the production and evolution of cultures*. Cheltenham: Edward Elgar.

Borch, C., & Kornberger, M. (2016). In *Urban commons: Rethinking the city*. II (2015), New York: Routledge.

Bryman, A. (2012). *Social research methods* (4th ed.). Oxford: Oxford University Press.

Cartiere, C., & Willis, Shelly. (2008). *The practice of public art*. New York: Routledge.

Deutsche, R. (1992). Art and public space: Questions of democracy. *Social Text, 33,* 34–53.

Euler, J. (2018). Conceptualizing the commons: Moving beyond the goodsbased definition by introducing the social practices of commoning as vital determinant. *Ecological Economics, 143,* 10–16.

Farquhar, J. D. (2012). *Case study research for business*. London: SAGE Publications.

Frischmann, Brett M. (2012). *Infrastructure: The social value of shared resources*. Oxford: Oxford University Press.
Gehl, (1971). *Life between buildings: Using public space*. Washington: Island Press.
Gombrich, E. H., Spanziani, M. L., & Moscone, L. (1995). In *La storia dell'arte* (1950), Leonardo.
Hardin, J. G. (1968). The tragedy of the commons. *Science, New Series, 162*(38), 1243–1248.
Harvey, D. (2014). In *Rebel cities: From the right to the city to the right to the urban revolution*. New York: Verso.
Hein, H. (1996). What is public art?: Time place and meaning. *Journal of Aesthetics and Art Criticism, 54*(1), 1–7.
Hess, C. (2008). Mapping the new commons. In *Governing shared resources: Connecting local experience to global challenges*. 12th *Conference of the International Association for the Study of the Commons*, Cheltenham, England: University of Glucestershire.
Hess, C. (2012). Constructing a new research agenda for cultural commons. In E. Bertacchini, G. Bravo, M. Marrelli, & W. Santagata (Eds.), *Cultural commons. A new perspective on the production and evolution of cultures* (pp. 19–35). Cheltenham: Edward Elgar.
Hess, C., & Ostrom, E. (2003). Ideas artifacts and facilities: Information as a common-pool resource. *Law and Contemporary Problems, 66*(1/2), 111–145.
Kelly, M. (1996). Public art controversy: The serra and lin cases. *Journal of Aesthetics and Art Criticism, 54*(1), 15–22.
Klamer, A. (2017). *Doing the right thing. A value based economy* (2nd ed.). London: Ubiquity Press.
Kopytoff, I. (1986). The cultural biography of things: Commoditization as process. In *The social life of things: Commodities in cultural perspective* (pp. 64–91). Cambridge: Cambridge University Press.
Krause K., & Senie, H. F. (2016). In *A Companion to Public Art*, Wiley Blackwell.
Lacy, S. (Ed.). (1995). *In Mapping the terrain: New genre public art*. Seattle: Bay Press.
Margozzi, M. (2001). L'arte negli edifici pubblici e la legge del 2%. In V. Cazzato (Ed.), *Istituzioni e politiche culturali negli anni Trenta, Ministero per i beni e le attività culturali*. Ufficio studi, Istituto Poligrafico e Zecca dello Stato, (pp. 123–135). Roma, tomo I.
Oldenburg, R., & Brisset, D. (1982). The tirdth place. In *Qualitative sociology*.
Ostrom, E. (1990). *Governing the commons The evolution of institutions for collective action*. Cambridge: Cambridge University Press.
Ostrom, E., & Hess, C. (Eds.). (2007). *Understanding knowledge as a commons from theory to practice*. Cambridge: MIT Press.
Pratt, A. (2017). The rise of the quasi-public space and its consequences for cities and culture. *Palgrave Communications, 3*(1), 1–4.
Romano, M. (2007). In *La Città Come Opera d'arte*. Giulio Einaudi Editore.
Senie, H. F. (1992). Baboons, pet rocks, and bomb threats. In H. F. Senie, & Webster, S. (Eds.), *Critical issues in public art: Content context and controversy*.
Sennett, R. (2018). *Building and dwelling: Ethics for the city*. London: Penguin Books.
Standing, G. (2019). *Plunder of the commons*. Pelican: A manifesto for sharing public wealth, New York.
Stavrides, S. (2014). Emerging common spaces as a challenge to the city of crisis. *City, 4–5*, 546–550.
Zebracki, M. (2012). Engaging geographies of public art: Indwellers, the 'butt plug gnome' and their locale. *Social and Cultural Geography, 13*(7), 735–758.
Zebracki, M. (2013). Beyond public artopia: Public art as perceived by its publics. *GeoJournal Special Section on Geographic Aspects of Vulnerability, 78*(2), 303–317.

Art and the City: Dialogues Between Space and Community

The Rocking Cradle of Creativity. Tales of Inertia and Frictions, Cultural and Urban Transformations, Creative Actions

Mariangela Dalfovo

Abstract

Through the metaphor of a rocking cradle, the author describes the relationship between cities and creativity. Creativity is intended in its wider meaning, encompassing a range of creative activities which contribute to urban and human regeneration and advancement. These processes often run faster than the city itself (city inertia), both in its spatial and administrative dimension. Different velocities of cultural and urban transformations cause frictions that can hinder creative processes. Focusing on the city of Bologna (Italy), the chapter highlights common challenges and potential solutions. Final remarks highlight the general importance of co-designing, co-governance, compromise (the "co-"paradigm), but also the specific role of people and places in governing the balance between power, problem and solution in order to nurture cultural commons.

1 Introduction. Culture and the City

What do we talk about when we talk about creativity? The last couple of decades have seen the rise of creativity as a popular concept. At European level, creativity has been seen as a means to build a shared culture while highlighting the value of the different local identities. At the national and city level, creativity has been regarded as a driving force for the economy, with investments made in cultural and creative industries (CCI) and the like. Increasingly, and particularly at the very local level of cities or city areas, creativity has in recent years become one of the ingredients of a much needed urban and human regeneration.

M. Dalfovo (✉)
Trento, Italy

E. Macrì et al. (eds.), *Cultural Commons and Urban Dynamics*,
https://doi.org/10.1007/978-3-030-54418-8_7

The word itself has nuanced, often multiple meanings. Some people have taken on the label "creative" themselves, somewhat blurring the lines between creativity, innovation and culture to the point of making others wonder if those are not just empty words rather than fundamental concepts. The following sections do not aim to define this word or subscribe to a specific, limited or prescriptive meaning, but rather to tell stories and report ideas about what creativity might mean in cities, and how it contributes to nurture and even generate cultural commons.

Creativity in the urban landscape can be about creating new values, products or services, or inventing new ways of making them work. Culture regarded in its wider sense is very close to creativity as intended in this discussion, be it for similarity or input-output relation. Inertia and frictions, cultural and urban transformations, creative actions, the challenges that people and places encounter "when things are moving"—and above all the specific solutions they put in place and that could inspire fellow citizens of another city—are some of the topics that are discussed in this chapter.

"Consciously producing culture" is not limited to the production of cultural goods or services and their placement within society, but it also means claiming a role in the formulation of norms and values that regulate that very society (Zobl and Klaus 2012). If we consider cultural production as a circular, and thus relational process that involves various levels of society, we can discover pockets of culture and creativity in unexpected places of the urban fabric. This means that citizens are cultural producers and as such have the right, duty and power to influence the context within which culture is produced.

Among the distinguishing traits of this process is its intrinsic dynamic status that triggers and nurtures a chain reaction affecting the surrounding context: the production of culture is not only dynamic per se, but it can directly and indirectly affect city structure and life. This state of movement, evolution and transformation is all but homogeneous. For instance, self-organised community centres, cultural phenomena or bottom-up innovative services usually go faster than innovation processes within the public administration or top-down development of infrastructures or urban areas.

These different velocities can be recorded on different levels of the civic scenario, but differences do not always bear negative effects. Sometimes the faster pace of creativity in an informal or non-institutional community can stimulate innovation on a much bigger scale, to the point of being recognised and developed by public administrations themselves. On the other hand, there are many instances where these different velocities cause frictions, which can hinder, stop or even reverse what begun as positive grassroots creative processes and urban transformations.

Sometimes city governments put in place solutions to face these challenges, which stand out as additional instances of creativity in the city. Going beyond theory and speculations, the following sections touch on some stories of creativity in the urbanscape. These are not presented as perfect, ready-made solutions, but rather as specific manifestations of creativity that can and should inspire equally specific responses to local issues and provide some more keys to the comprehension of the current paradigm and where it is leading the world.

In order to focus on a smaller portion of the spectrum, the examples that are used to highlight the relation between city, creativity and urban commons are drawn from a specific local context. Stories are pooled from the city of Bologna,[1] capital of the Region Emilia-Romagna in Northern Italy. Bologna is home to the most ancient university in the western world and well known for its history and tradition around participation, collaboration. The city is a fertile cradle for cultural processes and has developed quite some actions and research[2] in the topics of creativity, active citizenship and cultural urban development.

A note to the reader. Labels, such as creativity, innovation, culture, good and bad, are nothing but shortcuts that help people communicate in a more efficient way. For this very reason, the final sections of this chapter are divided into shorter paragraphs that make it easier and more efficient for readers to draw (or literally, jump to) conclusions.

2 The City, Cradle of Creativity

Cities can be considered as specific frames of space in time: comprised of both infrastructures and symbolic places, they are the product of local identity and express the relation and constant negotiation between past and future. As entities in perpetual evolution and change, cities vary through time. The spatial location, people that live there and those who pass by, institutions and government are elements that keep moving within the city determining its unique evolutionary path. This means that the pace of change of the city as a whole is connected to that of its building blocks, the interrelations among them and interaction with the surrounding context.

Because of their specific and heterogeneous nature, cities have always been the stage of cultural production in its manifold meaning. As introduced above, cultural production is a circular, dynamic process that involves various actors across society. Citizens, artists and institutions, actual and potential audience, managers and even places themselves are involved in the production of culture. Consciously avoiding the debate around "what culture is (and what it is not)" and adopting a permeable and open view with regards to culture and creativity, the range of what contributes to defining the cultural grounds of the present can be widened considerably.

[1]Bologna is the seventh most populous city in Italy with about 390,000 inhabitants and 150 different nationalities. Its metropolitan area is home to more than 1,000,000 people. Source: Wikipedia.

[2]In recent years the Region Emilia-Romagna has addressed the topic through extensive research. The Report on the creative economy in the Region (ERVET 2012 and 2018), extensively analysed regional data in order to feed into a creative development strategy. In 2019 the latest research was published in the book *Il valore della creatività. L'economia arancione in Emilia-Romagna* (Bologna, Il Mulino) edited by Michele Trimarchi. In the publication, the topic of creativity and the city was explored by the author of this chapter (Mariangela Dalfovo "Una mappa della creatività: esperienze e fermenti" in *Il valore della creatività*).

Cities are natural attractors for ideas, new inventions, creative minds. They are the centre of art and culture, the stage and frame where cultural values are negotiated and defined. Digital connectivity, international networks and transportation infrastructures allow cities to be extremely connected to one another and provide a fertile ground for comparison and dialogue. However, especially in the fast and interconnected present times, changing and evolving takes up an increasingly significant importance, not devoid of efforts and challenges.

Urban transformations take place on different levels. There is the development of infrastructures, such as bridges or squares, and the advancement of the "urban software", such as mobility systems or ways and rules for the city-user relation. Transformations also happen in the way people interact with the city and its elements, such as service providers who adapt the shape of a service to a new need or audience. City users themselves can be initiators of change, from the (creative, innovative) way they use a service to proper citizen-activated initiatives. All these different elements form an integral part of what shapes and dictates cultural and social transformations in the urban dimension.

The never-ending evolution process does not prevent cities from being perceived as specific or even immutable entities, from within and without. The transformation of their tangible aspects runs at a slow pace: the time span for a square to be built, from idea to ribbon cutting, may take well up to ten years. On the other hand, cultural and creative processes run at a much faster pace: cities are fertile ecosystems, "rocking cradles" where innovation can happen.

The image that a city conveys has very much to do with the cultural and social sphere, besides its looks and shape. Cities tend, however, to conserve inertia. That is, they tend to maintain their characteristics for quite some time despite generalised or local changes in the socio-economic scenario. Cities doing well (e.g. on tolerance, inclusion, services, etc.) tend to retain their positive characteristics for about a decade, while cities in decline find it takes decades to improve the quality of life.

3 *Urbanauts* Change (the Way They Use) the City

3.1 Socio-Economic Changes Pose New Challenges

The socio-economic changes of recent years pose important challenges to urban life and dynamics. Increased life expectancy draws policymakers' attention to the ageing population and their needs; a changed job market affects the separation and connections between life and workspace; gender equality battles reshape roles within families; higher education levels equip the population with a widened range of needs.

Institutional structures and grids often tend to be rather static when confronted with needs arising from a transforming society and new economies. Much of the change happening in cities is propelled by those population segments who are more likely to find themselves toggling between cultural, social, work and family needs. *Urbanauts* in the rocking cradle are bound to find creative solutions to their everyday urban life.

3.2 Altering Service Configuration. Cinenido (Bologna)

An example of an alteration in shape—in this case, of the cultural offer—in order to improve content accessibility without deteriorating its quality is provided by the *Cineteca di Bologna*.[3] Through its programme *Cinenido—Visioni disturbate* (literally, *disturbed screenings*) the Cineteca opens up to a specific audience segment. Since 2010, the programme offers morning and afternoon film screenings for parents with their young children (0–18 months old), providing a full range of services such as parking space for strollers, dim lights, softer sounds and "freedom to disturb", cry and nurse. If on the one hand, such service alterations need monetary investment in organisation and resources (e.g. opening times), it is evident how the social benefit, improved quality of life and even audience numbers outweigh the effort.

3.3 New Nodes on the Map: Coworking Spaces

Citizens themselves can modify the urban fabric and create new content and containers. Creativity is a useful tool to make activities and products compatible with work and life. The specific positioning of places in the urban fabric helps urbanauts draw more effective trajectories. This shifting and moving of people and routes has frequently contributed to the regeneration of urban areas that used to receive scarce attention and support on the part of public administrations.

Making the most of existing infrastructures, citizens have created new nodes on the map. This is true for coworking spaces, now a quite established phenomenon, usually located in well-connected spots. Initially set up on the cost-efficient solution of sharing office space and expenses, coworking spaces have quickly gained importance in social relations, culture, community building (Pais 2016). They have thus become hybrid places where a varied range of activities take place, including training, career fairs, social and cultural events and even welfare services.[4]

Evolution is not limited to the services they provide. From functional aggregators of heterogeneous workers, some of these places have naturally bent towards specialisation (e.g. culture and creativity, IT, etc.) and evolved as an interconnected ecosystem and even international networks. Pooling from the skills and knowledge

[3]Official site: www.cinetecadibologna.it.

[4]For instance, back in 2015 *Spazio Kilowatt* (now known as *Kilowatt*—www.kilowatt.bo.it) in Bologna started a pioneering nursery school for its co-workers' children. Today *Kilowatt* has become much more than a coworking space and the *KW Baby* (www.edu.kilowatt.bo.it.) is still up and running at the new location, where it keeps being co-developed and tested together with parents, educators and the University of Bologna, becoming a transferrable model.

of co-workers, some coworking spaces work almost as private companies providing integrated creative services, from design to event management, or as tech innovation labs and incubators (fab-labs, impact hubs).

3.4 Advocacy and Soft Power Change the System. Dynamo (Bologna)

Dynamo—la Velostazione di Bologna[5] provides another great example on the topic of shared space. Their focus being green mobility, Dynamo started off offering a wide range of services around bicycles for both local and temporary citizens (bike parking, rental, repair shop, bike tours, relax area, etc.) and soon developed its offer to address a wider range of city matters. Since its opening Dynamo has been both a producer and aggregator of social and cultural events (exhibitions, parties, markets, etc.), opening up its space to citizens and organisations.[6]

Dynamo started off as a dream. A group of active citizens who strongly believed in green mobility as an answer to climate, socio-economic challenges and that, as such, should be supported, protected and made easier for all. In 2016, Dynamo was among the winners of an open call issued by the local government to allocate public buildings to creative projects. Through this call, Dynamo settled in a quite peculiar although strategically located place, a former parking garage between the train station and the city centre.

Ideas that become real such as Dynamo can bring real change to cities. They can influence policies, legitimise or validate the changed behaviour of citizens and help create new, updated institutional rules. For instance, it was also thanks to Dynamo's support, advocacy and negotiation with the public administration and policymakers that in 2019 the "continued behaviour" of many citizens on (bike) wheels led the public administration to declare some Bologna streets "one-way except cycles".[7]

The value and importance of these people-driven hybrid organisations in the urban scenario is evident. Besides the leading—yet much varied—services provided, they contribute to the soft power of cities. Usually referred to nations but extendable to cities as well, the term soft power[8] refers to the ability to attract and co-opt, rather than coerce or pay (hard power) in order to obtain the desired results.[9] These organisations contribute not only to reach certain noble objectives such as

[5]Official site: www.dynamo.bo.it.

[6]In 2018, Dynamo issued a public call aimed at Third Sector organisation to share its space (as headquarters, meeting place, etc.). From April to October it also made its space available (and free Wi-Fi) as a study hall and coworking space.

[7]Paolo Rosato, *Bici contromano Bologna. "Il doppio senso è sicuro"*, www.ilrestodelcarlino.it, Bologna, 15/02/2019.

[8]The term was made popular in 1990 by Joseph Nye with his book *Bound to Lead* (Nye, J. S. (1990). *Bound to Lead: The Changing Nature of American Power*.).

[9]Source: "Soft power", en.wikipedia.com.

social or environmental sustainability, but also feed into what is called cultural diplomacy: the negotiation power that a state (or city) has thanks to its composing elements.

4 And the Cradle Rocks. Participatory Budgeting and District Labs

4.1 Participatory Budgeting and District Labs

The examples in the previous section illustrate creative urban transformations generated by bottom-up stimuli. However, some of this creativity trickles down—or filters up—to the level of public administration. City governments are tied to their citizens by a double-edged mandate that bonds them together in a two-ways relationship which should be founded on trust and responsibility. With relatively small territories under their control and a relative freedom from central governments, cities are the governmental level that is more open to innovation, creativity and experimental policies.

The city of Bologna is not new to creative actions and innovation. Since 2010, the city has promoted *Incredibol—Bologna's creative innovation*,[10] a region-wide programme to support creative innovation and cultural and creative industries. The programme provides coaching and training and issues several calls to support innovative start-ups and the internationalisation of the cultural and creative industries (CCIs). Through public tenders, it also manages the allocation of public buildings to such organisations and projects (such as the parking garage which is now home to Dynamo).

The problem of empty, unused and underused public spaces and areas is very dear to Bologna. In 2016, the city set up a participatory budgeting process to involve its citizens in public decision-making around strategic issues, policy development and to re-think the use of public space in certain areas of the city. *Laboratori di quartiere* (district labs, begun in 2017) are the main tool for participatory budgeting and stand as a space for dialogue between city-community to co-design and define the use, function and development of urban places.

In district labs, citizens suggest ideas for specific places or buildings in the area. Proposals range from use and function to actual urban development and regeneration, they are discussed, developed and then put up for vote. Successful proposals become projects that translate into actual budget lines and work plans in the public programme. In 2017 and 2018, around 7000 citizens participated in these labs and presented 60 projects for participatory budgeting. A total of 30,932 votes were cast to select the 12 final projects for implementation.

[10]More info at www.incredibol.net/en/.

The work-in-progress of selected projects can be monitored by any citizen through a dedicated webpage.[11] In spring 2019, one project was marked as completed and one project under construction, four projects at the stage of public procurement for the construction works, one at the stage of recruiting the project manager. The remaining five projects had yet to begin their route to implementation. For the third edition (2019–20) the total budget for participatory budgeting was doubled to 2 million euros, including the additional million allocated to activities (versus construction and development work).[12]

4.2 The Regulation of the Commons

Another important tool developed by the city of Bologna to foster and channel the creativity of citizens in order to take care of the common good is the *Regulation of the Commons*, also known as the *Regulation of Bologna.*[13] The document enforces the constitutional principle of horizontal subsidiarity,[14] which establishes that public administrations should support citizens in the development of autonomous initiatives of collective interest. This game-changing tool allows formally or informally organised citizens to establish partnerships (Collaboration Pacts) with city governments to take care of a public good or provide a service of general interest.

The Regulation represents a clear attempt to provide an administrative framework for citizen-driven activities that were already happening in the city, building on Bologna's long history and tradition of citizens' participation in decision-making.[15] The growing buzz around common goods is also connected with the historic moment marked by economic crisis and cuts in public spending. The Regulation on the collaboration between citizens and the public administration on activities aiming at the care and regeneration of urban commons was approved in Bologna in May 2014,[16] many other Italian cities soon followed suit.[17]

[11]"Bilancio partecipativo: realizzazione dei progetti 2017 e 2018" on www.partecipa.comune.bologna.it.

[12]During the Covid-19 pandemic of 2020 the municipality published an update. Participatory budgeting processes were stopped in order made those resources available for the current more pressing challenges.

[13]The full text in English and Italian is available on the website of the Municipality of Bologna www.comune.bo.it.

[14]Italian Constitution, art 118, par. 4.

[15]Entry: *Bologna Regulation for the Care and Regeneration of Urban Commons* at www.wiki.p2pfoundation.net.

[16]The Regulation was developed with the help of *Labsus—laboratory for subsidiarity,* a not for profit organisation inspired by Art. 118. Since then, Labsus has kept track of the debate, actions and circulation of the Regulation of the commons. www.labsus.org.

[17]As of early 2020, 211 municipalities have adopted the Regulation, sometimes with minor variations.

The latest national report on the state-of-the-art written by Labsus in 2019, counts more than 1000 recorded Collaboration Pacts across Italy[18] and analyses a sample of 830 pacts. A particularly interesting phenomenon highlighted in the analysis is represented by the so-called "complex agreements",[19] which are those pacts that specifically focus on the regeneration and reuse of buildings. With construction works, multiple actors involved and higher interests at stake (and, consequently, a higher added-value potential), it is in this sample that the most interesting instances of creative citizens expression are to be found.

5 The Community and the Commons

5.1 INstabile Portazza: From Virtual to Real to Virtuous

INstabile Portazza Community Creative Hub,[20] is an example of creative use of the Regulation. Started out as an urban and architectural regeneration project, INstabile soon became a "civic centre 2.0", an informal organisation that has something to do with entrepreneurship and everything to do with community, cooperation and social and cultural value. Located in Savena, a residential district in the southeast periphery of Bologna, the centre has a varied and hybrid role, aiming to be a community-led aggregator and coordinator of community and civil society initiatives.

The story of INstabile begins with a social street. Social streets were born in Bologna in 2013. People started to create virtual aggregative spaces (i.e. Facebook groups) for those living in a specific area or street. These communities often go from virtual to real, establishing or nurturing social ties through real relationships and social events. In 2014, in via Portazza (a street in the Savena district), people met at a social meal had an idea: reclaiming an abandoned building to answer the needs of the local community. The building was a former civic centre built in the '60s, which had been empty since 1984.

After many meetings within the community and with the public administration, the group signed an agreement with the Municipality through the Regulation of the commons. With the Municipality as third party guarantor, they were then able to stipulate an agreement with the public housing agency, owner of the building. While the owner took care of some major interventions on the building, the remaining renovation works were done by the local community, pooling from the

[18]The publicity and documentation of collaboration pacts depends on local administration, the actual total number of pacts is surely much bigger.

[19]7.8%, 65 pacts over the total sample of 830. Most agreements focus on parks, gardens or green space (46%), urban public space such as streets or squares (17%) and involve two parties (public-private) for small actions of urban care. Source: *Rapporto 2019 sull'amministrazione condivisa dei beni comuni* (by Labsus).

[20]Official site: https://www.instabileportazza.it

skills, competencies and resources found among its members and fulfilling the core principles on which collaboration pacts are founded.

This circular economy of resources is reflected in the governance mechanism, where decision-makers, implementers and beneficiaries coincide. The general assembly is supported by a coordination team who monitors projects and processes (horizontal governance). Community meetings are held regularly and allow citizens to suggest ideas and activities, and to participate in the structuring of the programme. The activity programme and services offered have a particular focus around culture, work and welfare. In 2018, INstabile's events were featured in the citywide Bologna summer cultural programme.

Working together, the community created a physical and relational space that local citizens can use, populate and fill with their ideas. This new kind of places that are fundamentally made of people are the "where" local communities express themselves and participate in redefining their own identity—and therefore, that of the city they are a part of. INstabile is a community centre but also an open space for projects and ideas, keeping a steady eye to the future, yet grounded in a fertile ecosystem of collaborations with public and private institutions and organisations.

5.2 From Spaces to Places

It is no coincidence that community experiences such as INstabile develop in urban peripheries. Often neglected by public and private investment, infrastructure and service development, peripheral and internal areas are where some of the more innovative instances of change are taking place. Populated by a varied mix of people—intergenerational, intercultural, etc.—these places are now increasingly reclaiming their right to updated infrastructures, services and resources. They do not wish to become a new "city centre" or hip area, but they are rather reclaiming their dignity and purpose as places for people.

The success of INstabile and the like is connected with specific factors. Local social capital, the knowledge and experience found among community members (architects, engineers, social innovators), the ability to create a productive relationship with the public administration, the knowledge of administrative procedures, the timeliness of the regulation on the commons. Peripheries have stepped in the spotlight, not just asking for resources, but also increasingly providing virtuous solutions that central areas and local government should take into account for further development and planning.

The discourse on peripheral and neglected areas was met with an increased interest in local development, leading to what has been called[21] a new course of social innovation. Private and public investment have shifted from assets or buildings to the support of holistic urban solutions that comprise social and community functions, often co-produced with not for profit organisations. This has

[21]Paolo Venturi, *È ora di inaugurare un nuovo ciclo dell'innovazione sociale—partendo dal 'senso' dei luoghi*, 24/02/2020, www.che-fare.com.

stimulated a shift from spaces to places, which, in turn, enables the convergence of the relational value with the practical use of spaces.

6 Challenges

6.1 Different Velocities Cause Frictions. INstabile, Dynamo, District Labs

However well some situations might turn out, it is undeniable that urban development, cultural processes and public administrations have a different pace. Running across the same urban scenario, the trajectories of change sometimes intertwine, sometimes collide: city inertia, the procedure-driven pace of bureaucracy and public administrations, the rapidity of cultural, creative and social processes interact in the construction of our present and future.

In 2018, INstabile was told by the local administration that some renovation works had to be done on the building (property of the public housing agency). With the space undergoing restoration, INstabile's activities were put on hold, waiting for the assignment of a temporary space, a smaller empty public building in the area. One year later INstabile finally got the new provisional space and could get started on the works and adjustments to make it suitable for their purposes.

Nevertheless, INstabile is, by definition, *unstable*.[22] Their "light structure" (not a formal organisation) actually allows them to be resilient, adaptive and flexible—three of the most fundamental keywords of present times. While waiting for the new, provisional headquarters INstabile kept on developing projects that could take place outside their space, such as a construction workshop with local university students to build a library. And yet, because INstabile is fundamentally made of people, being homeless for one year has made it extremely difficult to hold the community together.[23]

Dynamo, the cycle-green mobility centre mentioned above, went through a similar situation. In order to make room for some major renovation works that had to be done on the building,[24] Dynamo cleared out the affected area (event space bar, kitchen, stage, etc.). Works should have started in late 2018, to last 12 months, but in early 2019, the public tender was still tangled up in procedures and technicalities. For Dynamo this delay meant a prolonged stop of the cultural and social activities

[22]The name INstabile is a pun, being both adjective and adverbial of place. In Italian, the word "instabile" means "unstable", while the phrase "in stabile" means "in (the) building".

[23]As everything else, this situation became more precarious since February 2020, by the global pandemic Covid-19.

[24]The construction plan was approved in 2016, and consisted of necessary interventions (such as the heating system) on the event space, adding up to a total of 1.5 million euros co-financed by the Region and the Municipality. (Micol Lavinia Lundari, *Velostazione di Bologna, il Comune: "Il cantiere potrebbe partire anche fra un anno e mezzo"*, 15/02/2019, www.bologna.repubblica.it).

of the event space, which affected revenues, jobs and implied an interruption in the public social and cultural service.

As opposed to the natural flexibility of informal organisations like INstabile, structured organisations[25] have more tangible downsides. Given the uncertainty around when works would actually start, in early 2019, Dynamo launched a crowdfunding campaign to rebuild the event space and temporarily resume its activities. The space reopened in May 2019, while construction works began in September 2019. Over the course of 2019 Dynamo not only resumed social and cultural events, but it also reinforced a thriving public debate around the commons and the role of administrations in nurturing or hindering a sustainable and responsible management.

Participatory budgeting and district labs have their own challenges too. The implementation of projects selected in the first edition (2017) only started in 2019. It is no surprise that the route from idea to reality in the public sector is slow and full of procedures. What this means for citizens is that expectations are not met in the short term. The doubling of the budget for the third (2019–20) edition with one million euro allocated to activities might represent a reaction to the problem. With activities (festivals, exhibitions, courses, events), the lag between idea and reality is much smaller than with construction works. This can absolutely be read as the public administration's response to its own slowness.

6.2 The Dark Side of Active Citizenship (Plus Some Good News)

Recent years have seen the development of debate and actions around active citizens. Dynamo, INstabile, the Regulation and district labs belong to this process. With active citizenship increasingly considered as a miracle cure for deteriorating urban and social landscapes, horizontal subsidiarity[26] can become a double-edged sword. While it allows citizens to act upon a public good or provide a service of public interest, administrators might sometimes be led to think that they can delegate regular day-to-day urban care or take citizens actions for granted across time.

This flawed approach to active citizenship could thus become an obstacle: on the public administration side, to recognising the necessity of supporting these cultural processes, on the side of those very cultural processes, to striving and fighting for their own economic sustainability (and freedom). This also ultimately feeds the misleading paradigm of creative and cultural processes being the output of voluntary actions carried out for one's own pleasure and in one's own free time, thus "free" from any sort of monetary valorisation or compensation.

---

[25]As a legal entity, Dynamo is a cooperative organisation with 20 + employees. It provides an essential mobility service to both residents and tourists.

[26]Horizontal subsidiarity is the constitutional principle that regulates the relationship between government and citizens to take care of common goods and services, which is further articulated by the Regulation on the commons.

The recent Italian reform of the non-profit sector[27] (*Riforma del terzo settore*, law 106/2016) actually tries to address these issues by regulating and restructuring the sector and setting standards, indicators and boundaries that organisations must comply with in order to fall under the Third Sector Reform umbrella. There is a thriving debate in and around the so-called third sector, as many organisations (including those driven by active citizens) do not fall under the public or the commercial sector. These organisations, often operating in the social or cultural realm, are driving a new paradigm, where "common interest" is associated with "economic sustainability" rather than just with voluntary work.

The third sector is a fertile ecosystem where new ideas, skills and professions are being developed. Grassroots instances of creativity based on the two core concepts of community and place can build relevant answers to local needs. Working at the core of what is deemed most "valuable"—art, culture, society, urban space, etc.—, they often take common assets and concepts (home, school, factory, community, district, etc.) and return them to the community. Taken apart and freed from bureaucratic boundaries,[28] these assets are reframed through new social and creative purposes that respond to true community needs.

7 More Frictions and Some Grease

7.1 Causes on the Podium: One, Two, Three

The previous sections have outlined some stories of different velocities in the city, if self-organised citizen initiatives are virtuous examples, city governments must also do their part in nurturing these processes. Among the innumerable reasons that hinder the development of bottom-up, citizen-driven experience, there are three main causes. From the more evident to the deeper (and thus less visible) they are: (1) financial and human resources (how much/how); (2) the lack of managerial figures in the public administration; and (3) the priority of culture and creativity in political agendas.

The lack of financial and human resources is usually the first that comes to mind. Although scarcity of money and personnel does prevent the public sector from running fast enough and keep up with cultural processes, pointing fingers to the mere amount of resources can be an easy excuse not to address real issues.

[27]The reform involves more than 300,000 associative, cooperative and voluntary organisations, as well as more than six million volunteers, gathering them (i.e. associations, foundations, social enterprises, philanthropic entities, voluntary organisations, etc.) under the common status of "Third Sector Bodies". The Code for the Third Sector harmonises the bodies' characteristics and activities and establishes a national Register. The reform pushed the organisations to be socially and economically sustainable and has a strong focus on accountability (towards all stakeholders, including sponsors and communities). Many smaller organisations will probably be wiped away, whereas larger organisations will have to adjust and make important choices.

[28]Paolo Venturi, *ibid.*

The deeper challenges around resources are related to soft aspects (how budgets are managed, skills and competencies) rather than mere quantitative or hard factors (amounts of resources).

The lack of experienced managers within the higher ranks of public administration is linked with the "process" dimension highlighted above (how versus how much) and earns the second place. The public engine needs project managers, resourceful people capable of making strategic choices at the right moment and carrying them on. People with hands-on experience, ready to take risks and with a mandate linked to clear and measurable objectives, with knowledge of bureaucracy and procedures but above all packing people skills and the art of mediation and compromise.

This cannot really be possible without political backing: the key to unleashing a culture and creativity-based revolution lies with the top levels. The position innovative cultural and creative intentions and actions get on political agendas is the number one reason for which innovative experiences are subject to frequent hiccups. It is not only about mentioning culture, but specifically about what priority level culture and creativity are assigned in political agendas compared with the rest. Attributing high priority often requires making choices that might be risky, and sticking with them.

All in all, the true challenge lies with people. Many of the glitches in urban and human development processes lay in what could be called the bureaucratic and procedural evolution of guilt—a most ironical overlap of illuminist-inspired structure, socialist-derived control and catholic-inherited morals. The Bologna examples outlined above could be successful also thanks to a visionary (even though perfectible) public policy centred around culture, welfare and sustainable mobility. Courageous politics is not so easy to find, and always bears some room for improvement.

7.2 The Third Way Through the Threshold of the Future

The holistic or "combined" approach (top-down meets bottom-up) is a recurring mantra among scholars and policy experts. This has proved to be absolutely right: there can be no true paradigm shift if grassroots experiences are not met by institutional efforts and public policies. This is not limited to the recognition or acceptance of such grassroots practices, but it needs to translate into targeted public policies that nurture existing experiences and allow new ones to grow. It also means compromise, investment, risk and sacrifice.

The bottom-up side should be more sympathetic to the other party. Public administrations are often unprepared to provide relevant answers and generate adequate responses to innovation. This grey area could actually make room for negotiation and discussion to innovate the existing technical tools in order to facilitate access to common goods and to redefine the concept and idea of sustainability, measuring them on co-designed objectives.[29]

[29]Filippo Tantillo, *Quando i margini assediano le città: i nuovi centri culturali stanno cambiando la provincia profonda,* 17/02/2020 www.che-fare.com.

The encounter between bottom-up and top-down, between public and private, is an important node in the analysis and potential solution of frictions. The commons are known for their power to blur the clear-cut division between public and private and give birth to new hybrid ways, such as public goods managed by private organisations in the public or collective interest. All these grassroots experiences that populate cities and peripheries get to a point where, in order to scale up their cultural, social and civic value, they need to be properly processed and understood by the system. This can only be achieved through a productive dialogue with institutions and infrastructures.

Like public administrations, private organisations and individuals (e.g. artists and professionals) are also often unable to address and manage this delicate transition towards integrated solutions. Crossing the threshold from the present to the future paradigm can be made easier by the intervention of third parties who put aside personal or professional interest in the name of the public good. This is a call upon public servants, mediators or external organisations who can act as facilitators in this process towards a better future for all.

8 And There Is Hope. An Attempt to Drawing Conclusions

8.1 The Managerial Turn

Good news. A paradigm shift in people's minds is taking place, even where one would least expect it. In the public administration, some cities (such as Milan in Italy) are appointing managers recruited in the private sector to executive positions. The managerial approach introduced in public administrations enables a quicker implementation of projects to the benefit of citizens and their expectations. Being appointed by the local government, their mandate is usually limited in time, often project-based and almost always changing with a change of flag.

If regular administrative-nominated executives run at a slower pace and pay the price of a procedural approach to project management, they can, on the other hand, ensure more continuity in time. Is this a dilemma between swift and temporary versus slow and steady? There is no right answer, but there are attempts to find different shades of grey. In recent years, Bologna and other municipalities introduced flexible hours and telework for their employees and started to test a project and objective-based approach to work streams.

8.2 Space is the Place[30]

As seen through this chapter, one of the main issues or friction-factor around urban cultural commons is related to space. As introduced at the very beginning of this

[30]Disclaimer: the paragraph title does not refer to jazz composer and musician Sun Ra's Afrofuturist science fiction film released in the 1970s.

chapter, the spatial context is a fundamental element of the cultural production process, together with the interaction of the different actors across society. This is also true for urban transformation processes, which can be considered as cultural production themselves. The management of public space and the allocation of public buildings are, therefore, crucial subjects in the political discourse, regulation and innovative practices.

Most cities are aware of the importance of public space and the different pace at which processes, policies and the city itself run. How fast is the cradle rocking? How can it keep up with what is inside? City governments often find new ways to manage these processes and bypass their internal limits. The issue of priority levels does not only lie with the political agenda, but also with individual departments within the administration and what they feel needs to be prioritised. This is why the call for third parties, mediators and facilitators is fundamental even within administrations themselves, where they should act as translators, coordinators and guarantors of the public good.

8.3 New Tools Foster Cooperation on Cultural Grounds. Laboratorio Spazi (Bologna)

Besides political and administrative priority-setting, the Regulation of the commons and public-tender mechanisms for the allocation of buildings to cultural projects have shown their limits. Bologna, initiator of the Italian "revolution of the commons" through the first steps that brought to the Regulation, is on the front line to find more effective and sustainable solutions. In 2019, the city's *Fondazione per l'innovazione urbana* (Foundation for urban innovation) started a new project, *Laboratorio spazi*, which brought together cultural organisations to discuss the topic of public space and how the limited number of available buildings could be managed in a more efficient way.[31]

The Laboratorio Spazi started out with an internal analysis to appraise the existing administrative tools for space allocation and management. The second stage consisted of individual and collective consultations with cultural actors and civil society organisations aimed at developing new and better tools. The result was a new experimental procedure for building allocation. Instead of relying solely on the traditional application-selection process, selected candidates are called to present their project ideas to the group of fellow applicants and invited to formulate joint applications for the final selection.

This assembly works as a sort of co-designing platform, inspired by processes that spontaneously take place in grassroots organisations, social and community centres (such as INstabile). The process is coordinated rather than imposed from above and members have the freedom to choose if and with whom to join forces. This tool works towards a more efficient use of scarce resources through the

[31]More info on the project on the website www.fondazioneinnovazioneurbana.it and in the 2018 report *Per una nuova politica degli spazi a Bologna. Laboratorio spazi*, Bologna.

promotion of the "co-"paradigm. Co-existence, co-governance, co-programming and (more often than not) compromise are values that push cities in the right direction, working together in the name of a higher, common interest.

8.4 Common Good, Common Wellbeing

Urban commons also mean common wellbeing. The efficient and smooth running of public administrations, combined with a more managerial approach and an attitude to taking risks, often prove rewarding in the bigger picture. Cultural and creative processes that are born in cities can and should affect the management of the city itself, and should also be less strict with public administrations, who will continue to be tangled up in bureaucracy and procedures for the foreseeable future. Third party entities or individuals could be the catalyst of a true paradigm shift, taking both cultural producers and public administrators by the hand and helping them through the threshold between past and future.

The growing multitude of grassroots practices is a positive phenomenon, but in order to be scaled up and lead to diffused change, it has to be understood and digested by the system. By no means, this has to happen through radical change or value abdication, but it does mean that some experiences will have to change and grow and gain more structure in order to deal with hard institutional procedures, standards and times. Having the right credentials to dialogue or even partially "entering" the system gives them more chances to change it from within.

The regulatory function of the public sector is fundamental, especially in this process (even though incompetent people do exist and they must be confronted).[32] A well-thought and coordinated process is what makes it possible to adjust the trajectory of the present and re-frame processes and experiences: from the sum of individual interests to a higher collective interest.[33] This is the true and only cure to tackle the procedural evolution of guilt that cements the barrier to taking relevant, innovative, visionary, creative choices (and risks), on the part of any actors—public and private alike—across and beyond every urban level.

References

Carta, M. (2019). *Futuro*. Il Rubbettino: Politiche per un diverso presente.

Dalfovo, M. (2019). Una mappa della creatività: esperienze e fermenti. In M. Trimarchi (Ed.) *Il valore della creatività: L'economia arancione in Emilia-Romagna*. Il Mulino.

Nye, J. S. (1990). *Bound to lead: The changing nature of American power*.

[32]As urbanist Maurizio Carta wisely pointed out at a presentation of his book *Futuro. Politiche per un diverso presente* (2019, Il Rubbettino), "(…) la funzione regolativa del pubblico è fondamentale—poi ci sono gli incapaci, che vanno combattuti". At Due Punti bookshop in Trento on 21/02/2020.

[33]The concept of the shift from the sum of individual interests to the shared collective interest is drawn from Maurizio Carta's book *Futuro* (2019, Il Rubbettino).

Pais, I. (2016). Il « non formale » : una categoria per leggere le trasformazioni sociali?

Zobl, E., & Klaus, E. (2012). Cultural Production in Theory and Practice. In *p/art/icipate–Kultur aktiv gestalten. eJournal des programmbereichs contemporary arts & cultural production. Schwerpunkt Wissensc < z<haft & Kunst. Issue 1, Initiate: I am a Cultural Producer.*

Sitography

www.bologna.repubblica.it.
www.che-fare.com.
www.cinetecadibologna.it.
www.comune.bo.it.
www.dynamo.bo.it.
www.edu.kilowatt.bo.it.
www.fondazioneinnovazioneurbana.it.
www.ilrestodelcarlino.it.
www.incredibol.net.
www.instabileportazza.it.
www.kilowatt.bo.it.
www.labsus.org.
www.partecipa.comune.bologna.it.
www.wiki.p2pfoundation.net.

Public Space: Mapping the Physical, Social and Cultural Accessibility for the Creation of Urban Commons

Lidia Errante

Abstract

The focus on accessibility is a primary concern in the field of public space, as a right to be guaranteed by and for all the actors involved, both public and private. The objective of providing a good standard of accessibility can only be achieved through an accurate understanding of the physical and social conditions of public space: on the one hand, studying the socio-spatial dynamics; on the other hand through a desirable renovation of the design know-how, making accessible to administrations and designers the necessary knowledge needed to positively improve the success of urban transformation actions.

1 Introduction

Accessibility (noun) is defined, by Cambridge Dictionary as: the fact of being able to be reached or obtained easily; the quality of being easy to understand; the quality or characteristic of something that makes it possible to approach, enter, or use it; the ability to reach or enter a place or building.[1] The present time is marked by different forms of exclusionary dynamics that make the contemporary city socially and physically inaccessible. In this sense, the claim for accessibility can be considered a

[1]https://dictionary.cambridge.org/dictionary/english/accessibility accessed 04.02.2020.

L. Errante (✉)
Department of Architecture and Territory, Mediterranea University, Reggio Calabria, Italy
e-mail: lidia.errante@unirc.it

E. Macrì et al. (eds.), *Cultural Commons and Urban Dynamics*,
https://doi.org/10.1007/978-3-030-54418-8_8

major form of resistance from the erosion of the public realm, a shared value of the debate on contemporary public space and urban commons. The assumptions of this contribution are, in fact, that urban commons and public space are the two faces of the same coin, having a comparable socio-spatial structure, from which it is possible to improve the liveability, vibrancy, efficiency, health and safety of the city.

The role of public space has been widely acknowledged in the cultural debate as a mean to pursue quality goals within the urban transformation, with positive effects on the physical, environmental, social, cultural and perceptual level (De Capua and Errante 2019). Public space is the physical place of urban experience, in which and thanks to which, the transformations and contradictions of contemporary living take place and can be studied in the interaction between subject (individual or collective) and object (space and/or all the tangible elements that articulate it). These dynamics, defined as socio-spatial, are implicit in the primary infrastructural function of public space to connect the urban environment and to host the flows of people, goods and services (Ibid.). In this perspective, the common sense giving to public space as "design of the soil, drawing, *embellissement*, greenery, attribution of meaning to the void between the buildings" (Gregotti 1993, p. 2), cannot satisfy the renewed social and physical potential claimed for the contemporary city.

For more than a decade now, the UN documents have outlined the operative framework to reach urban sustainability and liveability, in light of the exponential increase of the population. Indeed, the UN claims for an institutional, regulatory and cultural review of urban planning to improve the access to services and to economic and social opportunities. In the future, planning and urban transformation tools will have to: monitoring and evaluating the performance of the city; provide for a certain degree of informality in the phase of urban expansion and management (subtracting this space from the dynamics of the market); aim to increase the level of democratisation of decision-making processes to increase citizens' awareness of their social and economic rights. The UN Word Urbanisation Prospects (UN 2014), confirm the need to address the principle of sustainability, equity and democracy, opening the debate to the understanding of the role of public space in this perspective. Within the 2030 Agenda and the Sustainable Development Goals, public space is acknowledged in the 11 Goal—Sustainable Cities and Communities, Target 11.7 that aims "by 2030, provide universal access to safe, inclusive and accessible, green and public spaces, in particular, for women and children, older persons and persons with disabilities" (UN 2015, p. 22).

Within the next paragraphs, the issue of accessibility will be discussed from an urban perspective, questioning: how the activation of commons can collaborate to create a robust and accessible, physical and social infrastructure of public spaces? How to guarantee a certain social, physical and cultural accessibility within limited administrative and financial resources? How the communing process can become an asset to improve the social and physical relevance of urban public space?

To answer these questions:

- public space and urban commons will be compared with respect to the literature;
- the issue of the commoning process will be addressed as an opportunity for the governance and the management of public space;
- socio-spatial dynamics will be investigated according to the need of monitoring and study them, in order to gain knowledge on the everyday life use of public space and empower local communities and local bodies;
- urban transformation practices will be explored towards a holistic perspective, to understand how quality goals can be translated into actions able to reshape public.

2 Public Spaces of the City: Between the Social and the Communal Meanings

Nowadays, the concerns on public space and on urban commons dominate the cultural debate, as well as the political agendas. The uprising interest on these topics can be justified on the basis of the increasing process of commodification of cities, leading towards a new model of public management. David Harvey argues that such "recent revival of emphasis upon the supposed loss of urban commonalities reflects the seemingly profound impacts of the recent wave of privatisations, enclosures, spatial controls, policing and surveillance upon the qualities of urban life […] and the potentiality to build or inhibit new forms of social relations (a new commons)" (Harvey 2012: 67). Next to the neoliberal critique, a powerful intellectual and social movement is claiming their power over the control and the decisions about urban transformation, in order to guarantee greater access of urban space and resources for all urban inhabitants (Foster and Iaione 2016: 283).

There is no doubt that urban commons and public spaces share the ground of the same sociocultural debate. Stephen Carr defines public space as "the stage upon which the drama of communal life unfolds" (Carr 1992: 3). From this perspective, the *publicness* of public space is enhanced by the presence of life that is communal, collective and shared between individuals that are simultaneously the actors and the audience of this drama (Errante 2019). At the same time, we have to acknowledge that urban public spaces and urban commons are not necessarily the same thing. A first distinction can be made in terms of participation, in fact, while in public space the citizens are passively involved mainly in leisure or optional activities, the commons suggests a direct and active use and maintenance of the space. Public space, as a common good of the city, can be considered a commodified space which plays a collaborative role with state and market, "crucial for capitalistic development" (Harvey 2012: 72). On the contrary, we can talk of urban common when a public space or a public good is triggered by a political action, when "social forces appropriate, protect, and enhance it for mutual benefit" (Ibid. 73). In this sense, David Harvey recognise the struggle over the balance of interests and actors that participate in the production, the access and the regulation of public space and public goods (Ibid.). If public space has to be triggered, i.e. if some kind of bottom-up sociopolitical and sociocultural interest is required, it is equally true that public space in itself is a social product (cf. Lefebvre). The Lefebvre's spatial triad assumes that public space is constructed within three main collaborative dimensions that represent a scale, a way to shape space, its specific tools and the actors able to use them. The representations of space—or how it is conceived—refers to how it is actually used as a bi-dimensional or tri-dimensional mean by professionals and planners; the spatial practice is related to how space is perceived through its design, its physical configuration; representational space is how the space is lived and used by the inhabitants, including cultural, political and intangible elements. (Lefebvre 1991). These considerations let us believe that it is a more convenient attempt to understand the analogies existing between public space and urban commons, rather than drawing a clear line to separate them.

Within the definition provided by the Nobel prize-winning Elinor Ostrom, commons are those communal goods and services whose property is not referable neither to public authority nor to private corporations, and can be identified on the basis of three elements: the common or collective property; the commoning attribute, as something depending on human decisions and activities; the autonomy from the market or state forms of management (1990). In this respect, a common is an object of collaboration, an activity carried out by people and a form of management and ownership (Bollier 2014). Some "value practices that are alternative to that of capital [...] are interlinked by commons networks" that "imply a plurality of people (a community) sharing resources and governing them and their own relations and (re)production processes through horizontal doing in common, commoning"[2] (De Angelis 2017: 10). In this respect, public space can be considered as a common-pool resource, something in which the community has a strong implicit or explicit interest into (Ibid.). On the other hand, can be also considered the needs of "urban reformers [that] are looking beyond the state [...] to make claims on urban resources and city space as a *commons* [...] as a way of resisting the privatisation and/or commodification of those resources" (Foster and Iaione 2016: 284).

In a broader perspective of "city as a commons" in which public spaces are indeed a collective resource, make a better use of the built environment needs a tangible effort in terms of urban improvement, which also imply the need "to provide a framework and set of tools to open the possibility of more inclusive and equitable forms of city making" (Ibid.: 285). As citizens, our material dependence on the capitalistic system "aimed at accumulation and profiteering" is the main obstacle to prove a real interest in the quality and quantity of resources that we use —and waste—in terms of biodiversity, social reproduction or in general, rhythms of life, work and production (De Angelis 2017). On the level of urban transformation,

[2]"[...] social systems whose elements are commonwealth, a community of commoners and the ongoing interactions, phase of decision making and communal labour process that together are called commoning". De Angelis 2017: 11.

private, public and collective interest, which usually may collide, can be harmonised in the understanding of the many shared needs, as well as in the mutual goals to achieve. As Foster and Iaione argue, horizontality, collaboration and polycentrism are the principles able to "reorient public authorities away from a monopoly position over the use and management of common assets and toward a shared, collaborative governance approach" in which the state has the role of facilitator (Ibid.: 289–290).

Another concern of this contribution is to understand what scalar, physical and functional properties public space and urban commons share. First of all, the cityscape. According to the perspective proposed by Foster and Iaione, the urban environment in itself, the man-made "urban landscape" is, in fact, the production of multiple layers of meaning and uses, it is habitat, home and place, tangible and intangible landscape "shaped and reshaped by the inhabitants that are drawn to them and the interaction among them" (Ibid.: 295). As already mentioned, the problem of resources consumption is not secondary within the urban history, especially nowadays, where we assist at over-consumption and over-congestion phenomena of rivalry use, for instance of land property rights. In this sense, land use and zoning regulations may have prevented over-consumption, reducing the potential rivalry in the use of urban space (Ibid.). On the other hand, this kind of regulation can be criticised from many angles, if we consider that squatters, an abusive and informal settlement that continues to be the only choice for many underprivileged citizens that are not in the position to get into—or are for some reasons excluded by—the formal housing market. Sometimes, in extreme cases, the illegal and unregulated consumption of land respond to a life-or-death priority needs that do not meet the ideal principle of fair distribution of resources, since those who are forced to act against the law are, in fact, exactly victims of the failure of that system. Another perspective of critique may be found in the many reasons blamed of the decline of public space. The zoning regulations has been the main means to pursue a rational city form, according to functional and capitalistic principles solely devoted to production. Such a mechanism has led, as a consequence, to the social and spatial fragmentation of many contemporary cities.[3] Such phenomena has compromised the spontaneous practices of territorialisation (Madanipour 2003), and the transformative process from space to place (cf. Norberg-Schultz 1980), "destroying the integrity of the individuals, isolating them from society and depriving them of any defence" (De Carlo 2013: 66), now labelled in formal categories (Sebastiani 2010: 238–239).

The disconnection between the two key elements of urban dynamics—society/space—has an impact on the decline of public space, worsened by the political inability to deal with the issue at the urban scale. As David Harvey argues, the "scale problem" carries analytical concerns that require very careful evaluation,

[3]Cities have been transformed by way of highways and automobiles in order to let people spread and circulate all over a territory, superimposing a traffic infrastructure over a socio-spatial one, regardless of what they spread across or at what cost is kind of approach has determined a fragmentation of public space as a whole, seriously affecting pedestrian mobility, accessibility and interfering with the many social, cultural and recreational activities of everyday life (Errante 2019).

since "as we jump scales, so the whole nature of the commons problem and the prospects of finding a solution change dramatically" (Harvey 2012: 69). For instance, it would be a mistake try to translate the collective organisation of small-scale solidarity into a global solution, that should be necessarily be incorporated into a hierarchical form (Ibid.: 70). Pivoting on Harvey's definition,[4] we can assume that the shared ground among commons and public space rely on the combination between the social and the administrative spheres.

For the purposes of this contribution, the erosion of public space and public life can be seen as an obstacle to the flourishing of a bottom-up interest or, on the contrary, the very incentive to gather a community around a common interest. In general, urban public spaces can fit into the definition of common-pool resource. In the perspective of Foster and Iaione (2016), public space is revived and qualified by its being relational, which can lead to different phenomena: on one hand, it is a precondition for knowledge exchange and social capital accumulation; and on the other hand, it can be crucial to its decline, due to its over usage. The authors refer to such phenomena as the "tragedy of the urban commons" which arises as a result of weakly or poorly regulated space in terms of public control or management that may degenerate to the decay of the space due to the conflictual presence of different users and uses (Ibid. 299). In these terms, public control is not to be intended as a call for over-secure, militarised space, which rules of usage are imposed by restricting municipal ordinances. Also, the management of urban public spaces not always imply the presence of a private actor, who is in any case limited by public norms in order to prevent any physical or social enclosure phenomena. In this sense, collective, bottom-up, or simply public-private involvement in the management of urban public spaces allows to distinguish a commodity from a common good, in the absence of a mercantile relationship between the actors involved (whether they are public or private) and the presence of a strong community behind it (Fig. 1).

3 Accessibility: A Multifaceted Concept

In order to further investigate the issues of public space and common goods, a terminological examination can clarify some nuances of the concept. Among the many features, Common goods and Public space share the etymological status of being a "twofold character" (De Angelis 2017). In respect of the common goods, Massimo De Angelis put together the substantive '*goods*', in terms of objects that have a social and use value, next to the adjective '*common*' to underline the plural value of such goods, exacerbate the meaning of common goods as "use value for a plurality", something that "satisfy given socially determined needs, desire and aspirations" (Ibid.). In this sense, the definition of public space can be way too

[4]Commons is defined as "an unstable and malleable social relation between a particular self-defined social group and those aspect of its actually existing or yet-to-be-created social and/or physical, environment deemed crucial for its life and livelihood" (Harvey 2012: 73).

Fig. 1 The faces of the residents involved in the redevelopment of a square in the Ciutat Vella, in the district of El Born, Barcelona, ES (2017). Credit: Lidia Errante

challenging, considering the origin of the two latin words *spatium* and *publicus*. In the first instance, *'space'* means *being open*, the indefinite place in which all the material thing are contained, their physical and proxemic configuration, the object of perception by each individual and a modality of representation and organisation of the everyday reality. The adjective 'public' refers, instead, to the quality of something being *accessible*, *common* to those who belong to the community of citizens, that can liberally use it or participate in it. In this terms, the *publicness* of public space is related to the citizenship, a condition that can reveal the possibility, for a public body, to deny the access to that space to whomever not belong to that specific category of citizens. Limitations on the use of urban spaces can be pursued in the attempt to repress, or suppress, habits and behaviours excluding certain social categories, like for instance indigent people, beggars, homeless, squatter or buskers (Mitchell 2003; Nemeth and Schmidt 2011).

Due to this complexities, Public space is a common-pool resource that ideally belongs to the definition of "open access commons" and also comfortably fits in the meaning of "limited access commons"[5] of the city. The main assumption of this paper is, in fact, that the *trait d'union* between public spaces and urban commons lies in the concept of accessibility, intended here in its holistic, multifaceted meanings. In this sense, the paper assumes that:

- The infrastructure of public space is the social, political and physical dimension of urban commons;
- Accessibility is a mean for the intersubjective use of space;
- Any transformation of the space, whether formal or informal, involve urban design;
- Physical, social and cultural implications of accessibility within the urban environment need to be studied individually and in their mutual interrelations.

Given these premises, the contribution will address the issue of accessibility through a relevant literature review. In the first place, Németh and Schmidt define accessibility as the overall quality of space that allows all the possible activities and opportunities for interaction and encounter (2011), a necessary basis for the attribution of social and civic significance to a place due to its importance within the everyday life. Uses, functions, activities, or more generally the opportunities that the public space offers ranges from the exercise of democracy to other passive recreational activities (cf. Marcuse); encourage interaction, thanks to certain abstract features of variety, flexibility, permeability and/or authenticity; allow the unexpected, immediate, unplanned uses (Németh and Schmidt 2011); support social cohesion—conceived as a sense of trust, cultural, economic and social wealth, that distinguish a community (Venturini and Graziano 2016). Following this logic, the

[5]Public goods are "open access", non-rival resources, as highways, transportation systems, public schools, etc., which access is guaranteed by their very public nature; the "limited access" commons can be considered as private spaces accessible for those who have the right (property right or membership) in order to protect a specific resource (cf. Foster and Iaione 2016: 293).

ideal public space is, in fact, a potential commons waiting to be activated. This condition of catalyst for social activities can be—or have to be—supported by the tool of planning and urban design, as well as by political and administrative choices. In this respect, within the whole discourse on the decline of public space and the arising of urban commons, accessibility has a main role, sometimes hidden between the lines, and certain dynamics seem to be more significant than others. In the following sub-paragraphs the implications of accessibility will be discussed from different angles, from the perspective of governance and management; urban design; social perception and awareness.

3.1 Accessibility and Management

Governing—and maintaining—commons within the urban environment, saturated as it is by capital investments (Huron 2015), in a contemporary phase of economic crisis and rolling back of public responsibility for funding and managing infrastructure, parks and public spaces (Bradley 2015), is a great challenge. Assuming the city as a commons, its governance and management appear as complex as the urban system in itself, in terms of individuals, cultures, institutions, laws, buildings, spaces and services. In respect of Public space and Common good, a tangible difference pertains to the modality of governance and management, in which the clashing interests of the public (intended here as the governmental bodies) and the private are clearly visible. Ostrom's perspective (1990) on natural-commons resources, can be applied to the whole urban contexts, considering Urban commons as new—or rediscovered—model of collective or public management of resources in the form of a social institution, to address political claims or to supply services that neither the market nor the State is providing to the population. The literature distinguishes the 'neighbourhood commons' (cf. Hess 2008), understood as local resources managed by their own community. To the last category belong community gardens, street-open markets and in general urban public spaces, as well as squatter houses, housing cooperatives and gated communities.[6] Given that heterogeneity, urban commons are not to be merely considered as a third kind of property next to the public and the private. Sheila Foster assert, indeed, that "collective management regimes in the urban context thus come to resemble a type of hybrid solution that is peculiar to its context, in part because of the government's existing regulatory and ownership role over the resources" (Foster 2011: 71).

Public space plays a central role in urban transformation policies, becoming an object of interest from both the public and private sectors (Madanipour 2005). In this respect, the commoning process and the social right at the core of it, are equally attractive as a market opportunity or may become a market niche, if not entailed

[6]The case of 'neighbourhood commons' are the closest to initial assumptions that public space is the physical and social extension (in this case, the neighbourhood) in which commons may be activated, and require a 'contextual definition' of the concept.

within a protest or a civil disobedience practice. Also, 'social innovation' and 'social entrepreneurship' projects can, indeed, be useful for public administrations and private actors to overcome the scarcity of economic resources (Ibid.). One answer to that rivalry can be to impose a new and flexible scheme of government control on the public space (Foster 2011). In the public/private dichotomy, David A. Super suggests as the private property and management of a resource can provide an undeniable degree of security, like a "form of insurance against certain kinds of threats to that individual value" (Super 2013: 1793). Similarly, the conventional bourgeois concept of public sphere proposed by Habermas, as an abstract space between society and the state, appeal for a corpus of private subjects that come together to discuss issues of public or common interest (Op. cit., 1962, Mazzette 2013). This position, which is exclusive of other unofficial or interstitial forms of public, is the basis of the "ideal legislation" around which the public and private agents operating on space (cf. Fraser 1990), by limiting the use of urban space in the attempt to inhibit behaviours that could undermine the order and the control imposed by the rules (Mitchell 2003; Nèmeth and Schmidt 2011).

Németh and Schmidt (2011) assert, regarding the private management of public space, that three main aspects have to be considered to prevent negative effects on accessibility:

- The access rules set by the private person in charge of the management of the space do not always deal with the public interest or the community needs, sometimes limiting the freedom of speech and protest;
- Private spaces can act as a marketing device for advertisements and brands, and their access can be restricted to unwanted subjects;
- Security, considered as freedom from crime against the person, is the main concern since September 11, and frequently used as a pretext to justify the previous points; it can be also observed that, in the face of a considerable and widespread increase of security measures on public space, these have actually increased the perception of insecurity of users.

In this terms, the private versus collective property right struggle within the commons can be seen in the perspective of private versus public access to urban spaces and services, considering the many options in terms of collaborative management, identify the right groups of users and rule of uses in order to achieve an horizontal cooperation within "public and private instrumentalities" (cf. Ostrom 1990). In fact, as Sheila Foster emphasises with reference to the case of New York's, in periods of reduced oversight and management by local governments, neighbourhood public spaces and urban parks have been perceived as "unsafe, dirty, prone to criminal activity and virtually abandoned" (Foster 2011: 96). In reaction to that emergence and as a direct response to what she called a "regulatory slippage", residents invested and mobilise resources to restore, maintain and preserve such spaces, becoming the so-called "Friends of [Park X]", often assisted by local governments in terms of technical assistance and training (Ibid: 96–97).

In leisure, as well as in the management of public space, the role of the local authority is shifting from being a provider or even a commissioner of services, into a partner which subsidises and facilitates social businesses.

Such consideration on collective management of urban space, whether is public or common, is a key premise to frame the complexity of factors and actors that can undermine the accessibility of a place. On one hand, the property regime, on the other, the agents in charge to regulate the access, may be able to set the rules of access and use to a place, its functions and activities—public, private or commercialised—as well as its physical transformation.

3.2 Urban Design Process Between Access and Accessibility

Addressing the issue of accessibility in relation to urban design is quite a tough job, most of all to avoid the misconception that accessibility in public space is solely related to the issue of architectural barriers. Of course, everyone needs for a better street to walk or bike the way to the workplace, car-free roads on which kids can safely go to school, and the right design choices can guarantee such requirement to the urban population. On the other hand, to address also the claim for more green, vibrant and inclusive public spaces, the tools of urban design have had to overcome their physical ray of action, embodying socio-spatial features like the design of the everyday life activities and the understanding of a community symbolism. For the purpose of this contribution, urban design is intended, in a more holist perspective, as a "design process", a collaborative work that "joining-up environments and places, professional and other actors with each other, with communities, and those who wish to invest" (Carmona et al. 2003: 290). This is a necessary clarification, in the whole discourse and in the specific issue of urban design, because of the key importance of public and private actors within any action of urban transformation, whether bottom-up. In the first place, for the long-term sustainability of the action in itself and on the other for the essential role of support that administrations and professionals can provide. Of course, this also implies that dialogue and compromises can be found and continuously experimented in many ways, always in the spirit that a well-designed and accessible public space is also the one that provides access to urban public service (Fig. 2).

Within the built environment, urban design can be a very successful tool to address social and physical accessibility, providing a variety of opportunities to people and enhancing the quality of living (Pasaogullari and Doratli 2004). According to Project for Public Spaces, NY (2000), public space accessibility depends on the degree of visual and physical connection to the surroundings, but also aesthetic features have to be considered in relation to the attractiveness a place. Also, Pasaogullari and Doratli (2004), assert that accessibility in public space is related to features as: the location of a place, its proximity and travel time; the physical and functional characteristics of street and transportation type; physical and functional properties in general; characteristics of comfort, safety, cleanness, maintenance and shelter; activities and facilities that attract more people and

Fig. 2 Flows of pedestrians and cyclists cross the road safely in Amsterdam, NL (2018). Credit: Lidia Errante

increase social interaction. In a more condensed perspective, a research conducted by Matthew Carmona and Filipa Matos Wunderlich on London public spaces, explore the idea that a successful design (and space) should tend to be: Evolving; Diverse; Free; Delineated; Engaging; Meaningful; Social; Balanced; Comfortable; and Robust (Carmona et al. 2019).

From another angle, it is interesting to notice that many cities have witnessed a position shift from an agnostic/managerial perspective to a role as an advocate for public space investments, increasingly for social reasons, producing efforts directed on the quality of everyday spaces in respect to (Carmona et al. 2019):

- the provision for pedestrian space within the city;
- safety measures for cycling routes;
- new and diversified recreational and leisure opportunities;
- the provision for outdoor spaces to support processes of densification (or to balance highly densified urban areas).

In this respect, can be mentioned several relevant international scenarios, able to explain this perspective in different times and context:

- Copenhagen and the case of Public Life/Public Space Studies and Strategies;
- Curitiba and the emergence of Urban Acupuncture;
- Bogotá and the urban mobility paradigm;
- The Tactical Urbanism approach;
- The experience of The City at the Eye Level in Rotterdam.

The first three experiences are mainly municipal-based, and have produced real multi-scalar paradigms of action replicated all over the world. In each case, the issue of urban mobility is central to the whole discussion, increasing accessibility in pedestrian routes removing physical obstacles, opening space for more walkable and safer streets, and providing more people with access to public transportation services. The following, last two practices, are instead more oriented towards a bottom-up perspective.

Copenhagen and the PL/PS Studies and Strategies.

The case of Copenhagen is pivotal, as the main paradigm that have triggered the contemporary debate on public space, started in the late 1960s. Between the 1970s and 80s, the city experienced a phase of profound urban renewal in which public space has a central role within the revitalisation of both central, residential and post-industrial peripheral areas. Indeed, Copenhagen is a pioneer in this field, as the first city to adopt an explicit public space advocate regime in 2006 (Carmona et al. 2019). Despite the economic crisis of 2008, the city made extensive public investments in the design, construction and maintenance of public urban space win the framework of the 'Metropolis for People' policy, mainly based on the theory and methodology of Jan Gehl (Ibid.). Gehl Architects was consulted by the municipality to develop the policy within three main goals: more urban life; more walking; and more people to stay longer (Ibid.) eventually achieving what now we know as Public Life/Public Space Studies and Strategies. On one hand, PL/PS Studies and Strategies deserve to be approached on a methodological level, precisely because of its widespread on a global scale.[7] On the other, it is also interesting to mention how the city administration has progressively shifted from this paradigm towards a "more iterative and co-creative process" (Ibid.). The so-called Gehl Method analyse the socio-spatial dynamics starting from the assumption that Public Space is every place of the city where public life is (Gehl 2011). On a methodological level, the central role of the individuals is the *fil rouge* of the whole process, entirely based on the understanding of the habits of citizens in public space through a systematic investigation and documentation of public life. Through a "look and learn" approach, the aim is to build a more understandable picture of the city that can be used as a political and operative tool, with the intention to improve urban liveability. The Method, also, begins and ends in the critical observation of

[7]The method is so well-known all over the world, that it was adopt for the Time Square transformation in New York City as well as for other urban renovation in the United States as San Francisco, Denver, Pittsburgh and Lexington. For Latino America and Caribbean Islands, it was also released a guidebook to instruct administrations on how to encourage the use of bicycle and evaluate the whole process of implementation.

public space: in the first phase to understand how it is configured and which human and non-human actors, formal and informal features, tangible and intangible characters to consider for the definition of transformation strategies; eventually to evaluate the results and the effect of such transformation. Indeed, the PL/PS Studies and Strategies are conceived to provide feedback to decision-making processes as an integral part of the planning or design processes (Gehl and Svarre 2013). The interaction between public life and space is highly unpredictable and cannot be analysed through fixed and immutable categories: at the same time, Gehl and Svarre suggest that a targeted study, however simple, may produce enough information to guide the process of urban transformation (2013). With this purpose, the methodological structure of PS/PL Studies and Strategies is replicable, adaptable to different urban contexts and according to further variables and necessity. Socio-spatial dynamics are: observed, in respect of the habits of people and according to the specific physical qualities of the studied space; interpret, identifying problems or potentialities; compared and benchmarked, in reference to other similar context, cases or best practices; and eventually translated into standards or quality goals, thanks to which elaborate and propose the proper strategy of transformation. The data collection is performed through direct and empirical approaches, making the method very close to micro-sociology. The extensive production and use of data make the results to be readable and understandable by public and private organisations, and easily translated and incorporated into policies. Within the 'Metropolis for People' such a method was used to "emphasises the provision of attractive public spaces and measurable objectives for their performance" (Carmona et al. 2019: 244). Despite the many positive results, the current adopted policy 'Community Copenhagen' is focused on "creating possibilities for citizens to become more engaged in the design and maintenance of public space and to develop urban life activities in the public realm" (Ibid.: 244). This new phase on urban transformation is, indeed, devoted to the urban experience rather than on the esthetical appearance of the space, probably accounting the many critiques over the city branding approach to "cosmetically address the greater issue within cities [...] do little more than speeding up the gentrification of older areas" (Koch and Latham 2017).

Curitiba and Urban Acupuncture.[8]

The case of Curitiba is one of the first examples of radical contrast to urban homologation processes. At the end of the 60s, the city was recently the capital of the state of Parana, with an increasing population. The instruments of transformation to support this growth would have transformed Curitiba according to the ideal model of Brasilia or São Paulo, extending the road infrastructure towards new

[8]The main references consulted for this section of the paragraph are: Lerner (2014). *Urban Acupuncture.* Washington DC| Covelo| London: Island Press; Adler (2016, Maggio 6). *Story of cities#37: how radical ideas turned Curitiba into Brazil's 'green capital.* From The Guardian—Cities: https://www.theguardian.com/cities/2016/may/06/story-of-cities-37-mayor-jaime-lerner-curitiba-brazil-green—capital-global-icon; Hernandez and Casanova (2014). *Public Space Acupuncture.* Actar.

and extended mono-functional areas. These forecasts, included in the Agache Plan, never came true, on the one hand, because of the lack of financial resources able to support the extreme infrastructural transformation of the city, and on the other hand, because of the opposition of the residents in the face of the feared destruction of entire historical areas. This "emergency" had the power to gather the urban community around the theme of the future planning of Curitiba and its conscious development. This "emergency" had the power to gather the urban community around the theme of the future planning of Curitiba and its conscious development. Since 1964, the Institute of Urban Research and Planning of Curitiba (IUPPC—Instituto de Pesquisa e Planejamento Urbano de Curitiba) elaborated the new Masterplan together with a team from the Federal University of Parana, led by a young Jaime Lerner, architect and planner, future mayor of Curitiba three times from 1971 to 1992. The idea of the new masterplan was to give main priority to pedestrian transit and public transport, instead of vehicular traffic and to integrate the flows according to the daily life activities of the city, focusing on economic ways of transportation serving the most disadvantaged section of the population. These aims have been pursued through:

- The hierarchisation of the main traffic routes structured according to a trinary system that directed the flows in five main roadways that crossed the city;
- The design of an Integrated Transport System based on fast transport throughout the territory and a differentiated line—called Interbairros—that interconnects the districts and terminals without passing through the historic centre;
- The metropolitanisation of surface public transport with the creation of the BRT (Bus Rapid Transit) system, which connects the south and north axes with the centre.

These actions allow the pedestrianisation of entire areas of the historic centre, which are designed according to the principles of occupation of urban voids and architectural and functional diversification, with a focus on services for citizens and the creation of new large parks and the restoration of historic buildings. The small-scale of the planned interventions and the progression of their individual development has led to the definition of the Urban Acupuncture approach, meaning the precise strategy of starting from a single intervention as an engine for the entire process of urban transformation. UA, in fact, is based on small actions of urban transformation, ephemeral interventions on public space, considering the city as a place for people. In this sense, wide space is given to the design of the activities within public space, forecasting the opportunities to create the right context for something to happen: from local markets to festivals to pieces of public art. This approach overturns the typically modernist and economically unsustainable concept of extensive top-down control of interventions, without being able to predict or govern their outcomes. The principles of Urban Acupuncture are inspired by the European ideals of public space, and in particular, by the approach of the PL/PS Studies and Strategies.

Bogotá and the Transmilenio.

At the end of the nineties, the city of Bogota was defined "unregulated, dirty and unattractive" (Rhinehart 2009), because of its ungovernable scale. The continuous population growth at that time was not supported by an adequate transport network capable of connecting the outermost residential areas to the centre, resulting in urban segregation, pockets of crime and widespread illegal building and forcing people not to live in urban space for fear of criminal reprisals (Ibid.). In this complex context, it was crucial the political effort of the two mayors who alternated from 1995 to 2003, Antanas Mockus and Enrique Penalosa. Both placed the civic engagement at the centre of their agenda, with particular emphasis on the proactive role of young people to counteract feelings of cynicism and apathy (Ibid.). This mission was translated into the Culture Ciudadana campaign, encouraging citizens to expose problems and possible solutions. The promotion and the dissemination of the campaign basically took place in public spaces, where events, happenings and participatory activities were being organised to gather information on the level of citizens' satisfaction. On the other hand, the profits from the battle against corruption and tax evasion have made it possible large investments on the improvement of public spaces, parks and the road network, implementing pedestrian and cycle paths with the aim to regain the human scale of the city (Ibid.). The TransMilenio system is a hybridisation between the surface metro and the bus, and runs along a fast lane separated from the car traffic. This has facilitated the design of safer pedestrian routes and crossings, and has dramatically contributed to the decrease in fatal car accidents, air pollution levels and fossil fuel consumption, as benefits related to the promotion of public transport use (Ibid.).

Another key issue is the direct engagement of citizens within the design process. In the above mentioned experiences, the well-being of the citizens are the main concern but their involvement is, in fact, mainly indirect and integrated within the analysis of the socio-spatial context and the validation of the results. Citizens are, in other words, used as a litmus test. On the other hand, the analytical and methodological structure elaborated within such municipal-based experiences, due to its open-source approach, has been further experimented and adopted within bottom-up and DIY urban transformation practices. According to Bradley (2015), DIY practices for urban transformation is occurring in tandem with the contemporary crisis and the rolling back of public responsibility for funding and managing infrastructure, but the recourse to such practices can have a strong educative role for both professionals and the collectivity, and also useful to public authorities as well. In the perspective of the creation of urban commons, another opportunity related to such learning-by-doing practices is the construction of practice open-source manuals, developed in a peer-to-peer relationship and shared by everyone to address self-management commons (Ibid).

Tactical Urbanism.

Founded by Mike Lydon and Anthony Garcia, the Tactical Urbanism movement is based on the will to develop a guide for urban transformation, acting on a wide range of urban scales. On one hand, the goal is also to inspire, empower and engage citizens, urban designers, land use planners, architects and policymakers to become key actors in the transformation of their communities. On the other hand, transforming squares and reimaging parking spaces as temporary places for the community. The intention is also to gain public funding and municipal support to make these actions permanent and effectively reshape the city. Tactical Urbanism aims at the re-appropriation of the city spaces through the elaboration of practices and actions that mobilise a counter-intuitive method. "Recognise the dysfunctionality of the norms, procedures and conventional tools of urban planning" can be challenged "the inefficiency and unsustainability of the onerous [...] mega-projects and long-term transformation scenarios of Plans as the only tools and factors of development (development, not growth) of cities" (Bazzu and Talu 2017: 18). The involvement of citizens is achieved through workshops, focus group, talk, online forums and questionnaires, public discussion and, eventually, practical DIY actions. Indeed, the motto "Short-term Actions for Long-Term Change" expresses the overall objective of Tactical Urbanism to act through "low-cost and short-term micro-projects as tools to ensure and promote the quality, accessibility and usability of the city" (Ibid.).

The City at Eye Level and STIPO.

The City At Eye Level (CAEL) is a network of professionals from different disciplines, led by the design group called STIPO since 2012, and united by the goal of producing knowledge about the physical nature of the city and public space as perceived by the human eye. The project is a partner of UN-Habitat, Project for Public Space and Gehl Architects, and closely collaborate with city administrations. The starting point of CAEL's research work is to study the relationship between buildings and the street section in Dutch cities, considered a key reference point for the naked-eye's perception of the city (STIPO 2016, 2017). In particular, the ground floors at the street level can be considered a particular form of semi-public space included in the public realm, according to Gehl's concepts of passive and active facades (Gehl and Svarre 2013). In this perspective, CAEL analyses the different types of "plinths" in relation to their specific functions—retail, commercial, social, leisure, residential—and identifies three level of intervention—building, street, context—in order to better plan the action. On the basis of these concepts, STIPO has activated numerous placemaking processes in collaboration with other design groups. One of these relevant cases is the ZOHO project in the Zomerhofkwartier district of Rotterdam, defined as a Climate Proof District that implements and integrates the Climate Adaptation Strategy applied to the neighbourhood scale with social innovation initiatives. The strategic programme of the area has been developed by STIPO and De Urbanisten, with the aim to provide safety measure for the area, exposed by a high risk of flooding during heavy rain events, through the design of a new public space (Fig. 3). The whole decision-making process started by a deep analysis of the climatic conditions of the area, parallel to the laboratory and participatory activities carried out with the inhabitants of the area. In the very genesis of this project, has been put to the test the value of

Fig. 3 Benthemplein watersquare, by De Urbaneisten. Rotterdam, NL (2018). Credit: Lidia Errante

inter-institutional and trans-disciplinary synergy of all the actors and tools involved to pursue the strategy. The first step was the realisation of the Benthemplein watersquare, the square designed by De Urbaneisten, but many other pilot projects were started thanks to the participation of the municipality, in the dual role of facilitator and co-financer of the interventions. The first positive effects are already evident in the new development of the area, north of the Centraal Station, where the presence of very wide railways and viaducts cause a major obstacle to reach the city centre. Indeed, this issue has become the subject of a further public space project, among which the Luchtsingel Bridge, by ZUS, the largest public infrastructure in the world to be financed mainly by crowdfunding (Fig. 4).

3.3 Social Accessibility and Urban Life: Between Knowledge and Awareness

The many connections between public space, urban design, accessibility and the activation of urban commons are very difficult to retrace in a coherent discourse, and of course, many nuances and key references may be lost in the attempt. On the other hand, some partial conclusion can be outlined, especially in relation to accessibility and the potential positive social impacts. Of course, the aim of accessibility in public space have to be related to the different perspectives of private, public and/or collective agents which, to some extent, can be harmonised within the urban design process. Also, as the above mention experiences have proved, urban design and public space can be used as means to visualise and give materiality to problematic situations, make them more perceivable and communicable to larger publics, inhabitants and visitors (Susser and Tonnelat 2013). Indeed, within a research-based approach, two main outcomes can be distinguished: the physical, tangible actions, necessary to the urban transformation and the analytical results. In a dissemination perspective, such analytical results are the necessary knowledge base to inform the citizens, which have—and strongly claim—the need and the right to be informed, educated and aware on their urban context, in order to be engaged. The central role of people in the decision-making of urban transformation does not necessarily imply participatory practices, opting instead for socio-spatial analysis that may result in small-scale, people-oriented, solutions of real common sense. Such an approach also helps to establish a trust relationship between public administrations, professionals and citizens, that consequently support the social cohesion and the collective efficacy[9] of an urban transformation. Another element to consider is, in fact, the widespread sense of disaffection by civil society and institutions, or more generally a loss of civic sense (Sitte 1953; Jacobs 1992), that can be recorded since the beginning of the capitalist urbanisation era, when the provision of public space was a mean for development and accumulation processes (Lefebvre 1991, 2003; Harvey 2012). In this respect, the efforts put on collective, collaborative, mutual supportive forms of management can be also seen as a claim for a more democratic access to resources, as well as both a social and individual empowerment, depending on how these communities are open to public participation. Of course, as Sheila Foster asserts: "the creation of a commons is directly connected to a shared willingness of the residents to be involved on many levels, including to maintain effective social controls in the community" (Foster 2011: 86).

In other words, accessibility is the overall quality of public space, crucial for the perception of the urban experience, and is a right to guarantee in order to "provide, by 2030, universal access to safe, inclusive and accessible green and public spaces…" (UN 2017). Such a goal can be pursued on the physical and the social dimensions, separately and together, but it is on its cultural dimension that accessibility may be appreciated. That is, the degree of interest and proactive attitude, the social involvement and awareness, the willingness to participate, revealed within a community to take part in the transformation. This, of course, implies an effort on behalf of administrations and professionals to create the conditions for this to happen, acknowledging that this is not always a smooth process, but read the context and trigger a collaborative process may hopefully lead to the creation of commons—and their sustainability over time.

[9]Management and design issues are crucial because "a lack of collective efficacy is highly correlated with the existence of social disorder in public spaces, enforced by violence or threats of violence. Violence in particular (or the fear of it) can prevent or impede the development of productive social norms and the collective efficacy necessary for neighbours to maintain effective social controls in their community" (Foster 2011: 86).

Fig. 4 Luchtsingel bridge by ZUS, Rotterdam, NL (2018). Credit: Lidia Errante

4 Maps, Topographies and Protocols: Tools to Spatialised Social Data

The process of commoning is, in other words, 'a social fact in space' as Maurice Cerasi (1976) would have said. In this sense, represent and spatialise the everyday life activities can be crucial to develop a strategy of knowledge, to devise a radical critique of traditional urbanistic models and their contradictions and to develop a science out of the understanding of urban phenomenon (Alves dos Santos 2014). Experiences such as those mentioned above, proves the need to overcome the fragmentary analysis approach typical of the industrial-based urbanistic tools, towards a socio-spatial attitude that can reveal processes of differentiation, segmentation, commodification and/or segregation within the urban environment (Ibid.). In these terms, retrace and highlight such social, cultural and economic dynamics in space is a mean to understand rather than control them. Bordieu (2018: 161) asserts that the city space is both physically and socially created, as "the distribution in space of different sorts of goods or services and also individual agents and physically located groups and endowed with opportunities for appropriation of these more or less important goods and services". The author further notes that "it is in the relation between the distribution of the agents and the distribution of the goods in the space that the value of the different regions of reified special space is defined". (Ibid.). According to that, the scale is again a key issue to consider, because it identifies (and defines) the class of users most economically and socially dependent upon the resource and who thus have the most incentive for collective action (Foster 2011). Also, in order to understand and spatialise socio-spatial dynamics, have to be clarified: the aim of the study; the needed tools; the actor involved; and the expected outcomes. In this paragraph will be explored the result of the doctoral research[10] conducted by the author and discussed in 2019, which aimed to formulate an interpretative, evidence-based and socio-spatial tool for public space, to support public administrations within policy-making and strategic goals for urban transformation, giving to them an independent source of information about the urban socio-spatial dynamics. The objective of this research starts from the assumption that most of these analytical tools, as well as those mentioned in the previous paragraphs, are not directly accessible without the mediation of particular consulting firms. On the other hands, as in the case of the 'Gehl method', the open-source methodological approach allows it to be partially replicable.

Understand the complex and ever-changing urban dynamics and translate them into spatialised data implies an interpretative effort, also considering the inevitable expected result to "implement the demand for a right to the city" within the "democratic forms of the design process" (Marcuse 2009). The aim of the study is

[10]The Doctoral research to which this paper refers to is: Errante (2019), Qualità dell'abitare urbano —Un modello interpretativo per lo spazio pubblico, 'Mediterranea' University of Reggio Calabria, Department of Architecture and Territory, Doctoral Research in Architecture and Territory—XXXI Cycle. Tutor: Prof. Alberto De Capua.

to develop a critical approach, an "evaluative attitude towards reality" that uses questioning in order to understand the world and "critically expose" the opportunity of a potential change (Ibid.). The 'critical theory of urbanism'[11] of Expose, Propose and Politicise, is a suitable structure to analyse the flows, experiences, practices of daily life within which people "develop the potential of the existing urban society" and use this knowledge to "inform the future course of such practice" (Ibid.). Mapping the socio-spatial dynamics in public space is particularly important in order to identify trajectories or patterns of behaviours that can variously overlap, criss-cross one another, move from a point in the space to another one. Also, in the words of Katz (2001) "producing topographies and countertopographies can be a way not only to reimagine a politics that redresses the toll of globalisation, but also actually being to build a practical response that is at once trans-local and strategically focused". Topographies are defined by Katz as proper political and analytical tools that can be used for a detailed description of the reality, mapping the position of the elements in the space at every geographical scale.

The interpretative model has been conceived to study the socio-spatial dynamics according to the methods suggested by the international cultural debate, in order to be:

1. socio-spatial, paying equal attention to the typological-formal architectural aspects and to the social ones linked to the dynamics of use and to the conditions of urban democracy;
2. political, to be a design-oriented tool to support the physical and social transformation of the built environment and the improvement of the quality of urban life;
3. qualitative, or quali-quantitative, in the techniques used;
4. flexible, so that it can be adjusted to the changing needs of urban living and contemporary public space;
5. informative, supporting the cultural debate and the experimentation of inclusive forms of design, management and programming of public space.

On a methodological level, the interpretative model is divided into three phases—Observation, Evaluation and Benchmarking—structured to be consecutive, concatenated and collaborative. Each phase is associated with the appropriate qualitative-quantitative, subjective and/or objective, direct and/or indirect data-collecting tools to gather information on the physical and social attributes of the public space. On a practical level, the model is targeted at local public

[11]The 'critical theory of urbanism' consists in expose, propose and politicise. Expose means to evaluate the existing system in its potential and its weakness, understanding the nature of the phenomena and the dynamics of previous fractures or crisis, in other words, "analysing the roots of the problem and making clear and communicating that analysis to those that need it and can use it". Propose means set strategies, targets and desired results, planning the work, make proposals, programs, demonstrating "the need for a politicized response". Eventually, politicize is conceived as "the political action implications of what was exposed and proposed" supporting the arrangements of the work by an informing action. This implies on one hand a "day-to-day politics" and on the other involving media and academic institutions (Marcuse 2009).

institutions, with the aim of providing a solid knowledge base to address, suggest and guide the formulation of quality goals and processes of urban transformation.

Observation

Provides data on the physical, social and cultural configuration of public space, in the past—according to historiographic and bibliographic sources, documentary tools, photographic, audio and video—and the present—mapping the physical and social attributes that configure the space. During this first phase, techniques of direct and empirical analysis are used several times during the day and the week, possibly with different climatic conditions, to record any change in the use of the space. The tangible and intangible characteristics of the space are then analysed and compared to the closest surroundings, to the role of the community and in relation to relevant events for the city. Its proximity is then observed in relation to the space-time relation with the main activities, places of interest and connection infrastructures, in order to define any disjunction of the system of public spaces and in general the quality of physical accessibility. The collection of all these information are summarised in two different documents: the diary of the observation, with comments and notes on the habits and uses of public space; and the behavioural maps, in which are noted the position and the action in space of each individual and group that was found during the observation phase.

Evaluation

Provides information on the objective and perceptual quality of public space according to five macro-indicators such as inclusion, relevance, attractiveness, comfort and safety, independently investigated with the assessment of objective and subjective sets of sub-indicators, scored from 0 to 3 used direct observation and interviews.[12] The objective and subjective sub-indicators correspond to each other in terms of subjects, weights and scores, allowing to highlight any discrepancies between the technical and perceptive evaluation for each indicator and sub-indicator. Among the subject of the evaluation are considered factors such as the social and functional mix of the space; its accessibility and safety, both physical and social; the presence of third spaces or commercial activities; the quality of the physical elements that articulate it; the variety of sub-spaces; the sensory complexity; the presence of elements of architectural or landscape value.

Benchmark.

Provides a framework of potential actions to support the elaboration of strategies, quality goals, intervention and/or transformation priorities, according to the emergencies detected by the results of the evaluation. For this purpose, the research provides the structure of a database that collects and organises the possible actions,

[12]The main reference used to define the evaluation phase, in its methodological structure; in the weights and measures of the indicators; in the method of representing the results; is the following research work: Mehta (2014) Evaluating Public Space, Journal of Urban Design, 19: 1, 53–88; Mehta (2007) A Toolkit for Performance Measures of Public Space, 43rd ISOCARP Congress.

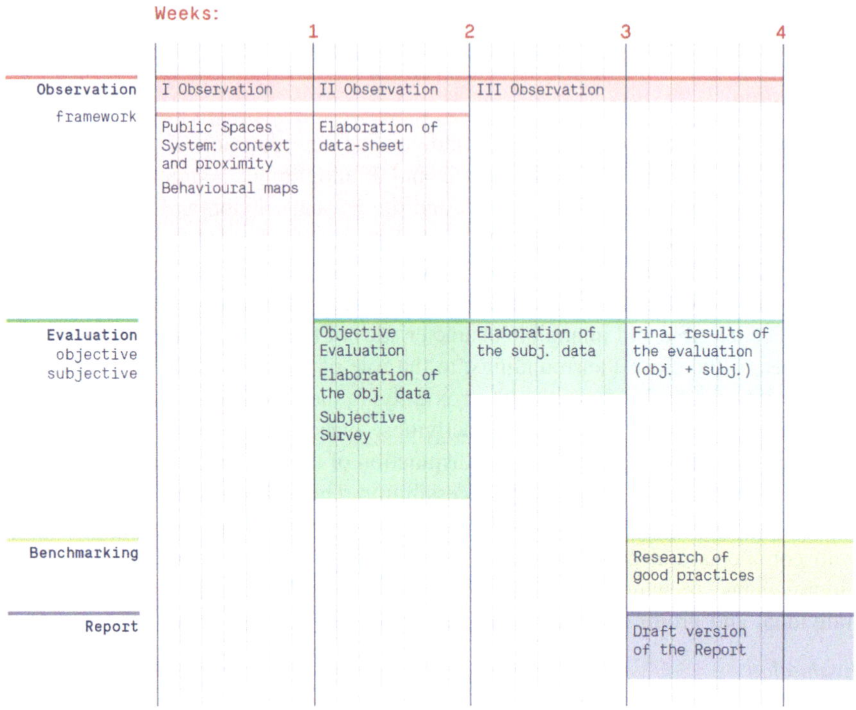

Fig. 5 The schedule of the phases developed over the four weeks

best practices and case studies that can constitute an adequate knowledge base. The analytical categories selected are technical execution, management and programming, as tools of a design process that encompasses the main steps of public space transformation.

The results of the model, in the succession of the three phases, are eventually summarised in a final report, which can be a form of dissemination for the benefit of the community in order to support a good public debate, thus increasing the knowledge and the awareness of citizens on urban issues. The model and the analytical phase can be completed within four weeks, and can be repeated over time to report any change in the habits of the citizens or to monitor the outcomes of an urban transformation project (Fig. 5).

5 Conclusion

The concept of the city as a commons suggests a wide sharing of the resources for the benefits of the inhabitant, particularly the disadvantaged, addressing the many and complex issues of urban inequalities (Foster and Iaione 2016). The driven force needed for this to happen may come from the administration as well as the urbanites, implying in both cases a political effort and a strong involvement. In all events, a strong action with long-lasting impact needs to be framed within a knowledge-based structure, to facilitate:

- the identification of key points in which to experiment innovative transformation or management actions;
- the retrieval of economic, professional and cultural resources needed to involve the interested actors and agents;
- planning the sustainability of the action over time, to ensure its survival.

These considerations are equally valid whether it is a bottom-up or top-down action, considering the commoning process as an intermediate step in the decision-making, as a smooth shift from the administrative to the collective competences. This transition can be facilitated in the clear understanding and the right distribution of roles between the different urban agents according to the objectives of an urban transformation strategy. In this respect, the activation of commons is not to be considered as a *panacea* for all urban diseases. In fact, as Foster and Iaione (2016) emphasise, commons can be used for many purposes: to increase the private wealth of single households; as a stock of resources that can be used to more fairly distribute social and economic resources; to improve the quality of life (and also the value of owned assets); to improve income and find or create jobs. Definitely, the shared amenities and the social inclusion fostered within a commoning process can be jeopardise by the economic results of the increasing value of housing and properties, which may attract private investors. Instead, carefully planning the sustainability of a commoning process towards a "makerhood[13]" model, can orient the efforts in the increasing of economic inclusion and urban liveability, using the reclaimed public spaces for people to learn skills, obtain access to job opportunities and social services (Ibid.). To do so, local administrations and policy makers have the key role to encourage this actions, providing spaces and distributing economical, professional and philanthropical resources to support the development of a long-term plan. On the other hand, local administrations have to be properly equipped with the right toolkit in order to achieve this complex tasks and fulfil their role of facilitators.

Many recommendations may be considered in this sense: Foster and Iaione (2016) suggest the "co-city" protocol, developed and experimented in five cities in Italy so far, is articulated in three main phases: mapping, experimenting and prototyping; Gehl Architects propose their method of Public Space/Public Life Studies and Strategies, experimented all over the world (Gehl and Svarre 2013); or maybe the City-Protocol proposed by Vincente Guallart for a Self-Sufficient city, which also involves environmental and energy sustainability. In any case, mapping,

[13]«The concept of "makerhoods"—urban planning and economic development strategy that seeks to unleash micro-entrepreneurs to strengthen communities through natural and affordable live/work accommodations—embodies this mix of inclusive, affordable, and shared space in which people can earn a living and still sustain themselves while establishing small businesses» (Foster and Iaione 2016: 341).

spatialise, visualise the urban issue is a necessary step to develop knowledge base, enabling tools to put together public and collective efforts. Participated processes, co-design practices, public debates, have all in common their position within an intermediate or final phase of the decision-making, or should I say, it very hard to verify their ideological continuity within the whole process. What this contribution suggests—in particular regarding the proposal briefly explained in paragraph 5—is that, especially nowadays, it is necessary to equip each city with tools for the analysis, the interpretation and the monitoring of the built environment and the socio-spatial dynamics, in order to support the urban transformation within investigation, strategies and actions, to achieve physical and social outcomes.

This can be realised by implementing the resources available to urban centres, which offer a perfect framework for this purpose, as the case of the city of Bologna has proved; establishing public space observatories would facilitate the creation of a structure to support public administration, taking charge of the dissemination of content and the training of facilitators in urban communing processes; professional bodies could also train architects and planners on the principals of the new urban design process[14] aimed at activating urban commons. In Italy, there are virtuous examples as the Observatory for Municipal Goods, in Naples and Bologna, whereas in other municipalities have only been adopted the common good regulations and the following lists of eligible goods. The absence of a comprehensive—national as well as local—mapping of the eligible urban commons preclude the opportunity understand them in a relational perspective, to each other, to the territory and to the claims of the community. Furthermore, it appears to be a widespread practice in Italy to associate urban common good with property confiscated from crime organisations, left unclear why other forms of urban property cannot be included.

All things considered, it is tangible that the city is not only an object of perception and enjoyment, but the product of the transformation of countless actors who can change and control the urban structure, its details, its growth and form, in a continuous succession of phases (Lynch 1960). In this sense, urban design, as a process, it is to be considered as an integrated activity, which scale is also the infrastructural one. Therefore, urban design has to overcome the physical sphere, becoming contaminated by the ethical one to address values such as urban democracy and social justice. In other words, it means that we have to consider public space no longer as a static object but as a moving and dynamic entity, as something that, once realised, is continually transformed by its users, modified by everything that happens inside and outside of it (Latour and Yaneva 2008). The physical configuration of the space acts as a solution of continuity between the administrative and management choices of urban policies and the way in which the communities perceive them (Lefebvre 1991). The design of public space can be considered as the binding elements within the socio-spatial dynamics. On the one hand, public space provides for tangible elements, on the other, it contributes to establish the more or less tacit behavioural rules allowed to use them (Gehl and Svarre 2013).

[14]The design principles can be summarised as: removable and reversable project; activation of underused spaces; self-managed proposals; recycle and reuse waste materials.

References

Adler, D. (2016, May 6). Story of cities #37: how radical ideas turned Curitiba into Brazil's 'green capital. From The Guardian – Cities: https://www.theguardian.com/cities/2016/may/06/story-of-cities-37-mayor-jaime-lerner-curitiba-brazil-green-capital-global-icon.

Alves dos Santos, O., Jr. (2014). Urban common space, heterotopia and the right to the city: Reflections on the ideas of Henry Lefebvre and David Harvey. *Brazilian Journal of Urban Management, 6*(2), 146–157.

Bazzu, P., & Talu, V. (2017). *Tactical urbanism 5—italia*. Sassari: TaMaLaCà Srl.

Bollier, D. (2014). In *think like a commoner: A short introduction to the life of the commons*. New Society Publishers.

Bordieu, P. (2018). Social space and the genesis of appropriated physical space. *International Journal of Urban and Regional Research*, 106–114.

Bradley, K. (2015). Open source urbanism: Creating, multiplying and managing urban commons. *Footprint*, 91–108.

Carmona, M. (2019). Principles for public space design, planning to do better. *Urban Design International, 24*, 47–59.

Carmona, M., Hanssen, G. S., Lamm, B., Nylund, K., Saglie, I.-L., & Tietjen, A. (2019). Public space in an age of austerity. *Urban Design International*, 241–259.

Carmona, M., Heath, T., Oc, T., & Tiesdell, S. (2003). *Public places—urban spaces*. The dimensions of Urban Design: Architectural Press.

Carr, S. (1992). *Public space*. New York, US: Cambridge University Press.

Cerasi, M. (1976). *Lo spazio collettivo della città – Costruzione e dissoluzione del sistema pubblico nell'architettura della città moderna*. Milano: Gabriele Mazzotta.

De Angelis, M. (2017). In omnia sunt communia—On the commons and the transformation to postcapitalis. M. Zed Books.

De Capua, A., & Errante, L. (2019). Interpreting public space as a medium for urban liveability. *Agathón—International Journal of Architecture Art and Design, 06*, 59–72.

De Carlo, G. (2013). *L'architettura della partecipazione*. In S. Marini (Ed.), Macerata: Quodlibet.

Errante, L. (2019). Public space and its challanges: a palimpsest for urban commons. In C. Benincasa, G. Neri, & M. Trimarchi (Ed.), *Art and economics in the city. new cultural maps* (pp. 191–198). Bielefeld: Transcript Verlag.

Foster, S. R. (2011). Collective action and the urban commons. *Notre Dame Law Review, 87*(1), 57–134.

Foster, S. R., & Iaione, C. (2016). *The city as a commons. Yale Law and Policy Review*, 281–349.

Fraser, N. (1990). Rethinking the public sphere: A contribution to the critique of actually existing democrac. *Social Text*(25/26), 56–80.

Gehl, J. (2011). *Life between buildings: Using public space*. Washington, DC: Island Press.

Gehl, J., & Svarre, B. (2013). In *How to study public life*. (K. A. Steenhard, Trans.) Washington, USA: Island Press.

Gregotti, V. (1993). In *Casabella il disegno degli spazi aperti*. (597/598), Editoriale.

Harvey, D. (2012). *Rebel cities: From the right to the city to the urban revolution*. London: Verso.

Hernandez, J., & Casanova, H. (2014). Public space acupuncture. Actar.

Hess, C. (2008). Mapping the new commons. Retrieved February 2020, from SSRN: https://ssrn.com/abstract=1356835.

Huron, A. (2015). Working with strangers in saturated space: reclaiming and maintaining the urban commons. *Antipode*, 1–17.

Jacobs, J. (1992). In *The Death and Life of Great American Cities* (Edizione Originale: 1961, New York: Random House Inc. ed.). New York, USA: Vintage Books Edition.

Katz, C. (2001). Vagabond capitalism and the necessity for social reproduction. *Antipode, 33*(4), 709–728.

Koch, R., & Latham, A. (2017). In *Key thinkers on cities*. SAGE Publications Ltd.

Latour, B., & Yaneva, A. (2008). Give me a gun and I will make all buildings move: an ANT's view of architecture. *Explorations in Architecture: Teaching, Design, Research,* 80–89.
Lefebvre, H. (1991). In *The production of space* (Original Ed.: La production de l'espace, 1974, Éditions Anthropos ed.). Oxford, UK: Basil Blackwell Ltd.
Lefebvre, H. (2014). In *Il diritto alla città* (Original Ed.: Le droit a la ville, 1968, Paris: Ed. du Seuil ed.), (A. Casaglia, & G. Morosato, (Eds.), Trans.) Perugia, IT: Ombre Corte.
Lerner, J. (2014). In *Urban acupuncture.* Washington DC| Covelo| London: Island Press.
Lynch, K. (1960). *The image of the city*. Cambridge: The Technology Press and Harvard University Press.
Madanipour, A. (2003). *Public and private space of the city*. London, UK: Routledge.
Madanipour, A. (2005). Public space of european cities. *Nordic Journal of Architectural Research, 18*(1), 7–16.
Marcuse, P. (2009). From critical urban theory to the right to the city. *City, 13*(2–3), 185–196.
Mazzette, A. (Ed.). (2013). In *Pratiche sociali di città pubblica.* Editori Laterza.
Mehta, V. (2007). *A toolkit for performance measures of public space.* Antwerp: Urban Trialogues.
Mehta, V. (2014). Evaluating public space. *Journal of Urban Design, 19*(1), 53–88.
Mitchell, D. (2003). *The right to the city and the fight for public space.* New York, US: The Guilford Press.
Nèmeth, J., & Schmidt, S. (2011). The privatization of public space: modeling and measuring publicness. *Environment and Planning B: Planning and Design, 38,* 5–23.
Norberg-Schultz, C. (1980). In *Genius Loci: toward a phenomenology of architecture.* London: Academy Ed.
Ostrom, E. (1990). In *Governing the commons: The evolution of institutions for collective action.* Cambridge University Press.
Pasaogullari, N., & Doratli, N. (2004). Measuring accessibility and utilization of public spaces in Famagusta. *Cities, 21*(3), 225–232.
Project for Public Spaces. (2000). *How to turn a place around: A handbook for creating successful public spaces.* New York: Project for Public Spaces.
Rinehart, N. (2009). Public spaces in bogotá: An introduction. *University of Miami Inter-American Law Review*, 197–211.
Sebastiani, C. (2010). Politica: governo collettivo dei beni comuni. In F. Bottini (Ed.), *Spazio pubblico—declino difesa, riconquista* (pp. 235–243). Roma: Eddiesse.
Sitte, C. (1953). In *L'arte di costruire le città* (Ed. or. Der Städtebau nach seinen künstlerischen Grundsatzen. (1889) ed.). (L. Dodi, Ed.), Milano: Officine Grafiche dell'Editore Antonio Vallardi.
STIPO. (2016). In J. L. Hans Karssenberg, (Ed.), *The city at eye level—Lessons for street plints* (II Ed. ed.). (Rotterdam: Eburon.
STIPO. (2017). In S. v. Jeroen Laven, (Ed.), *The city at eye level in the Netherlands.* Amsterdam: Uitgeverij Blauwdruk.
Super, D. A. (2013). A new property. *Columbia Law Review, 113*(1772), 1773–1896.
Susser, I., & Tonnelat, S. (2013). Transformative cities: The three urban commons. *Journal of Global and Historical Anthropology, 66,* 105–132.
UN-Habitat, United Nations Human Settlements Programme. (2017). *Global public space programme: Annual report 2016.* Nairobi: UNON, Publishing Services Section.
United Nation. (2014). In *world urbanization prospects.* United Nations.
United Nations—Human Settlements Programme (UN-Habitat). (2015). In *Global public space toolkit: From global principles to local policies and practice.*
Venturini, G., & Graziano, P. (2016). Misurare la coesione sociale: una comparazione tra le regioni italiane. *Impresa Sociale, 12*(8), 27–36.

Enhancing Human and Urban Capital: A Value-Oriented Approach

Danila Longo, Andrea Boeri, Rossella Roversi, and Serena Orlandi

Abstract

Cultural Heritage (CH), in its tangible and intangible dimension, can represent an extraordinary engine for sustainable transformation and reactivation processes in abandoned and underused urban spaces. The regenerative potential of CH requires the identification of innovative operating models and strategies, able to strengthen common resources, starting from the acknowledgment and the enhancement of human and urban capital. This value-oriented approach was experimented in the Bologna University area by the EU Horizon 2020 project ROCK—*Regeneration and Optimisation of Cultural Heritage in creative and Knowledge cities* (GA 730280) through a series of pilot actions. Among them, the temporary transformation of Piazza Rossini.

D. Longo (✉) · A. Boeri · R. Roversi · S. Orlandi
Department of Architecture, University of Bologna, Bologna, Italy
e-mail: danila.longo@unibo.it

A. Boeri
e-mail: andrea.boeri@unibo.it

R. Roversi
e-mail: rossella.roversi@unibo.it

S. Orlandi
e-mail: serena.orlandi4@unibo.it

E. Macrì et al. (eds.), *Cultural Commons and Urban Dynamics*,
https://doi.org/10.1007/978-3-030-54418-8_9

1 Introduction

Many urban and suburban contexts in Europe are affected, in different forms, by physical abandonment of spaces and by the exclusion of vulnerable and underprivileged people from social, economic, cultural and participation chances.[1]

The intense changes experienced by the EU cities over the last century due to the economic model and the market economy, have generated economic growth but have not created equal opportunities for all segments of population. The risk-of-poverty or social exclusion in the EU has steadily declined from its 2012 peak; however, progress in reducing inequality and relative poverty (AROP) has been modest and the income distribution is more unequal today than in the 1980s in almost all Member States[2]: in 2017, 112.8 million people (22.4% of the entire population) in the EU lived in households at risk of poverty or social exclusion.[3] Thus, inequality can therefore be considered one of the main socio-economic challenges in the EU. Risks of poverty or social exclusion are more pronounced for certain types of workers and vulnerable groups.

Educational attainment and skill levels play an important role in determining social inclusion and labour market outcomes. In EU there is still an employability threshold which a high number of people with low educational and skill achievements cannot cross.

Alongside the social consequences, the economic structural changes, the decline of traditional industries economic model and the globalization have led to significant shifts in land occupation patterns that resulted in the creation of so-called 'brownfields' across Europe, particularly in urban areas.

During the urban sprawl process, industrial uses dating back to the nineteenth century have been subject to a persisting displacement pressure and have been moved to peripheral zones or in other Countries, even extra UE. In addition, large areas previously occupied by large scale infrastructures, such as railway and harbour facilities, have been left vacant and constitute huge voids inside or in the outskirts of cities. These dynamics, in terms of pressures creating potentially derelict areas, have been reinforced by speculative land banking. The effect of these factors, along with problems relating to conflicts affecting the interest, use and ownership of the sites, led to a generally large extent of derelict land in urban areas: approximately 40% of the European cities are facing de-densification processes and the emergence of brownfield sites (Haase et al. 2014).

Abandoned and neglected areas can be both inside and outside the cities, can be open spaces or dismissed buildings, large brownfields or residential settlements, such as social housing districts. At present, a reliable estimation of brownfields and abandoned areas in EU is impossible, also due to the lack of a common definition of

[1]According with the Employment and Social Developments in Europe report in 2016 people at risk-of-poverty or exclusion in EU 28 were the 25,3%. European Commission Directorate-General for Employment, Social Affairs and Inclusion Directorate A (2016).

[2]European Union Statistics on Income and Living Conditions (EU-SILC) (2020).

[3]EUROSTAT (2019).

the concepts. Even where the European countries can provide estimates on the size of problem in their areas, the data are not directly comparable, and include different kinds of sites (Grimski and Ferber 2001). It is not a phenomena limited to suburbs: historical centres are not immune to the presence of disused areas or places where citizens live in a state of degradation and isolation.

A sustainable environment and inclusive economic development cannot be achieved without the reintegration of these sites and their inhabitants, when present, into the social, economic and cultural dynamics of the city. The strategies used by cities to deal with this challenge mainly focus on using the classical instruments of urban planning. Large-scale projects, based on top-down decision, are developed by master plans and investor planning and have sometimes led to economic failure, to real estate valorisation without social benefits or value redistribution, or to gentrification (Magdaniel et al. 2018). New strategies, approaches and solutions are needed to re-activate and re-generate neglected, abandoned urban areas and brownfields.

Although often considered anomalous, and associated with emptiness or lack of productivity, "empty lands" are often at the core of alternative uses by local communities that manage, plan for and otherwise engage with vacant spaces in a variety of both spontaneous or organized and ad hoc ways that represent a pluralism of values and can become Common Goods where culture and creativity enhance multidimensional and multi-scale impacts at urban, metropolitan and regional level. Value, in fact, can also be generated by the material and immaterial dimension of the layering heritage, related to identity and diversity that can be the base for a new value chain.

The following paragraphs propose some reflections about a value-oriented approach to urban regeneration, describing place-based and Cultural Heritage-led strategies, focused on the enhancement of urban and human capital. They are supported and experimented within the research framework of the ROCK EU—Horizon 2020 project (GA 730280), that is approaching its completion. Finally, a pilot action implemented in the city of Bologna is described as testing experimentation of the developed methodology and strategy.

2 Heritage-Led Regeneration Potentials in Historic Urban Areas

Historic urban areas are the principal result of the common Cultural Heritage (later shortened to CH), shaped by layers of values produced by cultures, traditions, experiences, recognized as such in their diversity.[4] Over time, the meaning of CH has been extended from single monuments and manufacts, identified as proper objects of art, to cultural landscapes, historic cities, and serial properties. Moreover, contemporary practice (ratified by ICOMOS at its Madrid General Assembly)

[4]Directorate-General for Employment, Social Affairs and Inclusion Directorate A (2018).

expands the concept of heritage beyond "tangible heritage," to the intangible dimensions of heritage as well; "this means the entirety of the capital of knowledge derived from the development and experience of human practices, and from the spatial, social and cultural constructions linked to it that may be encapsulated in the word 'memory'.[5]

CH can offer great opportunities to tackle contemporary urban issues. As stated in the UNESCO Recommendation on the Historic Urban Landscape, "urban heritage, including its tangible and intangible components, constitutes a key resource in enhancing the liveability of urban areas, and fosters economic development and social cohesion in a changing global environment. As the future of humanity hinges on the effective planning and management of resources, conservation has become a strategy to achieve a balance between urban growth and quality of life on a sustainable basis".[6]

In order to fully understand the potential of CH as engine for sustainable development, promotion of social cohesion, inclusion and equity, the idea of "heritage" must thus be interpreted in its broader and more extensive meaning, particularly in urban areas: CH is an expression of the ways of living developed by a community and passed on from generation to generation, including customs, practices, places, objects, artistic expressions and values.[7]

In this perspective, the Council of the European Union adopted on 20th May 2014 the fundamental document "Conclusions on cultural heritage as a strategic resource for a sustainable Europe", which has recognized Cultural Heritage as "a strategic resource for a sustainable Europe".[8] The same vision has been taken into account in several EU projects as a leading course of actions, e.g. Horizon 2020, and by the 2030 UN Agenda for Sustainable Development.

As part of human activity, CH produces tangible and intangible representations of the value systems, beliefs, traditions and lifestyles: a common 'urban capital', that configures the space of the shared identity, the memory of the urban system, the stable element in its dynamic change and, at the same time, the transformative potential that is continuously generated during the evolution of the urban process. Urban capital is combined and complementary with the more subjective dimension of the 'human capital' that sums up social and personal attributes such as knowledge, skills and creativity.

The use of the term/concept of 'capital' has the advantage of being immediately understandable, being transversal to different disciplinary areas; however, the term can be interpreted in a reductive economic sense as it embodies the reference to financial assets and to the ability to perform labour so as to produce economic value. This is why Saskia Saassen and other authors prefers the use of the term 'capabilities' instead of 'capital' (Saassen 2012; Borghi 2017).

[5]ICOMOS (2016).
[6]UNESCO (2011).
[7]International Council on Monuments and Sites, ICOMOS International Cultural Tourism Committee (2002).
[8]Council of the European Union (2014).

A systemic transformation, understanding historical city heritage as a common good, can offer the potential to generate new social, economic and sustainable environmental virtuous processes.[9] The presence of creative sectors, students, start-ups, social innovation and cultural activities can be seen as factors to tap the potential to regenerate neglected areas into innovation hubs by matching cultural and economic growth, education and training, sustainable and fair entrepreneurial opportunities.

Enhancing the regenerative potential of CH for historic urban areas requires the identification of innovative operating models and strategies, able to strengthen common resources starting from the acknowledgment and the setting up of human and urban capitals and according with an approach that recognizes them as values.

The applicative contexts of these strategies, the historic urban areas, are not limited to historic city centres but include all the layered urban territories that reflect the interaction over time between people and their surroundings. Also brownfields, suburban areas and disused infrastructural service facilities can be the expression of a strong identity shaped by the local social, economic and cultural history. Moreover, historic urban areas are not delimited by rigid borders: they are often inserted in or in continuity with the Cultural Landscape,[10] including gardens, parks and natural corridors, reflecting the strong association with human processes.

2.1 Human and Urban Capital as Common Pool Resources for the Re-Activation of Public Spaces

The contemporary city—both in the suburbs and in the central areas—represents a complex context of relationships within which encouraging and experimenting strategies and pilot actions aimed at overcoming urban and social deterioration affecting public spaces and communities.

The growing of population is increasing year-by-year the urban density, leading to the exacerbation of challenges related to sustainability and to urban management. Moreover, criticalities affecting urban spaces and services of common interest—essential to the satisfaction of numerous living needs and functional to the individual and collective well-being of communities—are partly attributable to the citizens' disaffection towards public spaces and services that are perceived as places of nobody rather than places of all. In a vision of the city that considers public spaces as urban commons, collaboration between institutions and civil society is an indispensable and required condition (Iaione and Arena 2012).

The Faro Convention (Fairclough et al. 2014) introduces the concept of "heritage communities" and recognises the "individual and collective responsibility towards cultural heritage", clarifying the importance of an inclusive and active engagement

[9]Council of the European Union (2005).

[10]Council of Europe. (2018). European Landscape Convention. Contribution to human rights, democracy and sustainable development. Accessed March 16, 2020, from https://rm.coe.int/council-of-europe-landscape-convention-contribution-to-human-rights-de/16807bffda.

of "everyone" as well as of the CH adaptive "sustainable use" so as to highlight its ancient and new meanings (Faro Convention 2005). This action of co-responsibility towards commons of collective relevance—concerning production, governance and care of public spaces—finds its resources in the mutual acknowledgment and involvement of the main actors of the urban ecosystem of stakeholders.

This shared responsibility towards the heritage can contribute also to shared value that underpins a common political design for Europe, providing useful inputs for establishing the forthcoming EU Urban Agenda as set through the Pact of Amsterdam[11] which identify in the partnership tool the way to collaborate on an equal footing in the development of common solutions to improve urban areas in the European Union.

In this scenario, human capital and urban capital are intended as active and operable material able to activate the potential transformations of urban areas, creating new networks, enabling different uses and triggering a deep relationship of identity recognition between spaces of the city and local communities.

Thus, "capital" is intended as a common relevance property, to be administered and managed in such a way that the interest of the whole community benefits from it: ideas, experiences, skills, time, relationships and knowledge invested in the management and care of what is common (Arena 2007). Civic resources and capabilities can trigger effective actions of regeneration and transformation through —and above all—the involvement of active citizenship. The development of social cohesion, new forms of participation in public life, the creation of opportunities for meeting and discussion and an assumption of responsibility towards the care of public "affairs" are secondary, but not less important, effects. A process through which understand the effective capability of urban territories and communities to respond to the turnaround that degradation and exclusion conditions of the cities require.

3 Possible Integrated Strategies of Boosting Values for Urban Regeneration

Reversing the abandonment and exclusion trend of historic urban areas goes through the identification of inclusive and integrated step-by-step strategies with a focus on the nexus between urban contexts, entrepreneurial processes and local governance mechanisms, and with the commitment to bring together and encourage individuals, groups and communities in delivering locally-tailored solutions.

In a progressive and people-place-based approach (Hopkins and Ferris 2015), the fundamental starting step point is the acknowledgment of what is already in place, in order to avoid financial, political, social, managing barriers and to make more effective the existing resources. The already existing blueprints—in terms of policies and practices, capacity buildings and connectivity—are to be linked with

[11]Urban Agenda for the EU Pact of Amsterdam (2016).

new networks of collaboration and co-production. The knowledge of local CH treasures, social and cultural opportunities, talents and resources, often unknown to citizens themselves, is fundamental also to stimulate the awareness and sense of belonging of local communities, and to disclose the existing urban and social capital as well as its potential in terms of knowledge, skills and abilities.

In this perspective, to leverage on a requalification based on the key existing enabling factors, and to rebalance urban processes and sustainable growth in historic areas, the possible strategy goes through the following challenges:

1. heritage-led regeneration combined with conservation, taking into account CH sensitivity to change without loss of its cultural/memory values, but opening buildings and spaces to different or unconventional uses and users, avoiding "museification", "touristification" and gentrification effects;
2. reversing the process of losing memory of heritage that inevitably afflict abandoned spaces through CH-led initiatives, starting from mapping the existing heritage resources to create a dynamic network of people/places linked to the involved areas;
3. light re-industrialisation and innovative manufacturing process linked to historic heritage can be promoted through site-specific and sustainable solutions for a progressive adaptive reuse of heritage to accommodate small scale advanced manufacturing, producers and local 'makers', craft workshops etc., sharing responsibilities and developing practical strategies for safeguarding community interests and increasing community values (spatial and relational ones) deriving from CH;
4. strengthening relations among communities and citizens for the value understanding, common generation and exchange; supporting the social, cultural and entrepreneurial initiatives and the related impacts on the socio-economic environment and the ability to actively contribute to community life, particularly overcoming the barriers for women, children, elderly and migrants;
5. up-skilling of workforce through specific programs to promote new entrepreneurship able to generate direct and indirect benefits on the local territories, with the support of local groups of interest as firms, academic players, agencies, and associations that facilitate the reskilling and up-skilling process;
6. peer production starting from the set of resources (human and urban capital) already available in the test bed sites and enhanced through co-design and co-working, pooling the individual efforts of different people, with different capabilities;
7. value re-distribution in terms of knowledge, capabilities, enabling spaces, enabling tools: even in cities with a high rate of innovation and wealth production, the risk is that the different areas grow at different speeds, leaving entire territories and population groups behind. In particular, the gap in access to digitisation and education contributes significantly to this risk;
8. application of skills and knowledges to be addressed through a cross-fertilisation approach among several disciplines such as architecture, urban planning and

real estate, data analysis, sociology, economy, joined in a collaborative network applies with the experimenting of new forms of partnership between public and private actors (companies, foundations, universities, associations, etc.).

Into this approach, some trends and drivers can be recognised as important key-factors to be considered in developing new approaches for Cultural Heritage regeneration. According with a literature review made by the authors, these factors are aligned mainly to the following macro-areas:

1. Social Trends and Drivers
   a. Population Growth and Urban Density (need for sustainable growth, new services, etc.…).
   b. Identity/Multicultural Cities/new citizenship and opportunities to access to CH contents (for migrants, poor, disabilities etc.…).
   c. Cultural Diversification (both people, services and activities in cities) to increase intangible CH productions.
2. Technological Trends and Drivers
   a. Digital Lifestyle and spread of ICT technologies. The diffusion of ICT (Information and Communication Technologies) devices gives resources and potentially useful instruments for ruling and effectively managing high level of complexity as those concerning cities. These instruments allow the collection and processing of high amount of information, also on real time, which is important for directing more effectively urban strategies and projects, fostering inclusive approaches and the overcoming of cultural barriers.
   b. Smart infrastructure and big data to monitor and analyze regeneration processes.
   c. Enabling technologies for accessibility and fruition of CH.
3. Economic Trends and Drivers
   a. Finance and investments to support the valorization of CH.
   b. Open innovation and community base financing for creative and cultural districts development.
   c. Creative and cultural industry and start ups linked to CH promotion and valorization.
4. Environmental Trends and Drivers
   a. Climate change and urban resilience applied in historic city contexts.
   b. Resource efficiency and circular economy in historic city contexts.
   c. Change of behaviour of cultural institutions and CH users.

5. Political/Governance

   a. Urban planning and urban integrated management for historic city context.
   b. New policies to increase collaboration between cultural and creative operators.
   c. Sustainable procurement policies for CH valorization.

Strategies, to be proved effective, must be tested and verified through pilot actions implemented in selected contexts; successful experimentations can allow the transition from the testing phase towards more substantial transformations. Actions may be designed and carried out in limited areas, as significant representative of larger contexts and as part of wider relational systems.

3.1 A Value-Oriented Methodological Approach: The EU—ROCK H2020 Project

The experience carried out by the ROCK—*Regeneration and Optimization of Cultural heritage in creative and Knowledge cities* project (grant agreement n° 730280)[12] can be considered a relevant example to better clarify the above described approach.

This project—funded in 2017 under the H2020 programme in the axis Climate—Greening the Economy, in response to the call "Cultural Heritage as a driver for sustainable growth"—is leaded by the Municipality of Bologna with scientific coordination of the University of Bologna and involves 10 European Cities and 32 partners.

ROCK overall objective—by relying on an Action Plan for regeneration—is to support a systemic transformation that imply historical city heritage as a common good, capable of generating new social, economic and sustainable environmental processes. The Cultural Heritage-led regeneration strategies promoted by the project, focus on historic city centres with the aim to transform the selected demo areas into Creative, Cultural and Sustainable Districts. The implementation of key actions is aimed at providing new ways to access CH, defining key policy issues and developing a sense of belonging to places. The demo areas are located in central urban sectors that, despite their geographical position and relevance in terms of CH, are lived and perceived as separate from the rest of the city, as well as characterized by the presence of physical and/or social degradation and by underused or poorly used spaces. The mutual exchange of Heritage-led good practices and regeneration initiatives is a very important strategic element: the 7 Role Model Cities (Athens, Cluj-Napoca, Eindhoven, Liverpool, Lyon, Turin and Vilnius), have already implemented successful processes of regeneration and support, through a mentoring action, the 3 Replicator Cities (Bologna, Lisbon and Skopje) in developing similar models in relation to their specific local contexts.

[12]Rock—Cultural Heritage Leading Urban Futures (2020).

The ROCK approach is based on a circular urban model, transferred from the economy model to the urban historic environments. It is based on considering CH as a product to which the same principles of saving and reuse can be applied. CH already in use for specific activities hides other unused potentialities if framed in a less specialized idea of culture: a value-sharing process that must steer city changes both in terms of physical environment and of mindset.

In particular, the underused, misused or abandoned spaces are interpreted as resources to be re-introduced into a continuous positive development cycle that regenerates existing elements, while preserving and conserving them. Creating a circular urban model implies connecting "systems" that were initially separated through not only technical but also organisational and institutional solutions and changes, to be adopted and adapted (Vernay 2013).

ROCK starts from the identification of the specific local systems articulated into:

- system of actors, which constitute the backbone of ROCK, to define the transformation needs, the collaboration pathways, the opportunity creation, fostering the circulation of knowledge and abilities;
- system of places, starting from the pilot areas of ROCK and understanding their relations with the whole urban contexts, circulating solutions, tools, strategies and results of experimentation, to foster the replication of the most effective ones in similar contexts;
- system of initiatives (bottom-up and top-down; collaboration, sponsorship, partnerships, etc.) to promote creativeness and cultural production from different sources, combining them in common projects of regeneration;
- systems of resources (physical resources, financial resources, human capitals) to promote a circulation of flows, overpassing the linear processes in the circular city, from extraction to waste, replacing them by circular processes.

ROCK pilot process is driven by a *research-action-research* methodology in which the combination of research and action play an essential role in heritage development procedures: research elaborates possible regenerative scenarios, according which site-specific actions are implemented in pilot areas, feedbacks and results are recorded, impacts are verified and recalibrated for the future, and new updated and adjusted scenarios are elaborated again with the support of the research.

The demonstration areas involved by the project are intended as experimental labs where testing and implementing successful practices. Bologna is one of the Replicator cities. A set of coordinated actions has been implemented in the University area–named "U-Zone"—with the aim to transform it in a Sustainable Cultural and Creative District by improving safety, mitigating social conflicts, attracting visitors and tourists, entrepreneurs and private investments, increasing pedestrian flows and slow mobility with new cultural routes.

Like many historic city centres, the U-Zone area is a very complex system of human and urban capitals where many different interests, conflicts and values converge.

The University sector is located inside the historic city centre where a large, mixed and open community of residents, students, homeless, pedestrians, tourists and cultural users daily inhabit, live and pass through with different needs and habits. The scenario of these human dynamics includes important CH testimonies, such as historical palaces, university buildings, the Municipality Opera House, Libraries, Museums, churches, streets, squares. "Via Zamboni"—characterized by the presence of a continuous system of porches which qualifies the image of the whole city of Bologna—is the road axis that physically and ideally crosses and connects the different elements that define this rich, conflictual and vibrant urban scenario (Fig. 1).

The increasing of the student population (about 80,000 students), the migration phenomena, the change in the number and composition of population in the centre (15,000 new residents each year, of which 9,000 Italian), the growing new tourism fluxes, have not been integrated in the social and relational asset of the area. These dynamics has generated phenomena of social conflict between different categories of users and triggered decay and disturb. In particular, the presence of the students, vital and positive per se, is turned into a problematic issue for the coexistence with the residents. The area stands out as one of the main places in Bologna where excluded people from urban dynamics gather and meet and it is perceived by the rest of the city as a separated part. So, nevertheless the richness of the U-Zone in cultural and artistic institutions and museums, this cultural heritage is not fully known and exploited by citizens and tourists.

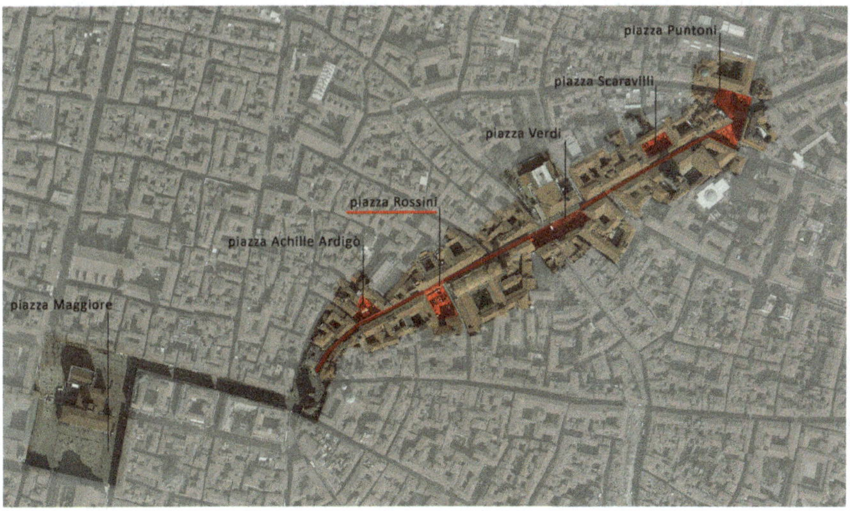

Fig. 1 The U-Zone Five Square highlighted in red, from left to right: Ravegnana, Rossini, Verdi, Scaravilli, Puntoni. The red line points out Piazza Rossini, object of the "Green Please: the meadow you don't expect" temporary project

The design the of the regeneration pilot actions is carried out through the 'living lab' approach. A process of community involvement (U-Lab) creates a local Ecosystem of Stakeholders (Institution, University and research area, association, students, citizens, companies) by relating new and existing blueprints, enabling co-designed and co-construction workshops based on cross-fertilisation among several disciplines (U-Atelier).

Practices of temporary adaptive re-use applied on public spaces with the involvement of communities are strategic tools to experiment an innovative way to build and shape a new shared identity in which people can recognize themselves.

The important role that open and public spaces play in the social and ecological balance of cities, can takes on new values linked to social significance in which inclusive design, co-planning, co-construction and co-management of public spaces are fundamental components of the process.

4 Testing the Enhancement of Urban and Human Capital in the Historic Urban Scenario: The Temporary Transformation of Piazza Rossini in Bologna

During the three years of ROCK project, different types of actions have been carried out in the "U-Zone", each one inserted in a global vision, concurring to achieve integrated targets and objectives, according with the specific character and vocation of spaces involved.

The experience of adaptive reuse of a an historical urban space of the U-Zone in Bologna, Piazza Rossini, is an opportunity to better explain the potential of shared, temporary, value oriented transformations. Afterwards the pilot experience implemented in Piazza Scaravilli—the U-Zone public space where "Malerbe" actions were realized (Fig. 2)[13]—Piazza Rossini goes on in the same direction, confirming the force of human and urban capital in urban regeneration dynamics.

The project for a temporary redefinition of the square, named "Green Please: the meadow you don't expect", is the result of a co-design and co-construction workshop for students promoted by ROCK actions with the coordination of Fondazione Innovazione Urbana: for a week, the public space was transformed from parking into a green pedestrian area.

The experimentation is part of a broader strategy of actions that systematically involved all other public spaces of the sector—as recalled by the name of the initiative, "The Five Squares" of the U-Zone—developed in synergy with the programming of Bologna Design Week and Researchers' Night in September 2019.[14] A proposal and an event dedicated to urban regeneration, optimisation of cultural heritage and its accessibility, the incentive and promotion of public space care, through the development of its potential by imagining and testing different and

[13]Dossier Piazza Scaravilli (2018).
[14]Le Cinque Piazze (2019).

Fig. 2 'Malerbe' temporary construction on Piazza Scaravilli, outcome of a co-design and co-construction workshop during U-Atelier phase of the project (coordinated by the Department of Architecture, University of Bologna): the parking area changed into a dynamic urban garden

unconventional uses, according to an environmental sustainability perspective (Fig. 3).

The five squares involved in the project are public spaces connected by the porches line of Via Zamboni, with different characteristics, transformed over time, dominated by the presence of important historical buildings with artistic and patrimonial value—home of equally important university, economic and cultural realities—whose systemisation reaffirms their interesting potential for the U-Zone of Bologna.

Piazza Giacomo Rossini has been always in use as a public parking area for cars and bicycles. It occupies the grounds of the ancient churchyard or cemetery of the Basilica of San Giacomo Maggiore. The others relevant building that define the square facades are: the former convent complex of Santa Cecilia, home of the 'Giovan Battista Martini' Music Conservatory; the late Renaissance front of Palazzo Magnani—currently used as a bank office—that inside preserves remarkable frescoes and a picture gallery open to the public; the Palazzina Lambertini, an example of eighteenth-century civil architecture; and the sixteenth-century Palazzo Malvezzi, current headquarters of the 'Metropolitan City' public body of Bologna. Due to the use and function it has always held, the beautiful square did not represent a place to stop, gather and socialize: pedestrians could only circulate on the narrow sidewalk margins next to the road lane, while the presence of the parked vehicles in the middle of the area interfered with the view towards its architectural scenario.

Due to the use and function it has always held, the square did not represent a place to stop, gather and socialize: pedestrians could only circulate on the sidewalk margins, sharing the location with cars, while the presence of the parked vehicles in the center interfered with the view towards its architectural scenario.

The temporary-reuse project, with the aim of proposing an unexpected perception of the square's space, experimenting with new uses and offering the opportunity to rediscover and appreciate the details of the architecture overlooking the square, has converted part of the parking area into an "unexpected" vegetable

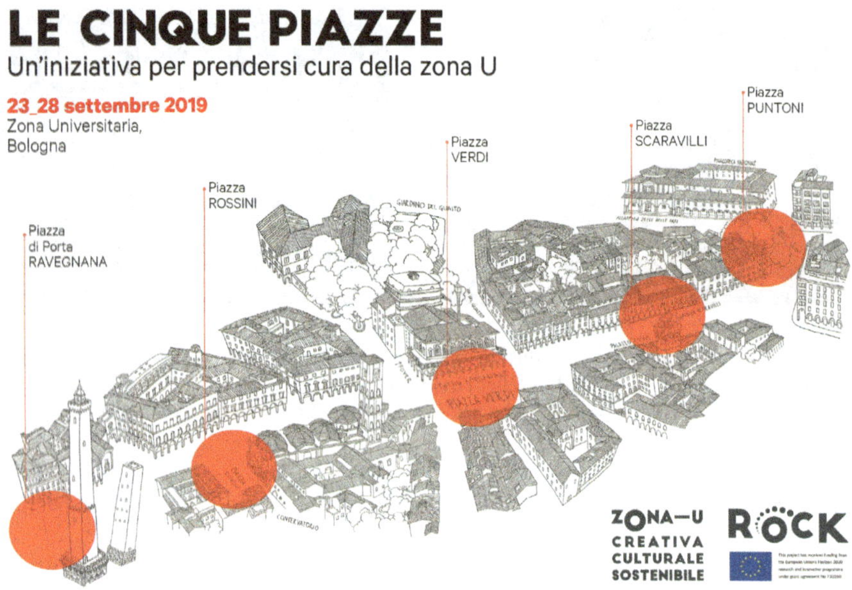

Fig. 3 The Five Square poster event. The five public spaces involved by the project are highlighted in red on the drawing

meadow, restoring the ancient churchyard of San Giacomo Maggiore. In a decentralized position, a large artificial flower—designed by Viabizzuno srl—illuminated the space during the night (Fig. 4).

The idea was born during the participatory laboratory "U-Lab" implemented on this specific area, which was attended by over 250 people and from which emerged the need to restore a social dimension to the square, enhancing the collaboration of all the actors of the territory (institutions, associations, students, etc.), and paying particular attention to greening and lighting.[15]

The intentions come out from the laboratory were later developed and directly realized through a co-design and self-construction workshop, which involved students, researchers and professors of the Department of Architecture of the University of Bologna.

The self-construction set-up was itself intended as a performative event: an active demonstration of re-appropriation of public space and its possible and unconventional use. In addition to students, the process involved various subjects—public and private ones—who coordinated, collaborated and actively took part in

[15]Dossier Piazza Rossini (2018).

Fig. 4 Concept of the temporary project "Green Please! the meadow you don't expect"

the various steps of the staging and the activities organization: University of Bologna, Fondazione Innovazione Urbana, Fondazione Rusconi, "Città Metropolitana" of Bologna, the Viabizzuno srl company, the BAG Studio architectural firm, the Music Conservatory and various cultural associations.

During the experimentation days, the citizens gathered freely on the green carpet, joined the various activities—scheduled and also born spontaneously—and enjoyed this usually passageway of the city in a different way, rediscovering and appreciating the details of the architectures that overlook the square. In a week almost 200,000 people passed by Piazza Rossini, providing a continuous monitoring of the area and showing appreciation for this new form of use.

Fig. 5 Self-construction workshop reportage. Day one: safe delimitation of the area and coverage of the asphalt paving with a plastic sheet

Following the citizens' consent for the initiative and sharing its aims and outcomes, the Municipality of Bologna established that the square will remain pedestrianized, starting a transition path that will transform definitively the square into pedestrian, from temporary experimentation to permanent construction (Figs. 5, 6, 7 and 8).[16]

[16]ROCK sperimenta e Piazza Rossini diventa pedonale—Zona (2019).

Fig. 6 Self-construction workshop reportage. Day two: installation of the flower light element and application of the rolls vegetable meadow

5 Conclusions

The response to the growing need of contemporary cities to re-activate and re-generate neglected, abandoned urban areas and brownfields requires the application of new strategies and new planning, design and governance models. The acknowledgment, the enhancement and the improvement of the value linked to all the components of urban and human capital, are key steps of an integrated and holistic approach, capable of driving participatory and community-place-based projects.

Cultural Heritage—understood as a common pool resource, in its tangible and intangible dimension—represents an opportunity on which the challenge of transforming cities into places of solidarity and real sharing between groups and individuals can be based.

The results obtained thanks to the transformation pilot actions in Piazza Rossini and the other public spaces of the Bologna U-Zone, confirm the value of an approach that—starting from the engagement of underused existing resources in terms of urban and human capital—is able to deal with contemporary challenges and positively affect the consolidated dynamics of urban contexts. The low-cost and

Fig. 7 Self-construction workshop reportage. Day two: break during the rolls meadow application

temporary changes, with low risks and low impact on the consolidated built environment, experimented by the ROCK project, proved their potential in turning temporary actions into a permanent transformation that will definitely return these spaces to citizens. The positive answer of the community showed that the proposals conceived and developed within the participated laboratories and the co-design workshops responded to the real need for different uses and the re-appropriation of the urban public space.

The challenge launched by the initiative, founded in particular on education in the care of public spaces, was met by the city with a sense of participation and responsibility that shows the possibility for new form of collaborative governance processes and models.

The critical reading of the factors that triggered the degradation and abandonment of urban contexts, the people-place-based transformations carried out through democratic and participatory process, the systemisation of different knowledge and skills, the application of research as an active tool, the acknowledge of the potential of Cultural Heritage and Heritage-led good practices, define a value-oriented approach that recognizes the potential of human and urban capital as resources and common goods to be exploited and deployed in urban regeneration processes.

Fig. 8 Self-construction workshop reportage. Day three: Piazza Rossini view from the windows of Palazzo Malvezzi, headquarters of the "Metropolitan City" of Bologna offices

As the historic built environment is an inclusive and comprehensive platform that cannot be understood or managed except through an approach that embraces all its complexity, the European policy for CH recommend "a holistic research agenda and an inclusive interdisciplinary approach" (Sonkoly and Vahtikari 2018), by means of a new vision and mission in heritage management.

The experience of ROCK pilot actions shows the crucial regenerative role of the integration of human, urban and heritage assets. The on-site actions allow to test strategies and to point out constraints, barriers and unexpected positive implications, as happened thanks to the described Piazza Rossini co-design and co-production experience.

However, to extend the scale of interventions and strengthen their potential, an integrated and long-term system of urban governance is needed, to learn and benefit from the test-bed sites actions and to explore ways to best reveal the relations between supranational, national and local policy (Veldpaus 2015). With this aim, ROCK project is developing the Integrated Management Plan (IMP), in which new targets have been established such as the importance of a common ground to define, assess and improve management systems, the mutual exchange of good practices and the evolution of improved management approaches as well as the provision of practical guidance and tools for day-to-day practice recognizing the increased number of stakeholders involved and the awareness of the diversity of governance and management problems linked to each specific country.

Thus, the legacy of ROCK project wants to overcome the experimental dimension of the specific actions by structuring a general methodology that can be replied, as a step-by-step approach, also in the future and in different EU cities.

References

Arena, G. (2007, June 5). *Cittadini e capitale sociale*. Accessed March 18, 2020, from https://www.labsus.org/2007/06/cittadini-e-capitale-sociale/.

Borghi, V. (2017). From knowledge to informational basis: Capability, capacity to aspire and research. *Critical Sociology, 44*(6), 899–920. https://doi.org/10.1177/0896920517705437.

Council of the European Union. (2005). *Council of Europe's Framework Convention on the Value of Cultural Heritage for Society FARO Convention 2005*. Accessed March 15, 2020, from https://rm.coe.int/CoERMPublicCommonSearchServices/DisplayDCTMContent?documentId=0900001680083746.

Council of the European Union. (2014, May 20). *Conclusions on cultural heritage as a strategic resource for a sustainable Europe*. Accessed July 5, 2019, from https://www.consilium.europa.eu/uedocs/cms_data/docs/pressdata/en/educ/142705.pdf.

Directorate-General for Employment, Social Affairs and Inclusion Directorate A. (2018). *Employment and social developments in Europe*. Accessed March 10, 2020, from https://ec.europa.eu/social/main.jsp?catId=738&langId=en&pubId=8110.

Dossier Piazza Rossini. (2018, June 12). Accessed March 18, 2020, from http://dati.comune.bologna.it/node/3518.

Dossier Piazza Scaravilli. (2018, June 8). Accessed March 18, 2020, from http://dati.comune.bologna.it/node/3509.

EUROSTAT. (2019). *People at risk of poverty or social exclusion*. Accessed March 14, 2020, from https://ec.europa.eu/eurostat/statistics-explained/index.php/People_at_risk_of_poverty_or_social_exclusion#Number_of_people_at_risk_of_poverty_or_social_exclusion.

European Commission Directorate-General for Employment, Social Affairs and Inclusion Directorate A. (2016, December). *Employment and social development in Europe 2016 European Commission*. Accessed March 10, 2020, from https://ec.europa.eu/social/BlobServlet?docId=16828&langId=en.

European Union Statistics on Income and Living Conditions (EU-SILC). Accessed March 17, 2020, from https://ec.europa.eu/eurostat/web/microdata/statistics-on-income-and-living-conditions.

Fairclough, G., Dragićević—Šešić, M., Rogač—Mijatović, L., Auclair, E., & Soini, K. (2014). The Faro convention, a new paradigm for socially-and culturally-sustainable heritage action? *Култура/Culture 8*(*8*), 9–19. Accessed March 15, 2020, from https://journals.cultcenter.net/index.php/culture/article/view/111/95.

Grimski, D., & Ferber, U. (2001). Urban brownfields in Europe. *Land Contamination & Reclamation, 9*(1).

Haase, D., Haase, A., & Rink, D. (2014). Conceptualizing the nexus between urban shrinkage and ecosystem services. *Landscape and Urban Planning, 132,* 159–169. https://doi.org/10.1016/j.landurbplan.2014.09.003.

Hopkins, E., & Ferris, J. M. (2015). *Place based initiatives in the context of public policy and markets: Moving to higher ground.* Los Angeles: The Center on Philanthropy and Public Policy.

Iaione, C., & Arena, G. (2012). *L'Italia dei beni comuni* (pp. 109–110). Roma: Carocci.

ICOMOS. (2016). *Cultural Heritage, the UN Sustainable Development Goals, and the New Urban Agenda.* Accessed March 17, 2020, from http://www.usicomos.org/wp-content/uploads/2016/05/Final-Concept-Note.pdf.

International Council on Monuments and Sites, ICOMOS International Cultural Tourism Committee. (2002). *Icomos international cultural tourism charter: principles and guidelines for managing tourism at places of cultural and heritage significance.*

Le Cinque Piazze. (2019). Accessed March 18, 2020, from https://www.fondazioneinnovazioneurbana.it/45-uncategorised/2087-le-cinque-piazze.

Magdaniel, F. T. D., Kask, K. D., Heijer, A. D., & Arkesteijn, M. D. (2018). Innovation reversing abandonment: a systematic literature review on regeneration of historic urban areas. In *25th Annual European Real Estate Society Conference. ERES: Conference. Reading, UK.* https://doi.org/10.15396/eres2018_89.

Rock—Cultural heritage leading urban futures. Accessed March 18, 2020, from https://www.rockproject.eu/.

ROCK sperimenta e Piazza Rossini diventa pedonale—Zona. (2019, October 10). Accessed March 18, 2020, from https://bologna.rockproject.eu/rock-sperimenta-e-piazza-rossini-diventa-pedonale/.

Sassen, S. (2012). Urban capabilities: An essay on our challenges and differences. *Journal of International Affairs, 65*(2 spring/summer), 85–95.

Sonkoly, G., & Vahtikari, T. (2018). Inn*ovation in Cultural Heritage Research For an integrated European Research Policy.* Directorate-General for Research and Innovation Europe in a changing world—Inclusive, innovative and reflective societies (Horizon 2020/SC6) and Cooperation Work Programme: Socio-Economic Sciences and Humanities (FP7). Accessed March 11, 2020, from http://openarchive.icomos.org/2323/1/KI0118044ENN.en(1).pdf.

UNESCO. (2011). *Recommendation on the Historic Urban Landscape, Introduction, point 3.* Accessed March 10, 2020, from https://whc.unesco.org/uploads/activities/documents/activity-638-98.pdf.

Urban Agenda for the EU Pact of Amsterdam. Agreed at the Informal Meeting of EU Ministers Responsible for Urban Matters, Amsterdam, The Netherlands. (2016, May 30). Accessed March 18, 2020, from https://ec.europa.eu/regional_policy/en/information/publications/decisions/2016/pact-of-amsterdam-establishing-the-urban-agenda-for-the-eu.

Veldpaus, L. (2015). *Historic urban landscapes: Framing the integration of urban and heritage planning in multilevel governance.* Eindhoven, The Netherlands: Eindhoven University of Technology.

Vernay, A.-L. (2013). *Circular urban systems: Moving towards systems integration.* Accessed from https://books.google.it/books/about/Circular_Urban_Systems.html?id=JN2JrgEACAAJ&redir_esc=y.

The Social Aesthetics of Cultural Commons

Letteria G. Fassari

Abstract

In this chapter Cultural Commons are placed within the framework of sociological aesthetics in order to grasp the imagery underlying this emerging social form. A series of questions revolve around the issue: what Cultural Commons reveal of the representation of collective life? From which imaginary do they emerge? What subjective orientation do they bring? Why, at the some point, they become an object of interest and debate? Since Cultural Commons are material, immaterial and imaginary spaces, we will consider them as a tension to re-space social experience.

1 Social Aesthetics

Social aesthetics refers to a sociological tradition, which includes both classics such as Simmel and Benjamin, modern and contemporary authors such as Kracauer, Adorno, Bourdieu, Jameson, Nisbet and Maffesoli, just to name a few (Harrington 2004; De La Fuente 2008; Mele 2013). Even in different historical moments and sometimes from not exactly convergent positions, the above mentioned scholars consider aesthetics, not as a pure object of science but a constituent part of it. As a branch of philosophy concerned the value and meaning of artworks, aesthetics has traditionally been focused on the evaluation of autonomous objects such as poems, painting, sculptures and more recently installations and performances. Classic philosophical debates considered the beauty of such art objects as universal. From a different perspective, sociological debates began to study the role of social, cultural,

L. G. Fassari (✉)
Department of Social Sciences and Economics, Sapienza Università di Roma, Rome, Italy
e-mail: letteria.fassari@uniroma1.it

E. Macrì et al. (eds.), *Cultural Commons and Urban Dynamics*,
https://doi.org/10.1007/978-3-030-54418-8_10

and economic conditions in regulating judgments of aesthetic value. The term "social aesthetics" concerns precisely the analysis of social processes activated by works of art considering them as objects, which generate forms of communication. Returning to Simmel one of the variations taken by his intertwining of aesthetics and social is the consideration of the forms of interaction as aesthetic forms. It is precisely this perspective, inspired by Simmel, at the basis of the reflection presented in the chapter.

With the essay Soziologische Ästhetik (2008), Simmel inaugurates a cardinal direction of sociological thought, at the same time paying attention to the subject and the society, on both philosophical and sociological level in order to integrate the value of individual difference with that of collective social belonging. This is the reason why Simmel considers the individualistic demands of modernity to be inconsistent, although it justifies their existence. Vital, social, cultural formal units are fragments of an impossible totality. Nevertheless, the way out of such impasse, intrinsic to modernity, is "relationality". In other words, without an interactive, dynamic, relational configuration, the individual is destined to remain eternally confined to an irremediable conflict between self and community, between self and others. Sociability is, for Simmel, a playful form of association that has no objective; it is intrinsic to the pleasure of being together. Sociability is an art form expressed through movement between the subject and the beauty of sharing. Society is socialization where dynamic forms of relationship give life to a reality of associating that becomes meaningful in the individual's life.

Simmel inspired the idea—still convincing—that life is a negotiation between rationality and imagination, individual and collective, material and immaterial, in which the subject acts incessantly to connect facts/objects through the continuous "compromises" with representations/ideal images. These are necessary negotiations since only the synthesis between rational and imaginary allows the individual to give meaning to existence (Simmel 1918).

The liveliness of Simmellian thought pushes us to place social aesthetics in an area of reflection on the border between imagination and social forms. Simmel, however, is not the only one to resort to the imagination. For example, Nisbet (1976), author of the book "Sociology as an art form", recalls the Weberian insistence on the importance of *Verstehen*, rooted in intuition and in the iconic imagination as the tension to understand the affective dimensions that permeate social life.

Continuing this excursus towards a particular meaning of the relationship between aesthetics, imagination and social, more recently than the classics, it seems impossible to evade the contribution offered by Cornelius Castoriadis and Jean-Jacques Wunenburger.

Castoriadis (1975) writes of the imaginary as a constant and essential creation of figures/forms/images. What we call "reality" and " rationality" are products of imaginary. Referring to institutions, he was interested to understand their symbolic nature because it is in such dimension, which the generation and the stabilisation of common form lay. Castoriadis believes that the functionalist interpretation based on the idea that the institution responds to "real" needs of society is inadequate. Social arrangements are generated from a symbolic frame in constant transformation or, better said, the social-historical world is socially woven in the symbolic. It is not a question of recognizing the importance of the imaginary as an autonomous and neutral dimension but of considering it as the constant production of the symbolic order. The scholar also clarifies the profound and never completely transparent relationship between the symbolic and the imaginary. In essence, the imaginary uses symbolic, not only to express itself but to exist, to move from the virtual to "something more" (ibidem p. 190). Inversely, the symbolic presupposes imaginary capacity.

Wunenburger (2008) referring to the functions performed by imaginary already present in ancient thought, extricates three orientations: one is the playful aesthetic function regarding the ability to anticipate social roles. Another is the cognitive function connected to find unexpected solutions or insights that do not follow the linearity of rational logic. A third is an institutional-practical orientation. It is this last that is pertinent to our thesis. According to Wunenburger, the imaginary not only satisfies sensitivity and thought but also constitutes the potency that underlies social action. The imagination is the basis of the energy that pushes individuals to act socially to change the status quo.

Obviously institutions are not only symbolic systems, but, following Castoriadis, we must ask ourselves why the generative symbolic tension becomes social forms. In this work, we will try to answer this question. Let us first try to understand which characteristics specify Cultural Commons.

2 Defining Cultural Commons

In 2012 in the book "Cultural Commons" by Bertacchini et al. the question of defining them is posed in terms that all commons are in some way Cultural Commons (Hess 2008 cited in Bertacchini), and this could represent the real challenge marking terminological boundaries.

Originally, the term common is referred to the common land used for grazing; it was used to describe, in general, the common environmental resources: earth, air, water, etc. Subsequently, the meaning expanded to include human-made shared resources. In particular, the term has acquired specific relevance in the field of knowledge including culture, health, information but also cultural heritage such as traditions or art.

By placing the question within the perspective of the rational choice, the problem translates into term of contributor's opportunism. Like natural commons, Cultural Commons are shared collective goods with one crucial difference; they are not resources that can be eroded by overuse such as pastures or forests (Ostrom 1990, 2002). Cultural Commons do not suffer from limited load capacity. The consumption of culture, information, etc. not only does not reduce its value but can be increased with their use and the interaction. Listening to music, enjoying a painting, or sharing a poem are not highly generative common cultural resources of value (Santagata et al. 2011). Although Cultural Commons are less likely to suffer from what is called the "common goods tragedy" (Hardin 1968), they are not entirely immune from social dilemmas. They can undergo the difficulty of passing from one generation to another without losing their value. Besides, following the critical theories (see para 5), they can be exploited the interests of businesses through privatization.

Instead, if we move towards social movements, drawing on a long history of protests, the defence of cultural heritage has been made by its own movements that can be defined as anti-capitalists. Examples could be the protest movements against biopiracy, the patenting of life forms such as plants and the exploitation of traditional knowledge of their varieties (see Shiva 1997); the *Open source movement* is also a challenge to maintain the software public ensuring its use but avoiding its appropriation. This movement has inspired similar initiatives to make creative works (literature, photography, music) information (Parker et al. 2007).

In the light of the above considerations and from a socio-aesthetics perspective, Cultural Commons are not merely "a resource" but imply the presence of a community and its orientation to preserve its heritage. According with Hess (2008), which defines commons as tension to see what is shared, we will try to understand why and how the logic of sharing becomes a social aesthetic form.

3 Cultural Commons as Social Aesthetic

In order to place Cultural Commons in an aesthetic-social perspective, it is necessary to make a premise. We will therefore start from considering contemporary narrative mainly centred on the transition from traditional capitalism—as Weber describes it—to contemporary capitalism. This step took place by pivoting on the double movement intrinsic to modernity relative to subjectivation and rationalisation, which in contemporary modernity tend to radicalize.

The unfolding of modern and the most recent changes—globalisation, affirmation of technologies, neoliberalism, etc.—has made it very difficult to keep these two poles united within a framework that enhances personal meaning and collective narration. The result is, therefore, a separation between actor and system and a fragmentation of the epistemological, cultural and social frameworks previously integrated into that representation of collective life that we call modernity. According to Magatti (2009), a contemporary partial and illusory re-composition is provided by a particularly useful paradigm, the neo-evolutionist one. It constitutes the epistemological background of the new neoliberal policies. The paradigm is entirely in agreement with the idea that the market logic could solve the problems of effectiveness and efficiency of the institutions; it is also perfectly compatible with biotechnological IT paradigms affirmation; but, above all, it weaves with the rising of individualist culture which makes freedom of choice its mantra against the rigidity of institutionalised life. As Foucault (2005) had anticipated, the emergence of the neo-evolutionistic paradigm is at the basis of the neo-liberal turn of social regulation; it produces a governmental modality of biopolitical power that undermines the subject in terms of autonomy and self-determination. The subject is the objective of a continuous solicitation to the self-realization, to self-government and personal autonomy.

The previously visible social powers are disarticulated and governed through economic modus—strategic and competitive logic, which is considered as natural or real. The disciplinary government that assimilates the conduct to an ex-ante rule is replaced by a very effective technique of governing lives that is exercised ex-post emerging from the standards used as qualitative indicators (Bazzicalupo 2006). In other words, the system presents itself by promising not to exclude anyone ex-ante, but it is individual behaviours that become standard, that is emerging from below.

From the sociological aesthetic point of view, it is important to underline what authors such as Boltansky and Chiappello, Magatti and Perniola highlight: without the imaginary of freedom neoliberalism could not have had this disruptive and pervasive force. The new spirit of capitalism (Boltansky and Chiappello 1999) is the result of the integration between this drive or the desire of individuals to be actors in their existence (Touraine 1981) and the reorganisation of the logic of capitalist accumulation centred on flexibility and innovation. Such spirit was also fuelled by some aspects of the philosophies that had supported the subjectivist turn of the 1960s as existentialism did. If in Protestant ethics, the commitment and success in worldly activities constituted proof of divine grace, in the new spirit of capitalism, the task of realising oneself coincides with the liberation from any constraint. In contemporary capitalism, the value of freedom of choice prevails over the stability needs of the group. According to this interpretation, the plot of social relationships characterised the loosening of cultural ties and solidarity is replaced by stripping of the social bond, which is reduced to its functional nature (Magatti 2009). Here, it is not a question of putting moral criticism into play. More simply inference is that the functional performance pushes the social experience to adhere to the new spirit of capitalism that requires enjoyment because the more one enjoys, the more one consumes (Lacan 2001; Recalcati 2010). Even if we assume the Lacanian perspective or if we turn to the Jungian one (Hillman and Kerényi 1991), enjoyment is opposed to desire because it has an element of compulsiveness and of not processing reality.

From the standpoint of radical sociology, Mark Fisher defines the phenomenon as “capitalist realism” (Fisher 2009). Fisher speaks of capitalist realism as a dreamlike form represented, for example, in the dystopian cyber nihilistic culture of the nineties. The pamphlet describes a transversal reading of the dominant imaginaries. Fisher’s thesis is straightforward: there are no alternatives to capitalism; the melancholic nostalgia for a future that no longer exists pervades culture, policies and consumption. Capitalist realism is the widespread feeling that not only capitalism is the only possible political and economic system, but also that any alternative is unthinkable today. Aesthetics has lost its meaning. From the translation of any cultural object into the monetary value, we have experienced the absence of tension between the opposites from which the symbol emerges. The meaning is enclosed in itself.

According to Fisher, capitalist realism has settled in our unconscious and occupies the whole horizon of the thinkable. The forms of resistance are so helpless and desperate that we cannot think opposing them. A moral critique based on topics such as poverty, hunger, wars, reinforces it because these are understood as inevitable aspects of reality. Any critical tension within capitalist realism is guilty of naive utopianism. Capitalist realism submits to us an infinitely plastic reality capable of being configured only in terms of the fungible present. In the capitalist realism, emphasis is on performance evaluation determined by the quantification of any form of work. We are not faced with a direct comparison between performances and results but between the duly quantified "representation" of performances and results. Furthermore, the performances are intrinsically communicative and permeate at all levels. That of evaluation and promotion seems to be a totalizing logic imposed and aspired by all. We are willing to yield to the pressure of the "representation" policy.

This long premise, before entering the heart of the aesthetics of Cultural Commons summarizes the hegemonic literature in defining the cultural characteristics of contemporary capitalism. To understand the imaginary of Cultural Commons, we must try to oppose these arguments with the empirical grounded work of François Dubet and particularly his definition of social experience. This concept can help us to get out of the desperate view of the critical theory in which capitalist realism seems to be the point of no return.

At the basis of Dubet's (1994) argument, we find the idea that social experience is not an uninterrupted flow but responds to different logics in tension. The scholar distinguishes at least three logics that I can only mention here. One of these coincides with the subject's need to be an actor of his own experience (subjectivation). Another is aimed at being rewarded for the commitment and skills within society (strategy). Finally, a third logic is that of wanting to feel part of a community (belonging). Experience is always the result of a combination of logics that come under tension. The experience Dubet will say is still dramatic in the sense that it emerges from a strenuous process of having to respond to logics in opposition to each other. It is possible that in particular historical moments, a logic of action will be remarkably present and widespread, but, in any case, it will come into tension with its opposites.

A vision where social action coincides with systemic prescription, it can only make sense if the actor is totally socialised but, as Dubet stated, *the actor is never fully socialised*. In other word, capitalist realism and other radical representations present themselves as interpretative models that are too clean to account for the experience that is defined by the combination of heterogeneous logics. What Dubet brings into play is the fact that social experience is inherently critical, as social researchers we always detect a "tension" between the system and the actor. On the actors' side, there is still a practice of justification, of critical reading of their experience. To make sense of their "experience" individuals are hooking it on criteria of justice, authenticity and truth showing a distance from it (*ibidem*).

In conclusion, if you accept the idea that social experience is composed of several logics, this necessarily implies an exercise of reflexivity as capacity for permanent criticism even within a domain system.

Returning to Cultural Commons through Dubet's work, we can hypothesize that Cultural Commons emerges as a compensatory and rebalancing response, an output of the critical capacity intrinsic to social experience that leads subjects to activate spaces in which they can feel themselves in the bond with others and with their own history. The Cultural Commons perhaps show the need for new social forms in which the moral norm is not the one imposed by the modernity institutions or the functional standards conveyed by the neo-liberalist but a relational social fabric, symbolically dense in which the dimension of sharing brings out the varieties of forms.

4 Relational Aesthetics as Tension to *Re-Spatialized* Social Experience

There are many factors, which influence the way we *spatialise* our experience and how this, in turn, re-configures the space. About globalisation, the process concerns the globality of risks, the pluralisation and pluri-localisation of subjectivity through communication, tourism, trade, migration, etc. As Morin (1986) had foreshadowed: each part becomes part of the world itself, the whole world is increasingly present in each of its parts.

The extensiveness and depth of the changes lead to what Knoblauch and Löw (2017) define as the "re-figuration" of space. It allows all structural layers from local to global to be represented as interconnected and intertwined. The re-figuration of space is a conceptualized process that emerges from the analysis of the collision, tension and conflict between different logics. Logics, which arise from below, defined by daily social, affective and imaginary actions (Löw 2016). In this sense, Cultural Commons are action of "spacing" (*ibidem* p. 134) in my view understood as subjectively oriented. They emerge from negotiations with material and imaginary elements but filtered by a subjective logic of action.

Cultural Commons present themselves as the response to the effects of globalisation as an end of the social (Touraine 2005). It can be hypothesized that they are configured as circumscribed relational structures that are probably more fragile but at the same time are bearers of subjectively oriented logics. They oppose a renewed spacing logic to the spatial compression of cultures and forms of life (Harvey 2010). In summary, as Alice Borchi (2018) said, Cultural Commons are seen as a way of reacting to commodification and precariousness; a way to feed the sense of belonging, the stratification of public memory, and the incorporation of cultural heritage as counteracting the negative impact of neoliberal policies.

This hypothesis finds confirmation in the essay by the philosopher Elena Pulcini, author of the evocative book *La cura del mondo: paura e responsabilità nell'età globale* (2009). In a most recent article on the relational aesthetics of Cultural

Commons, Pulcini (2013) defines Cultural Commons as the tension to reconstruct common being.

Interdependence and connectivity permeate the aesthetic of Cultural Commons. In the 90s, thanks to the rise of the network as infrastructure, as well as organizational and social forms, but also thanks to the planetary utopia by Pierre Levy, relational aesthetic emerges as the new *mantra*. In Lévy's conception the network is not only an isolated mechanism for the coordination of a limited set of activities but an ethical, political and epistemic-logical horizon in the process of sharing human society in this current social and technological phase of development (Lévy 1994).

The culture of the network as described by techno-enthusiastic conveys values of sharing, collaboration, and sociability. The technological infrastructures that characterize techno-nihilist capitalism (Magatti 2009), on the one hand generate entropy and self-destruction, on the other, produce relational goods as trust, friendship and solidarity. They can neither be created nor consumed, therefore cannot be acquired independently by a single individual because they depend on interactions and enjoyed when are being shared (Pulcini 2013). Relational goods, as Pulcini points out, grow with time and with relationships; unlike common goods (especially material), as already specified, if not used, they lose their value. Their essential characteristic is, therefore, reciprocity. What makes us so willing to exchange ideas, creativity, material and immaterial spaces with each other? For the author, that particular feeling that predisposes us to the solidarity to which we give the name of empathy or the ability to understand the other, to identify oneself (*Ibidem*).

Also in the field of contemporary art, the French curator and critic Nicolas Bourriaud analyses the artistic practices of the nineties in terms of relational aesthetics. Relational art includes those creative paths based on intersubjectivity and relationality with the involvement of the public, which becomes not only a spectator, but the architect of the work. As Bourriaud states (2001) the meaning seems to emerge from the installation of the forms, from how they relate to each other and the way they are organised in the artistic space. Bourriaud formulates a new concept of art space that becomes a social and physical space where artist and audience collaborate for the *opus*. Bourriaud's writings were debated and sharply criticised. The most important criticism is that of assimilating an aesthetic judgment with an ethical-political one of the relationships produced by the works. However, from a sociological aesthetic point of view, it seems to indicate that the metaphor of relationality is a crosscutting concept.

5 Relational Aesthetics as a Productive Force

In this concluding paragraph, we will address the risks of common goods from the perspective of critical theories. Negri and Hardt define biopower in the sense of conjunction between instrumental action of economic production and communicative action of human relations (Negri and Hardt 2000). The concept of *General Intellect,* which is a crucial concept of their theorising, describes the transformation of the nature of the workforce. Whereas previously, the labour force was defined primarily through physical rather than mental abilities, now, as Virno claims, it includes in itself the life of the mind (2001). Where previously capital could have been concerned only with how a worker can use an instrument or serve to a machine, today he is increasingly interested in minds, not only in the knowledge or information, but also in desires or imaginary. In this sense, the capital is interested in exploiting the social assembly, which includes machinery and broader social flows with particular interest in social bonds. These are exploited as shared infrastructure within which it is possible to create value (Lazzarato 1997). The criticisms of the autonomist Marxists certainly have a specific theoretical attraction.

According to Terranova (2004), digital economy constitutes the space in which externalities can be captured and valued, in which knowledge, communication, cooperation and sharing can be transformed into economic exchanges. In a word, the digital economy is the space in which Cultural Commons becomes productive.

So far I have tried to make clear some rhetoric within which Cultural Commons has been posed. I use the term rhetoric without any negative meaning but only as discursive form in order to understand the request for Cultural Commons. Each repertoire has its *raison d'etre*. However, referring to the social experience in the terms I have discussed above, it is essential to investigate whether, in what contexts, under what conditions and for what reasons the Cultural Commons can go further and become a common resource that wants to be preserved. As I have tried to show, it could indicate the return of the subject to society with their generative power of creativity (Touraine 1995).

References

Bazzicalupo, L. (2006). *Il governo delle vite. Biopolitica ed economia*. Bari-Roma: Laterza.

Bertacchini, E., Bravo, G., Marelli, M., & Santagata, W. (2012). *Cultural commons: A new perspective on the production and evolution of cultures*. Cheltenham UK: Edward Elgar Publishing.

Boltanski, L., & Chiapello, E. (1999). *Le nouvel esprit du capitalisme*. Paris: Gallimard.

Borchi, A. (2018). Culture as commons: Theoretical challenges and empirical evidence from occupied cultural spaces in Italy. *Journal Cultural Trends, 27*, 33–45.

Bourriaud, N. (2001). *Esthétique relationelle*. Paris: Les presses du réel.

Castoriadis, C. (1975). *L'institution imaginaire de la société*. Paris: Seuil.

De La Fuente, E. (2008). The art of social forms and the social forms of art: The sociology-aesthetics Nexus in Georg Simmel's thought. *Sociological Theory, 26*, 344–362.

Dubet, F. (1994). *Sociologie de l'expérience*. Paris: Le Seuil.

Fisher, M. (2009). *Capitalist realism: Is there no alternative? Hants*. UK: John Hunt Publishing.

Foucault, M. (2005). *Nascita della biopolitica*. Corso al Collège de France. (1978–1979). Milano: Feltrinelli.

Hardin, G. (1968). The tragedy of the commons. *Science, 162*, 1243–1248.

Harrington, A. (2004). *Art and Social Theory: Sociological Arguments in Aesthetics*. Cambridge UK: Polity Press.

Harvey, D. (2010). *La crisi della modernità*. Milano: Il Saggiatore.

Hess, C. (2008). *Mapping the new commons*. SSRN. Disponibile in https://ssrn.com/abstract=1356835. Last accedes May 10, 2020.

Hillman, J., & Kerényi, K. (1991). *Oedipus variations*. Dallas: Spring Publications.
Knoblauch, H., & Löw, M. (2017). On the spatial re-figuration of the social world. *Sociologica, Italian Journal of Sociology On Line, 11*, 0–0.
Lacan, J. (2001). *Il seminario. Libro XVII. Il rovescio della psicoanalisi*. Torino: Giulio Einaudi Editore.
Lazzarato, M. (1997). *Lavoro Immateriale: Forme di Vita e Produzione di Soggettività*. Verona: Ombre Corte.
Lévy, P. (1994). *L'intelligence collective: Pour une anthropologie du cyberspace*. Paris: La Découverte.
Löw, M. (2016). *The sociology of space: Materiality, social structures, and action*. Berlin: Springer.
Magatti, M. (2009). *Libertà immaginaria. Le illusioni del capitalismo tecno-nichilista*. Milano: Feltrinelli.
Mele, V. (2013). *Aesthetics and social theory*. Roma: Aracne.
Morin, E. (1986). *La Méthode III. La connaissance de la connaissance*. Paris: Edition du Seuil. (A. Serra, Trad. (1989). La conoscenza della conoscenza. Milano: Feltrinelli).
Negri, A., & Hardt, M. (2000). *Empire*. Cambridge, Mass.: Harvard University Press.
Nisbet, R. (1976). *Sociology as an art form*. London: Oxford University Press.
Ostrom, E. (1990). *Governing the commons: The evolution of institutions for collective action*. Cambridge. UK: Cambridge University Press. (Trad. (2006). Governare i beni collettivi. Venezia: Marsilio.
Ostrom, E. (2002). Managing resources in the global commons. *Journal of Business Administration and Policy Analysis, 30–31*, 401–413.
Parker, M., Fournier, V., & Reedy, P. (2007). *The dictionary of alternatives. Utopianism and Organization*. London: Zed Books.
Pulcini, E. (2009). *La cura del mondo. Paura e responsabilità nell'età globale*. Torino: Bollati Boringhieri.
Pulcini, E. (2013). Beni comuni: un concetto in progress. *Politica & Società Periodico di filosofia politica e studi sociali, 3*, 349–356.
Recalcati, M. (2010). *L'uomo senza inconscio: Figure della nuova clinica psicoanalitica*. Milano: Cortina.
Santagata, W., Bertacchini, E., Bravo, G., & Marrelli, M. (2011, January). *Cultural commons and cultural communities*. Paper presented to Sustaining Commons: Sustaining Our Future, the Thirteenth Biennial Conference of the International Association for the Study of the Commons, Hyderabad, India.
Shiva, V. (1997). *Biopiracy: The plunder of nature and knowledge*. Boston: South End.
Simmel, G. (1918). *Lebensanschauung*. Vier metaphysischen Kapitel. (Antinolfi, G. Trad. (1997). Intuizione della vita. Quattro capitoli metafisici. Napoli: Edizioni Scientifiche Italiane.
Simmel, G. (2008). *Soziologische Ästhetik*. Berlino: Springer.
Terranova, T. (2004). *Network culture. Politics for the information age*. London: Pluto Press.
Touraine, A. (1981). Le retour de l'acteur. *Cahiers internationaux de sociologie, 71*, 243–255.
Touraine, A. (1995). *Critique of modernity*. Cambridge, Mass: Blackwell.
Touraine, A. (2005). *Un nouveau paradigme: Pour comprendre le monde d'aujourd'hui*. Paris: Fayard.
Virno, P. (2001). *Grammatica della moltitudine: per una analisi delle forme di vita contemporanee*. Soveria Mannelli: Rubbettino Editore.
Wunenburger, J. J. (2008). *L'immaginario*. Genova: Il Nuovo Melangolo.

From Digitalisation to Crowdfunding Platforms: Fomenting the Cultural Commons

Carolina Dalla Chiesa

Abstract

Digitalisation has allowed various theoretical perspectives and empirical examples to emerge within both market and non-market realms. One of them is the so-called "crowdfunding": an online tool widely used for both commercial and non-commercial purposes. Cultural commons, digital commons, private goods and projects with public good characteristics can all benefit from accessing the "crowd's" support via money contribution and matchmaking supply and demand. This chapter argues that, due to its hybrid features, crowdfunding is overlooked as a tool that firstly promotes diversity, long-tail initiatives, "do-it-yourself" projects and creations of many sorts precisely because of its openness. By allowing that bottom-up solutions emerge without having to pass through traditional certifiers and gatekeepers, crowd-validation tools proportionate a fruitful environment for the "new commons" to thrive. The essay, hence, assumes a normative perspective by which social surpluses, positive externalities and increasing social welfare depend on users having access to digital infrastructures that convey diversity.

1 Introduction

Since the first appearances of the World Wide Web, scholars have attempted to theorise the uses and of the digital landscapes. Nowadays, the digital landscape is no longer considered a "novelty", although new ways of interacting, exchanging and trading are progressively implemented with the aid of digital tools. Digitalisation has

C. Dalla Chiesa (✉)
Erasmus School of History, Culture and Communication, Rotterdam, The Netherlands
e-mail: c.dallachiesa@eshcc.eur.nl

E. Macrì et al. (eds.), *Cultural Commons and Urban Dynamics*,
https://doi.org/10.1007/978-3-030-54418-8_11

become an inescapable path in the daily lives of people regardless of their social class, geographic regions and gender sometimes helping social, political and cultural agendas to face new upbringings. Digitalisation has also unveiled the power of algorithms in shaping consumption patterns especially in the case of sharing information, cultural goods and political agendas.

Digital infrastructures can both help bottom-up collective actions to develop more rapidly than the pre-digitalisation period and enhance markets that would otherwise suffer to reach consumers without a great deal of gatekeeper intermediation. That is the case for most of the cultural good traded privately, but also online petitions, voluntary aid, collective engagement and political activists that benefit from having access to larger audiences through online means. "Do-it-yourself" cultural expressions can also emerge within platforms devoted to long-tail[1] suppliers and their potential audiences, as it is the case for crowdsourcing and crowdfunding tools. Whereas crowdsourcing typically aims at engaging a large pool of consumers in the product development phase to better provide goods or services put at the test of user experience, crowdfunding makes use of a large pool of supporters to collectively fundraise initiatives that speak to their motivations: charitable giving, community engagement or only pre-buying innovative products as early adopters.[2] In all cases, the aid of many seems to enlarge diversity and the realisation of cultural commons.

Within crowdfunding platforms, the pressing need that independent ventures, niche artists and start-up initiatives have with raising funds make the case for a bottom-up solution in which projects are subject to the crowd's validation. This is represented in the "game-like" mechanism of "all-or-nothing" funding, meaning that a project only moves forward if the funding goal is reached and a sufficient crowd of supporters believes in it.

The chapter argues that crowdfunding is a hybrid commercial and non-commercial tool that facilitates, among other goals, that cultural commons become diverse and spread, due to the outreach of digital websites. As such, it would allow the emergence of niches driven by matchmaking of supply and demand. Online crowdfunding remains a perennial tool at the service of "long-tail" projects and small-scale entrepreneurs to test demand and innovate when traditional routes (certifiers, gatekeepers, banks, venture capitalists) seem unreachable. Hence, crowdfunding ideally allows cultural resources to be accessed on a larger scale due to promoting diversity of options and more competition in the market for cultural goods.

This essay does not conceptualise cultural commons per se, but rather the way through which online platforms can help their flourishing. The chapter starts with a brief historical outlook about optimistic *versus* pessimistic approaches to digitalisation that have guided scholars in the past decades. Secondly, it reviews the main

---

[1]The widely cited work of Anderson (2006) guides this assumption.

[2]The *equity crowdfunding* (Ahlers et al. 2015) type is not cited here on purpose as profit-sharing schemes are better understood in comparison to typical investment behavior and traditional financing models (i.e., bank loans, venture capital and angel investment).

features of shared infrastructures and how they connect to digital environments such as crowdsourcing and crowdfunding initiatives. It concludes by arguing that among various online platforms that allow the expression of cultural commons, crowdfunding can be regarded as a valuable tool for societies to access more diverse cultural options and enhance bottom-up initiatives to arise while bypassing gatekeepers and traditional institutions.

2 Two-Sided Digitalisation: Critical *Versus* Optimistic Approaches

Digitalisation has changed dramatically the forms of communication and interaction. It is unnecessary to point out the various ways through which the Internet has made human lives both easier and more complex. Whereas the changes it brought are consensual to most scholars, its consequences are not. To cite a few perspectives, the power of algorithms in shaping knowledge is often object of critical constructivist analysis of technology (Mager 2012) as much as the negative connotation of images without a referent grounded in the work of Jean Baudrillard.[3] In the first critical approach, also more recent, the digital world is a result of a political economy of algorithms; and in the second case, and more ancient, the digital represents the hyperreal condition: making the image more real than the real itself.[4]

This is a relevant approach to critically interpret consumerism within a virtual reality paradigm whereby citizens become consumers driven by a poverty of substance. Even though Baudrillard has not directly addressed the World Wide Web, his writings have unveiled provocative thoughts to interpret how the virtual means of communication and the excesses of media guide our daily lives (Nunes 1995). As Merrin (2001) says, these formulations tend to repeat the western political hopes whereby "the real" has to be defended.

On the optimistic side, scholars like Lévy (1997) have observed that the internet could become a "global village" once conceptualised by McLuhan and Powers (1986), whereby humankind is all interconnected. The "collective intelligence" of many would provide better grounds for decision-making of individuals, governments and groups through sharing knowledge in real time with the aid of the Internet. This is possible only if online infrastructures are in place in order to allow immediate interconnection—a discussion much present throughout the 1990s when

[3]Numerous scholars had influence his thoughts with regard to critically interpreting the fetishism of images—an aspect already discussed in the work of Marx as well as later in Walter Benjamin's *aura* (Merrin 2001). In general, the critical approach of the sociologists Adorno and Horkheimer (1997) had contributed to deny the benefits of reproducibility, of which digitalisation is a major result. As a consequence of this perspective, one can assume that digitalisation magnifies the effects of reproducibility.

[4]The underlying rationale is that one cannot know whether the signs available are a representation of the reality or the reality itself once the referent is absent. Baudrillard's observations on excessive consumerism says that "the referential substance is becoming increasingly rare" (1996, pp. 29–30), which means that we consume without referents.

much of the developed and underdeveloped world had not seen the daily effects of digitalisation to a greater extent.

This rather hopeful perspective about the new possibilities of the post-digitalised world is often enrobed with the notion of "democracy". Scholars have often used the internet democracy to imagine how societies can better foster open and free forms of expression. This techno-utopia[5] communicates that progress is based on access to infrastructure, machineries and digital tools that promote the progress of democracy around the globe. As a consequence, mankind would ideally become better informed in matters that involve collective decision-making.

Extensive studies like "The Wealth of Networks", by Benkler (2006), show the greater benefits that networked economies have in contrast to hierarchical structures. By favoring the importance of network versus hierarchies, Benkler's goal is to show how mankind can greatly appropriate shared infrastructures toward the benefit of us all. This utopian angle is also balanced with a more realist political economy of information understanding that often pushes hopes to a different path. In the long run, companies often make use of a network economy discourse in order to implement project-based performance and managerial tools that remain within typical industrial structures. As Boltanski, Chiapello and Elliott (2005) contend, management practices have greatly incorporated a so-called "neoliberal" rationale in which network structures are often used in favor or corporations augmenting profits while reducing the rights of the working class.

The first perspective overestimates the individual contrarily to the second, which amplifies the collective action aspect. Whereas the first skeptical approach emphasizes the individualist, rent-seeking behavior and some virtual loss of human connection, the second over-stresses the potential of collective action, bottom-up actions and freedom of expression. The first stream of thought seems perfect for the realisation of profit-making endeavors, private goods and excludability, whereas the second seems likely to flourish with non-profit firms, public or common goods and non-excludability. Although this binary narrative is not always perceived like that[6] in empirical settings, excessively hopeful and critical theoretical approaches can be opposed to a certain extent.

To stay within cultural goods domain, music and movie streaming platforms are exemplary cases of how recommendation systems instruct consumers on their related interests. On a broader scale, recent cases of democratic disruption such as fake news boosted by algorithms (Lee 2019) have also shown a facade of

[5]Techno-utopians typically describe a future reality in which the present conditions are improved with the aid of technologies and machinery that make our lives better (Dickel and Schrape 2017). Historically, different techno-utopias have been communicated, especially after the various Industrial Revolutions. The latest object of techno-utopia is digitalisation and its tools: crowdsourcing, blockchain, social media, etc. In contrast, critical perspectives have shown the limits of this approach as often the basic conditions of production and consumption are not overall changed after the introduction of new media devices.

[6]The advent of digitalisation and the information society as a precursor for flatter organisations is most often an utopic assumption. Pragmatic outlooks such as Brown and Duguid (2000), for instance, observe that a more balanced view is needed, given that desintermediation doesn't necessarily do away with intermediaries.

digitalisation that depicts self-contained domains of interest and nudging political support against democratic principles. Nevertheless, both examples cannot be put together under the same scrutiny given that one is motivated by a somewhat liberal in-demand consumption of music whereas the second case typically shades its funding sources, which makes democratic principles convulse to a certain extent.

These are instances where the motivation of agents behind the actions matter as they shape the infrastructures and their consequences. In the theory of institutional analyses proposed by Ostrom (1990), the incentives of users with building up collective or proprietary management of resources should be considered as they base the rules and the management of resources put in place. Some digital resource management tools can lead to collective-owned solutions whereas others can lead to proprietary enclosed systems. What is more, digital tools can be organized under a market domain where the exchange of supply and demand under certain rules prevail, whereas others fit better under non-market domain where open source and sharing cultural commons may prevail.

Just as in any "offline" domain, markets and non-market realms coexist with realizing commercial and non-commercial purposes together. This is also the case for online realms where tools for private realisation of goals coexist with publicly motivated ones. As the next section depicts, digital platforms can realise these commercial, non-commercial goals, and also a third case which entails a combination of both at once.

3 Digital Platforms: Commercial and Non-commercial Uses

Since the seminal work of Elinor Ostrom on the institutional characteristics and consequences of collective management of common resources, we know that the "tragedy of the commons" (Hardin 1968) can be avoided once alternative bottom-up management of resources emerges. Typically understood as rival and non-excludable goods, natural resources can always be on the verge of depletion. Alternatives exist for communities, countries and groups interested in maintaining their resources available, despite the threats of "free-riding" and "rational-choice"[7] action. With the dissemination of digital tools and social media websites, the commons have also been associated with sharing resources other than natural ones, such as knowledge, information, culture and heritage.

Cultural commons have been, thus, theorised as a derivation of the Institutional Analysis and Development Framework (IAD) matured by Ostrom's understanding of Commons governance. In this realm, open-source alternatives, Wikipedia (Madison et al. 2010), universities, "jam sessions" in music gathering, and other similar cases in which a community of practice both establishes its own rules and

[7]The Rational-Choice Theory depicts among other assumptions, the *homo-economicus* behavior, independent, utility-maximizer and rational for whom collective-dependent behavior would be atypical.

distributes ownership to a certain extent. The "new commons" (Hess 2008) exist without pre-arranged institutional frameworks. Usually they share the premise of implementing "joint ownership" which implies that non-proprietary systems are in place. As Ostrom (2010) observes, much work remained to be done in order to better grasp the institutional features of cultural commons, as these are common resources that do not fall under the same tragedy of depletion.[8] As Hess (2008) observes, these types of "new commons" exist without pre-arranged institutional frameworks.

Cultural commons can be observed in the empirical cases of communities of practices where open management standards guide the provision of goods. Within online environments, these new commons are better off managed in shared infrastructures driven by open-source ideals. This is the case for various free-software movements, "hacker groups" (Himanen 2001; Coleman 2013), "free culture" advocates (Lessig 2005) and other communities of practices where the technical aspects of digitalisation are intertwined with the morals of distributed networks.[9] These communities have already been widely observed, described and discussed as cases in which distributed systems lead to sharing knowledge and, therefore, social surpluses of many sorts.[10] Most often, these groups are aided by online platforms that can act either as free repositories or, as proprietary websites. The second case represents what we understand as "two-sided markets".

On the other side of the digital spectrum, empirical and conceptual observations have shown the emergence of two-sided market platforms, which act as match-makers between supply and demand (Rochet and Tirole 2003): a typical function of markets taken to the digital realm. Two-sided or multi-sided markets operate by charging one or two parties for the service provided to all, a matchmaking service in which suppliers more likely have better chances to meet their suppliers if entry-barriers are low and price structure meets the willingness to pay of consumers. In many cases (such as movies and music streaming platforms) the business model and its price structure are sufficient to prevent unauthorized copying of digital content. As such, platforms like eBay, Amazon, Spotify and others supply private goods created by third parties by charging a fee for online services.

Two-sided platforms can also benefit projects with a common purpose and public good characteristics as long as the matchmaking fee services are applied to one or more parties involved in the transactions. In this sense, platforms do not withhold content per se, but rather facilitate the transmission of a message to other parties, peers or consumers. Some examples of two-sided platforms that allow private goods, cultural commons and calls with public good characteristics altogether are GoFundMe (a donation crowdfunding website), Kiva (crowd-lending platform), Patreon (subscription website for creatives) and Kickstarter (a reward-based platform).

[8]To cite the famous "Tragedy of the Commons" (Hardin 1968) essay, based on which Ostrom (1990) develops an alternative analysis of how resources can be collectively organised in order to bypass both depletion and the "individual-rational" behavior depicted by neoclassical economics.
[9]Its antipodal case for "open-source" solutions is any product organised under "proprietary" systems.
[10]A comprehensive study about the heterogeneous groups that embody the notion of "new commons" can be found in Hess (2008).

Table 1 Taxonomy of types of goods according to the economic theory

	Private and club goods	Commons and quasi-public goods
Type of venture	Commercial ventures	Non-commercial ventures
Incentives	Monetary incentives	Non-monetary incentives
Agency	Individual agent	Collective agent
Platform role	Platforms as matchmaking supply and demand	Platforms as matchmaking collaboration
Motivation	Crowdfunding for pre-ordering in-demand products	Crowdfunding for supporting social causes

Source Elaboration of the author
In some cases, crowdfunding calls can exert both commercial and non-commercial motivations at the same time by offering a range of rewards that contain both products and gifts

Crowdfunding platforms can be interpreted as two-sided markets (Viotto-da-Cruz 2015) regardless of its user's motivations (commercial or non-commercial). As any two-sided market, crowdfunding ones charge one party for accessing consumers who buy suppliers' products. More than that, crowdfunding also charges suppliers of goods with no commercial value, whose *raison d'être* is better associated with the "gift-economy" principles (Klamer 2003). Crowdfunding, thus, acts as a singular case of a platform that articulates various types of goods and their producers' motivation. As long as suppliers pay the fees concerning the platform services,[11] both commercial and non-commercial projects can be found (Table 1).

More than other types of digital tools, crowdfunding accepts a wide diversity of products and motivations unlikely to happen in other similar cases. As the next section shows, this fundraising tool originates from the larger picture of crowdsourcing which also allows both commercial and non-commercial goals to be realised. In both cases of crowd-intervention, users can direct these tools to their self-interest goal at the service or not of common-purpose results.

4 From Crowdsourcing to Crowdfunding

Much before crowdfunding emerged around 2004 with the platform *ArtistShare*, crowdsourcing was already part of open-source groups,[12] coding communities, open-source engineers and software developers. For a long time, these communities of practices operated through collective agency principles and non-monetary

[11]A fee applied to the total funds achieved by the call. Kickstarter, for instance, charges 5% fee.
[12]It should be noted that even before digitalisation, social historians and sociologists observed how communities develop collective solutions for problems, such as Sennett (2012) depicted in his work. His argument is that cooperation is necessary for prospering societies and welfare. This essay, however, does not discuss pre-digitalisation periods.

incentives, to a certain extent. Online coding practices such as the ones fostered by *GitHub* platform ensure that knowledge is distributed and contributors can participate in a project by either helping in the development of a code or using it for future projects with the consent of the creators. *Wikipedia* also relies on dispersed curatorship of knowledge to build a widely accessed information tool. Some of these cases have been interpreted as a part of the so-called digital commons.

Firstly observed by Howe (2006), Crowdsourcing, simply put, "refers to the process of taking tasks that would normally be delegated to an employee and distributing them to a large pool of online workers, the 'crowd,' in the form of an open call" (Felstiner 2011, p. 1). This activity can serve individuals, firms and, especially, governments interested in the input of various people, amateurs or volunteers willing to contribute[13] (Brabham 2013). Such a participative online task may encompass monetary or non-monetary incentives, as both for-profit and not-for-profit ventures can benefit from it. Even though, sharing knowledge is part of most of open-source communities, "crowdsourcing" has been mostly associated with for-profit ventures and paid collective labor via online means. The case from Lego company (Schlagwein and Bjorn-Andersen 2014), for instance, shows that firms can provide complimentary incentives and, hence, benefit from a collective way of open innovation.

Within communities where this consists in the main mode of interaction for problem-solving, the unpaid/volunteer form of crowdsourcing is the main way through which innovative ideas and quick problem-solving happens. In cases of paid crowdsourcing (either via monetary incentives or prizes), outsourcing problem-solving can both connect firms with highly skilled consumers who can better assess the use of a product,[14] and provide remuneration to a project-based type of labor. Especially the paid crowdsourcing makes emerge new discussions with regard to open innovation systems and distributed intellectual property.[15]

Crowdsourcing combines bottom-up and top-down mechanisms, allowing both firms and governments to guide requests and receive crowd's support as an answer. From the supply perspective, incentives are quite clearer as finding rapid and clever solutions can be less costly if more people are involved (Schenk and Guittard 2011). Moreover, companies can rely on the knowledge, expertise and motivation of many while engaging with a motivated audience and ensuring, to a certain extent, demand in the long run. From the demand side point of view, incentives are also clear: money, engagement in a community or peer recognition through prizes.

[13]Examples of Hackathons (hacker marathons) conducted in various countries show the collective action of engineers and software developers toward the creation of applications, websites and solutions for public policy, firms and other institutions. Typically, Hackathons can be considered as a successful case of crowdsourcing that uses cultural common resources (such as knowledge and information) for public or private purposes.

[14]This largely contradicts the widely discussed notion in Economics that sellers know better and therefore quality assurance is of difficult signaling from the seller's point of view.

[15]Researchers such as Felstiner (2011) have observed the trade-offs of this labor contract.

Notwithstanding, the great majority of entrepreneurs lack funds to implement innovative ideas or to even start-up their operations. As Khavul et al. (2013) observe, banks find it difficult to serve the poor or informal ventures, so the funding gap ends up being partially covered by microfinance institutions, for instance, the ones based on crowdfunding. By enabling seeding entrepreneurship and innovation, crowdfunding supports entrepreneurs who are caught in a funding gap to start-up their projects (Bruton et al. 2014). For creative sectors, where labor informality is usually high, the low transaction costs and fast crowd support can become a short-term solution for "DIY" artists, independent creators and amateurs, besides the more business-oriented cases. For various reasons,[16] the cultural sector is much affected by the lack of financial resources to support their operations. It's within this realm that crowdfunding succeeds to attract the cultural sectors.

4.1 Crowdfunding Mechanisms and Definitions

The crowdfunding mechanism works by offering an online place for a campaign manager that seeks funds during a period of approximately 30–90 days. By stipulating a goal, the backers would be invited to contribute to the project within this timeframe and later expect rewards from their monetary contribution. If the online campaign succeeds by reaching its goal, the backers receive their expected rewards and the project managers carry on with the project. If not, typically, backers receive their contributions back. These transactions are mediated by a website[17] that gather funds, standardize communication and provide a web page where entrepreneurs and supporters concentrate their attention and other benefits depending on the platform services. As such, the model contributes to reduce the transaction costs of communication, administration and information searching, some of the features already observed by Agrawal et al. (2015).

Crowdfunding can be defined as a rapid and relatively open way of sharing ideas and asking people to contribute with money in exchange for a reward (tangible, intangible, monetary or non-monetary). One of the most cited definitions says that "Crowdfunding involves an open call, mostly through the Internet, for the provision of financial resources either in the form of donation or in exchange for the future product or some form of reward to support initiatives for specific purposes" (Belleflamme et al. 2014, p. 588). This funding model can quickly react to the pushed supply by long-tail producers. Amateurs who wish to professionalise their activities, small-scale projects, artists, independent creators and start-ups in the making can use this funding tool to subsidize at least initial operations or expansions depending

[16]Empirical data shows the effect of budget cuts in the cultural sector since 2008 in the aftermath of the economic crisis. Copic et al. (2013), for instance, show this impact in the EU member states.
[17]Kickstarter is so far one of the most well-known websites for this purpose (Mollick 2014).

on the development phase of an idea. Crowdfunding is, thus, an example of creative ventures realised in the "long-tail"[18] (Anderson 2006).

Up to this date, crowdfunding remains an important and stable tool for a wide range of specific purposes, especially the ones associated with cultural commons and some degree of collective participation. Given the specific characteristics found in these online calls, the next section selects the most relevant qualities to better support the emergence and maintenance of cultural commons, especially for the arts and creative industries.

4.2 Aspects of Crowdfunding Fostering the Emergence of Cultural Commons

As a non-market expansion of a market practice, some of crowdfunding features are more applicable to the "new commons" than others. Crowdfunding is not necessarily a cultural commons per se, but rather a tool that allows—among other purposes—that cultural commons become easily realised because of its digital features and diversity of expressions. The features described below are selected to represent how this funding scheme better represents the case for the public good, quasi-public good and common resources that require collective engagement for sharing knowledge, information and culture.

(a) *Stability*: due to the established design of platforms, these websites provide a relatively stable and open environment where the "rules of the game" hardly change. Crowdfunding has a *modus operandi* that suffers modifications with regard to its models rather than projects.
(b) *Anti-gatekeeping*[19]: crowdfunding platforms offer matchmaking of supply and demand with bypassing traditional market players. In most cases, traditional gatekeeping matters for quality assurance. However, in these cases, artists and creatives might not be able to reach a typical industrial organisation in their sectors.
(c) *Diversity of expressions*: when governments do not address the need of groups and populations, or when firms fail to provide goods that meet expected demands, crowdfunding can be useful to surge bottom-up solutions for problems of representation in both commercial and non-commercial cases. For commercially driven projects, this is mostly represented by the hypothesis of

[18]Especially in the case of cultural and creative sectors, which mostly utilize the so-called "reward-based model" (Mollick 2014). In this model, suppliers only offer rewards in exchange for money, but not any profit-sharing operation. Besides offering tangible and intangible rewards, suppliers also accept charitable contributions that do not request rewards in return. As the European Commission report (2017) observes, the cultural sectors tend to prefer this type of crowdfunding model.

[19]Certifiers and gatekeepers are used in the sense given by Caves (2000) as part of an industry structure that retains information and selects the suppliers who are able to access certain markets. As we argue in this chapter, crowdfunding can, to a certain extent, bypass such institutions in the short-run.

the "long-tail" which contends the importance of digitalisation to foster market exchanges in niche realms.

(d) *Time-perspective*: with regard to the timeframe, crowdfunding imposes the urgency for supporters to engage before the end of the campaign. If it reaches the goal, social benefits can be expected; if not, the money is returned to the backer. The time dimension in these campaigns runs faster than any government or bank funds, which can be helpful for charitable causes and collective solutions that require immediate action.

(a) *Non-rival access*: access to the campaign has virtually no barriers, which means that simultaneous engagements happen in a non-rival manner. After the campaign finishes and the exhibition takes place, the rivalry is subject to the over-consumption of the good,[20] which hardly happens in reality.

(b) *Semi-excludability*: with regard to "willingness to pay", supporters can choose a range of rewards and their respective prices. One can contribute with one dollar or more depending on their will to represent their engagement with a monetary value. When all contributions are made, the platform benefits from extracting a percentage of the total amount in order to maintain the activity of the website running with a stable system. This means that excludability does not relate to one single price, but to a range of different prices which, as a result, reduces the excludability component of crowdfunding calls.

(c) *Social surplus*: the bottom-up "crowd's" participation happens on the basis of money contribution on a platform, which denotes a minimal barrier for participation. However, because the social benefits spill over and contribution is also non-monetary,[21] the collective action is not confined to the Internet. As a consequence, collective action happens before, during and after the crowdfunding campaign. Once a socially driven cause is put forward or a niche finds its way in any potential market, social surpluses can be expected.

(d) *Risk-sharing*: especially for common resources where management is dispersed and institutional rules are collectively decided, risk attributions should follow the same pattern. In crowdfunding schemes, the risk is shared to the extent that if contributors do not contribute, demand may not be met because the good is not yet available in the market or because a hypothetical non-commercial project does not have other means to exist. And so, if suppliers do not supply, consumers do not consume.

Additionally, the platform also bears the risk of failure considering that its operations depend on successful fundraising campaigns. If that does not happen, platforms cease to exist unless they are based on charitable gift-giving by third parties.

[20]The "good" mentioned here is access to the exhibition only.

[21]For instance, by sharing the campaign online, taking part in the offline activities and supporting the organisation of collective action.

If these features are in place, crowdfunding can be used for "commons resource management"[22]—with the resource representing both (a) the access to cultural goods and (b) its way of managing it. By focusing on the function of such infrastructures, the managerial aspect of such tools becomes evident with, in theory, the reduction of transaction costs for producers. As much as the Internet in Frischmann's (2007) view is a commercial, public and social infrastructure, so crowdfunding is too—to the extent that it remains a tool with low-entry barriers.

In theory, the multiple-function of digital tools generates positive externalities by providing access to resources that otherwise would be allocated solely via individual willingness to pay. Because prices do not always match what is offered (due to the charitable aspect of the campaign), we can assume the existence of social surpluses. As a consequence, says Frischmann (2007), the diffusion of small-scale positive externalities could potentially generate aggregate social welfare. This is possible in light of a stable environment where the mechanisms are somewhat understood, shared and perennial yet subject to collective change (Ostrom 1990). The online form of crowdfunding can be regarded as a relatively stable structure, independent of typical state-market alternatives and rooted in the bottom-up dispersed, large-scale action. Those are the main features that support the emergence and continuity of cultural commons in the digital realm.

5 Conclusion

By moving away from glorified dilettantism of what technological progress can ideally provide, this essay has chosen the unpretentious path of unveiling the features of digital tools, common resources and their relation to the phenomena of crowdsourcing and crowdfunding. It firstly takes a historical route to describe the emergence of digitalisation, two main approaches and its derivations into more individualist or collectivist interpretations. And despite the criticised technological determinism of the aforementioned authors, this essay observes that the structures through which interaction happens are of much importance to understand the meanings attributed to them. As a typical two-sided market with non-market implications, crowdfunding is hybrid case of platform that allows a wide range of projects to happen and due to its technical features, cultural commons can greatly benefit from the low-entry barrier, low transaction costs and crowd validation that it proportionates. Especially for cases in which collective action is needed or when traditional routes for funding seem unreachable, this tool can facilitate the achievement of common goals. Much research is still needed in order to observe the limitations of this tool with regard to solving "funding gaps" or outreaching new networks. Nonetheless, it seems vital to take into account that the emergence of new

[22]This notion is supported on the premise that commons-resource-management is based on openness, does not discriminate who accesses and does not depend on the approval of a third party (Frischmann 2007).

digital platforms has helped cultural commons to thrive in the digital environments as much as any commercially driven solution.

References

Adorno, T., & Horkheimer, M. (1997). *Dialectic of enlightenment*. London: Verso.

Agrawal, A. K., Catalini, C., & Goldfarb, A. (2015). Crowdfunding: Geography, social networks, and the timing of investment decisions. *Journal of Economics & Management Strategy, 24,* 253–274.

Ahlers, G. K. C., Cumming, D., Günther, C., & Schweizer, D. (2015). Signaling in equity crowdfunding. *Entrepreneurship Theory and Practice, 39*(4), 955–980.

Anderson, C. (2006). *The long tail: Why the future of business is selling less of more*. New York: Hyperion.

Baudrillard, J. (1996). *The perfect crime*. Trans. Chris Turner. London: Verso.

Belleflamme, P., Lambert, T., & Schwienbacher, A. (2014). Crowdfunding: Tapping the right crowd. *Journal of Business Venturing, 29*(5), 585–609. https://doi.org/10.1016/j.jbusvent.2013.07.003.

Benkler, Y. (2006). *The wealth of networks: How social production transforms markets and freedom*. New Haven [Conn.: Yale University Press.

Boltanski, L., Chiapello, E., & Elliott, G. (2005). *The new spirit of capitalism*. London: Verso.

Brabham, D. C. (2013). *Using crowdsourcing in government*. University of South California. https://www.cbs.dk/files/cbs.dk/using_crowdsourcing_in_government.pdf.

Brown, J. S., & Duguid, P. (2000). *The social life of information*. Massachussets: Harvard Business School Press.

Bruton, G., Khavul, S., Siegel, D., & Wright, M. (2014). New financial alternatives in seeding entrepreneurship: Microfinance, crowdfunding, and peer-to-peer innovations, *Entrepreneurship Theory and Practice 39*. https://doi.org/10.1111/etap.12143.

Coleman, E. G. (2013). *Coding freedom: The ethics and aesthetics of hacking*. Princeton: Princeton University Press.

Copi˘c, V., Inkei, P., Kangas, A., & Srakar, A. (2013). *Trends in public funding for culture in the EU*. European Union, Brussels: EENC Report.

Dickel, S., & Schrape, J.-F. (2017). The renaissance of techno-utopianism as a challenge for responsible innovation. *Journal of Responsible Innovation, 4*(2), 289–294.

European Commission (2017). *Crowdfunding: Reshaping the crowd's engagement in culture*. https://europa.eu/capacity4dev/crowdfunding/documents/new-report-crowdfunding-reshaping-crowds-engagement-culture. Accessed 10 Jan 2018.

Felstiner, A. (2001). *Working the crowd: Employment and labor law in the crowdsourcing industry* (August 16). *Berkeley Journal of Employment and Labor Law*, *32*(1), 2011. Available at SSRN https://ssrn.com/abstract=1593853.

Frischmann, B. (2007). Infrastructure Commons in Economic Perspective. First Monday, 12(6), June, available at: https://firstmonday.org/issues/issue12_6/frischmann/index.html

Hardin, G., & American Association for the Advancement of Science. (1968). *The tragedy of the commons*. Washington, D.C.: American Association for the Advancement of Science.

Hess, C. (2008). Mapping the New Commons. In *12th Biennial Conference of the International Association for the Study of the Commons*, University of Gloucestershire, Cheltenham, England, July 14–18. Available at http://dlc.dlib.indiana.edu/dlc/bitstream/handle/10535/304/Mapping_the_NewCommons.pdf.

Himanen, P. (2001). *The hacker ethic, and the spirit of the information age*. New York: Random House.

Howe, J. (2006). The rise of crowdsourcing. *Wired 14* (6).

Khavul, S., Chavez, H., Bruton, G. D. (2013). When institutional change outruns the change agent: The contested terrain of entrepreneurial microfinance for those in poverty. *Journal of Business Venturing*, 30–50.

Klamer, A. (2003). Gift economy. In *A Handbook of Cultural Economics*, Edward Elgar Publishing.

Lee, T. (2019). The global rise of "fake news" and the threat to democratic elections in the USA. *Public Administration and Policy: An Asia-Pacific Journal, 22*(1), 15–24.

Lessig, L. (2005). *Free culture: The nature and future of creativity*. New York: Penguin Books.

Lévy, P. (1997). *Collective intelligence: Mankind's emerging world in cyberspace*. New York: Plenum Trade.

Madison, M. J., Frischmann, B. M., Strandburg, K. J. (2010). Constructing commons in the cultural environment. *Cornell Law Review* 4, May.

Mager, A. (2012). Algorithmic ideology. *Information, Communication & Society, 15*(5), 769–787.

Merrin, W. (2001). To Play with Phantoms: Jean Baudrillard and the Evil Demon of The Simulacrum. *Economy and Society*, *30*(1).

McLuhan, M., & Powers, B. R. (1986). *The Global village: Transformations in world life and media in the 21st century*. New York: Oxford University Press.

Mollick, E. (2014). The dynamics of crowdfunding: Determinants of success and failure. *Journal of Business Venturing, 29,* 1–16.

Nunes, M. (1995). From possible worlds to virtual realities: Approaches to postmodernism. *Style., 29*(2), 314–327.

Ostrom, E. (1990). *Governing the commons: The evolution of institutions for collective action*. Cambridge, UK: Cambridge University Press.

Ostrom, E. (2010). The institutional analysis and development framework and the commons: Response. *Cornell Law Review*. Issue 4, May.

Rochet, J., & Tirole, J. (2003). Platform competition in two-sided markets. *Journal of the European Economic Association, 1*(4), 990–1029.

Schenk, E., & Guittard, C. (2011). Towards a characterization of crowdsourcing practices. *Journal of Innovation Economics & Management, 7*(1), 93–107.

Schlagwein, D. & Bjorn-Andersen, N. (2014). Organizational learning with crowdsourcing: The revelatory case of LEGO. *Journal of the Association for Information Systems 15*(11), 3.

Sennett, R. (2012). *Together: The rituals, pleasures, and politics of cooperation*. New Haven, CT: Yale University Press.

Viotto da Cruz, J. (2015). Competition and regulation of crowdfunding platforms: A two-sided market approach. *Communications & Strategies 99*, 33–50. Available at SSRN https://ssrn.com/abstract=2741883.

William, M. (2001). To play with phantoms: Jean Baudrillard and the evildemon of the simulacrum. *Economy and Society, 30*(1), 85–111.

Experiences of Commons Between Antagonisms and Strategies

From Urban Commons to Commoning as Social Practice

Federica Antonucci

Abstract

A good city is like a good party, people stay longer than really necessary, because they are enjoying it. The vibes of places matter, feelings and perceptions play a crucial role in leading people's choices and behaviours when it comes to public space. Indeed, pages have been spent in addressing to the concept of atmosphere in social life a somewhat function. In this chapter, I will try to investigate why collective moods arise and to what extent they are effective in making and maintaining specific kind of urban communalities. In discussing the conditions of such processes, we should refer to what has been identified by David Harvey with the name of *commoning.* How different actors join together in a common governance of a certain public space? Or to put it differently, which resources contribute to increase social capital in a given urban setting?

1 Introduction to Public Space

In a situation where deep transformations cross contemporary societies and affect cities and their population, a crucial challenge seems to enrich and better articulate the public sphere. Public sphere comprehends a variety of realms, nonetheless political, social and infrastructural activities that take place on it. Public space is a paramount and crucial setting for social life. What happens there seems to have no

F. Antonucci (✉)
Department of Architecture and Territory, Mediterranea University, Reggio Calabria, Italy
e-mail: federica.antonucci@unirc.it

E. Macrì et al. (eds.), *Cultural Commons and Urban Dynamics*,
https://doi.org/10.1007/978-3-030-54418-8_12

equals. As a matter of fact, over the last years and increasingly at fast pace, public space is returning to be stage of claims (Mitchell 1995). Far in the past, public squares were an example of encounter and exchange according to the Greek idea of *agora* and the Roman *Forum*. Nowadays, we deal with a somewhat public space *renaissance*: after a persistent tendency which led spaces to be space of representation of governments rather than people and citizens, they are returning to be sites of resistance.

Consequently, planning public space becomes a complex and multifaceted duty: the usage and management of public space are functional to the production of sane and vibrant public sphere. The dichotomy between public space and public sphere is a recurring theme throughout urban studies' history: Michel de Certau in "The Practice of everyday life" highlights the paramount dual dimension of public space that he divides in 'place' and 'space'. Whereas the former involves a degree of physicality, the latter, instead, refers to 'a performed place'. To put it differently, he draws the attention to the ways in which people create their own meaning of space, individually or collectively, through their specific behaviours in space and put them to use (De Certau 1984). Indeed, the public space analysed in this paper combines features of physicality and public dimension as site of interaction and social practices.

2 Life in Public Space

Public space is made by streets, squares, parks, bridges and those dimensions are the ones we live more frequently. As everyone else, dwellers of any city wake up in the morning whether to go working or to school or somewhere else and to do so, all of us at a certain point walk on a soil of public space. If this is certainly true, questions about the meaning we address to the living of public space and our behaviours often arise. How do we live public space? Citizens' habits have changed over the years: it has become increasingly easy to find among citizens a general and depressive unsatisfaction and unhappiness, caused by the co-existence of many factors which has led to a mistrust and disaffection to the public life.

The new urban models' development strategies are part of this process and have brought to a substantial decrease in the quality of urban life. The kind of world it has built has brought society to a situation of mass alienation (Harvey 2012). Most people are not satisfied of their jobs anymore, dwellers are stuck in their cities' routine made of working hours, quick lunches and traffic. It seems that a general feeling of senselessness in what people do on a daily basis is taking over and within this daily grid, people have lost their will to interact and to socialize. It is also true that over the last years, city planners seem to have forgotten the importance of open and accessible spaces to the public and even when they actually did not, the risk of falling in the trap of pleasant, good looking but useless areas, is very high.

Undoubtably, many spectacular—and often partly publicly funded—urban projects in cities among the world have been developed winking to market and real estate forces. An example can be found in the Vessel project carried out in New York City. Lately, the city of New York has been scenario for a notable project which has involved the Hudson Yard area within a broader Manhattan regeneration project's costed 25 billion dollars. The Thomas Heatherwick–designed public installation, inspired in part by Indian stepwells, expands from a minimal footprint at the bottom to a 150-feet-wide diameter at the peak. The intentions behind the piece have well stated the desire to create a monument in Hudson Yards that engages, not overshadows, the surrounding towers, and a 'living room' for the public and residents who call the new neighbourhood home.

At the end of the project, residents have been asked to give feedback and assess the success of the Vessel and albeit dazzled by the physical structure, main concerns were addressed to the social utility of it. This conclusion lets us think that citizens' needs and desires are not correctly interpreted by the administrations and city planners, and not answered. In both cases, the supply and demands are far from the equilibrium point. Indeed, high-quality public spaces would encourage people to communicate and collaborate with each other, and to participate in public life.

In addition to this, consumerism forces have forged and drive citizens' behaviours and pushed them to the extent of a perpetual sense of unsatisfaction. Our societies rely on a strict economic system based on the assessment of values in monetary terms. What has no price, has no value because only the market determines price and values, while anything that stands apart from or against it is not just value-less but market-distorting (Standing 2019). We live in hyper-marketing society and current urban economies are still too far from the achievement of sane and vital social urban dimensions. Generally speaking, the standard economic approach to urban transition takes into account quantitative expansions by situating consumers in the last stage of the process: the growth and the size of the economy, the number of jobs and the exchangeable resources on the market that entail the government to be competitive on the international level. Consequently, such endeavours have brought people to be rigidly tied to market forces and being extremely dependent to exchange values.

In light of this, progressively an increasing number of scholars, practitioners and activists are attempting to elucidate why contemporary cities should require a new understanding of economics and culture able to overcome the economic framework in which our societies are now inscribed.

Consumers who happen to be primarily citizens should no longer be located at the final stage of the economic process. The assessment of space's production should be no longer based on a somewhat cost-benefits analysis, where rather much more attention should be addressed towards the external benefits deriving from an even and conscious use of public soil. Nowadays, we are in search of an alternative meaning to those provided by the monetary calculus and simple economic value: we are again desiring of being owner of our past, present and future.

3 Public Goods and Public Interest

Saskia Sassen argues who owns the city in an era of corporatising access and control over urban land and corporate buying whole pieces of cities, which is transforming the small and public into large and private across so many cities around the world? (Sassen 2001). Interdisciplinary intellectuals and a range of social movements reclaim control over decisions about how the city develops and grows and to promote greater access to urban spaces and collective resources for all cities' inhabitants. In other words, the right to the city, as articulated by the French philosopher Henry Lefebvre, which has manifested in efforts by progressive urban policymakers around the world to give more power to city inhabitants in shaping urban spaces (Foster and Iaione 2016). Those collective resources are not meant just as spaces and infrastructures, but also as an array of services and goods that belong to the citizenship. The term 'collective' sounds crucial in this analysis. Collective refers to something keen to be shared among a community interested in taking care of that certain good, because its use brings to a positive effect at 'collective' level. Within the economic theory, those goods are publicly provided and known as public goods. These ones respond to a dual feature: they are typically non-rivalrous and non-excludable: meaning that one's individual consumption of a good or service does not prevent another individual from consuming the same good; secondly, that if any person *X* in a group *Xn*…*X*, …*X* consumes it, it cannot feasibly be withheld from the others in that group (Cowen 1985).[1]

Typical public goods are national defence, healthcare systems, infrastructures of many sorts, education, culture and the arts. These goods' analysis encounters a major problem of inefficiency, namely the issue of 'free riding' and the difficulty of reaching the optimal provision. The problem with goods that are 'public' is that society needs them even if they fail in the market. In fact, lately the provision of these services and goods of public interests has been increasingly left aside by public administrations. So, what happens when the State fails in public goods provision? Which strategies and actors enter in the scene?

Grassroot movements, political actors, new forms of public-private collaborations are the new agents and shareholders dealing with this problem. Lately, if our societies have been experiencing, on the one hand, that fact that public goods' provision is considered highly risky due to its unprofitability and tends to

[1]The equivalence, public space-public good, has been explored by different scholars in accordance to different approaches. Among the others Ilaria Vitellio expresses it clearly in her text "Spazi Pubblici come beni comuni"; she explains that in order to split up the double dimension of space, the economic theory comes to help. In fact, before defining space as economic good, crucial is to deeply understand its nature. Indeed, spaces have a multifaceted identity: a physical place where things can happen and a place to craft a collective moral code. Among the theories that have influenced the practice of planning, the one adopting public goods' glance seems to be the most efficient. In fact, it allows to translate the physical dimension in economic features and to transmit the public dimension of space in the figure of the State and a modern citizenship. Indeed, the first characteristics, i.e. being the place of and for all can be read as non-excludability and non-rivalrous features of public goods (Vitellio 2005).

inefficiency, on the other, a strong desire of publicness is spreading throughout the citizenship. In fact, spottily (but more and more congenial to new societies) worthy initiatives are flourishing all over even though they often remain undeveloped due to either lack of representation or hostility in accepting them from the top. However, this imperfect overlapping could be greatly matched by increasing the amount of the so-called social capital, bridging bottom-up initiatives and top-down interventions. In this view, the development process based on horizontal subsidiarity[2] principles and addressed towards the generation of non-conventional public services can be seen as both necessary as challenging and unproductive. I found in scholars as Frischmann and Donolo interesting approaches in defining and studying collective resources' management by shifting point of view. When it comes to public goods, arguments are usually focused on the supply side, leaving unanswered many questions. On the contrary, a demand-side approach could pave the way for new insights; for example, we could start asking 'What drives the demand side of these resources?' and yet 'How should demand-side drivers affect public policy?' (Frischmann 2013). Indeed, over the last years a different demand of public goods, i.e. social cohesion, sustainability and sociability, has emerged led by new desires and needs to cope societal issues and to reconstruct a renovated public sphere (Donolo 2005).

Put it this way, a demand-side approach should facilitate a better understanding of the reasons why over the last years although plenty of initiatives have emerged, the most of them have resulted in unfruitful dialogue among public authorities and society. This has led to reactions from civil society, sometimes ending in abandoned or neglected spaces occupied illegally. Among many examples are Teatro Valle Occupato of Rome and MACAO of Milan.[3] Good examples of such a situation are those participatory experiences in which great investments in terms of analysis of public needs and hearing of social requests have poor and expected results. In the public goods' provision scenario, a school of thought has strongly argued that a

[2]The debate on subsidiarity is still evolving, albeit its pivotal role. The most recent definition highlights the importance of a strategic interdependency among civil society and public administrations at local level in order to explore new possibilities of integration to cope urban and societal challenges. Horizontal subsidiarity plays in a wide range of actions, involving at different scale and levels public administration and social actors (Foster and Iaione 2016).

[3]Respectively, Teatro Valle Occupato and Macao of Milano are two different examples which point out how a range of actions are undertaken by civic society to raise voice against privatisation and unmet needs. On 5 May 2012, a group of artists and professionals in the field of culture have occupied a 33-storeys abandoned skyscraper, which soon became Macao or "The New Centre for Arts, Culture and Research". Same fate awaited Teatro Valle in Rome, when back in 2011 a theatre of the Eighteenth century was occupied in the heart of Rome. The theatre had closed that year after the abolition of Ente Teatrale Italiano, which was the main public funding body within the Italian Theatre sector. In this case, the occupation was supposed to last few days, but instead the theatre has remained occupied for three years, until 11 August 2014, and by that time, the occupants, who defined their selves as "communards", developed a range of activities based on arts and culture.

co-governance model made by more actors (institutions, civil society) for the production of public goods should be necessary and this is the case, for example, of the cities as Bologna or Mantova. The idea of commons arises in this context: commons refers to all shared natural resources—including forests, parks, water—and all the social, civic and cultural institutions.

4 Introductions to Commons

Commons in modern times encompasses natural resources and yet public services and amenities, social justice systems but mostly our cultural and intellectual life, this means of course that social relations could be considered commons as well. Let me explain this latter. Literally, commons signifies something that is shared and universal, of general understanding and stake. Lately, the word 'commons' has been increasingly associated with the collective activity of working in the commons: even in the Magna Charta,[4] the idea of commoning as fundamental aspect of the commons as place where the commoners undertake collective actions, is particularly stressed. According to this fact, we can conclude that commons can be any setting where communal activities happen. To put it in other words, without community, commons have no reason to exist and thus without community commons do not exist (Standing 2019). The role of communities is crucial in the production of commons due to the intrinsic features of them that is that they need to be thought as reproduction resources rather than a thing tending to depletion.

The idea of commons is certainly rooted in our culture, and when we mention the commons, we do refer also to a private property on which the non-owners have certain rights and uses. Let me define the non-owners as commoners and indicate their use and rights as usufructuary right.[5] In fact, some of the commons can be seen as areas where albeit people live, they do not own the land, but still they benefit from it. Indeed, the important point when it comes to commons is that also the

[4]The Magna Charta is a document dated 1217: the charter placed implicit limits on the exploitation of natural resources and paid attention to the need to reproduce and preserve those resources.

[5]Specifically, with regard to the Italian framework, it is possible to recognize different approaches in terms of collective ownership: public goods and the so-called collective properties. If we think about the commons as ethic and civil value, both of the ownership's models can be encompassed in these two definitions. However, attention must be put towards the concept of collective properties, which origins from the idea of "civic uses". This particular case finds its roots in a crucial historical function: indeed, first of all they are the legacy of an ancient tradition of collective resources' shared management, which highlights the community's value in spite of the individual dimension. Secondly, civic uses taught us that a forward looking contribute to avoid depletion and the tragedy of commons. Civic uses both in public and administrative law, presents the collective rights of use and enjoyment of certain goods as one of the three cases which, together with the state property and the property itself, craft the notion of public property (Capone 2018).

non-owners have right to share it. The notion of common good finds its origin in a dual principle: on the one hand, it has to do with public interest, whereas on the other, it deals with the sustainability of our resources. On a political level, we are more interested in the first element. A common good is indeed the citizenship backbone and strictly related to the human being community well-being (Settis 2012). Interestingly enough, one of the first recall within a political context to this, appears in the U.S. Declaration of Independence (1776), where it was claimed that the purpose of governments was to secure the rights that all people have to 'Life, Liberty and the pursuit of Happiness'. That declaration ushered in a new era for governments and peoples across the globe with aspirations of liberty and happiness (Musikanki and Polley 2016). With regard to the theory of Commons, for many times, this latter was considered whatsoever opposed to the pursuit of happiness, since the notion of commons positions itself in contradiction with private property's principles in the individualistic framework of exclusive rights.

According to Howard Kaminsky, this dichotomy has been strengthened over the years due to societies 'features and beliefs: he argues that the commons goods' culture is for its nature elitist, whereas the proletariat individualism as leading factor of masses' pursuit of happiness results in a more diffused and easily embraceable idea for most of the people (Kaminsky 2003). If this can be valid for the American society Kaminsky knows and lives, it also true that such juxtaposition does not fit with the genealogy and nature of the common goods and the pursuit of happiness. On contrast, the theory of commons does not deny the pursuit of individual happiness, which finds its realisation in the collective effort. Plato argues that individual happiness can be reached by setting general and shared rules among individuals, which find expression in something capable of making feel people included and recognized: happiness is achieved in the good governance of the civil community which must be considered in its entirety. If the private owners become hostile instead of allies, they will drag themselves and the whole city to ruin, ultimately removing its part of happiness. Aristotle as well, although with a different perspective identifies the happy life—that is what nowadays we can detect as the good quality of urban and social life—with a better polis: that is to say, 'a polis brave, wise and just'. In order for the polis to be so, paramount is the absence of contrasts among individuals: polis and individual happiness are perfectly overlapped. Over the twelfth century, Tommaso D'Aquino follows in the reasoning stressing the idea of 'bonum commune civitatis', which by nature overcomes the individual 'bonum commune' due to the intrinsic human being's social feature (Settis 2012).

In this view, public happiness becomes a compulsory ingredient to accrue the quality of urban life, empowering and giving back collective, and thus individual, rights to the citizenship.

To say it with Standing: 'there is something comforting about the commons: their quality of just being there, part of our society, that adds to our sense of belonging' (Standing 2019).

5 Urban Common as Re-appropriation Strategy

Urban commons are such a wide topic, which moves its first steps from the notion of Commons as developed by Nobel Prize Elinor Ostrom. Applying the theory of Commons to the urban studies seems making a little of sense, due to the intrinsic characteristics of commons themselves. Typically, when referring to Commons, we do refer to natural resources such as fisheries, forests, grazing areas (Elinor 2006), namely common pool resources (herein after CPRs). Indeed, as both Hardin[6] and Ostrom explain, CPRs are characterised by the fact that they are non-excludable but rivalrous,[7] that is to say that the use of these resources by one person diminishes what is left for others to use. So, dealing with CPRs means addressing free-riding challenges. According to her, CPRs are resources that appropriators can use but whilst doing so, they contribute to diminish its value.

Within the urban studies, the notion of commons has been applied to cities and space, defining the urban commons as collectively shared resources that are subject to the same rivalry and free-rider problems. Therefore, when it comes to the urban level, more questions than solutions arise in terms of rules and ties that could weaken free-riding behaviours. Now, a sublevel in theory of Commons can be identified with subtractive and non-subtractive resources, that is to say that non-subtractive resources are those whose use does not reduce other consumers' benefits. This is the case of knowledge, for instance: using shared knowledge does not affect the pool 'knowledge', unless legal tools as property rights, copyrights and licenses do not regulate this (Landes 2019). Consequently, is this distinction applicable to the urban context? If we consider the urban domain, on the one hand, we should take into account elements such as roads and infrastructural systems, therefore, since the available space for traffic diminishes by adding an additional car, we can argue that we are dealing with a subtractive resource (Kornberger and Berch 2015). Yet, on the other hand, how could a city be a city without inhabitants using and living it? How could a public space be called public, if denied to the inhabitants? So, changing perspective, it won't be wrong arguing that the act of consuming the space contributes to increase its value rather than decreasing it. At this point, we could say that the value of space depends on additional factors than space itself that are proximity and density: proximity to other buildings and density of activities. That is to say that surrounding adjectives give light to it and the relation of space with other elements make it worthwhile (Howard 1965).

[6]The idea of commons comes down from the past and moves its first steps from Garret Hardin's famous article "The tragedy of commons". The seminal paper by Hardin represents the threshold beyond which every discussion was brought, emphasizing the controversial issues related to the delicate balance between benefits and costs.

[7]Rivalry and excludability are features belonging to all economic goods' categories. According to their nature, i.e. public, private or club goods, those two characteristics may change. As far as concern CPRs, they are not excludible but rivalrous. This means that one's individual consumption of a good or service does not prevent others from consuming the same good, whereas being rivalrous means that the use of these resources by one person diminishes what is left for others to use.

This made me reflect that within the city context, the only way to think about commons is as relational common, where on contrast, usage and consumption practices are a constitutive part of the production of the urban commons itself: consuming space is indeed a form of production. Are children playing in public gardens depleting that space? Are skaters using or abusing car parks? As many times happens, such a discrepancy marks theory and practice.

In fact, looking at the last years urban commons have been adopted as re-appropriation strategy of neglected, abandoned and many times denied public space. The use of space has become paramount in the claiming for essential and primary rights to the city, rights that are not affected by commodified financial and political urban stakes. The urban commons are born to produce an accessible and open space to the public and indeed to put it with Ostrom's words, the appropriators highlight its value—physical and symbolic—as key access to shared resources with the aim of re-creating a sense of publicness. This process raises many problems in terms of governance and rights' allocation among the users.

In claiming such spaces as common goods, what emerges is a new relationship between the world of people and the world of goods, for many times deeply entrusted to market logics. According to this view, the accent is no longer placed on the owner; in contrast, it falls on the role that a certain good plays in the society (Rodotà 2012). The debate on commons is nourished by the experiences of grassroot movements that give back subjectivity to widespread urban goods threatened by financial or real estate speculation. The relationship between political spaces and citizenship, understood as a practice of democracy, as a set of acts rather than as a stable condition (Nielsen and Isin 2008), constitutes one of the *leitmotifs* with respect to the growing privatisation and profitability of the collectively produced value.

As Mitchell shows, urban movements always demand a space of representation, a space where the agenda of public discourse can be challenged or re-directed by raising voice in the political forum (Calhoun 1992). In this sense, we can say that urban spaces are appropriated as public spaces, political spaces for debate and production of discourses. The right to having rights seems to take shape above all in the right to access public space under practical and symbolic forms.

6 The Need of Social and Shared Practices

Imagining the city as cobweb, kept together by strands, we can picture the commons as an aggregation node within it. The knots within a weave can hold the various threads of a fabric together, but too large or intricate knots can also grab the surface of the fabric. In the city, the nodes are made up of disparate elements with a strong distinctive character. The knots are the spots around which public and social life are articulated and those knots take place in public space.

Therefore, if urban public space remains the site where public life is consumed and the imagination and sense of identity of citizens are shaped, what is still missing is a proper investment to stimulate urban quality, which apparently has more to do with a cultural and social investment rather than economic. It cannot be expected that a culture of living together can flourish if the raw material of the community offers ever more torn and degraded scenes. In recent theories on urban space and the measurement of its quality, reference is often made to the presence of shared practices.

Why do shared practices seem so relevant in the urban quality discourse? We all agree that social and cultural quality both in public spaces and in cities are hardly measurable, and this seems one of the reasons why policymakers, for example, struggle to detect them and unleash it. At the same time, ideas are important as well. Successful ideas deriving from ongoing discourse have the power to make themselves realisable and able to be disseminated (Collins 2004).

Cities need to be empowered by activating their space through citizenship, cultivating a practical method that allows this process. If we agree on this, we can identify the practices that people share as encouraging ways to achieve this result (Klamer 2016). A practice denotes what people do in a given society and it is descriptive and reproductive of certain discourse.[8] Indeed, the city is above all a matter of practice, of giving shape to a common feeling in the urban space. In fact, space can be defined as the projection of social relationships and as a challenge in building a shared future (Cellamare 2018). In fact, the production of a common appears not only at the beginning and end of production but also in the middle, since the production processes themselves are collaborative and communicative commons (Hard and Negri 2009).

For a truly good life, it seems crucial to rely on different values than purely economic ones. We could also say that economic value is instrumental for the achievement of others like social and cultural values. Indeed, it seems that objectives as reciprocity, friendship, relationships and co-creation, in general, cannot be determined just with merely quantitative measures. People generate a range of goods and services by getting involved in networks, actions and activities and the

[8]At the beginning of the French Revolution, healthy and sanitary conditions in France were miserable as in the rest of Europe and the Country was in need of reforms, yet a deep economic crisis was at the core of the institutional stakes. Right after the end of the Middle-Age, the black plague ended to murder a third of the European population and when, thereafter, cities started to grow again in terms of inhabitants and dimension, hygienic conditions were still a legacy of the previous era. In London due to the high rate of population growth, new housing solutions were required, and more houses meant more pollution, contributing to increase the already existing unhealthy environment. A common belief addressed the risk of infection to airborne contagious, whereas the epidemy cause needed to be found in the streets' cleaning standards. Just then, a bunch of engineers realized that in order to overcome that decay, by acting as city's craftsmen, they could have been entitled to provide better life's conditions. Therefore, new smooth flooring flourished throughout cities with the aim of facilitate the cleaning. This is just to say that the underlying belief was that, by making the streets cleaner, inhabitants would have been less keen to make them dirty again, producing a sense of stewardship for something of common interest. And so it was (Sennett 2018).

outcomes produced contribute to keep the city vibrant and while improving the social quality of life,[9] i.e. by getting closer with the neighbours cleaning the streets or the public garden, they play a role in increasing the general wealth of the city. As a consequence, the issue cities face is to cultivate a practical method that allows for making urban qualities substantive.

At this point, following the above reasoning upon the rise of urban commons and shared practices increasingly spread all over the city, we should investigate whether differences or similarities exist between the two. Actually, when speaking of urban commons, we do refer to the relation capital registered in urban production, the so-called positive externalities that are anything but the territorial relationships among individuals: those relationships rely basically on features as proximity, reciprocity, collaboration and mutual exchange. The relational value collectively produced by the space is, therefore, central to thinking, identifying and claiming commons starting from the urban context.

It is precisely in the context of commons movements' that the concept of commoning starts to circulate and to be brought into focus with greater clarity. Also, in the analysis of the urban commons, it seems clear that the dichotomy subject/object is absorbed in a whole element: the community who produces and takes care of the commons is simultaneously producer and consumer, according to Lefebvre (Lefebvre 1968).

In this sense, the urban commons seem to share features with the intangible assets of public interest: besides the characteristics of non-rivalry and non-exclusion, they also share the features of being a non-established and fixed community, based on the fluidity and the irregularity of the variety of relationships existing with the resource. In light of the emersion of these communities not strictly related to the spatial fixity and proximity, the urban commons in many ways are similar to the commons of the intangible, especially when we refer to spaces aimed at producing cultural and social outcome. These spaces of production, although locally positioned, generate relationships spread all over the city. In this vein, it is possible to identify the practice of commoning as shared practice. That being said, to develop shared practices, clearly a supportive environment able to foster the intersection of the cultural and social sphere, which ultimately benefit the urban economy and would position cities in a more civilised system, is needed.

However, some cities are succeeding in this process, whereas others do not. So, it seems interesting reflecting upon the actors able to undertake the initiative in developing them.

In the following pages, we will analyse the role of social dynamics and collective actions in the creation of the so-called social value extracted and produced within the commoning framework. Furthermore, we will observe that interaction processes between public institutions and social organisations, under favourable

[9]Quality of life as paramount achievement for cities has become so relevant in the global discourse that the European Commission has tracked the quality of life in cities since 2004, and the United Nations has stressed the importance of the qualitative impact on urban life by funding studies and projects based on social inclusiveness, sustainability and participation (European Commission 2013).

circumstances, could enable abandoned spaces or neglected area of cities, to function as catalyst of local creative energies and incubators of social projects. Yet, examples of those experiences had reportedly failed in the collaboration of public administrations and civil society: many times, a too discretional political power has ended up arresting the creation of collective experiences.

7 Grande Come Una Città: The Roman Experience

Conversely to the idea that public space can be merely defined in spatial terms, as a particular set of configurations of urban design and construction, what said above suggests that public space is a 'co-produced' resource. That is to say, it only comes into being when it is activated by the presence of people according to dynamic and changing patterns and timetables.

'Grande come una città' is new-born movement in the city of Rome.

Over the last decade, Rome has experienced a deep crisis which has considerably affected the cultural sector: all started in 2008 right after the financial crisis when the public administration decided to slash the part of public budget destined to cultural public expenditure. In fact, in the cultural sector, particularly strong decisions have been taken due to the persuasion that those spaces with lack of revenue's utility, as cinemas, theatres and cultural spaces in general, were deemed to be commodified. At the time of budget's cuts, the government decision was taken in accordance with the implementation plan of spending review and consequently these measures had a particular impact within the cultural sector, targeting activities ranging from performances to exhibitions, education and research, in order for the government to cope with the international financial crisis and reduce the Italian public debt. This austerity was accompanied by an intensive campaign of privatisation of public services and goods up to the referendum on the ownership provision of water utilities (Belingardi et al. 2014).

Within this framework, many initiatives and movements have emerged with the aim of claiming back the city and its cultural spaces. These initiatives have taken different shapes: illegal occupations, co-governance models of public spaces' management, top-down and bottom-up actions.

In this light, *Grande come una città* seems an interesting experience due to its hybrid nature: in fact, the movement was born from an idea of the Cultural Department in the III Municipality of Rome, which covers such a wide area of the city of Rome: Montesacro, Val Melaina, Monte Sacro Alto, Fidene, Serpentara, Casal Boccone, Conca d' Oro, Sacco Pastore, Tufello, Aereoporto dell'Urbe, Settebagni, Bufalotta and Tor San Giovanni, and it counts 205.446 inhabitants.[10]

This is not a centrally located area of Rome but imbued of history and identity, where urban and social dynamics have always been its throbbing heart. The III Municipality is a neighbourhood where citizens live their daily life going to the

[10]Source: Comune di Roma, La popolazione di Roma. struttura e dinamica demografica, 2017.

market, talking down the street, going to work and doing all those normal activities that fulfil our days; but surprisingly such a wide and populated area lacks sites of cultural production and encounter. In such a vast territory there is only one library, a small theatre and a cinema, whereas a large shopping centre, where nearly 20,000 people enter every year is just behind the corner. Here it is a slot of public city, closed and empty, where public life is lacking; while instead a piece of private city, commodified, remains open until late in the evening and incessant flows of visitors go in and out. The name *Grande come una città*, literally 'As big as the city' is conceived as a manifesto to upscale urban policies on a bigger scope imagining the city as a common soil to explore, use and manage.

The project was born in 2018, when a community of people from the neighbourhood has gathered to think how to address local needs and issues: that occasion saw the birth of a new sort of community. On a voluntary basis, the inhabitants of the Municipality and all those interested in the cause set up a calendar full of cultural initiatives establishing a certain number of working groups—today there are 30 working groups and more than 200 organised public assemblies. Differently from other experiences, the creation of a method with the aim of highlighting the process rather than to the result, can be considered as the virtuous element of *Grande come una città* (Raimo 2019).

An example can be found in the occupation of the cultural centre Horus Club in the III Municipality, back in 2007 and 2009. After the second eviction, the building has been left and abandoned for ten years. Nowadays, Horus Club's doors are still shut down and due to its architectural constraints it has been saved from the financial speculation risk. However, although the building has remained untouched, something in the citizens aside it has changed: the presence of squatters and activists has functioned to activate new connections and dynamics with the result of giving new light to a neglected and traditionally peripheral area. Piazza Sempione, the square where Hours Club rises, has now become a new cluster for cultural activities; using and living public spaces of the city contribute to the pursuit of happiness at different scales (Blasi and Renzi 2019. We can thus say that individuals' happiness does produce an impact on the quality of everyday life, whereas on the other is key driving force for reviving local economies.

8 Concluding Remarks

Restoring cities is not just a question of constructing good-looking buildings and regenerating neglected urban areas, but rather is also about making sense of the accumulation of different urban dynamics and improving shared practices by fostering participation and inclusion (Polanyi 1994). Participation is an essential element for cities' development that can be increased by experiencing public spaces through re-education processes of civicness encouraged by politics: this can only happen if the whole city and its spaces are thought of as a learner/teacher community.

When politics is just used as synonymous for governance, the risk of failure is higher: Indeed, as much as Deliberations and acts are fundamental, the ultimate aim of public policies should be the construction and empowerment of sense of community. The emersion of a culture of the commons points out the evidence that abandoned or neglected buildings and spaces all over the city are the symptoms that it is not just a matter of re-use, whereas it deals with redefinition of values and need of a sense of common.

References

Belingardi, C., Giardini, F., & Pinto, I. (2014). *Spatial struggles: Teatro Valle Occupato and the (right to the) city*. Opendemocracy.

Blasi, L., & Renzi, V. (2019). *Rivendicare*. In Grande come una città. Reinventare la politica a Roma. Roma: Alegre.

Calhoun, C. (1992). Introduction: Habermas and the public sphere. In *Habermas and the Public Sphere. Studies in contemporary German social thought*. Cambridge: MIT Press.

Capone, N. (2018). Beni comuni, usi collettivi e comune: oltre la logica proprietaria. In *La rivolta della cooperazione. Sperimentazioni sociali e autonomia possibile*. Milano: Mimemis.

Cellamare, C. (2018). Nuove forme dell'urbano e processi di riappropriazione della città. In L. S. Olschki, Raccontare, *leggere e immaginare la città contemporanea = Raconter, lire et imaginer la ville contemporaine*. Torrerossa.

Collins, R. (2004). *Interaction ritual chains*. Princeton: Princeton.

Cowen, T. (1985). *Public goods definitions and their institutional context: a critique of public goods theory*. Review of Social Economy.

De Certau, M. (1984). *The practice of everyday life*. Berkeley: University of California Press.

Donolo, C. (2005). *Dalle politiche pubbliche alle pratiche sociali nella produzione di beni pubblici?* Osservazioni su una nuova generazione di policies. Il Mulino.

Elinor, O. (2006). *Governare i beni collettivi*. ricerche Marsilio.

European Commission. (2013). *Quality of life in cities*. Luxembourg: European Union.

Foster, S. R., & Iaione, C. (2016). *The city as a commons*. Yale law and Policy Review.

Frischmann, B. (2013). *Infrastructure. The Social Value of Shared Resources*. Oxford.

Hard, M., & Negri, T. (2009). *Commonwealth*. Harvard University Press.

Harvey, D. (2012). *Rebel cities*. New York: Verso.

Howard, E. (1965). *Garden cities of tomorrow*. Cambridge: The MIT Press.

Kaminsky, H. (2003). Citizenship versus the pursuit of happiness, bonum commune versus private property: A modern contradiction and its medieval root. *The Medieval History Journal*.

Klamer, A. (2016). *Doing the right thing. A value based economy*. London: SEC.

Kornberger, M., & Borch, C. (2015). Urban commons. In M. Kornberger, & C. Borch, *Urban commons. Rethinking the city*. New York: Routledge.

Landes, W. M. (2019). Copyright. In R. Towse, A *Handbook of cultural economics*. Edward Elgar Publishing Limited.

Lefebvre, H. (1968). *Le droit à la ville*. Paris: Anthropos.

Mitchell, D. (1995). The end of public space? People's park, definitions of the public, and democracy. *Annals of the Association of American Geographers, 85*(1), 108–133. Retrieved April 27, 2020, from www.jstor.org/stable/2564281.

Musikanski, L., & Polley, C. (2016). Life, liberty, and the pursuit of happiness: Measuring what matters. *Journal of Social Change*.

Nielsen, G., & Isin, E. (2008). *Acts of citizenship*. Zed Book.

Polanyi, K. (1994). *The great transformation: The political and economic origins of our time*. Boston: Beacon Press.

Raimo, C. (2019). Iniziare. In *Grande come una città. reinventare la politica a Roma*. Roma: Alegre.
Rodotà, S. (2012). *Il diritto di avere diritti*. Gius: Laterza & Figli Spa.
Sassen, S. (2001). *The Global city: New York*. London: Tokyo.
Sennett, R. (2018). *Costruire e abitare*. Milano: Feltrinelli.
Settis, S. (2012). *Azione poplare*. Cittadini per il bene comune: Einaudi.
Standing, G. (2019). *Plunder of the commons*. Pelican Book: A Manifesto for Sharing Public Wealth.
Vitellio, I. (2005). *Spazi pubblici come beni comuni. Critica della razionalità urbanistica*, pp. 9–20.

Cultural Commons and Historical Identity: The Experience of the Arbëreshë Community in Southern Italy

Emanuela Macrì

Abstract

This chapter aims to assess whether an ethnic and linguistic minority, such as the Arbëreshë community in Southern Italy, could be considered a specific kind of cultural common. Commons are historically defined as resources connected to natural sphere and enjoyed collectively. The idea that cultures may be analysed under the perspective of commons produces relevant theoretical constructs which are not strictly related to, and therefore not identifiable only with, common-pool resources. With respect to this issue, the chapter offers a systematic analysis of three important dimensions, belonging to a specific community, that can be considered crucial for the definition of a new concept of cultural commons: culture, spatial dimension, and community aspect. Some evidence, drawn from the theoretical analysis and case study method, offers an overview which led to considered Arbëreshë community a unique cultural commons, able to generate shared value from its rich, complex, and lively identity.

The author is grateful to Demetrio Guzzardi, Giulio Peta, and Lucio Franco Masci for their contribution to this research work as privileged observers. The usual caveat applies. The author is also grateful to the participants at the International Conference on "Cultural Commons and Urban Dynamics. New Economic Paradigm for a Complex Social Map", held in Catanzaro, October 2019, for their insightful comments and suggestions to an earlier version of this chapter.

E. Macrì (✉)
Department of Laws, Economics and Sociology, Magna Graecia University, Catanzaro, Italy
e-mail: emanuela.macri@unicz.it

E. Macrì et al. (eds.), *Cultural Commons and Urban Dynamics*,
https://doi.org/10.1007/978-3-030-54418-8_13

1 Introduction

The chapter aims at investigating the broad concept of cultural commons in order to analyse whether and how this concept may be used to define an ethnic and linguistic minority such as the Arbëreshë community in Southern Italy. Commons are historically defined as resources that are (or could be) enjoyed collectively. These resources may be part of the natural world as forests, oceans, and in broader sense natural resources. But they could also emerge from social realities such as the internet, scientific knowledge, creativity, conventional styles, or social rites. In this chapter, the attention is mainly given to cultural commons that are not strictly connected and therefore not necessarily identifiable with material common-pool resources. Despite the efforts aimed at consistently defining such commons where material and intangible variables coexist, they still prove complex and multi-dimensional, and can be interpreted from various perspectives.

Within such a conceptual framework the chapter focuses on a specific ethnic and linguistic community which seems to retain within its identity three important dimensions that can be considered crucial for the definition of a new concept of cultural commons: culture, spatial dimension, and community. The community is called Arbëreshë: the term comes from Arbëria, which is the denomination of the areas where an Albanian ethnic-linguistic minority live. It is the fifteenth century when Albanians, due to the Ottoman conquer, are forced to emigrate in Italy in Apulia, Calabria, and Sicily regions where they are hosted and then can establish their stable settlements. Since then the Arbëreshë people became part of the regional community, although they were able to keep their historical identity, language, traditions, and rites through the centuries.

Empirical evidence drawn on semi-structured interviews, with some privileged observers of this community, and document analysis offer an overview of the consistency of the concept of cultural commons to the Arbëreshë community. The chapter is organized as follows. Section 2 examines the theoretical framework. In Sect. 3, the Arbëreshë community and its history is briefly described. Section 4 explains the approach adopted. Sections 5 and 6 present and discuss the outcome of the empirical research. Section 7 offers concluding remarks and implications.

2 The Theoretical Framework

2.1 Defining Traditional and Emerging Concepts of Commons

Until twenty years ago only a few works focused on commons. The article of Coman (1911), published in the American Economic Review, about irrigation problems, can be considered the first contribution which traces the origins of the debate on commons. More than fifty years later the seminal work by Hardin (1968) focused on commons and collective action introducing the "tragedy of the commons". Hardin claimed that the only way to avoid the tragedy was to either privatise the resource or transform it in public property. Finally, Ostrom (1990) considers two possible ways to avoid the tragedy: the dilemma privatisation versus nationalisation on one hand, self-government on the other.

According to Ostrom's theory commons are not free to access spaces and resources but they are well-defined and self-managed by a limited group of individuals, based on rules and institutions that the community members know and are able to respect, applying predefined sanctions to those who do not enforce them. For the first time, Ostrom emphasizes the concept of institutional diversity, beside and beyond biological and cultural diversity, but especially she rejects the economic model based on the so-called *homo-oeconomicus* and on proprietary individualism.

There are further kinds of commons, which are not strictly related to, and therefore not identifiable with, common-pool resources. According to Edwards and Escande (2015), there are new categories of commons that include both physical and virtual communities. In the first type, we can include neighborhood commons, such as community parks, libraries, and so on; in the second type instead, we find open access repositories, blogs, virtual communities, internet, public radio and TV, shared music. Considering specific features we can focus upon neighborhood commons, knowledge or information commons, social commons, infrastructure commons, and finally cultural commons.

Within this general framework, commons related to cultural heritage can be identified with two sub-categories: the former is the generic "cultural commons" (cultural experience shared by socially cohesive communities), the latter is "research or education commons", usually supporting academic communities or focused on undergraduate students and school pupils. The former category needs further analysis which is being carried out in the recent years by many scholars.

2.2 The Development of Cultural Commons Theory: Toward a Shared Definition

One of the earliest contributions which refer to the notion of cultural commons was elaborated by Madison et al. (2010). They define the issue such as "environments for developing and distributing cultural and scientific knowledge through institutions that support pooling and sharing that knowledge in a managed way". Research is referred to knowledge, both scientific and cultural, and the paper tries to give it a new perspective, also considering knowledge from the point of view of a common pool focused on cultural production as information goods.

From this perspective, Solum (2010) elaborates his definition of cultural commons excluding "phenomena and processes that might be labeled as 'culture' but that are not usually described as information goods". Actually, he does not consider social norms, language, networks of social relationships among kinship groups, and so forth, but he defines cultural commons as only information production. Clearly, these definitions are still anchored to the discussion about traditional commons as natural resources, since economic debate ignores some important combination and reciprocal fertilisation among common resources and culture, from both the anthropological and artistic viewpoints.

The pursuit of this increased convention represents the prelude for a new definition of cultural commons, as understood in this chapter. In such a respect an important contribution is the book "Cultural Commons. A New Perspective on the Production and Evolution of Cultures" published in 2012. It argues that the economic issues normally applied to common goods, such as social dilemmas and free riding, should also be applied to the cultural and creative areas, in order for scholars and public decision-makers to elaborate effective guidelines aimed at crafting policy orientations. As Noonan (2014) claims "the book is an attempt to coalesce and influence the research agenda in this emergent area of inquiry".

In such a respect cultural commons can be seen, according to Bertacchini et al. (2012), as a set of resources expressed and shared by a community defined along three dimensions: culture, space, and community. Similarly, Marrelli and Fiorentino (2016) define cultural commons focusing on their spatial dimension. They also consider elements such as socially cohesive communities and the existence of a governance system based on social ties, over common pooled resource. The aim was to suggest a new orientation within a synergic framework of cultural commons, and to describe the creation and the eventual disappearance of cultural commons within local art market in Naples.

A wider and heterogeneous definition of cultural commons, which seems to be preeminent in literature, considers cultural commons such as commons created over social communication flows and composed by both information and attention. Sherman (2016) shares this definition and introduces the discussion on the adoption of a powerful management method for cultural commons, which is represented, according to his conclusions, by collective actions able to offer the spread of democratic options with respect to privatisation.

Other contributions have investigated upon boundaries and shared metrics of cultural commons definition, such as a container that can be filled and crafted within a strategic framework in which institutional goals clearly determine selection criteria and choice mechanisms end up defining cultural commons. Barrère (2018), for example, suggests a sharp breakdown among cultural heritage and cultural commons, in order for local governments to identify adequate management tools; Bruncevic (2017) analyses cultural commons from the legal perspective. With respect to this field of action the concept turns out to be unclear because, despite their permeability to even access, commons may imply limits on property rights and the appropriation of public domain.

3 The Arbëreshë Community in Southern Italy

The Arbëreshë community has moved to Italy since the fourteenth century. They were descendants of Illyrians, who originally lived in a wide area of Eastern Europe that extended from the shores of Danube River to Greece, like contemporary

Albanians. The Arbëreshë probably settled in Italy after the death of their national hero Giorgio Castriota Scanderbeg in 1468, when the progressive increase of the Turkish pressure led Albania to be a vassal state of Byzantine government. Many groups of the Albanian community came to Italy, including soldiers, families, mercenaries, farmers, shepherds, women destined for servitude (Liuzzi 2016). Also, the heavy earthquakes occurring in the same period may have exerted a notable influence on the migration to Italy.

Although the Kingdom of the Two Sicilies accepted these new populations within its borders, it settled them in isolated, neglected, and unproductive areas. Moreover, the socioeconomic dimension of the host territory seemed to be improper for coexistence with local populations, which immediately became hostile toward Albanian populations (Resta 1991). They lived in seven Southern Italy regions: the imaginary Nation of Arbëria composed by Abruzzo, Molise, Campania, Basilicata, Puglia, Calabria, and Sicily. See Fig. 1.

Over time, however, the Arbëreshë community has almost completely lost its identity in several regions, while in Calabria the community, counting 58.425 people who live in 33 towns and villages, mostly in the Cosenza province, still preserves its social, religious, and linguistic identity. The Arbëreshë community persists in 19 municipalities: 8 of them (Acquaformosa, Lungro, Firmo, S. Basile, Frascineto, Civita, Plataci, and Castroregio) are located in the mountain complex of the Pollino (northern part of the Cosenza province) while 11 (Falconara, S. Benedetto, S. Martino, Cerzeto, S. Caterina, S. Sofia, S. Demetrio, S. Cosmo, Vaccarizzo, S. Giorgio, Spezzano Albanese) are scattered east and west of the middle and lower sections of the Crati River (central-southern part of Cosenza province). They represent 46.3 % of the 41 Arbëreshë-speaking municipalities in Italy (Tagarelli et al. 2007).

According to Brunetti (2005), in the area among Calabria and Basilicata lots of Arbëreshë communities are located in mountainous areas away from the main communication routes. This uncomfortable condition of distance, also from other Italian communities, may have been the cause that allowed the Arbëreshë people to preserve their historical identity. This trait, composed mainly by three important aspects such as language, endogamy, and the Greek-Byzantine religious rite consolidated for the Arbëreshë community a strategic position of social differentiation with respect to the Italian community (Resta 1996).

Their language is based on two dialects: *tosk* is spoken in Southern Albania, while *ghego* is diffused in Northern Albania; through the centuries it has been handled orally, and such a practice contributed to contaminate it with the Italian language. In 1999 the act n. 482, enacted by Italian State, recognized the Arbëreshë language and tried to promote the linguistic and cultural enhancement of the community (La Barbera 2019). Also, it established the teaching of their ancient language within schools, and the activation of minority culture courses at university level, while inside public offices the Arbëreshë language can be used for institutional documents. In addition, subsidies are given for publishing and television broadcasters who use this language and finally within all Arbëreshë countries road signs can be written in dual language (Savoia et al. 2008).

Fig. 1 The imaginary nation of Arbëria. *Source* The web

The endogamy practice (marriage among the members of the community) is likely to have contributed to a gradual ethnic isolation process. The rationale of endogamy could be traced in the intention to keep a closed ethnic group, formed only by people from Albania, in order for the Arbëreshë community to consolidate and demonstrate its strength and cohesion (Liuzzi 2016).

From the religious point of view, the Byzantine Catholic Church is under the ecumenical jurisdiction of the Church of Rome, but it maintains and follows Greek Orthodox ecclesiastical rites and disciplines. It was February 13th of the year 1919 when Benedict XV, with the Bull "Catholici Fideles Graeci Ritus", canonically erected the Eparchy[1] of Lungro for Albanian worshippers adopting the Greek-Byzantine religious rite. Today it counts 30 Parishes: 25 in Cosenza province, two

[1]The Eparchy is managed by an Eparch nominated by the Pope. He is equated with the Roman Bishops, but before the ordination he can marry. The celebration of the mass is different from the Roman rite although it contains the same essential liturgical moments. For instance, the Eucharist is celebrated with fermented bread and wine while liturgical readings and hymns to Saints vary according to liturgical calendar.

in Potenza province, one in Pescara province, one in Lecce, and one in Bari. The Eparchy of Lungro is a *sui juris* jurisdiction of Greek-Byzantine religious rite which directly depends on the Holy See, like the Eparchy of Piana degli Albanesi in Sicily and the Exarchic Monastery of Grottaferrata in Rome (Vaccaro 2019).

4 The Analysis: Approach and Tools

The exploratory and descriptive research carried out on the cultural commons features in the Arbëreshë community based in Calabria starts from the theoretical analyses elaborated by Eisenhardt (1989), Yin Robert (1994), Sinkovics et al. (2016). The research method is developed along two stages. The first stage explores the economic literature and elaborates the features of appraisal and evaluation of cultural commons through a systematic review (PRISMA) proposed by Moher et al. (2009), as synthesized in Fig. 1, in order for us to adopt a clear selection process.

Scopus database has been used to select the studies. Reference lists of prominent studies and resources were also examined to include contributions that were not identified using a computer database search. After having fixed some limitations, such as the exclusion of contributions before the year 2000 and the exclusion of contributions from subject areas different from social science, arts and humanities, and economics, 140 studies were selected. These have been deemed to comply with inclusion criteria such as the presence of the "cultural commons" search term in article title, abstract, or keywords.

At this point, a single file of identified references was created, and duplicates were removed. The remaining contributions have been screened for eligibility through titles and abstract and 77 contributions were selected for full-text appraisal, but finally only 35 were taken into account. See Fig. 2.

The second stage has been carried out through the case study method (Yin 2002), specifically suitable to investigate the complex and dynamic nature of the cultural sector, and in particular the cultural commons field. Research activity has been carried out between May and December 2019. Data have been collected in two phases: a) information, historical documents, and publications available either on the web or in public libraries of the Arbëreshë community located in Caraffa, a small town of Catanzaro province; b) semi-structured interviews.

According to Gaskell (2000) the use of interview, in qualitative research, allows us to develop a deeper comprehension of a phenomenon. Specifically, semi-structured interviews adopt a common reference framework and allow the analysis to prove consistent. As Corbetta (2014) states, the trace of the interview constitutes the perimeter of the contents to be dealt with. Figure 3 describes the details of the investigation carried out.

The starting point for the elaboration of the content of the interview has been a specific definition of cultural commons provided by Bertacchini et al. (2012) and Marrelli and Fiorentino (2016). The authors similarly define cultural commons and

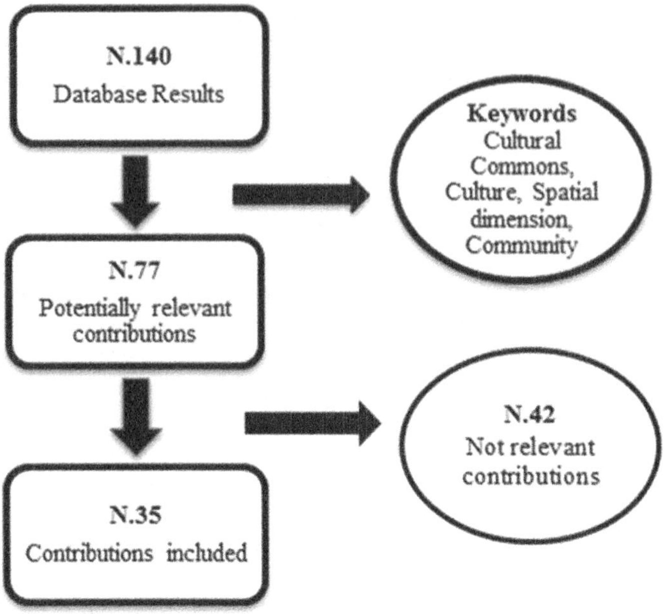

Fig. 2 Literature review. *Source* Author's elaboration

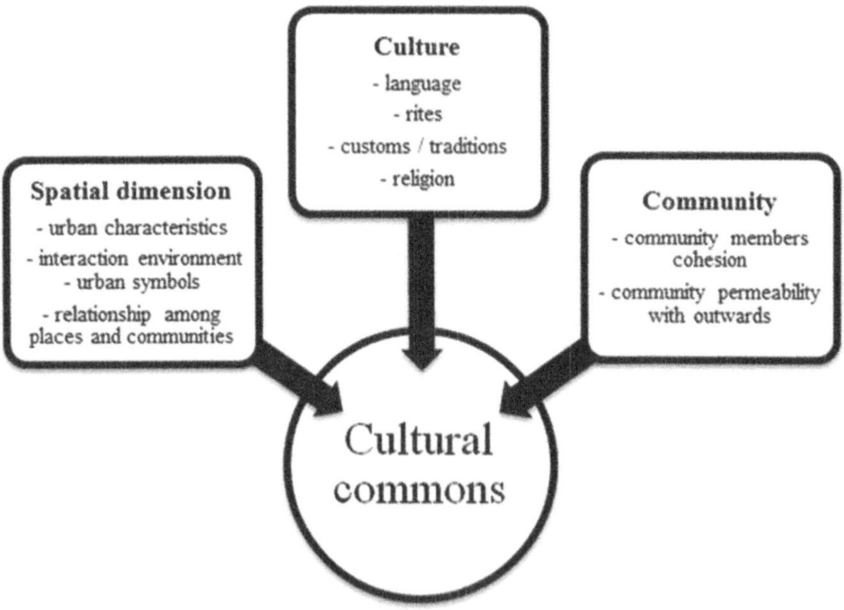

Fig. 3 Interview contents. *Source* Author's elaboration

used as characteristic elements a set of resources defined along three dimensions: culture, space, and the existence of a system of governance based on the social ties of a socially cohesive community.

Some qualified witnesses have been involved as holders of information about the Arbëreshë community. They are personalities generally involved in the preliminary stages of research (Corbetta 2014), and may be endowed with five features: high status within community, detailed knowledge of the phenomenon, willingness to cooperate, dialectical ability, and impartiality. As qualified witness, we chose three personalities from three different Arbëreshë communities of Calabria region: an elder member of the community as the guardian of collective memory, an historian of the Arbëreshë community, and finally an architect and urban planner, expert and scholar of urban settlements. They, respectively, came from Caraffa (Catanzaro province), San Demetrio Corone, and Santa Sofia di Epiro (both located in Cosenza province).

5 Main Outcomes

The aim of this chapter is to assess whether and how an ethnic and linguistic minority could be considered as cultural commons, focusing on the Arbëreshë community. The results are based on both primary and secondary data. Primary data were collected through semi-structured interviews aimed at verifying how the selected witnesses perceive and contextualise the three dimensions of cultural commons. Secondary data came from research articles, books and documents, and publications available in libraries, the web, and other sources.

5.1 Cultural Variables

Cultural variables were the first dimensions analysed; they consist in language, rites, and customs. Semi-structured interviews had the aim to verify how these aspects had been preserved and dealt with through the generations, and investigate whether these elements were similar or different to those present in contemporary Albania.

The Arbëreshë language, with its several facets, is presently spoken especially among the elderly and adults of the communities; its prevailing oral adoption and diffusion might have contributed to the disappearance of some words and expressions. Experts report that slightly less than half of the Arbëreshë words correspond to the Albanian language, while about 15% of the remaining glossary could have been coined by the Italian-Albanian writers who, in their stories and poems have crafted neologisms that have been later grafted into common language and adopted by the Arbëreshë community.

Finally, a remaining part of the Arbëreshë language derives from contaminations with the Italian language and particularly with many dialects of the areas where the communities were resident. As for the Italian dialects which may differ from each other even in the same Regional territory, also the Arbëreshë dialects vary quite a lot within communities settled a few kilometers away. Although the Calabria Regional Government has issued an act aimed at preserving traditional language through its teaching in schools, unfortunately it has partially disappeared, mainly due to the attitude of new generations to adopt a sort of homologous jargon.

The most popular rites, preserved and transmitted orally, have religious origins: Epiphany, Cult of the Dead, Holy Week, and Easter. In the Epiphany day, the solemn liturgy in the church is followed by a general gathering of the believers around a fountain in the town center; the Eparca and all the Papas[2] proceed with the blessing of the waters. This rite recalls, through a song, the descent of the Holy Spirit into the Jordan River during the Baptism of Jesus Christ. The Eparca submerges the cross in the water for three times, holding the candle holder and a sprig of rue in his hands. Finally, a white dove is flown to the fountain in order to reproduce the sacred image of the descent of the Holy Spirit on Jesus as he left the Jordan.

The cult of the dead, according to the timetable of Byzantine Greek rite, is celebrated at the beginning of spring and is based on the popular belief that for eight days Jesus Christ grants permission to the souls of the dead to leave the underworld and return to the places where they had lived. In some groups boiled wheat is used to commemorate a deceased person, it is blessed by Papas in the home of families who have suffered the loss of someone, and eventually exposed in the Church.

For the Arbëreshë communities, Easter represents the most important religious rite of the year. Passion, Death, and Resurrection of Jesus Christ are relived by the believers thanks to the rich Eastern symbolism. The celebrations begin on the last Friday before the Holy Week, when groups of young people headed by the Papas sing to believers waiting for them to give eggs as reward.

During the Sunday before Easter, the Eparchs on the back of a donkey cross the main course of the towns directed to Cathedrals to relive the entrance of Jesus in Jerusalem. Holy Thursday and Holy Friday host the celebrations of Passion and Death of Jesus Christ, while Holy Saturday opens with the prayer for the Resurrection, ad at midnight the Papas knock three times on the church door, symbolically blocked by the devil. Then the believers can get in to celebrate the Resurrection. Finally, during the Easter day prayers and songs create a spiritual atmosphere, and traditional costumes can be appreciated when women parade in the streets and squares, distributing red eggs as symbols of the cyclicity of life and immortality.

Within the Arbëreshë communities many traditional customs are still preserved and crafted. They are different from town to town, nevertheless they keep traits of homogeneity. Often communities preserve their traditional customs inside museums, although a few families still keep the original ones with them. Suits are normally being crafted by the same tailors, therefore their specific features can prove mixed and unusually combined with each other also when related to different

[2]They represent the equivalent of the priests of the Roman rite.

local groups. Furthermore, it seems that until the sixties many Arbëreshë people, both women and men, still used typical costumes daily, but gradually this habit was lost and today they are used only for specific religious and popular events.

Popular culture is mainly formed by songs, dances, and legends. It has always been transmitted orally, and this may have been caused by the widespread illiteracy in the past. Each community used some people as historical memory of the place: they were given the function to preserve and transmit the traditions toward the new generations. As mentioned earlier for the traditional customs, also popular traditions appear to be different among towns and groups. A common popular element is nostalgia for the lost homeland Albania and for the death of Scanderbeg. In fact the most important dance, called Vallje, commemorates Scanderbeg's victory over the Turkish army, which occurred on a Tuesday after Easter. In such a way, the Arbëreshe community remains ideally connected to its epic past. This dance strengthens the cultural identity and the social cohesion.

5.2 Spatial and Urban Variables

In cultural commons, the value chain is strongly influenced by the features of the physical environment where the interactions among the community members occur and develop. The research investigates the urban model of both primitive and contemporary settlements trying to highlight the symbolic places of the Arbëreshë culture. From the urban point of view the most important specific element of identity was, and still is in many communities, the so-called *gjitonia*.

It is a set of houses, usually three or four, which follow curved lines and have no edges; they are shaped in a concentric form with openings facing a small common area, similar to a small square, which is shared by all homes. Finally, within this area there are narrow alleys leading to other *gjitonie*. The families sharing these spaces usually establish deep relationships of fraternity and friendship among them, as well as material and spiritual sharing. For the Arbëreshë community, the *gjitonia* represents an extension of the houses beyond the walls: within it there are stone slabs where people sit to spend their time and do small hand jobs. In fact, the ancient homes had a circular shape, with the oven in the middle of the structure, in order for the residents to cook and to keep their places warm.

On a larger scope, the *rione* is a circular district shaped around a fountain and a small church. Both in *giitonie* and in *rioni* the circle is the symbolic and functional shape adopted in order for the resident group to share actions and benefits, and at the same time to enjoy the favorable omen related to the reproduction of the celestial sphere. Although these structures could not be built when parts of the community moved to the suburbs, they are still alive in historic centers and hamlets, where most of the houses are still in use, and not only by the elderly but also by young people who preferred to re-populate the places of the ancient Arbëreshë tradition.

5.3 Community Dimensions and Features

The last aspect examined in this section is related to the cohesion degree within the Arbëreshë community itself, and its permeability to the Calabrian people. Attention to ethnic minorities represents a very discussed topic by academics, policymakers, and social groups; its interpretation might combine technical and sentimental views, due to the intensive flows of migrants affecting many coastal areas of the Mediterranean Sea. New perspectives of analysis can be useful from the historical, linguistic, and anthropological perspective, shedding new light upon such a complex and controversial phenomenon.

In the past centuries, the cultural and social condition of the Arbëreshë community in Calabria Region (but, in general, anywhere in Italy) proved quite difficult. At first, the Arbëreshë had been welcomed but very soon cultural differences exploded and they were considered usurpers and, consequently, confined in places located far from the urban centers, in unproductive areas. Then the relationship between the two communities was conflictual. Over time, however, a slow and gradual process of integration has occurred, and despite the many difficulties the Arbëreshë were unanimously acknowledged and accepted as a community, and respected as a nation.

Until a few years ago, the Arbëreshë communities seemed to be not permeable. The reasons may have been manifold: among them the geographical location implying a long distance from other communities hence a high degree of isolation, and the religious identity acting as a glue within each community.

The first eco-system where social relationship developed was the neighborhood, being also considered a powerful educational place and a hub of personal relationships. In fact, daily social relationships with neighbours used to take place within *gjitonia*, the most important dimension of social life after family.

The community lives within these spaces, considered almost as small States, with their own natural laws based on solidarity and mutual respect; neighbours exchange among them both material goods such as food and spiritual goods such as comfort and solidarity. This is emphasised in particular times such as the death of family members. Nowadays the degree of internal cohesion of the Arbëreshë community still remains high, but there is also a high degree of permeability with the Calabrian community, especially among the new generations. The complex relationship between tradition and innovation, typical of each community, has led to flattening the differences and to a wider co-operation, and such a new unity has generated new cultural goods.

6 Discussion and Implications

A definition of cultural commons appears to be quite complex, for a variety of reasons. Certainly, difficulties arise from the need to identify the "culture" galaxy, a delicate combination of different disciplines whose methodological approach and technical tools contribute to define its features and values. From the anthropological point of view, for instance, culture could refer to the set of social expressions of a defined community, while according to conventional wisdom culture could refer to the practice of the arts in both tangible and intangible forms. From many perspectives culture ends up being identified with the source of a value chain where relationships are quite crucial. According to Donati and Solci (2011), relational goods are produced by relations among individuals or communities, accompanied by defined aspects that may limit their boundaries. Moreover, this particular type of goods postulates the knowledge of other subjects involved in the exchange, and requires an investment of time to build networks, in which monetary investments are not so important.

A relational good is produced in what Bruni and Zamagni (2004) define civil economy, in which the principle of reciprocity appears to be the most specific. At the base of reciprocity there is the action of a subject (*homo reciprocans* or *cooperans*) who carries it out in order for relationships with other subjects to be activated, kept and strengthened, and not merely rewarded (Bruni 2009). Cultural commons could be considered as a set of cultural resources shared by socially cohesive communities, interpreted in the broadest sense: a cultural district, the traditions of an indigenous community, and many other possible examples. The clear and evident aspect is represented by the fact that the resource shared by the community or group increases its value when people adopt it and exchange it; if there were no relational components the cultural commons probably would not exist.

According to De Moor (2013), the theory of commons refers to a different type of approach in which a new view of individuals as members of a community is being shaped. The "rational individuals" who are generally in competition with each other, change their objective-function, generating and getting value (what textbook wisdom would define "utility") from connections, interactions, collective orientations, and actions.

For *homo cooperans,* the commons represent a new arising phenomenon and source of value, beyond the mere market and state frameworks. The methodological individualism loses strength, in favor of a more collective and shared value hierarchy, and new kinds of goods, services, and actions are crafted. In such a respect, connections among people generate new resources and mutual social solidarity, so we can speak of generating social capital through the enjoyment and exchange of cultural commons. In such a complexity, in which a sharp complication is generated by the quick evolution and transformation of the society and of its dynamics, culture commons can be seen as a relational good produced and enjoyed by the participants in a particular action or in a specific event, or an external reality able to generate value and to satisfy human needs of a relational type (Donati 1994).

7 Concluding Remarks

This chapter aimed at examining the application of cultural commons theoretical features to the identity of a community settled far from its territorial roots and its original network of relationships, and interacting with a different culture. In such a perspective, the evolutionary dynamics affecting this identity are intensively influenced by the many features of cultural commons as a source of shared values both intangible and locally established, within the continuous dilemma between the preservation of cultural identity as it originally was shaped on one hand, and melting some of its features with the local habits, language, values, and beliefs on the other hand. Rather than a struggle, it appears to be an evolving process that we can consider an active cultural commons.

The case of the Arbëreshë community resident in Southern Italy, here examined, can be quite eloquent in offering a living field for analysis, and therefore confirming the complexity of cultural commons as unsteady and dynamic phenomena. The multifold nature of cultural commons, the variety of disciplinary perspectives needed to analyse them, and the multiple layers required for institutional responses to be crafted in order for arising and unpredictable problems and controversies to be effectively faced, make our analysis quite complex. The research carried out cannot reach clear cut conclusions, and further analysis is needed.

The generativity that characterizes the creation of commons can be seen as an opportunity for re-articulation aimed at filling the gaps inadvertently or indifferently opened by a stable and self-reproductive system. Hence what better opportunity, offered by a natural element such as an ethnic and linguistic minority community, can serve as a counterpart to the analysis of cultural commons concepts? The three dimensions of cultural commons allowed this research to achieve interesting results, able to enrich the economic analysis of cultural commons.

Cultural aspects that characterise the Arbëreshë community are related to language, rites, traditional customs, and popular culture. Language, with its several facets, is presently spoken especially among the elderly and adults of the communities, it has been handed down mainly in oral form and the Italian State recognizes and promotes it through a specific act. Rites as Epiphany, Cult of the Dead, Holy Week, and Easter are the expression of a tradition deeply rooted in the community as long as traditions, symbols, aesthetical signs, and styles.

Spatial and urban structures are anchored to two fundamental pillars belonging to the Arbëreshë community *gjitonia* and *rione*, that are not only considered as urban elements but as extensions of the houses beyond the walls where social relationships with neighbours take place, animated by feelings of solidarity and mutual respect. Finally, within communities is present a high degree of internal cohesion, nevertheless external relationships are gradually expanding, proving encouraging signals of integration and cohabitation with other communities, allowing both sides to accumulate an intensive shared social capital through time. The Arbëreshë community, as this research highlights, generates shared value from its rich, complex, and lively identity, that can be considered a unique cultural commons. In such a respect, this research work should be considered the preliminary step for further research and investigation, within a multi-disciplinary approach.

References

Barrère, C. (2018). *Cultural heritage: Capital, commons, and heritages*. The Oxford Handbook of Public Heritage Theory and Practice.

Bertacchini, E., Bravo, G., Marrelli, M., & Santagata, W. (2012). *Cultural commons. A new perspective on the production and evolution of cultures*. Massachussets: Edward Elgar Publishing.

Bruncevic, M. (2017). *Law, Art and the commons*. Routledge.

Brunetti, C. (2005). *Dalla negazione al riconoscimento*. La condizione giuridica delle minoranze linguistiche, collana dellIstituto Mezzogiorno Mediterraneo, Soveria Mannelli, Rubettino.

Bruni, L. (2009). *Dizionario di economia civile*. Città nuova.

Bruni, L., & Zamagni, S. (2004). *Economia civile. Efficienza, equità, felicità pubblica*. Il Mulino.

Coman, K. (1911). Some unsettled problems of irrigation. *The American Economic Review, 1*(1), 1–19.

Corbetta, P. (2014). *Metodologia e tecniche della ricerca sociale*. Ed. Il Mulino.

De Moor, T. (2013). *Homo cooperans. Institutions for collective action and the compassionate society*.

Donati, P. (1994). *Teoria relazionale della società*. Franco Angeli.

Donati, P., & Solci, R. (2011). *I beni relazionali: che cosa sono e quali effetti producono*. Bollati Boringhieri.

Edwards and Escande. (2015). *MS20: White Paper European cultural commons*. Project Acronym: Ev3 Grant Agreement number: 620484 Project Title: Europeana Version 3.

Eisenhardt, K. M. (1989). Building theories from case study research. *Academy of Management Review, 14*(4), 532–550.

Gaskell, G. (2000). *Individual and group interviewing. Qualitative researching with text, image and sound*, pp. 38–56.

Hardin, G. (1968). The tragedy of the commons. *Science, 162*(3859), 1243–1248.

La Barbera, N. (2019). *Gli Arbëreshë d'Italia: la storia e gli insediamenti*. Solfanelli Editore: Chieti.

Liuzzi, A. (2016). Old and new minorities: The case of Arbëreshë communities and Albanian immigrants in Southern Italy. *Migration Letters, 13*(2), 258–268.

Madison, M. J., Frischmann, B. M., & Strandburg, K. J. (2010). Constructing commons in the cultural environment. *Cornell Law review, 95*, 657e659.

Marrelli, M., & Fiorentino, P. (2016). Cultural commons and local art markets: zero-miles contemporary art in Naples. *City, Culture and Society, 7*(2), 117–122.

Moher, D., Liberati, A., Tetzlaff, J., & Altman, D. G. (2009). Preferred reporting items for systematic reviews and meta-analyses: the PRISMA statement. *Annals of Internal Medicine, 151*(4), 264–269.

Noonan, D. S. (2014). Charting a new cultural commons research agenda. *Journal of cultural economic, 38*(3), 287–290.

Ostrom, E. (1990). *Governing the commons: The evolution of institutions for collective action*. New York: Cambridge University Press.

Resta, P. (1991). *Parentela ed identità etnica, consanguineità e scambi matrimoniali in una comunità italo-albanese* (pp. 7–357). Franco Angeli.

Resta, P. (1996). *Un popolo in Cammino, Migrazioni albanesi in Italia* (pp. 7–119). Besa.

Savoia, L. M., Altimari, F., & Manzini, M. R. (2008). *Studi sulle varietà arbëreshe*. Sezione di Albanologia: Università della Calabria. Dipartimento di Linguistica.

Sherman, Z. (2016). Primitive accumulation in the cultural commons. *Review of Radical Political Economics, 48*(1), 176–188.
Sinkovics, R. R., Richter, N. F., Ringle, C. M., & Schlaegel, C. (2016). A critical look at the use of SEM in international business research. *International Marketing Review*.
Solum, L. B. (2010). Questioning cultural commons. *Cornell Law Review, 95,* 817.
Tagarelli, G., Fiorini, S., Piro, A., Luiselli, D., Tagarelli, A., & Pettener, D. (2007). Ethnicity and biodemographic structure in the Arbëreshe of the province of Cosenza, southern Italy, in the XIX century. *Collegium antropologicum, 31*(1), 331–338.
Vaccaro, A. (2019). Nel Centenario di istituzione dell'Eparchia di Lungro (1919–2019). Aspetti storici di una presenza neo-bizantina nell'Occidente cattolico (Secc. XV-XX). *Palaver, 8*(2), 225-280.
Yin R. K. (1994). *Case study research: Design and methods*. Sage publications.
Yin, R. K. (2002) *Applications of case study research second edition applied social research methods series*, Volume 34.

Migrant Cultures. Contributions of NGOs and Community-Based Organizations to Safeguarding Intangible Cultural Heritage in Santiago, Chile

Pascuala Migone

Abstract

This article examines how NGO and community-based organizations perceive their contributions to safeguarding migrant intangible cultural heritage in Santiago, Chile. Through the thematic analysis of 15 in-depth interviews with organizations' representatives, the study found the existence of three main values of ICH for the social inclusion of migrant communities: making immigrant visible and appreciated; strengthening their communities through reinforcing their identities and social ties; and revealing its economic potential. In achieving them, the following contributions of NGO and community-based organizations emerged: the creation of spaces, the promotion of sensitization actions and the creation of associations and empowerment within migrant communities. Moreover, specific operational features of these organizations were found: an inclusive and participation-based work, in situ and progressive knowledge and limited resources and voluntary nature appeared as relevant for the realization of these actions.

1 Migration, ICH and Social Inclusion

Migrant communities include expatriates, exiled, refugees and asylum seekers who have left their countries for different reasons and settled elsewhere (Naguib 2013). Within growingly multicultural contexts, Intangible Cultural Heritage (ICH)—in its dynamic nature—acquires new dimensions and poses new challenges for migrant communities and receiving societies. One of the first questions refers to their social inclusion: 'a process which ensures that those at risk of poverty and social exclusion

P. Migone (✉)
Santiago, Chile
e-mail: pmigonew@gmail.com

E. Macrì et al. (eds.), *Cultural Commons and Urban Dynamics*,
https://doi.org/10.1007/978-3-030-54418-8_14

gain the opportunities and resources necessary to participate fully in economic, social, political and cultural life and to enjoy a standard of living that is considered normal in the society in which they live' (Commission of the European Communities 2003, p. 9). It is then a normative concept, insofar it is considered desirable to promote conditions that favor the inclusion of individuals and groups into society (Abrams et al. 2005).

Conventional approaches to social inclusion mainly emphasize the enhancement of opportunities, access to resources and respect of basic rights for people who are disadvantaged on the basis of sex, age, disability, ethnicity, origin, religion or economic or other status (UN 2016). While these are fundamental, there is a gap regarding ICH—as a crucial element of an integral migratory policy—and the potential role non-State actors can play. ICH safeguarding actions, from protecting to sensitizing, have been argued as crucial in maintaining cultural diversity, promoting intercultural respect and dialogue and building resilient and socially integrated migrant communities (Kurin 2004; Bendix et al. 2013; Van der Zeijden 2017). In other words, safeguarding migrant cultural expressions can have a relevant role in fighting these prejudices and fostering their social inclusion in a new territory.

The main international framework for ICH is provided by the 2003 UNESCO Convention for the Safeguarding of ICH. The treaty not only gives guidelines and support for inventories and safeguarding policies, but particularly highlights the importance of a non State-centered approach (Kurin 2004; Severo and Venturini 2015), bringing attention to the need for State parties to actively involve the different actors—communities, groups and relevant NGO—that play a significant role in sustaining intangible practices (UNESCO 2003). It has been claimed NGO and alike organizations can build relationships with communities beyond the capacities of State institutions, bringing more dynamism where governments often remain too bureaucratic and rigid (Lewis 2014); offer agile support at different levels; and take intermediary roles between communities and other actors. In sum, they have the potential of making a productive contribution to ICH safeguarding efforts and community participation in the field (Kurin 2007; Lewis 2014). Despite this potential, it has been claimed they are not sufficiently mobilized for these purposes (Jacobs 2014a, b).

Since the nineties, Chile has received increasing flows of immigrants, mainly coming from other countries of the region: Venezuela, Peru, Haiti, Colombia and Bolivia. While the 6.6% of the population they currently represent may seem low compared to European countries, it has doubled in the last four years and reached one of the highest rates in Latin America[1] (INE 2019). While Chilean governments have progressively acquired international commitments in the field of human rights and established certain guarantees, the current migration law and policies have often been criticized as insufficient and ineffective in satisfying their basic needs—from entry permits to labor integration, health, education and housing—and in

[1]The fact that in only a few years Venezuelan immigrants surpassed Peruvians -the biggest foreign community in Chile since the nineties- illustrates this rapid growth and changing nature of the phenomenon.

tackling discrimination and social exclusion (De las Heras 2016). In the field of ICH in particular, only isolated initiatives exist, no expression is officially recognized in the ICH national inventory and a systematic and extensive policy is absent.

In response to this, Non Governmental (NGO) and community-based organizations (CO) have stepped into work for the social and cultural inclusion of newcomers, fighting for their needs and interests at different levels. NGO have been especially aimed at providing orientation about basic rights, giving free legal assistance, supporting labor insertion, developing proposals to influence public policy and collaborating with educational platforms to install an intercultural discourse. CO, in turn, have arisen spontaneously at a more local scale, from migrant communities themselves and other sectors of civil society, with different levels of formalization and purposes (e.g. promoting specific ICH expressions or teaching Spanish) and a frequent emphasis on participation (Martínez et al. 2013).

Considering these potential roles of NGOs and Community Organizations (COs) in safeguarding ICH, there are good reasons to assess their contributions regarding migrant communities in particular. On one hand, research that has looked at the role of relevant actors in migrant ICH safeguarding has addressed the contributions and limitations of public policies and private initiatives (Van der Hoeven 2019; Van der Zeijden 2017); museums (Naguib 2013; Van der Zeijden and Elpers 2017); and educational programmes (Vlachaki 2007). In Chile, in particular, studies such as the one by Caba and Rojas (2014) have focused on the symbolic dimensions of specific migrant ICH expressions as mechanisms of social inclusion. While there is also literature on the role of NGOs and COs in responding to migrant needs and supporting their social inclusion (Gadea Montecinos and Albert 2011; Garreta and Llevot 2013), they mostly focus on political organizations, overlooking the role of ICH. In this way, the study was aimed at bringing together the topics of migrant social inclusion and ICH safeguarding by looking at the contributions of these organizations within these processes, making an addition both to the field of ICH safeguarding and migrant social inclusion. By focusing on the contributions of non-traditional heritage organizations and in a non-European and highly multicultural city, the study hopes to contribute to the critical heritage perspective and its questioning of the power relations underlying heritage processes (Smith 2011). By analyzing the role of NGOs and COs in migrant ICH safeguarding processes, it also hopes to expand the field of critical heritage studies to a social inclusion issue: migration, bringing these two theoretical perspectives together.

2 Methodological Framework

In order to respond to the research question, a qualitative approach was employed, as it allows a rich and in-depth understanding of social phenomena (Klein and Myers 1999). It is also the most suitable for the interpretation of experience and meaning (Daher et al. 2017), in this case, of how these organizations perceive their contributions to migrant ICH safeguarding.

As previously stated, the choice of Santiago as a case study responds to the fact that the city concentrates the largest proportion of transnational migration in the country (Departamento de Extranjería y Migración de Chile 2018) and that, while numerous organizations have arisen to safeguard migrant ICH, there is a lack of empirical evidence regarding their roles. It was expected this case would serve as a relevant example of the potential contributions of these organizations, adding to previous research in the fields of ICH and migrant social inclusion.

The data collection process started with the construction of a comprehensive list of national and international NGO totally or partially dedicated to safeguarding migrant ICH in Santiago, by looking through the information available on their websites. While there are many NGOs that work for the social inclusion of migrants in Santiago, only four of them have a cultural aim. In the case of COs, the situation was different: a large number of formal and informal associations are dedicated to safeguarding migrant ICH in Santiago. Also, given time limitations and that several COs don't have a website or social media page, creating a comprehensive and updated list was not a feasible task.

A purposive sample of four NGOs and eleven COs was selected from this universe, under the following criteria: (i) being completely or partially dedicated—through one or more initiative—to the task of safeguarding migrant ICH; (ii) a minimum of six months of activity at the time of the data collection process, in order to favor an up-to-date and accurate understanding of the topic and (iii) in the case of COs, prioritizing the greatest diversity possible in terms of the nationalities involved, considering most of them target specific national communities.

In the case of NGOs, sampling was easy, considering it included all the four organizations previously identified. In the case of COs, a snow-ball strategy was pursued, starting with a couple of organizations that provided introduction to other key respondents. As shown in Table 1, most NGOs were aimed at promoting the social and cultural inclusion of immigrants without focusing on a specific community; while COs approached ICH safeguarding from different angles, and in most cases focused on a specific national community.

The data collection process took place between April and May 2019, gathering data through secondary sources and semi-structured in-depth interviews. Secondary data included ten available websites (given that five CO did not have one) and all fifteen Facebook pages of the organizations.[2] These sources provided relevant factual information about the mission and vision of the organizations and, in some cases, a description of their activities, which served to adapt some of the topics of the interviews. The decision of not including them as a main part of the analysis responds to the fact that the amount and depth of the information provided was very diverse.[3]

[2]Following the confidentiality agreement made with the respondents, a detailed list of the sources is not provided, since the links of the websites and Facebook pages identify the names of the organizations.

[3]While all four NGOs had updated websites with thorough descriptions of their aims and activities, a significant amount of the COs did not have a website. Also, while all had Facebook pages, some of them were inactive or the information provided in them was scarce or outdated, making a systematic analysis difficult.

Table 1 List of organizations

Interview	Type	Interest group	Focus of migrant ICH-related initiatives
1	NGO	General	Promotion, management and sensitization on CH
2	NGO	General	Social and cultural inclusion of migrant communities
3	CO	Colombians	Social, political and cultural inclusion of Colombian community
4	CO	Dominicans	Social and cultural inclusion of Dominican community
5	CO	Africans	Promotion and sensitization on ICH of African community
6	CO	Colombians	Promotion and sensitization on ICH of Colombian community
7	CO	General	Social and cultural inclusion of migrant communities through performing arts
8	CO	Haitians	Social, political and cultural inclusion of Haitian community
9	CO	Ecuadorians	Promotion of Ecuadorian ICH
10	CO	General	Social and cultural inclusion of migrant communities
11	NGO	General	Social, cultural and religious inclusion of migrant communities
12	NGO	General	Social and cultural inclusion of vulnerable migrant children and their families
13	CO	Peruvians	Promotion of Peruvian ICH
14	CO	Peruvians	Social, political and cultural inclusion of Peruvian community
15	CO	Haitians	Social and cultural inclusion of Haitian community

Source own elaboration

Interviews have the advantage of gathering information in a flexible or non-standardized way, and thus resembling everyday life situations. Being semi-structured, they included open-ended questions and considered possible modifications during the conversation (Whiting 2008), which was especially convenient considering the diversity of organizations and profiles of the respondents. Fifteen in-depth semi-structured interviews with representatives of these organizations were carried out through Skype sessions.[4] Considering ICH was not always the main focus of these organizations, interviewees were selected based on the fulfillment of three criteria: (i) knowledge about the project they were involved in,

[4]Given that fieldwork in Chile was not feasible due to economic and time limitations, conducting online interviews was considered the best alternative. Skype interviews present both advantages and drawbacks. Some of its limitations are that they require access to high-speed internet and demand digital literacy, which may limit the selection of respondents (Deakin and Wakefield 2013). However, it provides the possibility of synchronous and interactive communication, being as similar as possible to an onsite interview (Hanna 2012). It also solves potential time and place limitations of face-to-face interviews (Janghorban et al. 2014), as it was the case of this study, where the researcher and interviewees were based in different countries.

(ii) ability to provide detailed experiential information (ensured by their direct involvement in ICH-related initiatives), and (iii) willingness to take the time for a conversation (Whiting 2008). Interviews were conducted in Spanish and had an average length of 49 min.[5] Basic ethical considerations were taken: the purpose of the study was explained, and the anonymity and use of the results for academic purposes only was guaranteed. Participants provided written consent for their participation and the recording of the interviews.

The conversation started with general questions aimed at characterizing the NGO or CO in question, both in terms of their actions and operational approaches: their vision, aims, targeted communities, level of formalization, working teams and funding were discussed. Later, the conversation focused on their view on the extent of the social inclusion of immigrants in Santiago, in order to introduce the topic and connect it to their work. This was followed by a discussion on ICH and its roles in the life of migrants, and how safeguarding actions can be related to their social inclusion. Finally, the interview delved into the specific initiatives developed for migrant ICH safeguarding, including goals, involvement of migrant communities, lessons learned, emerging challenges, cooperation networks and how these actions may be contributing to social inclusion. The topic list was specific but flexible, enabling alterations and being perfected as the data collection progressed.

The data analysis process started with the transcription of audio recordings verbatim, using an online tool.[6] This, along with the examination of personal notes, enabled an initial familiarization with the data. Later, a thematic analysis was conducted, which allows the interpretation, reduction and comparison of the data into relevant categories (Strauss and Corbin 1990). The qualitative software Atlas.ti was employed, providing assistance for an efficient organization and interpretation of qualitative data (Smit 2002). Initial labels were created in an inductive manner, resulting in the identification of 111 codes and 31 quotes that reflected key ideas. Seeking a rigorous analysis, successive readings of the data were carried out: codes were reviewed, merged and organized, keeping the research questions at the center of the analysis. During the process, the data was compared and contrasted. Finally, these codes were categorized into three main themes: ICH values, NGO and CO actions, and NGO and CO features. In the results section, a thorough explanation of these topics, the relations between them and their interpretation in light of the theoretical discussion is provided.

[5]The complete processes of data collection and analysis were carried out by the researcher without any major difficulties, until the point of saturation was reached.

[6]Interviews were recorded in mp3 format using an external device. Notes were also taken during the interviews, as a precaution to not lose any relevant information and personal insights generated during the process. The transcribing tool employed is available at https://transcribe.wreally.com/.

3 Findings and Implications

In this chapter, the findings of the study are discussed, in order to respond to the research questions. The first section is dedicated to the ICH values that are seen as relevant for the social inclusion of migrants and the actions of NGOs and COs that are perceived as contributing to achieving them. These values are the visibility and appreciation of immigrants, the strengthening of immigrant communities and the economic potential of ICH. The actions, in turn, are the creation of spaces, the development of sensitization initiatives and the promotion of migrant empowerment and associations. In the second section, particular features of the approach these organizations take towards migrant ICH safeguarding are discussed, as they are perceived as playing a relevant part in achieving these contributions. Moreover, the main challenges they face in developing them are discussed (Fig. 1).

3.1 ICH Values and NGO & CO Actions

Visible and appreciated: creating spaces and sensitizing Chileans

One of the key qualities of ICH mentioned by most respondents was making migrant communities visible and promoting their appreciation. ICH is embodied; attached to a living bearer by definition (Kurin 2007; Maillard 2012). It follows that expressing it in more or less public instances results in making its practitioners visible while doing it.

Although this does not guarantee their acceptance or appreciation, it is mentioned by a large majority of interviewees as contributing to raising interest or at least curiosity towards migrant cultures and, in best cases, to a gradual departure from preconceptions and the image of an 'other', whose traditions are unknown and thus feared or rejected:

> Nobody loves what they do not know. I have met many people who have preconceptions of migrants, but when they know what they eat, what they dance, how they speak … at the beginning the migrant has the figure of the foreign, the stranger, and it is normal for people to feel a little distrust. Cultural expressions, in the end, help overcome these preconceptions. (Male, 38, religious NGO for migrant social inclusion)

As this interviewee explains, ICH—in its multiple domains—has the potential of making Chileans gradually more receptive to arriving foreigners. The positive effects of publicly expressing their culture were particularly highlighted by Ecuadorian and African CO representatives, as they argued communities with a smaller presence in Santiago sometimes face even more ignorance and prejudice. While visibility is the more immediate possible outcome, the appreciation of migrant cultures is also often mentioned. Shifting from the image of the 'stranger' to a welcomed member of society is described as a gradual process, clearer in cases of more longstanding migrations:

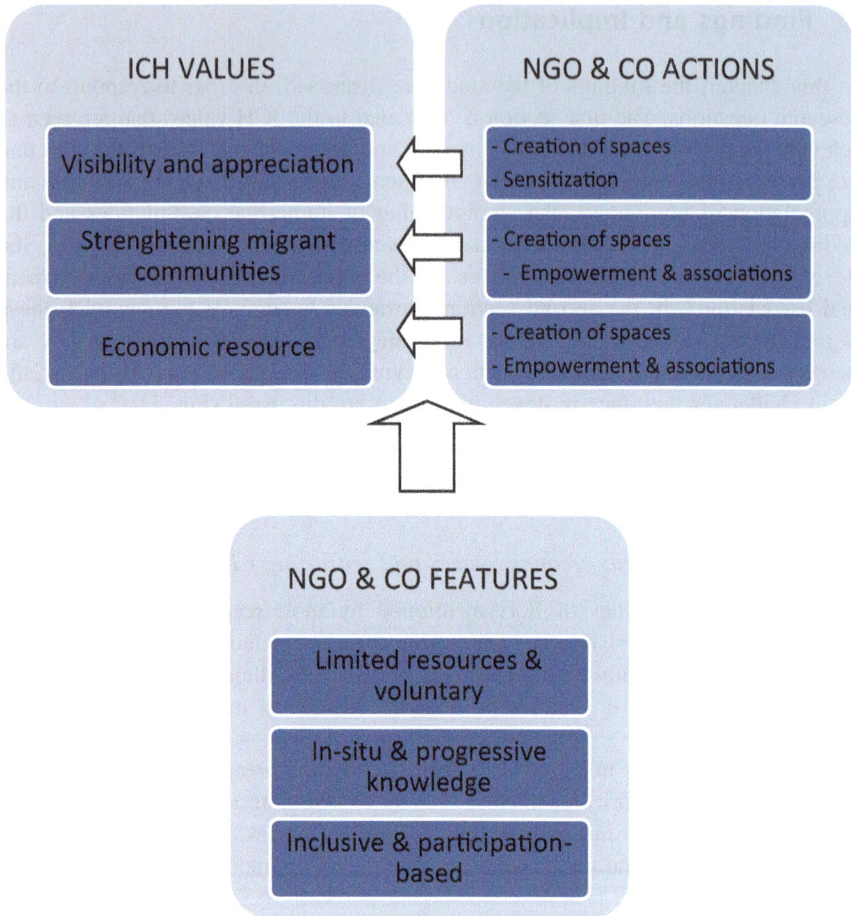

Fig. 1 Outcomes'chart

> Although there are people who see it as a clash, as a stranger, they realize they are people who maintain their traditions, and that for us, with the passage of time, will become common. As with Peruvian food, at first, maybe we were affected by the spices … now it is something that is very standard in Chile. (Female, 31, CH NGO)

The example stated here was given by several interviewees. Being one of the first waves of Latin-American migration at the beginning of the nineties, the evolution of the social inclusion of the Peruvian community is more visible compared to more recent migration processes. While discrimination still exists, their situation was described as clearly different since their arrival, attributing a great extent of this change to the role played by their gastronomy and the business ventures born around it. Their cuisine is signaled as one of the key entry points to Santiago's society: it initially raised curiosity, then interest, and is now largely appreciated.

Similarly, Peruvian festivities are more 'institutionalized' today than other migrant celebrations. In this line, several interviewees argued the recognition of the potential richness of migrants' culture may vary significantly according to the migrants' origin (e.g. Haitians are often described as more discriminated and their culture less known) and also across different Chilean social groups (e.g. according to age or socioeconomic status).

In this context, organizations are seen by their members as having a key role through two main safeguarding actions: the creation of spaces and the promotion of sensitizing processes. The first refers to platforms for ICH safeguarding in a broad sense. All NGO and CO representatives argued that, according to their availability of facilities and human and financial resources, they provide several spaces for migrants to practice their ICH. Their contributions range from lending a room to practice a cultural expression, to producing or supporting the realization of ICH events, such as the celebration of the Migrant day festival, National holiday festivities and cuisine workshops.

As argued in previous literature (Jacobs 2014a, b; Kurin 2007), organizations often take a 'bridging' role here, by mediating between migrant communities and concerned authorities, in order to facilitate the access to public and private venues. According to the interviewees, the bigger the organization or the better its reputation—which is mostly the case of long-trajectory NGO–, the more likely it is they can fulfill this contribution. These are ways in which they work on the goal of making migrants visible and hopefully appreciated, by exposing the receiving society to experiencing their cultures in first person:

> I feel the manifestation or intervention in the public space collaborates with this action [to reduce discrimination] because it allows the persons, in a moment of their daily life, to observe a cultural manifestation and be interested, or to understand that they also have cultural manifestations like us, and from there, accept what they are seeing, living. (Male, 46, NGO for migrant ICH diffusion)

As the quotation illustrates, these initiatives—especially when they take place in the public sphere, where they can reach more people and, especially, those who not necessarily intended to witness these expressions—facilitate spaces for intercultural encounter, where the distance between host and newcomer can be shortened. In this way, the use and creation of spaces appeals more to the *living* aspect of ICH (Kurin 2007) than to rational arguments, in the sense that it relates to a direct and recreational experience of their culture; to the awakening of empathy and appreciation. While this may or not be enough to break negative associations, it is seen as an action that definitely supports this goal, especially impacting in communities with a high presence of migrants.

For several interviewees, both NGO and CO members, a good indication is that the attendance of Chileans to their periodically stable events—such as yearly celebrations of national holidays—while varied, has progressively increased and involved family audiences. A few CO representatives pointed out that, in some cases—with the consent of the migrant communities involved—celebrations themselves have become multicultural, including artistic performances by Chilean and other nationalities, underscoring the dynamic aspect of ICH (Ladrón de Guevara and Elizaga 2009). While some challenges or limitations of the roles of NGOs and COs are raised here, they will be discussed in the second section of the results, dedicated to their organizational context.

The second contribution of NGOs and COs for the visibility and appreciation of migrant communities is sensitizing the Chilean population. Guided tours across migrant neighborhoods, educational and reflection activities in schools and public offices, participative theater plays and gastronomy workshops are some of the very diverse initiatives aimed at shaping new ways to include migrants. These actions seek to trigger an active reflection within the receiving society, either through a rational identification and challenge of preconceptions, intercultural conflicts and xenophobic attitudes; or by resorting to arguments on the richness of cultural diversity. Positively highlighting shared roots and features with other Latin American countries—from our shared colonial history to a Latin-American 'culture' of celebration—are good examples of this. In other cases, sharing interesting features of immigrant cultures that might be unknown for a large proportion of the public are mentioned as a successful tool, as this Congolese interviewee illustrates:

> Our aim is to inform, to share, because there is a lack of knowledge in Chile regarding Africa. There are people that think Africa is a country, who don't know there are 55 countries, that we have different flags. Where there's Africa, there's jungle and poverty. We tell them no, in Africa we have culture, dance, gastronomy. We try to change the switch on the image of Africa. (Male, 34, African CO)

In this way, these safeguarding actions entail a more 'externally-oriented' perspective, as it targets the receiving society. Here, organizations understand this role as crucial in promoting the right of migrants to express and share their culture; challenging existing preconceptions in everyday situations; actively re-educating the receiving society and creating awareness, reflection and change on social inclusion issues. While NGOs usually rely on more available resources and have a broader aim towards social inclusion, the actions of COs, while having a smaller scale, are also making important contributions from their specific fields of action. Contrast is often made here with the current government and mass media, portrayed by most of the interviewees as delivering incorrect or deliberately false information that promotes negative images around them, as it was mentioned in the introduction. While these actions do not definitely solve discrimination, they are described as relevant tools in problematizing and challenging it.

Strengthening migrant communities: spaces, empowerment and association

More 'internally-oriented', a second potentiality of ICH expression is strengthening migrant communities, both by affirming their identities and enhancing social ties. As ICH is essentially related to identity (Kurin 2007; Smith 2011), to practice it is said to allow migrant communities to maintain a sense of belonging and connection to their land and history and to strengthen them as a group through the reinforcement of this shared identity.

> When I celebrate the day of my National Holiday, I am connecting with something that, perhaps, I did not even consider in my country, but now I am away it has an added value … to listen to the national anthem, to eat the things that are eaten there, which for me was something routine, to listen to the music, to see the dances, to talk to others who speak like I do … it is like that. The connection with your country, your land. (Female, 40, Colombian CO)

As this interviewee explains, some of these common identity features—from knowledge to experiences—are even enhanced with the distance to their place of origin: a pride, an appreciation for their own history and culture becomes more apparent. This identity aspect does not mean ICH expressions cannot change, adapt or mix. Being essentially dynamic and sensitive to context (Ladrón de Guevara and Elizaga 2009), the re-territorialization of these cultural manifestations will, in many cases, entail a re-signification: they might change while still maintaining the features that, for its practitioners, tie them to their identities or origin. About half of the respondents gave examples of ICH adaptation or fusion: traditional Latin-American carnivals, religious celebrations and national cuisines that have acquired new features and shapes are seen as cases where ICH has adapted while still maintaining traditions at the center. This often results from the already mentioned convergence of common features—such as ethnical roots or similar historical pasts[7]—over national differences:

> I tell people, when they tell us 'hey, you eat weird things', no, we eat the same cow, but with different seasoning, that's all. (Female, 47, Ecuadorian CO)

As this interviewee effectively shows, this does not mean the specificity is eliminated, but that it is the similarities that often stand out or are made visible. In fact, this synthesis is usually referred to as something that happens spontaneously from the exchange between different cultures, and that is seen as a possible source of strengthening for migrant communities.

Regarding social ties, ICH expressions usually involve the participation of more than one individual, and are shared with others, either in public or for specific audiences. In this way, expressing their ICH also entails meeting and sharing with both co-nationals and other migrant communities, as this interviewee exemplifies:

> Here, in the Italian Parish, 19 different collectives participate, each one with its different celebrations during the year … religious celebrations, with a very high cultural heritage value that is not only gastronomic, folkloric; it is rich in dances, typical dances, crafts presentation … It has been like a cultural amalgam. The religious space is an intercultural mediator that makes different cultures know each other. (Male, 38, Catholic NGO for migrant inclusion)

In this way, these instances allow the creation of new social ties that provide support at different levels, from emotional (in general, given by friendship ties) to practical (e.g. orientation on legal or labor aspects); aiding in strengthening migrant

[7]Historical events that strongly marked Latin-American societies, such as the colonial era or 20th century dictatorships, are good examples of this shared past.

communities. Since it was mentioned that many individuals arrive to Santiago on their own, without a close social network, these instances become crucial:

> I think for them, and they have also expressed it, these are meeting spaces between them, not only with Chileans, but among them. Of discussion, of exchange of ideas … generating networks, friendships… because the immigrant often lives in solitude. (Male, 28, Haitian CO)

Regarding this potential of ICH in strengthening migrant communities, the contribution of organizations in creating and supporting spaces is again mentioned: theater plays, music events or gastronomy workshops are platforms that fulfill not only the purpose of allowing migrants to be seen by others, as discussed before, but also as important moments to encounter other members of their communities. Here, NGOs and COs see themselves as creating spaces for migrants to share with other co-nationals, exchange information, create social ties or simply have fun, finding 'a piece of home' in sharing their ICH, as this Ecuadorian interviewee illustrates:

> There are games for the children, food stands, they play football, and then you hear the accents, the dialects, the jokes, and it's like, in one day, being in our country (…) it's like that day they dedicate themselves to being 100% Ecuadorian and they do not limit themselves to talking, laughing, joking as they do there, they do not have to 'be good', you see? (Female, 47, Ecuadorian CO)

A second contribution of these organizations in strengthening migrant communities refers to promoting migrant empowerment and associations. In line with the 2003 Convention, interviewees argued they take an important role in encouraging the empowerment of migrants, by providing tools and installing capacities[8] for them to be able to fully develop in Santiago. Some examples are teaching Spanish to non-speakers,[9] as being able to communicate is an essential first step to navigate Chilean society at any level; giving guided tours around Santiago to show them potentially useful points of the city; offering artistic workshops to children; and providing relevant legal, organizational, entrepreneurial and funding training to carry out their ICH-related projects, for instance, in how to formulate a project or apply to public funds. The following quotations not only show this diverse range of tools provided, but also their potential impact in migrants lives:

> It is basic for human coexistence to be able to communicate, and in order to organize. Through language we name the world, and we can also transform it. They will hardly be able to function fully if they cannot also interact in the majority language. (Male, 28, Haitian CO)

> I see it in the lives of the people we work with, in a concrete way. How their quality of life changes, how they grow up, how they have related to other people … We started *Don't be afraid* with an open casting, people who danced in a non professional way came, and now, one even studies dance. (Female, 40, theater NGO)

[8]What Jacobs (2014a, b) calls 'capacity building', as explained in the theoretical section.

[9]Especially Haitians, as they are one of the latest big waves of Latin-American migration and one of the communities that face more difficulties in terms of their social inclusion in Santiago.

Secondly, these organizations promote the creation of formal and informal associations of migrants and of networks between different migrant organizations, to share information and deal with different issues relating to being immigrant. As it is also the case for empowering initiatives, these safeguarding actions are aimed at accompanying processes more than leading them (Smith 2011; Jacobs 2014a, b), pushing communities to be active regarding the promotion of their ICH.

An economic resource: spaces, empowerment and association

About half of the interviewees mentioned that, beyond their evident cultural value, certain ICH expressions might also be economic assets (Rizzo and Throsby 2006; Naguib 2013) in the sense that local knowledge, traditions, crafts and skills can become a source of income for arriving migrants:

> It allows culture to become a work tool. And then, they could perfectly enter the labor field. Young people, who make workshops, teach percussion or dance, could perfectly work in a school. You can perfectly have an agreement with a cultural center, or a space, or a municipal gym, and build a salsa school. (Male, 46, NGO for migrant CH diffusion)

As this respondent explains, from teaching their traditional music, dances and cuisines, to selling their crafts, ICH has the potential of becoming a 'working tool'. While the potential is there, it is mentioned as very incipient and as unlikely to be found as the main sustenance of arriving migrants. Only the case of the already mentioned Peruvian cuisine was referred to as an ICH expression that is both profitable and well-positioned in Santiago, in the sense that it is a renowned gastronomy, that restaurants and other businesses can be found all over the city, and that its bearers are often able to sustain themselves through it. Other examples, such as selling traditional crafts, are seen as very isolated and only potentially profitable.

The commodification of CH or the appreciation for its exchange value (Naguib 2013) is a complex topic. On one end, there is a risk of instrumentalization by third parties (e.g. the tourism industry) that see a profit potential and unrightfully appropriate it and endanger it (Villaseznor and Zolla 2012; Smith 2015). On the other, it is a potential source of wellbeing, projecting ICH as a viable and ongoing practice (Kurin 2007), promoting its sustainability and ensuring the persistence of its bearers.

The role of NGOs and COs in encouraging migrant empowerment and associations is again seen as relevant, in the sense of providing useful tools and training for different stages of the commercialization of ICH expressions, from food handling to accounting or applying to public funding. Also, they often encourage the formalization of these initiatives through associations, as the previous quotation pointed out. The contribution related to the creation of spaces is also present, as these organizations argue they provide platforms for migrants to share their ICH-related enterprises and create the conditions to offer their products or experiences. Taking mediation roles (Lewis 2014) in obtaining a permit to sell edible products; providing stands to sell their crafts in festivals; or remunerating them for musical and dance presentations are some concrete examples in this line. This topic was not further deepened by the respondents, being more of an incipient or potential value than a widespread phenomenon in Santiago.

3.2 NGO & CO Operational Features

Specific aspects of the rationale and operational approach these organizations take towards migrant ICH safeguarding are discussed in this section, as they might be contributing to how they pursue the previously mentioned contributions. Here is where stronger contrasts—both in terms of strengths and difficulties—are made with other relevant actors, especially public institutions.

In situ, *horizontal and progressive knowledge*

It is often highlighted that the expertise of these organizations is given by the fact they are territorially anchored: they are working *with* or—in more horizontally-based organizations—*from* the specific communities, situating ICH practitioners as the main carriers of knowledge and organizations as more of supporting actors (Jacobs 2014a, b). This approach provides a crucial strength: detailed, concrete and up-to-date information that constitutes the main input for their actions. For instance, regarding the challenges specific migrant communities face in terms of their social inclusion; or the ways in which they are currently expressing their culture in Santiago. It follows from this that these organizations are progressively and continuously updating their knowledge:

> Of course it has evolved [the organization], because migration in Santiago has changed. Each project is growing and strengthening. 'Salsa la Primavera' used to last a couple of hours, now eight days. Before, it was a dance show and that's it. Now there is a deeper cultural issue regarding salsa culture and migration, which requires an evolution. We bring guests, invite people of other nationalities, do a variety of activities, like talks, music clinics, meetings of music lovers, everything that grabs the salsa culture. (Female, 40, Colombian CO)

As this interviewee illustrates, through direct contact with the needs and desires of the concerned communities, the knowledge and safeguarding actions of these organizations are constantly evolving, acting as catalysts of local knowledge and taking accompanying roles (Smith 2011; Kuutima in Bendix et al. 2013), in a continuous learning and professionalization process. In this way, this in situ and progressively constructed training is considered key to promote ICH in a non-reductionist or elitist manner, as previously discussed (Kurin 2007). It is also highlighted as an advantage over public institutions that are limited to 4-year terms and subject to the change of political tendencies: the actions of previous governments are often undone due to different understandings on how to deal with migration. In some cases, an even stronger contrast is made with the current government, seen as openly promoting discriminatory policies towards migration.

Inclusive and participation-based

In line with a horizontal and non-reductionist creation of knowledge, active migrant participation is always described as a key principle within these organizations. Again, the contrast with State institutions is frequent, where these organizations are portrayed as more in tune with the bottom-up principles the 2003 Convention promotes (Broccolini 2013). While it is a strong part of their discourses, it is important to note that the effective levels of involvement described are very varied.

Especially in larger NGO, initiatives are mostly led by members of the organizations.

While they involve migrants in all of the initiatives that concern them, this is often done for specific phases—such as consulting them in the design, giving them a central role during events or taking into account their evaluations of the activities —rather than all stages of the design and implementation processes. A more extensive participation is here considered desirable, but difficult to achieve given the already mentioned limitations of time and human resources. In these cases, consulting or involving migrants in specific phases and installing capacities are seen as partial solutions. In this sense, there is still space for a more plural and horizontal recognition of ICH (Smith 2011; Jacobs 2014a, b), where these organizations prioritize supporting and accompanying over leading roles. In turn, within territorially situated COs that are formed by migrants, most of the work is described as completely collaborative, taking a horizontal approach to decision-making processes and the design of their activities:

> This principle of horizontality is permanent, in every space: in the teachers' assembly we plan and evaluate the lessons together; during the lessons we work together with the students … there are no hierarchical spaces; conversation is always on a horizontal level. From the beginning, we have always wanted the students not to be just students, but organizers. (Male, 28, Haitian CO)

This interviewee shows how, at every stage of the design and implementation of their language courses for Haitian communities, a democratic logic underlies. While in this case the organization was created by Chilean citizens, most of the sampled COs are formed by migrants themselves, eliminating the issue of 'involving' them. Given this characteristic and existing resources limitations, this principle is often extended to the creation of collaboration networks with similar organizations, in order to share information and join forces for the implementation of their activities.

In this participative philosophy also lies a difficulty: levels of participation and active involvement from migrants are often described as low, due both to the existence of other priorities in their lives—especially for more vulnerable groups— and different kinds of 'participative cultures' in every country of origin. For example, the Ecuadorian interviewee mentioned citizen participation levels in that country are usually low, which is also reflected in this new environment.

An important risk was also mentioned regarding the actions of NGOs and COs in terms of promoting the visibility and appreciation of migrant communities: the flipside is that, when these initiatives are not carried out with the active involvement of migrant communities, but take a paternalistic instead of an accompanying approach, there is a risk of producing opposite effects. For instance, of hiding or reproducing existing power conflicts under an illusion of symmetry between cultures; or reducing a specific culture to the validation of a single ICH expression. An example of the latter is the promotion of a national festivity celebration in a specific environment, such as a school or working place, and reducing the social inclusion of the migrant community to that single action of celebrating their culture. In other cases, an instrumentalization of migrant individuals is mentioned. For example, one interviewee mentioned that in the last years, it became 'trendy' to include migrant topics and individuals in theater plays, without a true interest in their social inclusion. The importance of seeing migrants as the ultimate arbiters of the value of their ICH (Severo and Venturini 2015) is often highlighted as something to keep at the center of these organization's work; to treat them as active and strong subjects, capable of identifying their difficulties, opportunities and possible contributions to Chilean society, and taking part in valuable exchanges instead of being 'accultured'.

Limited resources, self-management and voluntary work

Finally, a relevant feature of these organizations is a limited availability of resources and a self-managed and voluntary nature. Scarce financial resources are mentioned, almost in every interview, as one of the main challenges, which limits their choices and the time they can dedicate to their primary purposes, since generating new resources is a constant preoccupation and demands significant amounts of time and creativity. This is especially the case for NGOs and COs that focus on festivals and massive events that require extensive planning efforts and expensive infrastructure.

While types of funding and working teams are as diverse as these organizations, a common feature is that, in most cases—with the exemption of larger NGOs–, funding comes from self-sustaining activities. Some are in the context of their main initiatives (e.g. charging an entrance fee to their ICH events) while others are specifically aimed at raising funds (e.g. raffles and food sales). Another frequent source of income is private donations, usually from members themselves and, in some cases, sponsoring companies. Lastly, applying to public funds is mentioned by half of the respondents.

This limitation of resources is tied to the voluntary nature of most of these organizations: only in a third of them stable members receive a salary, usually being the case of NGO with a good position and long trajectory in the fields of migration or CH. In smaller NGOs and every CO, participation is completely voluntary. Especially in the case of the latter, all members have jobs outside the organizations, forcing them to work on their free time, becoming more energy consuming and limiting certain areas of their work (e.g. being able to contact State institutions, only available during working hours). In some cases, this can entail a challenge in terms of their motivation and commitment towards the organization. However, it can also be an advantage, as it is said to be more likely that members will act in a coherent and honest way towards the purposes of the organization, and for unstable members to spontaneously offer their support to their activities, with the only motivation of spreading their culture.

Finally, resource limitations and instability are not only financial, but also spatial. A significant number of respondents pointed out the existing difficulties in the access to public spaces:

> You have to look for them, but it's complex … we make a carnival where different traditional expressions of Latin America meet and we have difficulties getting permits, to do these activities that are free, for the community … it is not the same as if there is a run,

> when the whole Alameda[10] closes for the day, or if the Pope comes … for things that have to do with rescuing our most ancestral identities, there is no space, there is no respect. (Female, 47, NGO for migrant social inclusion)

As this respondent illustrates, they directly or indirectly refer to a lack of support from governmental institutions, mentioning there are not enough spaces for migrant ICH expression and that the access to public spaces is highly dependent on political tendencies, especially, to how favorable to migration is the Municipality involved. High levels of bureaucracy in obtaining consents and a very restrictive policy regarding musical performances or the number of attendants (compared to other activities undertaken in public spaces), are mentioned as examples of the difficulties in facing Municipalities, that often affect the execution or continuity of ICH activities. The current government is often portrayed as not making culture in general a priority, not guaranteeing the right of migrants to express their culture just like any citizen, and even promoting policies that openly reject migration. This lack of support reveals a limitation in the potential broker roles discussed in previous studies (Jacobs 2014a, b; Lewis 2014) and supports the general assessment of NGOs and COs not being sufficiently mobilized in supporting ICH safeguarding processes (Jacobs 2014a, b), despite their potential contributions.

4 Concluding Remarks

The study was aimed at exploring how NGOs and COs understand their contributions to safeguarding migrant ICH expressions in Santiago, Chile. In doing so, it brought together the topics of migrant social inclusion and ICH safeguarding through the role of these organizations, whose potential relevance has been previously overlooked.

Certainly, the social inclusion of migrant communities is a complex and multi-dimensional topic, as it seeks the conditions for a full participation in the social, cultural, economic and political spheres (Abrams et al. 2005). Without the intention of making generalization or reducing migrant social inclusion to a single realm, the study revealed the potential of culture—and ICH in particular—in this field: making immigrant visible and appreciated; strengthening their communities through reinforcing their identities and social ties; and showing its economic potential emerged as the main values of ICH for the social inclusion of newcomers. In achieving them, relevant contributions of these organizations emerged, being fulfilled both *externally*—by promoting spaces and sensitizing actions that target the receiving society—and *internally*—by facilitating spaces, promoting associations and empowering migrant communities.

Naturally, some limitations must be taken into account: a reduced availability of financial, spatial and human resources; and the risk of reproducing the power relations these actors intend to overcome (Broccolini 2013; Kuutma in Bendix et al.

[10]Alameda is one of the main avenues in the center of Santiago.

2013; Smith 2011) are relevant challenges. However, they are not enough to overshadow their contributing actions and, especially, some of their operational features: it is their inclusive, participative and horizontally-constructed knowledge what seems to have progressively fueled their work for the social inclusion of migrant communities. In other words, it is this direct and longstanding work with them what seems to provide an extensive expertise around their practices, needs and desires, making their actions both adequate and flexible, in line with the dynamic essence of ICH (Ladrón de Guevara and Elizaga 2009) and the bottom-up approaches promoted by the 2003 UNESCO Convention (Kurin 2007; Severo and Venturini 2015).

In this way, the study contributes to the expansion of non-Eurocentric empirical evidence on horizontal and dynamic approaches to ICH safeguarding (Kurin 2007; Lewis 2014), in a setting marked by a rapidly growing immigration process where non-State actors have taken relevant roles. Moreover, findings support critical heritage perspectives and expand them to the field of migrant social inclusion. Touching upon power issues, the study shows the role of these organizations in making intercultural conflicts, elitist discourses and potential challenges in the re-territorialization of ICH practices visible (Smith 2011; Caba and Rojas 2014) and, in turn, promoting sensitization, dialogue and appreciation of cultural diversity as social inclusion devices.

The study also provides a good starting point for further research. Considering it is based on a single-actor point of view, there is a risk of blind spots and overly optimistic insights. In this way, the understanding of the role of these organizations would be enriched with the perspectives of other relevant stakeholders, from ICH bearers to museums, schools and governmental institutions. Comparative perspectives on the topic would also be very valuable, in order to find similarities and differences in the work of these non-State organizations that could sharpen the knowledge on their specific contributions and particularities.

Finally, regarding the ICH policy field, the study could have relevant implications for the design of more well-targeted State actions, where the in situ, horizontal and progressive expertise of these organizations is recognized and supported. ICH expressions are as living and dynamic as the migrant communities that carry them, and policies aimed at ensuring the persistence and social inclusion of immigrant practitioners and promoting cultural diversity as a value must recognize these aspects to ensure the viability of ICH expressions.

References

Abrams, D., Hogg, M. A., & Marques, J. M. (Eds.). (2005). *The social psychology of inclusion and exclusion*. Psychology Press.

Bendix, R., Eggert, A., & Peselmann, A. (2013). *Heritage regimes and the State*. Göttingen: University Press.

Broccolini, A. (2013). Il patrimonio culturale immateriale in Italia e la convenzione UNESCO del 2003: territori, reti, musei. [Intangible cultural Heritage in Italy and the 2003 UNESCO Convention: territories, networks, museums] *SIMBDEA*. Retrieved from http://www.simbdea.it/.

Caba, S. & Rojas, M. (2014). Patrimonio migrante. Construcción social inclusiva e identitaria de la comunidad peruana en Santiago de Chile. [Migrant Heritage. Inclusive and identity social construction of the Peruvian community in Santiago, Chile]. *Estudios Avanzados. Universidad de Santiago de Chile*. 22. Retrieved from http://www.redalyc.org.

Commission of the European Communities. (2003). Joint Report on Social Inclusion. UNDESA, Expert Group Meeting on Promoting Social Integration, Helsinki, July 2008.

Daher, M., Carré, D., Jaramillo, A., Olivares, H., & Tomicic, A. (2017). Experience and meaning in qualitative research: A conceptual review and a methodological device proposal. *Forum Qualitative Sozialforschung*. https://doi.org/10.17169/fqs-18.3.2696.

Deakin, H. & Wakefield, K. (2013). SSkype Interviewing: Reflections of Two Ph.D. Researchers. *Qualitative Research.*

De Las Heras, M. (2016). Los migrantes como sujetos del sistema de protección social en Chile. [Migrants as subjects of the social protection system in Chile]. *Centro de Políticas Públicas UC*, 11.

Departamento de Extranjería y Migración de Chile. (2018). Estadísticas de migración.

Gadea Montecinos, M. E., & Albert, M. (2011). Asociacionismo migrante y renegociación de las identificaciones culturales. *Política y Sociedad (Madrid), 48,* 1.

Garreta, J. & Llevot, N. (2013). Las asociaciones de inmigrantes africanos. organización, proyección y actuaciones. *Revista Internacional de Sociología*, 71:1.

Hanna, P. (2012). Using internet technologies (such as Skype) as a research medium: A research note. *Qualitative Research, 12,* 239–242. https://doi.org/10.1177/1468794111426607.

INE. (2019). *Estimación de Personas Extranjeras Residentes en Chile: 31 de diciembre 2018.* Santiago: Instituto Nacional de Estadísticas y Departamento de Extranjería y Migración.

Jacobs, M. (2014a). Cultural brokerage. Addressing boundaries and the new paradigm of safeguarding intangible cultural heritage. Folklore Studies, TransdisciplinaryPerspectivesand UNESCO, 115.

Jacobs, M. (2014b). UNESCO, brokers and critical success (f)actors in safeguarding intangible cultural heritage. *Volkskunde. Tijdschrift over de cultuur van het dagelijksleven.*

Janghorban, R., LatifnejadRoudsari, R., & Taghipour, A. (2014). Skype interviewing: the new generation of online synchronous interview in qualitative research. *International journal of qualitative studies on health and well-being, 9,* 24152. https://doi.org/10.3402/qhw.v9.24152.

Klein, H. K., & Myers, M. D. (1999). A set of principles for conducting and evaluating interpretative filed studies in information systems. *MIS Quarterly, 23,* 67–94. https://doi.org/10.2307/249410.

Kurin, R. (2004). Safeguarding intangible cultural heritage in the 2003 UNESCO convention: A critical appraisal. *Museum International, 56,* 1.

Kurin, R. (2007). Safeguarding intangible cultural heritage: Key factors in implementing the 2003 Convention. *International Journal of Intangible Heritage*, 2, 10–20. Retrieved from http://www.rijh.org/.

Kuutma, K. (2009). Cultural heritage: An introduction to entanglements of knowledge, politics and property. *Journal of Ethnology and Folkloristics, 3,* 5–12. Retrieved from http://www.jef.ee/.

Ladrón de Guevara, B. & Elizaga, J. (2009). Diagnóstico para la conservación de patrimonios culturales en uso activo: propuesta metodológica. [Diagnosis for the conservation of cultural heritages in active use: methodological proposal] *Conserva. Revista del Centro Nacional de Conservación y Restauración*, 13.

Lewis, D. (2014). Understanding the role of non-government organizations (NGOs) as cultural brokers: A review of approaches. *OsterreichischeZeitschrift fur Volkskunde, 3,* 293–298.

Maillard, C. (2012). Construcción social del patrimonio. [Social construction of heritage]. *Hecho en Chile. Reflexiones en torno al patrimonio cultural.*

Martínez, J., Soffia, M., Cubides, J. D., & Bortolotto, I. (2013). Migración Internacional en Chile: tendencias, políticas, normas y participación de la sociedad civil. *Publicación Red Internacional Scalabriniana de Migración*, pp. 117–224.

Naguib, S. (2013). Collecting moments of life. Museums and the intangible heritage of migration. *Museum International, 65,* 77–86. https://doi.org/10.1111/muse.12035.
Rizzo, I., & Throsby, D. (2006). Cultural Heritage: Economic analysis and public policy. *Handbook of the Economics of Art and Culture.* https://doi.org/10.1016/S1574-0676(06)01028-3.
Severo, M., & Venturini, T. (2015). Intangible cultural heritage webs. Comparing national networks with digital methods. *New Media & Society, 18,* 16116–1635. https://doi.org/10.1177/1461444814567981.
Smit, B. (2002). Atlas.ti for qualitative data analysis. *Perspectives in Education, 20,* 65–75. Retrieved from https://journals.co.za.
Smith, L. (2011). *All heritage is intangible: Critical heritage studies and museums.* AmsterdamseHogeschoolvoor de Kunsten: ReinwardtAcademie.
Smith, L. (2015). Intangible heritage: A challenge to the authorised heritage discourse?. *Revista d'etnologia de Catalunya, 40,* 133–142.
Strauss, A., & Corbin, J. (1990). *Basics of qualitative research: Grounded theory procedures and techniques.* London: Sage.
UNESCO. (2003). International convention for the safeguarding of the intangible cultural heritage. UNESCO general conference, Paris, 17 October 2003. Retrieved from http://www.unesco.org/.
United Nations. (2016). Leaving no one behind: the imperative of inclusive development. Report on the World Social Situation 2016. *Economic and social affairs.*
Van der Hoeven, A. (2019). Networked practices of intangible urban heritage: The changing public role of Dutch heritage professionals. *International journal of cultural policy, 25,* 232–245. https://doi.org/10.1080/10286632.2016.1253686.
Van der Zeijden, A. (2017). 'Super-diversity' and the Changing Face of Intangible Cultural Heritage: the Case of West-Kruiskade'. *International Journal of Intangible Heritage. 12.*
Van der Zeijden, A., & Elpers, S. (2017). Intangible heritage & the museum in an age of superdiversity. *IMP Intangible cultural heritage & museums project.* Retrieved from http://www.ichandmuseums.eu/.
Villasezñor, I., & Zolla, E. (2012). Del patrimonio cultural inmaterial o la patrimonialización de la cultura. [About intangible cultural heritage or the patrimonialization of culture]. *Cultura y RepresentacionesSociales, 6,* 75–101.
Vlachaki, M. (2007). Crossing cultures through the intangible heritage: and Educational programme about migration in Greece. *International Journal of Intangible Heritage,* 2, 93–102. Retrieved from http://www.ijih.org/.
Whiting, L. S. (2008). Semi-structured interviews: Guidance for novice researchers. *Nursing Standard, 22,* 35–40. https://doi.org/10.7748/ns2008.02.22.23.35.c6420.

Feminist Movements in the City: New Strategies of Commons in Latin American Context

Carolina Gallo Garcia and Elena de Oliveira Schuck

Abstract

In the wake of a new wave of feminist movements in Latin America, this chapter seeks to analyze the city as a gendered space where gathering of protesters may propose new forms of organization. In the context of the emergence of conservative forces and democratic disruptions, street movements present forces of resistance to the growing socio-spatial segregation, violence, and discrimination. Thereby street movements claim for a more inclusive urban agenda. This chapter presents a critical gender approach to urban space based on three cases of feminist bottom-up organizations addressing inclusive public space policies in the region. We identify these as examples that dispute the traditional narrative between public and private, proposing new forms of organization of the urban public space based on the notion of the commons.

1 Introduction

In the contemporary context of the debate on urban public space, announcements of its decline (Sennett 2014) and "death" (Jacobs 1992) emerge as responses to excessive privatization of urban life, making it necessary to bring to scrutiny the traditional meanings about the constitution of public spaces. Starting from the understanding that such a notion of a decline of the public "man" (sic) (Sennett

C. G. Garcia (✉)
State University of Campinas (UNICAMP), Campinas, Brazil
e-mail: c261209@dac.unicamp.br

E. de Oliveira Schuck
Brazilian Center of Analysis and Planning (CEBRAP), São Paulo, Brazil
e-mail: elena.schuck@cebrap.org.br

E. Macrì et al. (eds.), *Cultural Commons and Urban Dynamics*,
https://doi.org/10.1007/978-3-030-54418-8_15

2014) means looking at the past as the holder of a lost ideal to be rescued. It is necessary to question in what terms—practical and ideological—these promises of a plural public culture were contemplated in urban life.

Deutsche (2008) pertinently inquires who was considered a citizen in these great remote civic scenarios that so many authors recall. She also questions for whom the city was once more public before. When proposing to reflect on the spaces of social minorities—women, homosexuals, foreigners, workers, and ethnic minorities, Deutsche (2008) brings up a central issue by proposing an always controversial and disputed character of public space, so that we can call it that.

In this context, it is intended to reflect on the notions of urban public space as a public good from a gender perspective that highlights its complex and disputed character. To this end, this chapter presents a critical gender approach to urban space based on three cases of bottom-up organizations that point out to more democratic, feminist, and even public spaces. We identify these as examples that dispute the traditional narrative between public and private, proposing new forms of organization of the urban public space based on the notion of the commons (Harvey 2012).

2 The Gendered City: A Mutual Production

> [Spaces] are gendered in a myriad different way, which vary between cultures and over time. And this gendering of space and place both *reflects and has effects back on* the ways in which gender is constructed and understood in the societies in which we live. (Massey 1994, p. 186, italics by the author)

Historian Perrot (2007) seeks to unveil historical evidence of a persistent asymmetry in the uses of the city from a gender perspective: public men and private women. More recently, some authors in the field of urban planning and architecture (Muxí 2006; Agrest 2008) have brought to the center of the discipline's debate the need to not only make differences in the uses of spaces visible but also to question the broad processes of making women invisible as subjects of urban life.

In this sense, it is noted that physical space—architectural, open or closed spaces, public or private—corresponds to a social structure, that is, the social place occupied by certain subjects tends to be reproduced in the material spatial structures, which corroborate the perpetuation and reproduction of the social and economic conditions of these agents (Bourdieu 2013, p. 134). In hierarchical societies, spaces are also hierarchized, to function as a "spontaneous metaphor of social space" (*ibid*). In these, social distances are inscribed in the physical world, thus producing direct implications for the constitution of identities and possibilities of forging or not belonging to certain spaces.

In a context of increasing financialization of cities (Harvey 2005), the place occupied by certain agents in the urban physical space increasingly tends to reflect their position in the social field. Thus, the social structure tends to be reified in the possibilities and impossibilities of the appropriation of physical space that each social group has so that space becomes a directly tangible effect of symbolic power (Bourdieu 1999).

To think of the city from a women's perspective, feminist criticism sensitive to the issue of space brings to the center of the debate the dominant significances in the disciplines of urbanism. These significances idealize the functional city and urban policies as a type of universal experience, markedly masculine, oriented toward the use of automobiles and presenting the territory as a neutral space.

Jacobs (1992), although not openly a feminist, was certainly one of the first female writers to launch a feminine perspective on the city, proposing urban planning that took into account the space for its users. By making an ode to the importance of the vitality of the sidewalks—busy, with a plurality of people, of encounters, a mixture of commerce, homes, and leisure—it produces a reinforcement of "public life," due to the inevitable coexistence with difference. Jacobs, who actively fought the construction of the Lower Manhattan Expressway in her neighborhood in the 1950s, is an exemplary case of what Harvey (2012) argues: public goods such as public spaces, cannot automatically be equated to commons—they must be appropriated by citizens through political action so they can constitute commons.

As Butler (2015) states, it is the bodies gathered in their plurality that can claim the public. In her text, there is a direct criticism of the supposed neutrality of the public sphere and public space, especially the dominant notion that all public space is already, by nature, public: these are always disputed to conform the common. Collective claims, when submitted to perspectives that recognize asymmetries in the socio-spatial relations of the order of class, gender, and race, must bring the bodies together in public space: "The claim of equality is not only spoken or written, but is made precisely when bodies appear together, or rather when, through their action, they bring the space of appearance into being. This space is a feature and effect of action." (Butler 2015, pp. 88–89).

Thus, to think of the city as a determined and determinant space for gender relations is to recognize that transformations within the scope of such relations must be exposed as a substantial parameter in the changes that have occurred in space. In a perspective aligned with feminist geography, it is understood that the modern dichotomy between public and private has provided spatial articulations that reify gender inequalities. According to Perregaux (2005, p. 183): "[...] spatial organization and gender construction are interdependent, as part of power relations that engage other forms of domination as well, such as race, class, and sexuality."

Massey (1994, p. 179) states that "spaces and places are not only themselves gendered but, in their being so, they both reflect and affect how gender is constructed and understood." In other words, Massey reinforces the idea of interdependence when thinking about the issue of limiting the mobility of women, either due to the absence of a good public transport network, either due to the fear of harassment or because the city has been planned mostly for cars, such limitations have been crucial for the subordination of women in certain socio-cultural and historical contexts. The city is identified as a key spatial scale through which these relationships are formed and perpetuated (McDowell 1983). In this sense, space can be affirmed as determined and determinant to the constitution of gender relations. Considering that every social relationship is the result of power relations and that space is fundamental in every power relation (Foucault 1984), it can be said that social relationships are spatially and materially based, which therefore favor articulations that reiterate and reproduce inequalities.

We hope to have made clear the argument of this chapter so far: social relations have a spatial and material basis, and as such, these bases can contribute to the perpetuation of asymmetries such as gender—there are co-implications between gender and space as inseparable dimensions from understanding socio-spatial dynamics (Massey 1994; McDowell 2000). However, it is necessary to escape from a binary perspective, as highlighted by most of the contemporary feminist thought: to think public space and common practices in contemporary times, it is necessary to understand it relationally. In this sense, in the final part of this chapter we present new forms of production of the common (Harvey 2012) that take shape in the streets of Latin American cities and are led by women's movements.

3 The Common and the Debate on Marginalized Identities: Notes for Thinking the City

> In the city, the common is an inherently relational phenomenon. [...] usage and consumption practices are a constitutive part of the production of the urban commons*: in fact, consuming the city is nothing but the most subtle form of its production*. (Kornerger and Borch 2015, p. 7, italics by the authors)

When dealing with the possibilities of producing the common in urban spaces from a feminist perspective, firstly it is necessary to distinguish between public urban goods and urban commons: their borders are fluid and "dangerously porous" (Harvey 2012, p. 79). According to Harvey, urban public goods tend to be easily co-optated by neoliberal logics, whereas the constitution of the common-the author emphasizes social movements that achieve an urban dimension—has a revolutionary, reformist, and anti-capitalist dimension.

A diversity of collective demands brought together, such as Tahrir Square in Cairo and Syntagma Square in Athens are public spaces, but become urban commons when people assemble to make demands and express new political views. The streets are public spaces that are transformed into the common of a revolutionary movement by collective action (Harvey 2012). The author does not highlight any feminist march, but these examples may include Women's March on Washington (2017), *Ni Una Menos* in Latin America (2016) and Black Monday in Poland (2016) as emblematic cases of urban mobilization incited by feminist collectives. These are examples of commoning.

> The common is not to be construed, therefore, as a particular kind of thing, asset or even social process, but as an unstable and malleable social relation between a particular self-defined social group and those aspects of its actually existing or yet- to-be-created social and/or physical environment deemed crucial to its life and livelihood. There is, in effect, *a social practice of communing*. (Harvey 2012, p. 73, emphasis added)

In this way, the struggles to appropriate the public spaces in the city for a common purpose are ongoing and permanent (*ibid*). As the author highlights, the "traditional left" struggles for grappling the revolutionary potential of urban social movements. They are often dismissed as attempts to deal with limited issues (women's marches are definitely seen as one) and therefore not a revolutionary movement. As we will see further, those feminist public claims usually bring dear demands to the left movements, such as the right to housing, accessible and sustainable public transport, public health issues, among others.

These movements can also be associated with the idea of counterpublics, proposed by Nancy Fraser (1990): the author argues that the public sphere becomes truly public through counterpublics, which would be discursive subaltern arenas produced in opposition to the notion of a neutral and unified public.

> […] where members of subordinated social groups invent and circulate counterdiscourses, which in turn permit them to formulate oppositional interpretations of their identities, interests, and need". (Fraser 1990, p. 67)

In refusal to understand the public sphere as bourgeois and unified, this vision also confronts the Habermasian rationalist theory, verifying that all consensus is a result of modes of domination and therefore of exclusion. The widely disseminated notions of public space as the ground where consensus must be produced are then replaced by the notion of containing publics and counterpublics as a "plurality of competing publics" and "always conflictual" (Fraser 1990, p. 61) that contests the exclusionary norms by elaborating alternative political discourses.

By presenting the cases in the third part of this chapter, we argue that these emerge as waves of responses to the growing democratic disruptions and the emergence of conservative forces in Latin America. The scenario of major setbacks in social rights is followed by eruption of social movements struggling against the increasing violence associated with discrimination based on gender, race, class, and sexuality. These forms of discrimination produce different experiences in the living of cities, affecting unequally those who have or do not have access to jobs, policies, and public facilities. The struggles for rights led by women have incorporated both urban and broader themes of social justice, but which indelibly cross materialities and territories, since all human action depends on material support:

> it is equally true that the collective actions collect the space itself, gather the pavement, and animate and organize the architecture. As much as we must insist on there being material conditions for public assembly and public speech, we have also to ask how it is that assembly and speech reconfigure the materiality of public space and produce, or reproduce, the public character of that material environment. (Butler 2015, p. 81)

Thus, the locus of the effectiveness of feminist marches must not be diminished: they take place in the space where power relations are produced and reproduced—the city. Agrest (2008) verifies a suppression of the feminine as a symbolic resource to the space built by modern architecture and urbanism, suggesting that both the materiality and the logic inherent in urban public spaces corroborate the perpetuation of social relations that are, as mentioned, always produced by and through space. Yet, paradoxically, the city remains as the scenario for public expression of the feminist struggle for excellence: by moving to the urban space, where they are ideologically suppressed, women produce resistance against hegemonic discursive orders against the dominant structures that determine unequal urban relations (Garcia and Schuck 2018).

> [...] the square and the street are not only the material supports for action, but they themselves are part of any account of bodily public action we might propose. Human action depends upon all sorts of supports-it is always supported action. We know from disability studies that the capacity to move depends upon instruments and surfaces that make movement possible, and that bodily movement is supported and facilitated by non-human objects and their particular capacity for agency. (Butler 2015, p.72)

In Notes Toward a Performative Theory of Assembly, Butler (2015) shows an approximation of social manifestations in public spaces, advocating them as key pieces in the production of crises in the *status quo* of democracy as a universal right that is given. When addressing how the possibility of physically and politically claiming for public spaces is not something given to everyone, but, rather, it complies with the asymmetric notion of the public sphere. Thus, the concept of public space also becomes the subject of scrutiny by the author, who understands the city as a space for political action for excellence.

> In the case of public assemblies, we see quite clearly the struggle over what will be public space, but also an equally fundamental struggle over how bodies will be supported in the world - a struggle for employment and education, equitable food distribution, livable shelter, and freedom of movement and expression, to name a few. (ibid, p. 72)

Considering data that shows a marked social, political, and economic inequality of the gender order in Latin America, we think that this phenomenon is inseparable from urban matters in the context of mutual incidence between social space and material space. It is, therefore, appropriate to present feminist and urban social movements, which increasingly seek to dispute the narratives between public and private and present as potentially revolutionary urban-based movements in Latin America.

4 Three Cases in Latin America: Feminist Urban Contestations

As presented so far, in this section, we briefly present a critical gender approach to urban space based on cases of bottom-up organizations that point out to new possibilities for more democratic and inclusive public spaces: a feminist urban squatting movement, the *Ni Una Menos* movement, and the Chilean women's movement that obtained global projection through digital networks in 2019. We identify these as a few examples that dispute the traditional narrative between public and private, proposing new forms of organization of the urban public space based on the notion of the common. These three cases may be organized from two central axes for gender-sensitive urban debate: (1) the struggle for decent housing associated with gender violence; (2) mobility, fighting gender violence, and state violence.

(a) **Feminist Squatting: Mirabal Reference House**

Here is a case of squatting that aims to protect women in situations of violence, especially domestic, but also from state violence due to evictions. In research on squatting undertaken by women during the 1970s in London, Ward (2017) outlines a historical picture of massive urban occupations that responded both to the aspiration of social and political movements—such as the feminist and lesbian movement—and to the effects of inequalities in urban development. Although the author's object of analysis is to produce a historical view at the phenomenon of intense occupation movement in regions full of unoccupied properties, it is worth noting both the recurrence of the housing problem in populous urban centers and its direct association with gender and class inequalities. Ward (2017) goes back to how the housing issue was especially difficult for women alone with children, due to the long waiting lists for social housing, and highlights the role that such occupations played as centers of reference for women, including victims of violence. In presenting this historical perspective on housing struggles from a gender perspective, she suggests that these urban occupation policies in the 1970s may connect with twenty-first century "occupy" movements and feminist organizations in favor of safe housing for victims of domestic violence.

The Mirabal Women Reference House appears on November 25, 2016, in a disabled and abandoned children's shelter, located in the city center of Porto Alegre, Brazil. It was occupied by about 100 activists, in order to create a reference space for women at risk and violence. The date and name given to the occupation pay tribute to the three Mirabal sisters, Dominicans murdered by the *Trujullista* regime in the 1960s, who would later become Latin American symbols of women's resistance.[1] The initial objective was to guide the need for shelter, given the great demand[2] for more emergency shelters for women in situations of domestic violence, in addition to requiring public services and public assistance policies.

Coordinated by the *Olga Benário Women's Movement*, the Reference House operated at the address between November 2016 and September 2018. Since September 2017, a working group had been created to manage the dispute for occupation of the property, in order to seek an agreement in meetings with members representing the State Government, City Hall, Public Ministry and Public Defender's Office. Between June and September 2018, there was a long period of threats of repossession and judicial suspensions, until the beginning of September 2018 when the repossession of the property was completed. Since then, the occupation has been transferred to the former Benjamin Constant State School. The state

[1]November 25 was declared by the United Nations in 1999 as the International Day of Nonviolence Against Women.

[2]As reported in 2016, the municipality had only one shelter for this purpose, with 48 places to welcome victims of domestic violence, even though the city has records of the occurrence of violence against women every 45 min.

government transferred the school property offered to Mirabal for municipal management, which in turn was committed to providing space for the use of the Reference House.

The new reference house was, however, far from the city center, creating some problems of displacement and accessibility to public goods for residents. In this sense, the situation of vulnerability of women in the occupation is reified by the new adversities of displacement, which socially affect the possibilities of restructuring the lives of these women who arrive at the House, considering the central role of space for the constitution of social agents. This debate refers to the imbrication between gender, race, and class as determinants of the different possibilities of the subjects to live and move. It is possible to think about the situation of female occupants from what Federici (2012) identifies in several studies as the "feminization of poverty" around the world, since there is a direct association between intensification of poverty and urban spatial segregation (Maricato 1996). As stated by Rolnik et al.:

> For women, the location of housing far from employment centers and public facilities or the absence of an efficient and accessible public transport network are particularly damaging aspects. Living in a distant place means, for them, greater difficulty in finding a job, greater expense of money and physical wear due to the long displacements they need to make. (2011, p. 17)

Thus, we highlight how the access to housing is central to social reproduction, since the domestic sphere is still the primary space for the performance of reproductive work. From the need to leave the home where violence is perpetrated, women are deprived both of their homes and of the network of sociability and support provided by family, friends, and neighborhood. Thus, the absence of a network for effective coping of the problem of gender-based violence is directly related to the debate on housing.

Violence against women can be considered a public problem, given its structural character and therefore must be tackled at the institutional level. It is worth noting that the failure to implement and/or violate the basic right to housing results in very specific consequences regarding the vulnerability produced from gender violence perspective. In this sense, Mirabal's repossession in 2018 leads us to reflect not only on the absence of the State in the management of gender violence, but also on the aggravation of the situation of these women. They are relocated and need to forge new support networks and new forms of resistance that are mediated by the self-managed organization of the Reference House.

For Rolnik et al. (2011), the violation or non-realization of the right to housing has specific consequences for women, which is central to the promotion of autonomy, the preservation of physical and psychological integrity and the fulfillment of other fundamental human rights. Therefore, incorporating the gender perspective into the debate on the right to housing and the city is necessary, since both rights are deeply imbricated and the difficulties in realizing these rights affect women in specific ways. However, what can be seen from the case study is the annulment of women—especially those racialized and coming from poor social classes—as a subject of law both before the aggressor and the State itself when this is absent in the provision of protection.

Today, even though displacement is a central issue for the occupants, concerns have been exacerbated by new threats of eviction: throughout 2019, a breach of the agreement previously established by the Porto Alegre City Hall was reported on Mirabal social network. In an audience with the Human Rights Commission of the Legislative Assembly of the State of Rio Grande do Sul, an agreement was reached between the State, City Hall, and the Movement to ensure the work carried out by the Reference House. During a year of negotiations with public entities, the space assigned to the Reference House is constantly under new requests for repossession required by the Porto Alegre City Hall itself, which fails to comply with an agreement previously established among other public entities, civil society, and other instances of the City Hall itself.

However, until the present writing of the chapter, the Reference House resists, and it is necessary to recognize the political power of occupations such as Mirabal, which are organized around anti-hierarchical principles and collective work, necessary to claim better living conditions for women broadly. This movement and similar ones in Latin American cities emerge due to its reformist potential: the case of Mirabal is a feminist urban phenomenon claiming the right to the city seeking to tackle the diverse inequalities of gender, race, and class, precisely by producing spaces of struggle and resistance.

(b) ***Ni Una Menos* and *machista* violence**

In another work (Garcia and Schuck 2018), we dedicated ourselves to the analysis of the posters wielded in the *Ni Una Menos* protests. Proclaimed as "a collective cry against machista violence", this movement emerged in Buenos Aires in 2015, with *Plaza del Congreso* as its first stage, in addition to a hundred squares throughout the Argentine country. It affirms the "beginning of a new path" and its main objective is to give voice to the feminist cause. There follows a public declaration to fight patriarchy and femicide, crimes that killed 275 women in one year in Argentina (2015–2016), and which places Brazil in 5th position in the world ranking according to the World Health Organization (WHO), with 4.8 homicides per 100,000 women. The movement in Argentina emerged as one of the most prominent and mediatized protests against gender violence in recent years, echoing in several Latin American countries.

With the objective of protesting against gender violence and, above all, against femicide, the movements express power in challenging gender violence, at the same time that they break with the very ideology of domestic confinement. When they move to the urban space, where they are ideologically suppressed, they produce counter-hegemonic and contestative resistance to structural male domination. The movement managed to organize and star in one of the feminist marches with the greatest media reach, gathering around three hundred thousand people. Among the hundreds of images produced in the media coverage, combative speeches referring to the issue of the right to the city are identified. The suggested hypothesis is that the occupation of the streets by feminist protests against macho violence is not a matter of chance, but rather, results as a fundamental element for understanding the movement itself.

The rhetoric of blaming victims of harassment and / or various forms of sexual and gender-based violence perpetrated in cities is commonly associated with certain inappropriate conduct by women to enjoy public spaces. The contestation of this rhetoric attests to the unequal constitution of these spaces, especially in regarding the right and possibility of access to them. The assignment of responsibility to women for their own safety in urban spaces shows the aspects of such asymmetries: the imposition of codes of conduct for the enjoyment and circulation on the streets, dress, and proper posture—in addition to the temporal issue, when the night becomes even more excluding and determinant—they are elements of common sense that demand confrontation.

The profusion of posters can be organized into two broad sets of ideas: the rejection of violence and the claim for egalitarian rights, especially the right to the city. These posters are dissident speeches, aligned with the logic of the counter-publics (Fraser 1990), which contest the systemic gender inequalities and show the political character of the dispute for urban public space: "these counterpublics emerge in response to exclusions within dominant publics, they help expand discursive space" (*ibid*, p. 67).

The slogans wielded on the posters can be read as alternative narratives, evoking dissent and exposing the fissures of an alleged democratic public space. By rejecting binary interpretations of the city and the impossibility of erasing the multiplicity of experiences in it, *Ni Una Menos* proposes to think about escapes from the strategically established order throughout the construction of dissent discourses. By playing with new speeches, affirmatives and bodies that disturb the apparent order established in the city, we suggest that the movements provided escapes to the hegemonic images that allude to the public space as something consensual.

In addition to a spillover from the private to the public, these discourses attest the fact that social movements need, as noted by Butler (2015), to insist on the existence of material conditions for public protests and speeches. This means thinking that space is not neutral, but rather a condition for the profusion of new speeches: both the protests and their speeches reconfigure the materiality of public space. Thus, the voices of the streets seem to emanate the claim to the most fundamental of rights: the right to the city as an elementary way to exercise citizenship. At the basis of the meaning of democracy in the polis is publicity—that is, the right to speak and be heard, for the purpose of political recognition for negotiating differences. In the poster that supports the phrase "I don't want to feel brave; I want to feel safe," we verify a demand for equality based on the negotiation of a position of refusal to the current terms of usufruct of urban public spaces.

Among numerous phrases, we highlight (a) "We want ourselves alive and free. The streets are ours"; (b) "Not one less, it is not the victim's fault, it is machismo"; (c) "Sorry for the inconvenience, but they are killing us"; (d) "One day, I will no longer be afraid to walk on the street, I will no longer be afraid to die for your machismo"; (e) "My cleavage is not an invitation to follow me"; (f) "Let me walk quietly down the street"; (g) "Using public space does not mean that my body is public too".

These are some examples of phrases associated with themes of repudiation of violence, demands for equality, and the right to the city. In the vast majority of sentences, it is possible to verify the unfavorable situation of women to enjoy their full rights as citizens in public spaces. These protests are definitely shaped by the expression of subordinate counterpublics. They are parallel discursive arenas, in which women represent a social group subordinated to patriarchal power, imposing, in turn, the circulation of their counter discourses. Such counter discourses allow them to formulate alternative interpretations to their identities and differences.

(c) **Women's March in Chile: Production of the Digital Common**

Since November 2019, Chilean women's marches have garnered international media coverage mainly due to the great impact of the hymn "*El violador eres tu*"[3] created by the collective *Las Tesis*. The collective originated in Valparaiso released the hymn[4] for the International Day to Combat Violence Against Women, on November 25th. However, due to allegations of abuse in anti-austerity protests and against President Sebastián Piñera that have taken over the Chilean streets since October 2019, the song was first presented on November 20. In choreographed action, women take public plazas wearing black blindfolds to intonate the song.

According to data from the Gender Equality Observatory for Latin America and the Caribbean (OIG)[5] of the Economic Commission for Latin America and the Caribbean (ECLAC), at least 3529 women were killed in 2018 for gender reasons in 25 countries in Latin America and Caribbean. The data put several countries in the region at the top ranking in femicide issues.

The scope of these women's protests was global, attracting reproductions of music and choreography in different cities around the world, such as São Paulo, Buenos Aires, Istanbul, London, Paris, and New York, among others. Several performance videos circulating on social media have also obtained thousands of views around the world. Although the advancement of the neoliberal prescription is present in most countries of the world, what draws attention is that, among all Chilean protests, it is specifically the protests of Chilean women against the violence that have become a phenomenon of worldwide circulation resulting in a transnational common production.

[3]"The rapist is you."

[4]The lyrics are followed by a choreography repeated by demonstrators blindfolded in black fabric. "Patriarchy is a judge/ Who judges us because of us being born/And our punishment is the violence you don't see/It's femicide/Impunity for my killer/It's the disappearance/It's the rape/And it wasn't my fault, nor where I was, nor how I dressed/You were the rapist/You are the rapist/They are the police/The judges/The state/The President."

[5]Available at: https://oig.cepal.org/pt/indicadores/feminicidio-ou-femicidio accessed on 03/20/2020.

These great marches then became mobile, fluid, and global through information technologies, which contribute to the circulation of images and narratives that cross borders, overcome censorship, and become part of the protest itself. The filming of truculent actions by the police produces a kind of "counter surveillance" of these actions. Moreover, thus, those bodies on the streets are required by the media to have an event, one that exists in a global arena (Butler 2015, p. 94). Once again, space takes on a central role for all social action, even though digital media allows to form a digital common.

These protests also constitute the logic of counterpublics as new ways of contesting systemic gender inequalities—and, above all, urban space as a locus of discursive disputes. The Chilean demonstrations, which had more than 1 million participants, have no defined leadership, nor a precise list of demands: it is a widespread criticism of the neoliberal economic system, which, behind the apparent success of macroeconomic indices, hides a profound social discontent. Associated with a broader dispute against austerity policies, it is worth remembering that the trigger for the protests occurred after the increase in the price of subway tickets, added to a series of pre-existing economic policies that generated profound discontent. In this sense, it is evident that "the city is not a frictionless agglomeration of commoners, but rather a site for ongoing contestation about what counts as common and who counts as commoners." (Kornberger and Borch 2015, p. 15).

In these common production insurgencies that articulate collective demands, there is "the spontaneous coming together in a moment of irruption; when disparate heterotopic groups suddenly see, if only for a fleeting moment, the possibilities of collective action to create something radically different" (Harvey 2012, p. 17). That is, as public assembly as Butler (2015, p. 80) argues, they affirm in a new way the right to have rights:

> The right to have rights is one that depends on no existing particular political organization for its legitimacy. Like the space of appearance, the right to have rights predates and precedes any political institution that might codify or seek to guarantee that right; [...]. The right comes into being when it is exercised, and exercised by those who act in concert, in alliance. Those who are excluded from existing polities.

Therefore, it is under the circumstances of these ephemeral actions of commoning of those who are excluded that Chilean protests and feminist protests conform. They contest specifically violence against women in protests, but also violence in everyday life. Undoubtedly, Kornberger and Borch (2015) are right in proposing that the use of places increases their sense of common when they are used, shared—and we add—politicized by struggles that present their constitutive exclusions. The concept of an urban common is strengthened precisely by the gathering of several commons, which in the public space intersect in a dense network and show the formation of a plural urban collective to historically marginalized voices.

5 Final Considerations

Despite the symbolic exclusion, the daily practices of women in cities do not cease, and it is necessary to highlight that these practices escape the power of space organization technologies. In other words, somehow, architecture as well as discourses symbolically establish a reality of social space in the material space of the city. Such symbolic systems—visual, discursive—clash in the public arena when we read "We want ourselves alive and free. The streets are ours." *Ni Una Menos* and other feminist movements such as the Chilean Women March and feminist squats guide new articulations, possibilities of discursive production and polyphonies of political practices in the field of feminism.

In the case of Mirabal Reference House, we highlighted as the (im)possibilities of displacement and urban mobility also impacted and limited the survival options for these women: it is a spatial distance that reinforces social distance and prevents women from overcoming adversities. Throughout this chapter, we have worked to show how issues of the right to the city, gender violence and their disputes with the state and neoliberal policies are intersected. We perceived that some experiences of spatial distances concretely reiterate social distances (Bourdieu 1999), resulting in aggravation of difficulties faced by women in a situation of violence. However, it is due to their reformist potential that these movements emerge: they are urban and specifically feminist phenomena that demand social justice and the right to the city, seeking to fight diverse inequalities of gender, race, and class, precisely at the same time, and to produce spaces of resistance that are always based on communing.[6]

References

Agrest, D. (2008). À margem da arquitetura: corpo, lógica e sexo. In K. Nesbitt (Ed.), *Uma nova agenda para a arquitetura*: antologia Teórica 1965–1995 (pp. 585–599). São Paulo: Cosac Naify.

Bourdieu, P. (1993). La Misère du Monde. Portuguese Edition: Bourdieu, P. (1999). A miséria do mundo. Editora Vozes: Petrópolis.

Bourdieu, P. (2013). Espaço físico, espaço social e espaço físico apropriado. *Estudos Avançados, USP 27* (79), 133–144.

[6]This chapter was written in the first semester of 2020 while the Covid-19 virus erupted worldwide causing a pandemic. As world leaders and sanitary authorities determined lockdown and social isolation measures to flatten the statistical curve of infections and deaths, many feminist collectives pointed to the risks of rising domestic violence. Quarantine is a situation that puts women at risk, because femicides primarily occur at home, according to *Observatorio Ahora Que Si Nos Ven* in Argentina. Under lockdown measures in March 2020, Argentines took to their balconies, banging pots, hanging green and purple handkerchiefs (that represent abortion rights and *Ni Una Menos)* to declare their outrage over machista violence. The abrupt change on world public spaces configuration due to quarantine, however, does not eliminate the challenge of seeking for inclusive and more equal spaces. On the contrary, on quarantine times, we face the challenge of rethinking the limits between domestic and public spaces, about the right to the city, and also about new forms of resistance.

Butler, J. (2015). *Notes toward a performative theory of assembly*. Cambridge: Harvard University Press.

Garcia, C., & Schuck, E. (2018). Movimentos feministas na cidade e suas discursividades. *Revista PerCursos, 19*(40), 141–159.

Deutsche, R. (2008). Visiones públicas. In R. Deutsche (Eds.), *Agorafobia* (pp. 25–52) Col. Quaderns portàtils. Barcelona: MACBA.

Federici, S. (2012). *Revolution at point zero: Housework, reproduction, and feminist struggle*. Brooklyn: PM Press.

Foucault, M. (1984) Space, knowledge, and power. In P. Rabinow (Ed.), *The foucault reader* (pp. 239–256). New York: Pantheon.

Fraser, N. (1990). Rethinking the public sphere. A Contribution to the Critique of Actually Existing Democracy. *Social Text*, No. 25/26, 56–80.

Harvey, D. (2005). *A brief history of neoliberalism*. New York: Oxford University Press.

Harvey, D. (2012). *Rebel cities: From the right to the city to the urban revolution*. New York: Verso.

Jacobs, J. (1992). *The death and life of Great American Cities*. New York: Vintage Books.

Kornberger, M., & Borch, C. (2015). Introdutction: Urban commons. In C. Borch & M. Kornberger (Eds.), *Urban commons: Rethinking the city* (pp. 1–21). New York: Routledge.

Maricato, E. (1996). *Metrópole na periferia do capitalismo*: ilegalidade, desigualdade e violência. Hucitec, Sao Paulo.

Massey, D. (1994). *Space, place and gender*. Minneapolis: University of Minnesota Press.

Mcdowell, L. (1999). Gender, identity and place. Understanding feminist geographies. Spanish Edition. Mcdowell. (2000). Género, identidad y lugar. Un estúdio de las geografias feministas (P. Linares, Trans.). Madrid, Cátedra.

Mcdowell, L. (1983). Towards an understanding of the gender division of urban Space. *Environment and Planning D: Society and Space, 1*, 59–72.

Muxí, Z. (2006). Ciudad Próxima: Urbanismo sin género. *I.T.* (75), 68–75.

Perregaux, M. (2005). The city as gendered space: A reading of three literary texts in the light of feminist geography. *SPELL, 17*, 179–194.

Perrot, M. (2006). Mon Histoire des Femmes. Portuguese Edition: Perrot, M. (2007) Minha história das Mulheres (A. Correa, Trans.). São Paulo: Contexto.

Rolnik, R. et al. (2011). *Como fazer valer o direito das mulheres à moradia?* São Paulo: Labcidade/ FAUSP.

Sennett, R. (1974). The fall of public man. Portuguese Edition: Sennett, R. (2014). *O Declínio do Homem Público*: as tiranias da intimidade (L. Watanabe, Trans.). São Paulo: Companhia das Letras.

Can Social Fractures Affect the Legal Framework? Towards an Institutional Craftsmanship

Verena Lenna, Roberto Randazzo, and Michele Trimarchi

The merchant persuaded the shepherd that the pasture and the forest were the right place to build a beautiful mansion. He could benefit from rents and sales, much more than his present earnings. The shepherd agreed and accepted the deal.
The herd suspected that something could spoil their pasture and decided not to move. When the shepherd tried to fell the trees and scythe the grass, he was prevented to even entering and soldiers had to be called in, to evict the herd. The sun was setting. From amongst the trees Elinor the magician appeared. She surveyed the scene, in silence. When the shepherd started to complain, pointing to the norms and traditions, Elinor simply stated: "This place is not yours, it belongs to its users".
(from *The Tale of Commons*)

Abstract

The relationship between urban communities and local administrations is necessarily complex and dynamic, often contradictory and even conflictual. Considering the proliferation of civic initiatives and their struggle for rights, our hypothesis is that the interest of communities and the public interest can be very different. The final outcome of their interaction is strongly determined by the

V. Lenna
IUAV, Venice, Italy

KU Leuven, Belgium

R. Randazzo
Lawyer in Rome, Barrister at the Supreme Court, Rome, Italy

M. Trimarchi (✉)
Department of Laws, Economics and Sociology, Magna Graecia University, Catanzaro, Italy
e-mail: trimarchi@unicz.it

E. Macrì et al. (eds.), *Cultural Commons and Urban Dynamics*,
https://doi.org/10.1007/978-3-030-54418-8_16

interpretation of the existing legal norms, as an expression of the prevailing political view. Urban commons allow us to rethink the interaction between the regulatory framework and the social ferments. The appropriation of neglected buildings and vacant sites questions the legitimacy to violate the law in the name of the common good; symmetrically, the design of ad hoc regulatory frameworks can lead to the institutionalisation of community-based initiatives, at the expense of their political value, and raises new questions about their representation and the related responsibilities. Which institutional approach can prove effective in supporting commons-oriented urban actions? How can they redraw the relationship between community and administration? How can we balance public and community interest? This chapter addresses these complex issues, by exploring three different cases of commons-oriented action. We suggest that they may provide us with useful insights in view of adopting an institutional craftsmanship being built in between flexible regulation and finely tuned co-operation.

1 Introduction

Rome, Italy, year 1886. Villa Borghese is a private park, legally owned by the Borghese family. The resident community, as well as visitors, voyagers and temporary residents, normally use the park to enjoy leisure time. Suddenly, one day Marcantonio Borghese decides to close the park by forbidding the access to visitors, and Leopoldo Torlonia, then Mayor of Rome, sues him on the basis of the ambiguous nature of Villa Borghese as *res in usu publico* combining private ownership and public right of entry; such a condition should prevent the owner from denying access to the park. The argument proves successful, and the Court imposes the re-opening of Villa Borghese, as Pasquale Stanislao Mancini, the plaintiff's attorney, had sustained in the appeal brief.[1]

The case is eloquent under various perspectives: it shows how a bundle of different rights can gravitate towards the same resource. It highlights the need for legal regulations to conciliate opposite interests. It suggests the relevance of shared interests in recognising the legitimacy of uses, such as leisure, educational and cultural activities, the fulfilment of needs. However, at the same time it points out the delicacy of balancing a multiplicity of specific expectations, rights and uses that could prove divergent or even conflicting, thus questioning the consistency of their formal representation.

[1]The appeal, *Del Diritto di Uso Pubblico del Comune e del Popolo di Roma sulla Villa Borghese*, was published in 1886 (Di Porto 2013). The case is described in Marella (2017). The final decision of the Supreme Court was adopted on 9 March 1887.

Commons have a long history. Their 'ancestors' are quite old, considering that in ancient times many forms of collective and shared property were ordinary, and that, as Marella (2017) sharply argues, also referring to Thomas (2002), "individual property in Roman Law, which the dominant view has traditionally represented as the noble ancestry of modern private property, derives 'by subtraction' from the legal regimes of common and public goods, so that individual property itself was even unconceivable without taking into account the regulation of non-private goods" (p. 73).

Through the centuries many forms of common action have been established, responding to economic, social and cultural aims in the broadest sense. Many of them disappeared or have been forgotten, crushed by the priorities of public and private forms of property. From land and agricultural entitlements—as in the case of '*usi civici*'—to Community Land Trusts, from urban commons to *Wikipedia*, the phenomenology—and consequently the theoretical interpretation and elaboration—of commons proves rich and varied.

Ranging from commons as shared practices in a material setting and their 'tragic' implications (Hardin 1968), to commons as converging purposes able to generate sustainable management of shared resources (Ostrom 1990), the economic approach to commons focuses upon the balance of a set of different interests achieved by overcoming the usual binary approach: on the one hand the public, driven by State distortionary action, on the other hand the private, driven by the rules of the marketplace bound to equilibrium and efficiency. A third area proves indeed eloquent and useful, taking many historical experiences as virtuous and effective cases of commons, and elaborating consistent interpretation for the many emerging phenomena that conventional wisdom cannot consider unless labelling them as 'anomalies'.

The Marxist narrative of commons focuses on the resistance to processes of accumulation by dispossession. Federici (2011), Swyngedouw (2011) and Harvey (2012) are just a few among the most eloquent scholars on the topic, although from different standpoints. Urban commons are thus conceptualised as a contemporary expression of the right to the city. Their value proves crucial in a period of radical transition, when the urban fabric is anaesthetised by increasing processes of financialisation; when, together with urban land, what is dispossessed is the power to decide and the possibility to inhabit in the broad sense of the word.

Urban commons are ad hoc projects, which need to be instituted (Dardot and Laval 2014), thus every time defined in relation to site-specific conditions and purposes, triggered by the needs of the involved communities, and adjusted to the existing regulations. As complex experiments that simultaneously redefine juridical architectures, spatial configuration and uses, while establishing socio-economic and cultural alternatives, urban commons require an interdisciplinary perspective, so that their holistic and pragmatic approach to the management of resources could be seized, as the source of a radical innovation. It is under this angle that we will look at the three cases examined in this chapter. Our reflections are situated in the space where local forms of governance take shape by interweaving three layers: (a) the legal infrastructure and its design of rights and duties, opportunities and prohibitions, whose features are generality and abstraction; (b) the administrative regulations and its range of possibilities and constraints, incentives and bureaucratic trails, whose rules are (should be, at least) crafted with reference to the local specificities; (c) the social ferment and its desire to establish and consolidate shared views and practices, whose actions are forced to combine informal fertility and formal processes.

The most evident, and frequent, problem arising from the combination of these three layers in the everyday practice of urban communities is twofold: on the one hand, the purposes of the actors located in the different layers are often reciprocally conflicting, and in any case their plain consistency cannot be granted in advance; on the other hand, the difference in their space and time framework naturally implies a sort of institutional dissonance due to the diverging interpretations that each layer advocates, either formally or informally. Among these the conception itself of property rights, as well as the definition and scope of public, collective and private interest.

Considering the endemic rigidity and slowness of central legislation, the complex range of interests and goals within local regulation, and the heterogeneous bundle of needs, desires and views perceived and pursued by the urban communities, this chapter examines urban commons as a factor for institutional transformation. As an alternative to a rigid regulatory attitude, urban commons seem to suggest the possibility of practicing an institutional craftsmanship underpinned by a finely tuned co-operation, thus transforming the relationship between the urban community and the local administration.

The chapter is divided into three sections. The following section will examine three cases of urban commons related to a variety of situations and featured by a variety of factors. The third section will focus upon them by adopting the 'morphology of the folktale' (Propp 1968) as a tool aimed at identifying and comparing roles and actions. At first, we will recognise and describe two main characters: the urban community and the local administration. Then we will highlight the recurrence of a plot, according to which their relationship—either struggle or co-operation—appears to be constantly defined and mediated by the interpretation of the existing legal infrastructure—our third character—with its design of rights and duties, opportunities and prohibitions.

Such an interpretative grid allows us to expose the ineffectiveness of the existing legal framework due to its natural abstraction and generality and the consequent slowness in responding to emerging phenomena and their multiform, ever-changing nature. As a result, urban commons risk to be either institutionalised or repressed. What is lost in both cases is the possibility of a more radical and substantial transformation of the legal framework and policies. In the fourth section of this chapter we will argue that a different approach should instead recognise the capacity of communities' interests and actions to transform legislation, policy and therefore the *modus operandi* of urban administrations. By elaborating a synoptic interpretation of the transactions across the three levels at stake we will draft possible institutional approaches and tools aimed at responding to the emersion of increasingly multiform bundles of uses, and the related bundles of rights, many examples of which can be found in the urban commons.

2 Three Cases of Urban Commons

2.1 Neglected Areas: Illegality and Social Subsidiarity

On 7 February 2019 the police evicted a group of activists from the "Asilo Occupato", a former kindergarten located in the central area of Turin, via Alessandria, in the Aurora neighbourhood, occupied since 1995. Social anarchists —as they defined themselves—claimed the right "to disrupt the strategies of power and open the doors of freedom"; through the years they were held responsible for criminal activities mostly against the State. Structured as a small company, with clear organisation, roles and functions, they were accused of carrying out many violent actions in several Italian towns, mainly consisting in arson attacks against banks, embassies, and other symbolic places. In the attempt at exerting some influence upon the national policy on migration, one of their main targets were the Centres for Accommodation and Repatriation (formerly CIE), whose management was considered biased and incorrect. In the wide police action following the Turin eviction a sort of handbook was found in various places: *National textbook of the violent anarchist*, whose conception and elaboration was attributed to via Alessandria occupants. After the eviction, a protest was performed in the area, and many damages had been recorded against both persons and buildings.

The group had re-occupied the building after a quick and short eviction in 1998, and had started a diffused action against the "mechanisms of exploitation, exclusion and repression" (Falconieri 2019): their protest and critique towards the State could also be expressed through effective daily actions of care and social assistance. With the occupation they took care of an otherwise abandoned building in a degraded neighbourhood, waiting for speculative plans to be realised and for the consequent gentrification to expel the poorest residents of the area.[2] Bianchin (2019), resident in the Aurora neighbourhood for twenty-five years, living just in front of the Asilo, remembers not only the coming and going of the guests, but also the community garden, the repainting of the façade, the dinners organised to collect funds for poor tenants, in the attempt at preventing their eviction, as well as to cover the trial expenses of anarchists in jail.

The local community had coexisted with the occupied 'Asilo' for more than twenty years. While many complained about the problems that the situation allegedly generated, others appreciated the daily gestures of solidarity of the occupants, and the courage to stand against the speculative transformation of the Aurora district. On one side, the social anarchism and the right to the city; on the opposite side of the scale, the charges of having established a subversive association and carried out the related criminal activities. Both actions were motivated by

[2]These processes already affect the other half of the Aurora neighbourhood, where a sort of smart-working district is being developed, following the urban renewal of this former industrial area started in 2012. Its flagship project, the 'Nuvola' complex by Cino Zucchi, triggered a substantial rise in the real estate property values, according to Osservatorio Immobiliare della Città di Torino.

the conviction that the State and the local administration were uncapable to manage the neighbourhood, when not fueling inequalities. Was it just angry romanticism?

The reactions to their eviction, that was defined "an intervention for public safety"[3], were manifold. Satisfaction was expressed by the Mayor Ms Chiara Appendino and many other local and national politicians, as well as by police officers; Appendino also announced that Turin Municipal Administration was already planning to devote the building to associations, nonprofits and organisations active in the field of social services, while denying any possibilities that the building itself could be sold within a wider plan of real estate disposal and sale. After the eviction, a small crowd tried to protest against the police, while many anarchists were arrested in many parts of Italy. Not all the neighbours were unconditionally happy about the eviction. Looking back at the 25 years of occupation the words of Bianchin (2019) reveal the contradictory feelings not unfrequently triggered by occupations, between fear and pride, conformism and disobedience. Acknowledging their illegal status and witnessing the troubles occurring in the building, Bianchin remembers their 'arrival': "In the first years we hoped that the building would be cleared: as everybody, we thought that their presence would degrade the area. They were crooked and dirty—at least it seemed so to our aesthetical sense—dressed in black and 'poor'. Poverty always scares, also when it is not ours".

The area had been degraded for a long time before the occupation: the noisy presence of a disco had generated thefts and damages, disturbing the neighbourhood with the many parked cars, and screams and troubles until late at night. Two streets away, a supermarket was used as the gathering point of drunk and desperate individuals, illegally recruited as cheap labour force. Drug trafficking and crimes proliferated—and still persist—with fights and frequent wounds, sometimes killings. Compared with such a violent repertoire, the occupants were never "robbing, stabbing, burgling. Clearly, 'occupying' is an illegal action. But, if the Municipal Administration did not need that kindergarten (was it really so?) it was not so unreasonable that somebody would use it in a different way and, why not?, as a social centre. […] An abandoned and unused space is a waste" (Bianchin 2019).

Two concluding reflections. The former concerns the conditions for the very existence of an occupation, as an illegal action by definition. The issues of property violation and public security, by referring to the legal framework, call upon the political will of administrators, who will have to interpret the law in between the pressure of investors and the needs of the concerned communities: in between ideology and consensus building. Negotiations and tolerance of the *status quo* can be achieved also in consideration of the social value of the activities squatters often organise. While making room for the alternative and the deviant, in the words of Castel (1995), they certainly offer support and solidarity, but at the same time they operate as safety valves, impeding more severe explosions of rage. The latter reflection concerns the issues of representation, responsibility and coexistence of rights that occupations inevitably raise. To occupy an abandoned space means to

[3]Words of the Mayor, Ms. Chiara Appendino, as reported by the press.

give it back to everyone, the Squat movement asserts.[4] While an unconditioned access would certainly lead to the tragedy of the commons, questions arise concerning the establishment of a substantial participatory governance. This dilemma invites us to reflect, on the one hand, on the conciliation of the goals and needs of a community, fulfilled by a given resource which they have direct access to and govern; on the other hand, the need to redefine the ways and contents of representation towards any institutional, social and informal counterparts.

2.2 Dismissed Spaces and Creative Re-appropriation

On February 2014, the Prefect of Rome rejected the proposal of formally approving the Statute of the newly established "Fondazione Teatro Valle Bene Comune". A few months before the new regulations had been crafted by a group of occupants with the legal assistance of Stefano Rodotà, formerly professor of Civil Law, Chairman of the Lower House of the Italian Parliament, and President of the Authority on Privacy. The ambition of this unusual Foundation was to create a new 'institution' based on common goods—*beni comuni*—and their management, a form of 'collective property'. Although the purpose was to address the complexity of unregulated phenomena with a versatile approach, the Prefect simply rejected the Statute arguing that it lacked the basic legal assumptions. This ended up denying the legal personality of the Foundation, and thus stopping the process of rehabilitating the commons in the legal landscape; collaterally, the emersion of further organisations sharing orientation and strategy with the occupants of Teatro Valle was also prevented.

"I am aghast—commented the director and actor Hossein Taheri, one of the occupants—they want to chop off the legs to a three-years' experience, pretending that nothing ever happened. They will not stop us, we will go on with our project also thanks to our agreement with the citizenship, with the subscribers of the Foundation. I believe that the problem is that we established the venue of the Foundation in the Theatre. We are citizens engaged in a project that institutions did not want to understand, we wrote to the Mayor Ignazio Marino, and to the Ministry for Cultural Heritage and the Performing Arts Massimo Bray, but did not receive any replies" (Giannoli 2014). After the failure of such a project and a period of silence the main Theatre of the city, the national Teatro di Roma whose main house is Teatro Argentina, a few blocks away from the Teatro Valle, started a programme labelled "Interludio Valle" consisting of exhibitions, installations, conferences and many other activities except performing arts. It could be interpreted as the acknowledgement of the urgency not to abandon such a historical building on the one hand, and to admit the persistent inability (or, according to many, the unwillingness) to take care of it on the part of the Municipal Administration, owner of the building, on the other hand.

[4]www.radar.squat.net.

The story started in 2011, after the disposal of the Italian Theatre Authority (ETI-Ente Teatrale Italiano) as part of a long-lasting wave of cultural austerity combining slow reductions and peak withdrawals in financial support, associated to growingly byzantine regulations, regularly performed by a sequence of governments of different political colour but showing equal indifference to culture and the arts.[5] Publicly funded, with very small box office revenues, the Italian theatre system has never seriously explored any market options and still prefers competition to co-operation, since the main struggle is to get funds out of a limited general amount. Teatro Valle was among the houses directly managed by ETI. Suddenly abandoned, there was no possibility that either a public or a private company could take over (similarly to what Teatro Duse, another former ETI house in Bologna, experienced in the same period), leaving a range of professionals (artists, technicians, administrative staff) without a job. Cultural workers, activists and citizens decided to directly manage it, by occupying its venue and starting a commons-oriented, experimental model of governance. Many shows were offered by external theatrical companies and single artists with no fees to the then "Teatro Valle Occupato", allowing workers to get their salaries from the ordinary box office revenues. After this favourable start, the occupants realised that their project needed to grow up.

The 'shapeless community' of the early period—in the words of Stefano Rodotà—had generated a "new subject, endowed with the right and the method to establish a dialogue with other institutions. From now on the walls of this building and its management concern the interaction with the participating local authorities; they cannot prescind anymore from its real existence, evenly" (Lo Gatto 2013). The prevailing atmosphere was wishfully romantic, reminding famous social struggles of the past, and combining idealism with a more pragmatic search for funds. The rules and *modus operandi* adopted by the occupants for the Foundation were somehow unrealistic, if we consider the specific needs and rhythm of theatre life: the season must be drafted at least one year in advance, continuity grants cultural and strategic reliability, the structure and the decision-making processes need to be structured and smooth: a theatre, like many other enterprises, works like a clockwork, and even a small friction can compromise the whole productive endeavour.

The Statute appeared to be "a wishful document based upon assembly decisions, short-time turnout and a sort of improper use of the label 'common', although no real approach to the culture of commons was actually present in the internal regulation" (Lenna and Trimarchi 2019). Although the Statute clearly referred to the values and principles of a commons-oriented governance, the financial framework was quite conventional (core activities, public calls, public funds) also aiming at the required

[5]The Italian legislation dealing with the performing arts is featured by a sequence of partial innovation aimed at granting survival of the organisations through monetary funds, while at the same time generating financial difficulties that will be faced by the next act, at its time inducing new forms of weaknesses. It regularly follows this uneven path, although the government normally promises a general reform, and the beneficiaries of funds patiently wait for it to be crafted, approved and introduced (Sabatini and Trimarchi 2019).

inclusion in the beneficiaries' category[6]; voluntary donations were included among the possible revenues, not really far from corporate sponsorship, membership programmes and the like: the label sounded more ambitious than reality. Among the principles were "solidarity, non-discrimination, promotion of workers' rights and dignity, environmental protection". The difficulty to conciliate a participatory approach in decision-making with the adhesion to an economic model based on competition (though formally rejected), as well as the idealistic principles with the concrete funding needs, ended up revealing the weakness of the experiment. A community needs to share not only motivations but also solid rules. In the case of Teatro Valle, the declared interpretation of the performing arts as tools aimed at political action, and the idealistic organisation may have strongly contributed to the refusal of a constructive dialogue on the part of both local and central governments.

2.3 Unmanaged Places and Grass-Root Initiative

Among the Italian towns, Bologna may represent a unique experience for many reasons. The oldest University was founded here in the year 1088 A.D.; from 1506 to 1859 it belonged to the Pontifical State ruled by the Pope (and it gave Cardinal Lambertini, as Pope Benedict XIV, to the Catholic Church); after the Second World War, it was considered the 'moral capital' of the Italian Communism. Its varied history makes it a non-prejudicial town, combining a provincial orientation, a cosmopolitan atmosphere, a hedonistic reputation and some frugality in its politics. Social and creative ferments are not rare in Bologna (Trimarchi 2019), also in consideration of the cultural variety characterising the city. Rather than the outcome of a homogeneous sensibility, they are often engendered by conflicting views. In a magmatic town, projects, visions and actions end up building a sort of involuntary framework whose energy triggers further intuitions.[7]

The combination of social sensitivity and creative attitude has led to some unique experiences based upon the search for a sort of social optimisation able to overcome the usual protocols shaping everyday life. Among these, a pioneering project is 'Social Street' that has generated a wide fallout of similar experiences in many other towns: almost 500 social streets in the world, involving 100,000 people, showcase the sound need for a similar project. The rationale of the initiative is quite simple, grounded in the acknowledgement of a schizophrenic approach to urban life: isolated in their neighbourhood, people normally interact with strangers through the web; is it possible to valorise proximity in various exchanges, from personal to commercial, adopting the web as a facilitator? "From virtual to real" was the claim of the first Social Street, in via Fondazza, and social networks were

[6]Access to the FUS (Fondo Unico dello Spettacolo) financial support requires the previous inclusion in one of the categories of theatrical organisations regulated by State laws, whose formal labels and substantial requirements often change. When the requirements are not fully satisfied such funds are not given.

[7]The many projects related to the communing orientation of many social groups and cultural organisations in Bologna are examined and discussed by Mariangela Dalfovo in this book.

used to build an intensive connection among people sharing the same urban area. As a consequence, the sense of belonging is not defined by political, religious or cultural beliefs, but simply by a shared living environment and the related territorial representation of the (collective) self.

Virtuous and fertile, Bologna is not always unanimous in interpreting its creativity: its professional and social milieu tends to institutionalise many artistic ferments and phenomena, thus (involuntarily?) blurring their message. An example is the 2016 exhibition of street art in Palazzo Pepoli (part of the municipal museum network): "Street Art - Banksy & Co." was at the centre of a harsh discussion due to the inconsistency between street art as the channel of antagonist language on one hand, and museums as the sanctuaries of institutional acknowledgement on the other. Quite similarly, outside the museum the municipal administration evicted many homeless families occupying a neglected building or activists managing a social centre (Xm24, via Fioravanti, 2020). In many cases, occupations were considered—as the press reported—a response to a weak housing policy on the part of the municipal administration, whose interpretation of social needs proves—as in many other towns—uneven, in the evident attempt at building an institutional identity on one hand, and pursuing general consensus on the other, despite the heterogeneous needs of its resident community.

Within such a contradictory framework Bologna crafted an innovative kind of institutional tool, managing to deal with urban commons as diverse, site-specific experiments. On 19 May 2014, the Municipal Administration approved the "Regulation on forms of collaboration between citizens and Administration for care and re-generation of urban common goods". Proposals can focus upon material goods (streets, squares, arcades, gardens, parks and green areas, buildings, etc.); immaterial goods (social inclusion, education, training, culture, environmental sustainability, re-use, sharing, etc.); digital tools (websites, applications, social networks, digital training, etc.). The scope is quite wide, and this allowed many registered associations and informal groups to draft more than five hundred projects. More than half of the submitted project have been transformed into pacts. Since the establishment of the Regulation, more than two hundred towns in Italy have introduced similar legal frameworks aimed at facing the unregulated features of institutional and social initiatives that capture emerging needs and views, whose novelty and unpredictability does not fit the conventional framework and the existing norms.

In such a respect, due to the effectiveness of what first appeared as an experiment and eventually revealed itself as a versatile protocol, similar legal frameworks are becoming systematic, thus recognising a pro-active citizenship at the core of a horizontal interpretation of subsidiarity. The idea itself of 'active citizenship' has been introduced in the Italian Constitution with the 2001 reform, by changing the Art. 118, par. 4: "The State, regions, metropolitan cities, provinces and municipalities shall promote the autonomous initiative of citizens, both as individuals and as members of associations, in carrying out activities of general interest, on the basis of the principle of subsidiarity". This principle is in fact at the core of the services provided by LabSus (labsus.org), the national Laboratory for Subsidiarity that acts like a hub for both unstructured intuitions and existing experiences, which certainly help active citizens to consistently elaborate and carry out projects focused on urban commons; it also provides local administrations with a range of technical tools and strategies aimed at finely regulating specific initiatives in their territory. Ambitiously, this could be the sort of platform pursuing the metamorphosis of the existing legal framework, being suggested and fueled by a heterogeneous landscape of urban initiatives. In such a respect, a versatile reformulation of property rights and a consistent redefinition of criminal law seem to be the two sides of the same coin.

3 Institutional Dissonances

3.1 Urban Tales

Although different from each other, the three cases discussed in the previous section are characterised by common elements. The 'analysis of the tale' by Vladimir Propp (1968) proves useful to recognise recurring plots and purposes behind case-specific differences. While the actual characters are different, roles and goals are very similar. There is always a hero, a villain, a helper, but who? There is always a lack at the origin of the action, which one? What is the reaction? And how is the recognition of the hero performed? The answers to these questions are necessarily ambivalent as a result of the plurality of interests at stake and of the site-specific conditions under which the actions unfold: according to some citizens the hero is the municipality, according to others the heroes are the squatters. The repetitiveness of the plots, on the other hand, reveals rigidity: an incapacity of listening and of institutional creativity that are arguably the main lack—more cultural than administrative—urban commons are reacting to. Whether it is about inefficiency and a consequent subsidiary initiative, or about exploitation and the consequent disobedient response, some sort of lack is at the origin of the stories of occupations and urban commons, triggering the interaction of the two main characters and initiating a transformative process.

The most active and creative character is the community, which in the name of shared motivation and needs acts by combining informal fertility and formal processes. The second character is the local administration, which operates by referring to, and by interpreting, the existing legal framework, swinging between interpretative openings and constraints, most of the times in pursuit of consensus. As a sort of magic wand (a 'magical item' in Propp's words) law enforcement can legitimate and trigger co-operation, conflict, even reciprocal indifference between the local administration and the urban community. Quite often, like in popular tales, one wins over the other; in some cases—more rarely—a happy ending is in view.

Stories of urban spaces, occupations and commons reveal an unbalanced framework where many actions converge and generate eventual synergies or conflicts. Whether the story starts from inefficiency and subsidiary initiative, action and reaction, or even unjust exploitation and illegal response, in every case the diversity of interests at stake clearly emerges. This is what fuels the story and triggers the interaction of the two main characters, thus initiating a transformative process that will deploy its trails until the unavoidable confrontation with the impersonal but sharp third character: legislation.

This section examines the features and the orientations of the two characters, and the potential of the 'magic' agent. Firstly, the urban community and its response to the infrastructural voids and asymmetries characterising the current socio-spatial conditions. Secondly, the approach of the local administration and its diverse options ranging from indifference to stewardship, within its short-period horizon. Finally, the ambiguities and controversies related to the legal framework, its value hierarchy and its rigid principles; it is a crucial device that should prove able to incorporate and balance the interests of diverse individuals and communities.

3.2 The Plural Space of Rights and Shared Interests

Written in 1974, against a background still echoing the student protests of 1968 and the critique to the State as an entity "[flattening] the social and cultural sphere,[…] [enforcing] a logic that puts an end to conflicts and contradictions" (Lefebvre 1991: 23), *La production de l'Espace* theorised the concept of the production of space, as a result of the dialectical interaction of three dimensions: the perceived, the conceived and the lived spaces.

The spatial practices—or perceived space—are the space "which embraces production and reproduction, and the particular locations and spatial sets characteristic of each social formation" (Lefebvre 1991: 38). Each society produces, and would not exist without producing, a specific space: therefore, the Medieval space or the space of the Renaissance society is different from the space of the industrial society. Representations of space—or the conceived space—are "the space of scientists, planners, urbanists, technocratic subdividers and social engineers, as of a certain type of artist with a scientific bent—all of whom identify what is lived and what is perceived with what is conceived […]. This is the dominant space in any society (or mode of production)" (Lefebvre 1991: 38). Representational spaces—or lived space—are the space as directly lived through its associated images and symbols, and hence the space of 'inhabitants' and 'users', but also of some artists and perhaps of those, such as a few writers and philosophers, who describe and aspire to do no more than describe. This is the dominated—and hence passively experienced—space that the imagination seeks to change and appropriate. It overlays physical space, making symbolic use of its objects (Lefebvre 1991: 39).

Space is not only produced, but it is also conflictual. Space is where differences survive and continuously emerge, thus resisting the homogenisation process determined by the space of accumulation. "The dominant form of space, that of the centres of wealth and power, endeavours to mould the spaces it dominates (i.e. peripheral spaces), and it seeks, often by violent means, to reduce the obstacles and resistance it encounters there" (Lefebvre 1991: 51). Class struggle is what prevents the abstract space of domination, of capitalism from erasing all differences. "The forms of the class struggle are now far more varied than formerly. Naturally, they include the political action of minorities" (Lefebvre 1991: 55).

Since the years of these theorisations, which largely influenced the work of the following generations of geographers and planners, socio-spatial contradictions and differences increasingly emerged, breaking the abstract space of consensus and of security required for the processes of accumulation to unfold. Neglect or exploitation of urban areas was interpreted as unbalanced management of rights and engendered a variety of reactions aimed at substituting the institutional inefficiencies with shared actions, converging towards the common goal of reconquering the right to use common resources. In fact, groups of residents consider static compliance, conventional protest and even material exit not anymore sufficient to counterbalance the dispossession generated by biased choices on the part of the municipal government.[8]

Under these conditions, what can prove difficult is the interpretation of the urban community as a bearer of interests. Excluding the conventional rights normally considered and protected by Constitutions and laws, and supported in each advanced democracy, the range of interests and expectations related to the urban community appears to be very wide. In fact, the proliferation of rights and interests has been the object of very different interpretations. Some scholars consider it as the consequence of neoliberal policies and a threat to the contemporary concepts of democracy and justice (Armony 2004; Supiot 2010). At the same time, a pragmatic understanding of democracy recognises the possibility of a plural landscape of needs and rights, not necessarily competing or corresponding with a general interest (Urbinati 2013). Empirically, the analysis of urban dynamics related to every single case could reveal converging positions and ultimate, common purposes, possibly leading to some form of either institutional acknowledgement or shared societal understanding of the interests at stake.

An insightful case is that of Cinema Palazzo, located in San Lorenzo district in Rome, and analysed by Marella (2017). Having been dismissed by the previous owner and abandoned for many years, it was rented to a private company in order for the place to be transformed into a casino. The former movie theatre was then occupied by a mixed informal group of residents, artists and students, who were promptly sued for their 'moral responsibility' of the abrupt dispossession. The claim was rejected by the Court, according to which occupiers had been motivated by "a genuine political interest" and not for economic goals; the occupation was then "virtuous" having been acted by what the decision itself described as a "pacific multitude".[9]

Marella (2017) observes that "in this case as in others (former Asilo Filangeri, Teatro Valle, former Colorificio Toscano) it is possible to talk of a 'virtuous

[8]On the growing role of 'action' as a further choice aimed at overcoming Hirschman's 'loyalty, voice and exit' range of citizens' feedback to institutional dynamics, see Lenna and Trimarchi (2019).

[9]Tribunale di Roma, VII Sez. Civ., Sent. 8th February 2012.

occupation', because this kind of occupation activates a virtuous circle of utilities production by 'freeing' real estates and areas from owners' misuse whilst, at the same time, using them 'properly', e.g. by organising Italian language courses for migrants, free sport activities, cultural happenings, afterschool activities, free-access libraries, etc".

Given the arbitrariness of defining a common good in the name of which a given action could be approved, such an argument may prove controversial. As in the case of Aurora: which communities benefit from the eviction from the 'Asilo'? Which communities was that a common good for? On the other hand, these cases also show how subsidiary actions could fill the void of representation, thus proving legitimate. While a specific community could be non-authorised to adopt decisions instead of local government, in some cases it could counterbalance its absence, with actions aimed at the pursuit of recognised collective interests.

3.3 Local Regulation: Steady or Proactive?

Being characterised by a wide and diverse range of mutable desires and needs, society continuously challenges the existing uses of space, and the related balances between public, collective and private interests. Leaving the private interest aside—since its role is not among the issues dealt with in this chapter—we can observe that public interest should be general, while collective interests tend to be site-specific and pursued by heterogeneous groups. Drafting an effective regulation can prove quite challenging for the local administration, not to mention all those cases where goodwill has been distorted by indifference, speculation, or by the pursuit of specific interests.

It is evident that both neglected areas and speculative projects exert a negative impact upon the resident community. In most cases, they end up amplifying inequalities and conflicts among different communities of the same town. In such a respect, it is therefore quite predictable that residents—as well as bearers of a shared interest not necessarily localised in the same area—will probably react to either a long-lasting abandonment or to speculative plans by occupying the concerned spaces in a variety of ways, as Lenna and Trimarchi (2019) examine with reference to a range of international experiences. This leads to a further institutional dissonance, generated by the choice on the part of local administration to remain idle until the occupation appears to be bearable by the urban community. In simple words: until the critical mass of informal, illegal and even criminal action often associated with occupation does not trespass the threshold of tolerance.

This continuous friction is featured by the multiple timing of actions and reactions, due to the different time horizons of general law, local administration and the urban community: while legislation tends to be subject to slow changes, normally motivated by consolidated social shifts, administrative action is based upon a much richer toolbox; its versatility proves more effective in fostering specific interests, through bureaucratic pauses, sudden accelerations, uneven communication and often some interpretative effort aimed at capturing local voters' opinions.

The evident absence of a solid strategy in urban governance gives room to unpredictable and potentially conflicting actions, triggered by a variety of motivations, from romantic dreams to social protests, from speculative to criminal projects, and the many possible combinations of these goals. Even in a physiological setting, where only honest civil servants and entrepreneurs interact, such an uneven structure of decisions and actions can sharpen social conflicts and urban contradictions. To make things furtherly complicated, the inconsistency, instability and weakness of the local administration in establishing clear goals end up encouraging corruption as a quick way to bend regulations and to accelerate the pursuit of private interests, at the expenses of a just and democratic governance. A weak body facilitates pathologies.

The local administration is a layer where rigid rules are often bypassed by unstructured action, due to a twofold goal: seeking consensus on the one hand, and balancing a variety of interests, not coinciding with the public interest, on the other. While regulatory loopholes and uncertain areas could be dealt with by adopting common sense views, this strongly depends on the ability of local government to establish a dialogue with members of its community, keeping in mind that most of the times administrative actions end up being selective, thus unavoidably generating further conflicts and dissent.

3.4 The Tables of the Law

General and abstract as it needs to be, the legal framework acknowledges and regulates social change, economic innovation and cultural shift. Whatever violates these boundaries is illegal; norms strictly and clearly define and list the deviating actions and behaviours, although the formal regulatory boxes can be sometimes overcome by either innovative or unpredictable events whose intentions and features do not perfectly fit the stated prohibitions; this implies a wide area of possible actions and interpretations. Such a feature of every legal system explains why often legislation proves late: social movements and actions continuously force the existing boundaries and their realm of what is institutionally established and conventionally accepted. Triggered by either inefficiency or rigidity, they act as a transformative force. Legal frames, on their side, require occasional phenomena to become systematic in order for their conflicting interests to find a new formal balance.

As far as urban commons are concerned, de facto they arise, flourish, decline and perish while violating, adapting to, or succumbing to a variety of civil and criminal law norms and regulations. In such a respect, the severity of criminal law violations strongly depends on the structure of civil law entitlements, and might suffer from the different frameworks and time horizons of civil and criminal law, whose value hierarchies exert a strong influence upon the different degree of urgency assigned to the various issues to be dealt with. Not only this dissonance ends up determining the inclusion of some specific action as a criminal offence in the light of the protection given to the corresponding civil right entitlement, but also the weight of sanctions visibly changes according to the civil law priorities.

The definition and structure of property rights are crucial for the governance of commons and their sustainability. Despite the growing privatisation of urban land (Sassen 2014), despite the variety of practices aiming to reclaim dispossessed built and unbuilt patrimony, and despite the implications of both processes for the governance and the project of the city, surprisingly architects and urban designers are currently approaching property issues in a very superficial way (Lenna 2019). While their projects may encourage and make new approaches to the use of resources possible, these are seldom supported by a consistent approach to ownership which remains unchallenged. On the other hand, in the most recent years jurists are intensively reflecting about the need to reconceptualise property rights according to the emerging approaches to the use and enjoyment of resources, as in the case of commoning practices.

Among them Pierre Crétois, who suggests that property should be "*répensée par l'accès*", i.e. as a function of the right to access (Crétois 2014). His theorisation goes in the direction of the interpretation of property as a bundle of rights, as suggested by Schlager and Ostrom in 1992. This theory was first introduced by the economist John Commons in 1893, and was later developed by the jurist Wesley Hohfeld in 1913. By recalling the medieval approach to the use, management and ownership of land, it was meant to replace the absolutistic understanding of property. The Italian juridical debate directly refers to this theory. Tracking back the deconstruction to Pugliatti (1954), an eloquent critical discussion on the evolution of property is offered by Maria Rosaria Marella who focuses upon the commons as a legal concept, and explores the wide grey area between the formal poles of purely public and purely private interest: "The commons represent the epitome of the crisis of the public/private dichotomy in property law" (Marella 2017: 63).

A few cases are discussed, showcasing the need for a more subtle regulation to protect the unusual but not infrequent common enjoyment and management of resources: a common fishery in the Venice Lagoon (state properties can be considered common goods "when they are devoted to the fulfillment of people's fundamental rights" such as the right to enjoy the environment, according to the judgement of the Italian Supreme Court, 14 February 2011, n. 3665); a pond in a village in the State of Punjab (India) where the local government's favour to a local developer has been evaluated as a violation of common rights, the pond being the source of water for drinking, washing and watering cattle for the whole community (Supreme Court of India, civil appeal no. 1132/2011).

By exploring a variety of situations and the growing legal, economic and sociological literature on the commons, Marella (2017) observes that "the commons provide a good example of how it is possible to challenge the public/private and state sovereignty/market divisions as major ideological frameworks that enable the dispossession of what is produced in common" (p. 64). This implies that, rather than simply elaborating a 'third way' between the public and private property, a more realistic approach could re-establish the theory of property as a bundle of rights (Hohfeld 1913), thus providing "a theoretical foundation to the commons" (*ibid.*).

In the absence of such a reconceptualisation of property rights, in many cases urban commons may need to start with some sort of violation. In addition, further legal barriers could be used to prevent and dismantle occupations and other forms of action occurring in public areas. In the recent Italian experience, it is in the name of 'security' that very restrictive regulations have been introduced with the so-called 'security act'[10] (*Decreto Sicurezza*). The concern for safety is being increasingly instrumentalised to prevent or repress ongoing demonstrations and occupations of both private and public spaces, although the right to demonstrate is constitutionally granted (art. 21 Cost.).

To sum up, while it is not impossible that existing legal institutions could be reinterpreted in order for us to recognise a commons-oriented approach to the use of resources, this requires a political willingness which so far proved absent, to say the least. The inadequacy of such an institutional posture is furtherly highlighted by the more or less genuine interest expressed by a growing number of municipalities for the urban commons. The adoption of regulatory frameworks, however, leaves the topic of property rights unchallenged, while security-biased interventions end up dismantling the urban commons. In such a situation, a general legal orientation would allow to recognise the cultural shift urban commons are expressing, beyond the contingency of the different initiatives and of the politically coloured favour of local administrations.

4 What Do Commons Have in Common?

4.1 A New Spirit of Time

The European democracies shaped their national civil, administrative and criminal legislation during the past century, when the economic and social paradigm seemed to be stabilised by the promise of a redistributive welfare state, with no perception of the crises and revolutions that since the 1960s started to disrupt the existing social and cultural structures. Not surprisingly, therefore, the current legislation lacks the fluidity that would allow it to face contemporary societal challenges. Among the others are a massive urbanisation, growing socio-spatial inequalities, the multiplication of often conflicting interests, engendered by a diverse society.

The heterogeneity of urban communities is reflected in the growing distance between a wide variety of collective interests and the public interest. The word 'collective' describes something that is common to a given group, either locally or thematically defined, and necessarily specific of that group. In the name of the

[10]The act 4 October 2018, n. 113, "Norms on public security, prevention and contrast to terrorism and mafia" tightened prohibitions and sanctions for many actions already included in the criminal offenses, widening their scope to pacific demonstrations, in response to a generic and quite often atmospheric demand for 'law and order' based on the rejection of migrants and whatever form of dissent. It was followed by a second 'security act': act 15 June, 2019, n. 53, aimed at furtherly tightening prohibitions and sanctions for both migration and demonstrations.

principle of representation, the public interest is supposed to be recognised as universal, and in theory it should prove relevant for the urban community. When that is no longer the case, many problems are generated by the slowness that central legislation reveals in interpreting and supporting societal evolutions. Therefore, the only possibility is the technical interpretation of laws and regulations, when their drafting allows lawyers and scholars to adapt their letter to society's changing spirit.

On the other hand, what would be the threshold for recognising the interest of a community as publicly relevant? How could it work for the rights and interests of smaller communities? How could they exert their legitimate influence upon public decision-making processes, and in general the political and social dynamics? There are neither rules nor established thresholds for the recognition and protection of an emerging right, although the constitutional norms protect minorities. The rise of participatory forms of democracy and governance, and the symmetrical crisis of representativeness seem to suggest that, at the very least, the logic of ritual democracy is no longer sufficient to fulfil the deflagration of rights characterising the contemporary society. However, a fragmented landscape of needs and rights also raises questions. How to deal with conflicting interests? How should the interactions with the public administration be managed, so that the different social groups and counterpart could have a voice?

Despite the clear difference and the consequent incomparability among the urban commons, as they emerge from the experiences examined above and the myriad of possible dynamics not considered here, some common features may allow us to elaborate a synoptic view where the three sides of a triangular interaction are analysed. Although the cases discussed in this chapter are related to the Italian legal, economic, social and cultural eco-system, we observe that *mutatis mutandis* there are many similarities among the commons experiences in the various countries, since the institutional framework adopted within the industrial paradigm is endowed with a common backbone.

4.2 Urban Trialogues

Observing the narratives of the urban commons, the constant presence of the elements described and discussed in Sect. 3 allows us to elaborate a synoptic grid aimed at describing the recurrent dynamics, and suggesting possible orientations that can overcome the observed rigidity. The interactions among the three levels are defined 'trialogues': their outcomes can be very different, ranging from constructive co-operation to violent clash. The combination of the three levels—central legislation, legal administration and urban community—ends up generating indefinite possible outcomes, and emphasises the need for clarity on the part of each side.

The reciprocal interactions among the three actors of urban commons strongly depend on the position that each of them is taking and keeping, both in general and with reference to the specific experience. Considering the strategic goals and interests, the scope for action, the constraints and obstacles of each side, we can focus upon the possible outcomes of their interaction. In a logic sequence, the first 'move' is normally performed by the local administration, whose action can vary between the poles of neglect and indifference at one extreme, and of exploitation driven by private interests at the opposite one.

The figure below outlines the possible trialogues, whose features can be easily recognised in the case studies described in this chapter. The red dots represent either actions or reactions, depending on how the narrative is framed. At the origin of urban commons, communities react to various degrees of action—or inaction—on the part of the municipal administration, whose position is located along the central line in the figure, ranging from neglect—not rarely aggravated by the collusion with speculative plans—to pro-active regulations aiming at the stewardship of resources and making space to participation. In any case, the abandonment and the eventual decay of public patrimony elicits a reaction on the part of the concerned communities, with the purpose of re-appropriating resources that otherwise would be subtracted to public use.

Community-based initiatives can be very different, from taking care of a community garden to the occupation of either private or public buildings for artistic or social purposes. However, subversive purposes are not related to any specific activities. A community garden can go a long way in mobilising the attention of the whole city, and preventing the umpteenth speculative project.[11] Within the framework of the existing legislation, to act or to disobey appears to be a sort of constrained choice, depending on the purposes and the conditions of the initiative. The municipal administration, at its turn, counter-reacts by referring to the current legislation (the line at the top of the figure) and its interpretation, by applying rigid boxes to magmatic changes, with attitudes that range from repression to tolerance to regulation, as represented by the arrows. Consequently, the relationship between the administration and the communities involved in a given initiative can be simply confirmed or variously reshaped, as represented by the line at the bottom: between the extremes of antagonism and participation there is space for transitional dynamics centred either on the agonist co-existence of diverging positions or on negotiation.

[11]As it happened in the case of the community garden "Potagers Boondael Ernotte Akarova", which filed an action against the municipality, to prevent the enforcement of a land use plan which would have dismantled the garden to make room to further housing projects and, ironically, a community centre, in a part of the city characterised by sharply rising land value. The Potagers won the case before the Conseil d'Etat in May 2018. http://www.tuiniersforumdesjardiniers.be/2018/05/17/potagers-boendael-ernotte-akarova-victoire/.

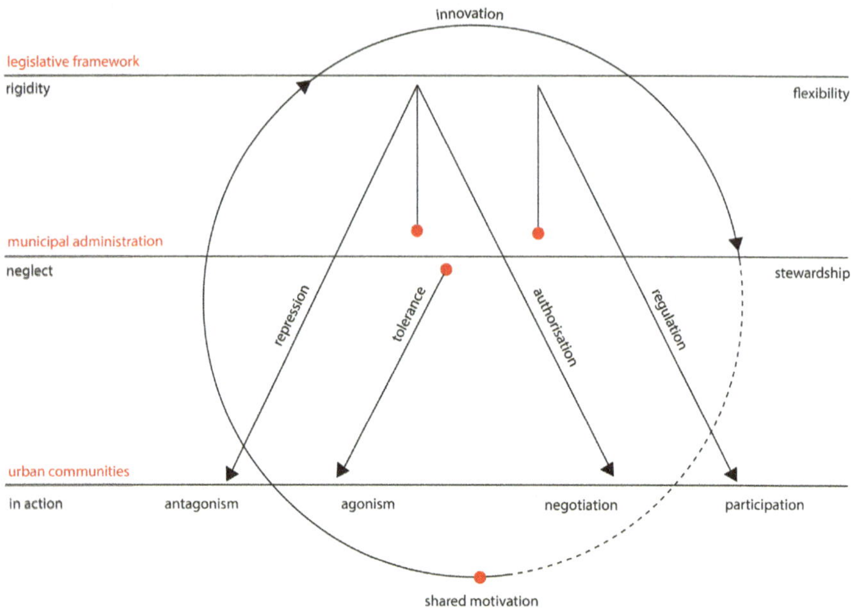

Urban commons often start as occupations. Besides filling institutional voids, they are often inspired by largely shared values such as care, responsibility, socio-spatial justice, participation and self-expression. In the attempt at building consensus, or in the name of genuinely shared ideological premises, local public administrations often adopt a tolerant attitude. However, as we showed above, the status of illegality of occupations is what makes them fragile and legally authorises their dismantlement, even when what is at stake is the right to housing and the only violation is the occupation of an otherwise abandoned/unmanaged space and no other crime is committed. Therefore, as soon as the troubles associated with the occupation trespass the threshold of conventional safety (not necessarily on the part of a majority: sometimes the dissent of an influent group may prove sufficient) or diverging interests prevail, evictions are the legal answer of administrations. Of course, it is a political response to a problem whose complexity cannot be reduced to a single action.

While the evolution of societal needs and the emersion of conflicting rights should induce a radical transformation of the systems of governance, the trialogues illustrated in the figure show that, on the contrary, innovation risks to be paralysed or neutralised by rigid attitudes and inadequate legal frameworks. Is there any chance that our *deus ex machina* could perform as a flexible magic wand, acknowledging the actions, the values, and the desires of the communities? If that would be the case, what role would the administration play? How would this change the relationship with the communities?

The circular line in the diagram allows us to imagine what a different approach would be engendered. The starting condition of the new narrative would be the recognition of the capacity of communities to actively contribute to the fulfilment of their needs and rights. With this background, the legal framework would have the purpose to empower rather than to regulate, and to make possible the continuous redesign of the sets of compossible rights (Steiner 1977). Rather than being the magic wand in the hands of the administration, such a legal framework should work as a toolbox, providing the actors with the basic elements for a do-it-yourself approach, suggesting principles, methods and criteria more than preconceived formulas.

Therefore, to begin with, the illegality of a given practice, instead than being an a priori label, could be pondered in relation to a background of emerging values and rights. In fact, if the purpose is that of recognising and amplifying the transformative capacity of the urban commons, the problem is not the lack of pacts, agreements and participatory platforms allowing the establishment of a horizontal system of governance. On the contrary, the problem is that those formal boxes end up suiting only conservative practices rather than more radical and truly innovative experiments, the latter being suppressed from the beginning by a rigid understanding of illegality, as we explained above. The possible way to face such complexities is what we can define 'institutional craftsmanship'. The first step, we suggest, is to reshape the regulatory framework as a common ground and a system of attunement, allowing communities and their administrations to constantly adjust the relationship, in the name of a co-responsible, collectively built governance.

5 Concluding Remarks: De Jure Condendo

Urban commons can generate a change in a landscape that seems to be bound to record a merely dimensional growth. Their origin and evolution introduce new, often unexpected values and dynamics. Until now the legislative framework, the social conventions, the established protocols are not crafted to accept the emerging needs, desires and views which commons respond to. As stranger bodies, urban commons perturb an apparently stable system, and end up creating frictions, sometimes fractures among the different actors involved in this complex multifold interaction, thus highlighting the urgency of an institutional transformation. This may imply various interventions aimed at effectively adapting the current legislative grid, the local administrative approach, and the strategies of urban community towards a truly collaborative decision-making process. This means not only establishing clear goals, but also monitoring the adoption of adequate and accessible tools, fine-tuning actions to the contingent changes, and pursuing sustainability within a horizontal subsidiarity framework.

At the local level, the introduction of a toolbox aimed at facilitating and encouraging the dialogue among social groups and with the municipal administration appears to be crucial, also in view of its selective power. The frameworks that aim at regulating the urban commons, however shaped, end up on the one hand extracting value from condescending practices; on the other hand, crowding out genuine antagonist and subversive projects. The latter, in fact, not only arise from a critique of institutions and their *modus operandi*: they are also often associated with illegal actions. Due to their illegal features, they can be easily delegitimised, although they often fill institutional voids by providing the weak components of the urban community with support and assistance they would not obtain otherwise. Therefore, any legal framework aiming at amplifying the transformative capacity of the commons and of any other initiative should make room also to the understanding of the contingently illegal, the fragile and the disobedient, for example, considering and evaluating—with the needed caution—the conditions that triggered an alleged illegal action and that could represent a partial exemption from the criminal responsibilities.

Consistently, an administration aiming at empowering its diverse community would gradually reduce competitive calls for projects, whose main effect is the fragmentation of the efforts and capacities of local associations and organisations and would rather identify the forms of collaborative frameworks supporting reciprocities and transversal collaborations, thus allowing also the fragile and emerging initiatives to exist and find their way. This would induce community-based projects, aimed at managing urban commons, to adopt a medium time horizon and to point at the cultural, social and economic impact they can generate upon the resident community, within a transparent negotiation where each actor plays an active role. Furthermore, in such a framework shared motivations and processes would aim at a co-operative governance of resources independently from the specific purposes, thus crafting and consolidating effective paths to social inclusion.

References

Armony, A. C. (2004). *The dubious link: Civic engagement and democratization*. Stanford: Stanford University Press.

Bianchin, M. C. (2019). Lo sgombero dell'Asilo occupato e le confessioni di una cittadina perbene. Volerelaluna. 4th March https://volerelaluna.it/in-primo-piano/2019/03/04/lo-sgombero-dellasilo-occupato.

Castel, R. (1995). *Les métamorphoses de la question sociale. Une chronique du salariat*. Paris: Fayard.

Crétois, P. (2014). La propriété répensée per l'accès. *Revue Internationale de Droit Économique, 3,* 319–334.

Dardot, P., & Laval, C. (2014). *Commun*. La Découverte, Paris: Essai sur la révolution au XXIe siècle.

Di Porto, A. (2013). *Res in Usu Publico e Beni Comuni. Il Nodo della Tutela*. Torino: Giappicchelli.

Falconieri, G. (2019). Torino, i 24 anni dell'Asilo Occupato. La lotta agli sfratti e la guerra al CIE. Il Corriere delle Sera. Cronaca di Torino. 8th February.

Federici, S. (2011). Women, land struggles, and the reconstruction of the commons. *The Journal of Labor and Society, 14,* 41–56.

Giannoli, V. (2014). Teatro Valle, il prefetto boccia lo statuto della nuova Fondazione. Repubblica. Roma. 12th February.

Hardin, G. (1968). The tragedy of the commons. Science. *New Series, 162,* 1243–1248.

Harvey, D. (2012). *Rebel cities. From the right to the cities to the urban revolution*. London: Verso.

Hohfeld, W. N. (1913). Some fundamental legal conceptions as applied in judicial reasoning. *Yale Law Journal, 23,* 16–20.

Lefebvre, H. (1991). *The production of space*. Oxford: Blackwell.

Lenna, V. (2019). *The project of property as emancipation. A community land trust in Brussels*. unpublished manuscript, IUAV Venezia and KU Leuven.

Lenna, V., & Trimarchi, M. (2019). For a culture of urban commons. Practices and policies. In Benincasa, C., Neri, G., & Trimarchi, M. (Eds.), *Art, economics and the city. New cultural maps* (pp. 205–242). Bielefeld: Transcript.

Lo Gatto, S. (2013). Nasce la Fondazione Teatro Valle Bene Comune. Che cosa è cambiato? Teatro e Critica. 19th September https://teatroecritica.net/2013/09/nasce-la-fondazione-teatro-valle-bene-comune.

Marella, M. R. (2017). The commons as a legal concept. *Law and Critique, 28,* 61–86.

Ostrom, E. (1990). *Governing the commons. The evolution of institutions for collective action*. Cambridge: Cambridge University Press.

Propp, V. (1968). *Morphology of the Folktale*. Austin: University of Texas Press.

Pugliatti, S. (1954). *La proprietà nel nuovo diritto*. Milano: Giuffrè.

Sabatini, F., & Trimarchi, M. (2019). Regulating the stage: Storms, wrecks and lifebelts in the Italian experience. *Athens Journal of Mediterranean Studies, 5*(2), 105–120.

Sassen, S. (2014). *Expulsions. Brutality and Complexity in the Global Economy*. Cambridge, MA: Belknap Press.

Schlager, E., & Ostrom, E. (1992). Property-rights regimes and natural resources: A conceptual analysis. *Land Economics*, pp. 249–262.

Steiner, H. (1977). The structure of a set of compossible rights. *The Journal of Philosophy, 74*(12), 767–775.

Supiot, A. (2010). *L'Esprit de Philadelphie. La justice sociale face au marché total*. Paris: Seuil.

Swyngedouw, E. (2011). Depoliticized environment: The end of nature, climate change, and the post-political condition. *Royal Institute of Philosophy Supplement, 69,* 253–274.

Thomas, Y. (2002). La valeur des choses. Le droit romain hors la religion. Annales. Histoire. *Sciences Sociales*, *57*(6), 1431–1462.

Trimarchi, M. (2019, editor). *Il valore della creatività. L'economia arancione in Emilia-Romagna*. Bologna: Il Mulino.

Urbinati, N. (2013). *Il bene e il giusto*. Udine: Forum Edizioni.

A New Urban Agenda: Interpretation and Action

At the Fringe of Human Freedom: The Concept of Space and Time Within Urban Settlements and Among Nomads in Antiquity

Raffaella Frascarelli

Abstract

The aim of this research is to identify in the early urbanism of the ancient Near East and in the nomadism of the Eurasian steppes the signs of a sociocultural dimension close to our concept of *commons*, particularly in relation to mobility in space and the control of time, also exploring how contemporary art collective practices are the generators of a new aesthetics of the real, *the living commons*, through the ongoing artistic researches of Filippo Berta and Julien Bismuth.

1 Space and Time Commons

The hypothesis of this study is that a dimension akin to the commons may have been ubiquitous, perhaps also due to the non-existence of sociopolitical forms and technologies being able to impose a structured control over time and space. This condition would have been subject to alterations that would have modified the human relationship with space and time to the point of causing the loss of awareness on the real value of impartial sharing, consequently favouring mediated and codified forms that would have deprived individuals of their right to access material and immaterial resources equitably. To relate a conception of commons intimately dependent on issues raised by our society's emerging notion of commons

R. Frascarelli (✉)
Nomas Foundation, Rome, Italy
e-mail: frascarelliraffaella@gmail.com

R. Frascarelli
Research Unit's Laboratory Sociological Aesthetics, Department of Sociology of Cultural Processes and Sociology of Contemporary Cultures-DiSSE, Faculty of Political, Sociological and Communication Sciences, Sapienza Università di Roma, Rome, Italy

E. Macrì et al. (eds.), *Cultural Commons and Urban Dynamics*,
https://doi.org/10.1007/978-3-030-54418-8_17

to a remote past that we can imagine more than reconstruct might seem a hazard. But it is a risk worth taking, especially by evoking the ability of the commons to generate not only practices instrumental to the disempowerment of neoliberalism, but also sociocultural know-how qualified to deconstruct a rationalist knowledge of the past, cultivating theoretical spaces necessary not for revolutions or reformism, but rather for explorations such as those of contemporary aesthetics.

The attempt to question any rigid formulation also resounds in a definition of *the commons*, the meaning itself of "good" in constant transformation. Hardt and Negri (2017) provide some explanations on natural commons and social commons: the earth and its ecosystem; the immaterial common of ideas, code, images, and cultural products; material commodities produced or extracted by cooperative forms of social labor; metropolitan and rural social territories; social institutions and services aimed at health, education, housing, and welfare. Another appropriate description of commons is the one provided by *Commons Transition and P2P: a primer* within The P2PF Library (https://welcomecdn1.p2pfoundation.net/wpcontent/uploads/2017/09/commons_transition_and_p2p_primer_v9.pdf).

2 Archaeological Negotiation

In this research, the birth of the city in Mesopotamia may have signed a noteworthy episode in the transition to a sociocultural form of regulated freedom, a condition symbolically increased in its space-time abstraction and diminished both materially and sensorially in its actual space-time dimension. In the case of the nomadism of the Eurasian steppes, its limited engagement with common goods was altered during its historical transformation into a series of steppe empires (Xiongnu, Türk, Mongol), wherein space and time would find a correspondence in the creation of visual commons. The chronological framework focuses on two different historical periods and cultural contexts: Uruk early urbanism (3500–3200 BCE) and Eurasian steppes' nomadism during the transition from the Bronze Age to the Iron Age. While Mesopotamian textual sources demand a thorough examination of their ideological aspects, even in the presence of a rich material culture, the absence of written sources for nomadism is integrated by a pictorial apparatus represented by the vast repertoire of petroglyphs scattered in the Eurasian steppes.

Within a multidisciplinary framework, it is also necessary to consider the relationship that historical archaeology has intertwined with capitalist modernity and colonialism (Liebmann and Rizvi 2008; Lydon and Rizvi 2010; Croucher and Weiss 2011; Leone and Knauf 2015; Gorshenina et al. 2019), especially the influence exerted in the realization and deconstruction of colonial historical representations (Said 1978). Archaeology implies a loss of data in the process of communication between the issuer (stratigraphy, artefact, monument, etc.) and the receiver (archaeology), and the tacit creation of a cultural apparatus negotiating between translation and reality. Indeed, the desire to approach the hard sciences makes us envision a time machine that, once the methodological and theoretical coordinates have been entered, is able to faithfully return the image of history. But it is only a mirage. Such a vision of a perfectible archaeology is only desirable if we are aware that the result can never be achieved. The reconstruction of the past can only ever be a precarious construction concerning academic disciplines that engage with distantiation such as archaeology and history. In the general desire for an understanding of contemporaneity and a definition of the paths of the archaeology of the present (Graves-Brown et al. 2013), a critical approach to archaeology, history, and religious studies can be part of that *other modernity* (Lash 1999) that looks *at* and *for* differences.

3 Early Urbanism Ideology

Human sciences dealing with antiquity agree on the fact that nomadism precedes urbanism and that, with the advent of the city, both ways of life coexist on all continents. More problematic is a unanimous definition of *city*: numerous studies focusing on the appearance of the city highlight the differences among settlement, urbanization, city, urban society, urban site, and state (Childe 1950; Tönnies 1963; Weber 1966; Nissen 1988; Mazar 1992; Algaze 1993; Liverani 2006). Even more challenging is the ideological question of the first city: while the UNESCO World Heritage Tentative List considers Jericho/Tell es-Sultan the oldest city/proto-city in the world, those looking for the oldest of the cities should not ignore 12,000 years old Göbekli Tepe (Schmidt 2000, 2001, 2011), one of the greatest megalithic monumental architecture in the world, whose discovery raises more than one issue. It is indeed problematic and challenging not only to establish the very nature of Göbekli Tepe, but also to place it within the theoretical framework on the neolithization. The criteria of UNESCO's Nomination Text emphasize these exceptional features (https://whc.unesco.org/en/list/1572/documents/). Notwithstanding the debated function of Göbekli Tepe, it is hard to believe that its surrounding area did not host communities structured according to a certain rate complexity, possibly already highly specialized, characterized by social differentiation, and likely as cohesive as such a massive enterprise requires for its designing and construction, people possibly living in tents or other arrangements made from perishable materials. Furthermore, considering megaliths as temples, sanctuaries, and ritual places can also be obsessions bequeathed by a certain archaeology which, before anything else, keeps on tracing the origins of what would later be defined as "religion" in the prehistory (Notroff et al. 2016). An alternative view considers Göbekli Tepe as a domestic place, a space where people lived in and maybe also performed their rituals (Banning 2011), suggesting that any interpretation is still hypothetical. Moreover, for anyone who wants to consider the extent of a site as something not to be underestimated, Göbekli Tepe (126 ha.) is by far broader than Jericho/Tell es-Sultan PPNA town (4 ha.) and even larger than Uruk (100 ha.). Indeed, returning to question the notion of *city*, other settlements may have also existed, perhaps even larger than Göbekli Tepe, Jericho, Uruk, and built from materials whose traces dissolve more easily than raw brick or stone. It is very likely that still many "first cities" or more simply cities await to be discovered by an archaeology eventually open to self-criticism and interdisciplinarity.

3.1 Technologies of the Intellect and the City

Beyond these considerations about the *first city*'s issues, in the Ancient Near Eastern Studies, Uruk is unanimously considered the first city:

> Without a doubt, one of the most significant turning points in the course of human history was the transition from a prehistoric society to one that was historic in the fullest sense of the word. This transition was, and still is, referred to in various ways. Those scholars who primarily look at aspects of urban settlement, call it the 'urban revolution'. Those who place emphasis on sociopolitical aspects, refer to the emergence of the 'early state'. Those who privilege the socio-economic structure (social stratification, labour specialization), speak of 'the origin of complex society'. And finally, those who take the origin of writing as a result that gives meaning to the entire process, and see writing as an unparalleled instrument for providing knowledge of past societies, call it 'the beginning of history' tout court. Without underestimating the importance of the ideological and historiographic implications in the choice of a definition, it is nevertheless unmistakable that they all refer to the same process, but in different ways. That process was so pervasive and multifaceted that it changed human society from top to bottom (Liverani 2006:1).

Despite the definition chosen to outline such a transformative process, the effects of what is called *urban revolution* have attracted the analysis of several scholarly disciplines which have created the image, and maybe the myth, of the very first city. For the purpose of this research, Uruk is the symbol of a society determined on exercising its power over natural space and human time: a place where, thanks to a targeted use of writing and mathematics, cuneiform, and sexagesimal system, a restricted number of people assembled the apparatus needed to change the instinctive and unrestricted access to space and time. Aiming at measurability, standardization, and efficiency, such a society dispossessed the community of its personal autonomy by both restraining access to space and compressing time. This extractive ideological mobilization is not pleasant. To quote Liverani: "It could not realize itself without the use of factors that transcended the natural tendency to self-sufficiency and self-reproduction. Those would range from physical coercion to ideological persuasion" (Liverani 2006, pp. 62–63). Persistently in a balance between their authoritative and generative domains, *technologies of the intellect* (Goody 2000) provide a significant contribution in shaping and influencing such a newborn urban community. Traditionally defined by its densely settled space and complex organization, urbanism is a dimension where political authority and individual agency demand a consistent negotiation among political, economic, and cultural actors, a process that gives rise to different endeavours. Circumstances such as the strategic management of technology and productive forces, the creation of labor needs, the incorporation of rural countryside, the organization of trade and exchange networks, the establishment of staple food politics, the administration of environmental matters, and the control of social apparatus, all contribute to creating wealth, prestige, and power, especially for the élites of overseers. Somehow, the city may also foster the formation of ideological boundaries, partitions, and divisions that over time gives rise to kingship, empire, nation-state, and experiences where the control of space and time is dominant.

In Mesopotamia, such a *diminutio* mirroring this process of space-time restraint is reflected in a specific economic structure, i.e. property. The right to property appears in Sumerian and Akkadian boundary stones, *kudurru*, recording land-tenure transactions from the Uruk III (Jemdet Nasr) period onwards (Gelb et al. 1991). The public or private dimension of possession has come a long way to meet the scrutiny of jurists, philosophers, economists, and historians of political doctrines, until it turns into the modern concept of property: a thorny path developed not without light and shadow, most of all when considering the space as the target for conquest, be it as vast as North America as in the famous Johnson v. McIntosh case (Rose 1985) or as small as an apartment as in the case of housing policies in Nazi-occupied Paris (Backouche et al. 2017).

One of the most important poems of the Mesopotamian literature, the *Enūma ilū awēlum*, "When the Gods Were Man" or Epic of Atraḫasīs (Foster 1996, p. 161), shows how possession and forced labor are two inextricable experiences that require the use of time. In the Old Babylonian version, the Anunna and Igigu divinities enjoy equal rights until the Anunna impose the forced burden of labor to the Igigi, a discriminatory situation that leads to conflicts and rebellions until the wise god Ea suggests the creation of man to do the work of the Igigi. Beyond this myth, such a divine and anthropomorphic community that quarrels to force someone else to work and to bear the burden in their place seems to be a metaphor of an ancestral equality whose pact was ruinously broken. Matured at the highest levels of the Sumerian pantheon, such a protest ratifies the early stage of the labor commodification process, also endorsing an experience of slavery and eventually promoting the categorization of the human slave as property (Verderame 2018). Within this process of space and time's control it is already possible to detect the seed of one of the main distinctive aspects of modernity where rationalization and production are considered emancipatory forces despite their afflictive restraint. Before communities were subdued to production and property, with limited access to their own space and time, the public sphere charged with redistribution roused a certain degree of inhomogeneity. In Uruk, for example, while provisioning of meals shows an intra-societal dimension also mediated by commensality (Liverani 2006), the same cannot be said for activities such as writing and calculating that remained accessible only to a limited number of people, i.e. the administrative space-timekeepers, who reallocate the benefits primarily to those who have the control of such technologies. Early written sources prove that, among other obligations, law is also born in response to a demand for ruling space and time: discrepancy between laws and their implementation can be detected in all the tireless Mesopotamian juridical reforms, from Urukagina to Hammurabi (Roth 1997; Westbrook 2003). Aimed at harmonizing law and litigation, these reforms also preside over the temporal frequency of compulsory offerings, one's obligation to service, the punishment of debts, the control of properties, the legislation of slavery, and imprisonment. Justice, law, and rights are subject to the king's decision and, as Hammurabi reminds anyone who doubts, he is the only one who can exercise the right to determine what is true and just. Normativity can be seen as the *verso* of a situation that on its *recto* records a persistent tension to re-establish a state of just, fair, impartial accessibility to space and time.

Assuming that the early Mesopotamian city is the birthplace of the material and symbolic possession and control over space and time, it would be a mistake to regard the modern city as the arrival point of this process of space-time restraint, especially if one considers its role in the promotion of individual freedom, but it would be equally misleading not to recognize the early symptoms of a condition aimed at diminishing natural rights. Indeed, awareness of *natural rights* emerges much later with Plato, Aristotle, and the Stoics, a path that will mature towards *human rights* through Hugo Grotius, Thomas Hobbes, Baruch de Spinoza, Samuel von Pufendorf, John Locke, and whose legacy is detected in Martin Buber, Jürgen Habermas, Gabriel Marcel, and Emmanuel Lévinas (Ishay 2008). Looking at the past with modern eyes, it is also desirable to imagine another sociocultural framework: alongside the written sources and monuments produced by the elites in order to exhibit their embodied, objectified, institutionalized cultural capital (Bourdieu 1986) and hegemony (Gramsci 1976), beyond their hard-to-access discourse created to maintain the power (Foucault 1971), other social forces create their own imaginary and worlds, beyond resisting or opposing.

4 *Perpetuum Mobile* of the Eurasian Steppes and the "Outside World"

Moving from the urbanism of the ancient Near East to the nomadism of the Eurasian steppes, Soviet and Russian scholars have carried on the most authoritative researches: as Anatoly M. Khazanov observes in his magistral *Nomads and the Outside World,* "It is of course not surprising that a major study of nomadism should emerge from Russia. Russian history and consciousness—whether through education or through a genuine folk memory—is pervaded by an awareness of the nomad problem, more so presumably than any other European nation" (Khazanov 1994: ix). Indeed, past (Klejn 2017) and present (Kradin 2011) Russian archaeology must cope with the issues of thousands of years of nomadic past, a mobile sociocultural, political, and economic force whose historical role is already mentioned in the Ur III texts (2100–2000 BCE) which ideologically reports the uncivilized tent-dwellers, Shimashki people (Michalowski 1986), a refrain recurring in Akkadian, Neo-Babylonian, and Neo-Assyrian sources as well (Ivantchik 2005). At the origin of Eurasian steppes nomadism, in the second millennium BCE, an increasing aridity prompts populations such as those from Timber-Grave Culture (Srubnaya) and the Andronovo Culture, previously living on farming-pastoral economies (i.e. hunting, river-fishing, and gathering), to find new strategic adaptation in response to such major ecological changes, turning themselves into specialized nomadic livestock breeders (Vinogradov and Epimakhov 2000). The shift from a sedentary lifestyle to nomadism implies the adoption of other strategies, as in the case of mobile architectures made by tents and waggons (Faegre 1979) which Greek sources from Aeschylus (Prometheus Bound 708.10) to Herodotus (Histories 4.46), and Strabo (Geography 7.3.17) describe as an oddity, a technology that reminds the ability of swiftness, on the one hand frightening settled communities and empires when conflicts with nomads arise, and on the other, contributing to building the wealth of those same communities and empires when there is an opportunity for trading activities with nomads.

The fluid, fluctuating, undulating nomadic *perpetuum mobile* considered by Kenneth Dean and Brian Massumi as "Nomadic-Extreme countervailing tendency to the State-Extreme" is a disorienting social experience:

> Nomadism, like its statist counter-extreme, is not reducible to a particular economic or political system. It is a mode of being in geosocial space that may assume many forms, all of which nevertheless share a common dynamic. Nomadic formations are those which value motion over fixation, variation over order; which affirm the spaces between stops rather than bee-lining to a promised land; which reach a resting point only to use it as a relay to a future move; which have no finality, only process; which skim the surface rather than implanting a symbolic edifice or superimposing a code or statistical grid; which "occupy space without counting it" rather than "counting space in order to occupy it" [Deleuze and Guattari 1987:477]; which involve "arraying oneself in an open space" rather than arranging a closed space around oneself, fortress fashion [ibid. 353, 380]; which smooth without striating (Dean and Massumi 1992, pp. 74–76).

The first enemy of such an unseizable fluidity is China: its relentless pression on non-Chinese territories occupied by nomads, the construction of long defensive walls—even before the Great Wall—to prevent invasions, and its expansionist policies. These strategies prompt those social transformations that give rise to the Xiongnu empire and its conflict with the Han dynasty (Di Cosmo 2002). Chinese sources like those provided by the historian Ssu-ma Ch'ien and by literary texts such as *Shan-hai ching* (Classic of Mountains and Seas), *Huai-nan-tzu* (The Writings of the Huainan), and *Shih chi* (Records of the Grand Historian) describe nomads through different ideological and historical perspectives. Greek sources, in particular, such as Homer, Hesiod, Herodotus, Hellanikus, Hippocrates, Ktesias, Eudoxos, Dinan, Apollodoros of Artemita, and Scylax (Gardiner-Garden 1987a, b, c, d), expand historical, ethnographic, anthropological, geographical details, focusing on cultures, traditions, folklore, and myths, but they also contribute to the creation of the negative myth of the *barbarian* and its controversial legacy within modernity (Potts 2014, pp. 431–443). More so than the Greek sources, the three centralized and bureaucratised great territorial empires—i.e. China, Sasanian Persia, and Rome—offer an ideological counter-narrative that in time reinforces the stereotype of barbarians, betraying the attempt to contrast a model of leadership based on political and human negotiation and flexibility, attitudes regarded as an awkward problem for the divinely legitimated kingship rooted in Persepolis, Chang'an, and for the *ius-* and *lex*-based authority of Rome. In the mediaeval period, nomadism draws the cultivated ethnographic observations of Persian historian Rashid al-Din in his *Jāmiʿ al-*

tawārīkh (The Compendium of Histories) and Arab historian Ibn Khaldun in his *al-Muqaddima* (Introduction), while with the advent of modernity it attracts the enquires of Montesquieu (*Spirit of Laws*), Adam Smith (*Lectures on Jurisprudence*; *Wealth of Nations*), Kant (*Doctrine of Right*), and Hegel (*Philosophy of Right*). Archaeology, anthropology, and history have gone from being exoticizing agents to being the object both of colonial lust and postcolonial guilt. Their critical and analytical perspectives are now effectively merging in the wake of their transformations (Khazanov 1994, pp. 1–14).

4.1 Nomadic Trading and Power

Although early nomads chose not to adopt any form of writing, the establishment of the nomad-ruled empires sees the advent of an elite that expands an interregional trading system lasting, along the Silk Road, over the course of millennia. These rhizomatic networks were destroyed in the seventeenth century by the Russians and the Manchu-Chinese partition of Central Asia. Coined in the nineteenth century, the Silk Road is a label gathering other ancient labels, that is the many roads created by the interaction between nomadism and other political entities, be they empires, kingdoms, or other political entities in the past (Kuzmina 2008). Some of these earlier roads include the Tin Road that contributed to the Bronze Age metallurgical industry; the Gemstones Roads of lapis-lazuli from Badakhshan that reached the Urals region (Sintashta and Ushkatta cultures), Egypt, Syria (Ebla), Anatolia, India; the Gemstones Roads of turquoise from Sogdiana and Bactriana that stretched to Mesopotamia, Egypt, Anatolia; the Gemstones Roads of jade from Khotan and Yarkand's mines that were almost entirely purchased by China; the Horses Road required to fulfil the military aspirations of China, Persia, Egypt, Babylonia; and finally the Silk Road that first connects China to Rome, Byzantium, and Venice. "The catalytic role that mobile pastoralists had in shaping the connections among regional civilizations and in promoting diverse institutional alignments across Eurasia throughout history" profoundly impacts the economy and social organizations, influencing cultural ties that will foster a process of sociopolitical and technological growth across Eurasia and beyond (Frachetti 2012, p. 21).

The leadership of these commercial networks is reflected in the funerary apparatus: *kurgans* reveal the determination of nomadic elites to flaunt their power, often emulating the Chinese and Ancient Near Eastern empires (Cunliff 2015) and displaying the rich diversity of cultural artefacts from the steppes region (Jettmar 1967; Piotrovski 1973–1974; Davis-Kimball et al. 1995, 2000; Aruz et al. 2000; Bunker 2002). Among the hundreds of thousands of Pre-Scythian and Scythian period, *kurgans* spread in the Eurasian steppes, the case of Arzhan cemeteries (Grjaznov 1984; Chugunov et al. 2004) in the Tuva region truly conveys the complexity of a hierarchical community of the eighth and ninth centuries BCE, betraying the accumulative ideology of an emergent leadership that, once it acquired more power, grew to be less interested in showing its supremacy in large burial structures easily exposed to looting (Toshio 2013).

4.2 On Space-Time Visual Equality

The Eurasian steppes extend over the immense 9000 km of grassland ecozone diversity stretching from Eastern Europe to the Pacific Ocean (Koryakova and Epimakhov 2007). At first glance, it seems a socioeconomic space that can only be exploited by way of ambitious physical and cultural strategies. In fact, this abundance of pasture and cattle demands tireless commitment, and requires working across huge distances, through control of the trading networks, while extreme temperature ranges and no shrubby vegetation challenge daily survival. The management of the environment constitutes a vigorous human commitment. Compared to those people living in the *outside world*, it is not surprising that the immersive experiences of such a wild space and time dimension awaken shamanic beliefs in supernatural forces and magical rituals. In some historical moments, shamanism even exceeds the limits of the steppes to creep into the Indo-Iranian world (Gignoux 2001). The Tibetan *Bön* and Buddhism (Eliade 1964), the Sufi Islam (Amitai 1999), all manifest a shamanistic influence that would profoundly fascinate Western culture as well (Francfort and Hamayon 2001).

Such an immaterial experience of space and time emerges from the non-elitist visual culture represented by the immense repertoire of petroglyphs spread throughout the steppes (Sher 1994; Blednova et al. 1995; Kubarev and Jacobson 1996; Mar'jašev et al. 1998; Sher et al. 1999; Jacobson et al. 2001; Jacobson-Tepfer et al. 2006). Despite the lack of writing, this nomadic mimetic imaginary is a language that has the potential to create, collect, and redistribute complex sociocultural codes. As a space-time aesthetic capacity, the incorporation of wandering gives birth to a cartography of de-territorialized signs where content-expression discloses a kind of multiplicity ad infinitum (Deleuze and Guattari 1987), even suggesting the existence of wandering artists/painters (Lorblanchet and Bahn 2017). Indeed, this immense repertoire of pictorial signs appears to be a visual text conceived to maximize the relationship with nature and facilitate its understanding. The ubiquity of Eurasian steppes petroglyphs seems to answer to the need for maintaining a high level of communication, a flow of figurative information, which documents the nomadic routine necessary for survival. The experience of such a nomad aesthetics is reminiscent of the physics of a stationary object that is set in motion and increases its acceleration. As speed equals space and time, and acceleration equals speed and time, this nomadic condition gives rise to an amplified experience of space and time. Such an intensified nomadic aesthetics fosters egalitarian space-time/nature effects, above all the open access to this visual vocabulary composed of signs that are not fenced in by any enclosure or wall but are displaced everywhere and are comprehensible to anyone even in the most inaccessible places. In contrast to the private or multiple-collective property of livestock such as reindeer, horses, cattle, and camels (Khazanov and Schlee 2012), since land and water sources are considered commons, can this egalitarian space-time/nature accessibility be the result of communal practices involving the use of pastures and water resources? Is such freedom to experience and to manage space-time/nature a medium to promote the creation of shared values, strengthening kinship, community, and tribal bonds, encouraging the adoption and the spread of visual codes endorsing a concept like that of our commons?

5 *Commonism*'s Contemporary Aesthetics

On the hypothesis that a sociocultural dimension akin to the contemporary concept of commons in relation to mobility in space and the control of time has always existed, the issues raised so far cause more questions than answers. This, in turn, deflates or reinforces the sense itself of such a reasoning. In our time, the matters of mobility in space and the control of time have become an issue involving the reflexivity of an embodied global community, be it that of migrants or of minorities and ethnic groups. Nomadism should not be intended exclusively as the freedom of exploring the space: it is a sociocultural need, a form of communal expression manifested by *new nomadic subjects* (Braidotti 2002). Choosing to avoid any self-centred comfort zone, on the contrary leaning towards others, our self undergoes a metamorphosis: "The reflexivity of modernity extends into the core of the self...the self becomes a reflexive project" (Giddens 1991, p. 32). When the artist is the individual who assumes a further in-depth plunging into this core of the self, then "the symbolic, the imaginary, and the reality" (Lacan 1982) merge together to transform the global reflexivity into universal consciousness, and the self moves towards commonism (Dockx and Gielen 2018). Both individual and collective, subjective and intersubjective, participatory and relational, this emancipatory experience that is morally shared, communally created, and can neither be determined nor measured, bought nor sold, is an evocative metaphor for our commons. The artist's commitment is bestowed with a capability responding to the *quality of life* (Nussbaum and Sen 1993), a social farmer whose soil and seeds are those provided by the surrounding otherness as can be discovered in the aesthetics of the ongoing artistic research in Filippo Berta's *One By One* and Julien Bismuth's *Hiaitsiihi*.

One By One is based on the unachievable attempt to count all the razor-like metal barbs of the state borders defined by barbed wires. Where the border transforms the lives of the people who live alongside it, the artist invites the inhabitants of the bordering areas to act an impossible performance: counting the endless barbs of the barbed wires installed along the borders of Serbia, Montenegro, Macedonia, Turkey, Greece, Cyprus, Bulgaria, Hungary, South Korea, North Korea, Mexico, and the United States. Impregnating social and geopolitical space with powerful symbolic effectiveness of deterrence, the border is also a fiction: neither the controller nor the controlled have full control. Demarcating between different rights, while barbed wires create positions and personal histories allowing different experiences of borders, the counting performance offers the opportunity to bring back precisely those rights to the material essentiality, to the universal of calculus. Invited to count the barbs, individuals living near the borders can choose to live space either as a bilateral dimension of themselves and others or as a condition of proximity which implies a cultural expansion that breaks down the very sense of boundaries, revealing the ethical impulse behind this aesthetic project (Maffesoli 1991). Counting becomes the action generating vital impulses able to trigger aesthetic connections that are at the same time trapped and freed in the performance: the tension between life and form provokes the art of life, the aestheticization through which individuals can truly engage with the profound meaning of living and sociability (Simmel 1911).

As Étienne Balibar reminds us, the key role of Europe as a community in redefining a *global public sphere* (2004) and facing their *borders'contradictions* (2016) suggests radical political undertakings that must guarantee a process of collective social reality. Analogical weapons are back in fashion. Barbed wires can push away, dismiss, separate, injure, and even kill visible standards-symbols of the invisible but material sovereignty exercised by market and technocracy. Before being inalienable rights, can the unrestricted mobility in space and the freedom to control time be considered common goods? Following the legal paths that society traced so far, how can we merge it with the idea of the commons? Escaping from the poverty that neoliberalism has been implementing in their homelands, how far should those who are looking for a new life travel before their rights under Article 13 of the Human Rights Universal Declaration are recognized?

Hiaitsiihi by Julien Bismuth started when the artist accompanied the anthropologist Marco Antonio Gonçalves for two stays with the Hiaitsiihi people in 2016 and 2017 in their autonomous land on the banks of the Maici river in the Amazon rainforest of Brazil. Known as the Pirahã by their neighbours, this semi-nomadic group calls itself the Hiaitsiihi, which means "a body (*ibiisi*) living in a layered cosmos". Hunter-gathers who continue to fish and hunt with bows and arrows, the Pirahã have been living in symbiosis with the Amazon rainforest for centuries, most of the year without shelter from the elements and relying only on the most essential material objects for their subsistence. They have no political structures, no economic or societal inequalities, and no obligations other than those of survival, enjoying and preserving Amazon resources, rather than consuming and depleting them. What one could call their culture consists primarily of the songs they sing and stories they tell in their singular tonal language, which can be whistled, spoken, or hummed: their cosmology is incarnated in the stories, songs, and rituals which punctuate and accompany their daily activities. As a matter of fact, the Amazon forest is a global common that the Hiaitsiihi live on without exploiting. Most of all, they enjoy a freedom of movement into several space-time dimensions, material and immaterial. As Julien Bismuth says: "During their rituals and their dreams, the Hiaitsiihi believe they can travel in space and in time, they can visit other worlds, included ours. All languages and cultures are different answers to the sole question of life, an enquiry that does not need a solution. Hiaitsiihi have found their answer to the question 'how to live here', they have found a system for living together without politics, economy, competition, individual property, and as such they have achieved the dream of the early anarchist thinkers. Their relationship to material objects is as minimal as can be imagined. Their way of life is based on the preservation of their autonomy, be it with regards to us or material objects. I have never seen a group of people living together, enjoying life together with such pleasure and happiness". Gaia's physiology (Volk 1998), politics of multiplicity (Viveiros De Castro 2019), cosmos (*idem* 2012), and non-human processes and agency (Haraway 2016) can be the compasses to trespass the limitation of our rationality and enter into ontology.

How can we connect with the ideas and ideals opened up by these nomadic artistic projects? Some possibilities are those offered by the contributors of *This Deleuzian Century: Art, Activism, Life* (Braidotti and Dolphijn 2014). Their *vitalist* or even erotic approach to these questions stems from aesthetics while breaking down barriers of any kind, allowing us to discover previously unimaginable perspectives and horizons. Mobile creative perspectives change the world and provide us to see what is unseen. As for the discovery of the vast previously unknown pre-Colombian anthropic network that the Amazon forest has preserved hidden for centuries (Levis et al. 2017): maybe the question itself of urbanism in the past will eventually disappear the day we will realize or accept that it is just a matter of perspective.

6 Conclusion

The process of restraining space and time can be at the origin of the loss or alteration of sociocultural practices based on the exercise of a non-instrumental and inclusive, individual, and collective freedom. As a result of non-homogeneous experiences triggered by conditions of necessity, the alteration of this social mechanism would have caused a profound transformation in the relationships among individuals, giving rise to mixed experiences of hegemony and resistance in relation to space and time. Do the nomadic cultures of the Eurasian steppes and the early urbanism of Mesopotamia contain the signs of this alteration? Though the full resolution of this question remains out of reach, an aesthetics eager to translate the voices of a multitude turned into an *assembly* is flourishing (Hardt and Negri 2017), a *supercommunity* (Aranda et al. 2017) whose social interaction revitalizes from solidarity, inclusion, understanding, and otherness.

Making an emotional infrastructure together (Nomeda and Gediminas Urbonas 2018), while keeping our minds constantly interconnected in the virtual borderless place of the Internet where the space-time dimension loses its physical restraints, another intersubjectivity is awakening our innate need to explore and share space and time on a deeper level. Maybe the future holds a new experience of living together and, as a settled and motionless space, the city will disappear. In its place, cities will exist just as nomadic experiences, fenceless travelling cities of human communities who will be able to share space and time without any restriction with *Motus* as the instrument to measure the degree of freedom of our society.

References

Algaze, G. (1993). *The Uruk world-system*. Chicago: University of Chicago Press.

Amitai, R. (1999). Sufis and Shamans. Some remarks on the Islamization of the Mongols in the Ilkhanate. *Journal of the Economic and Social History of the Orient, 42*(1), 27–46.

Aranda, J., Kuan Wood, B., & Vidokle, A. (Eds.). (2017). *Supercommunity. Diabolical togetherness beyond contemporary art*. London/New York: Verso.

Aruz, J., Farkas, A., Alekseev, A., & Korolkova, E. (2000). *The Golden Deer of Eurasia: Scythian and Sarmatian treasures from the Russian Steppes: The State Hermitage, Saint Petersburg, and the Archaeological Museum, UFA*. New York: The Metropolitan Museum of Art.

Backouche, I., Gensburger, S., & Le Bourhis, E. (June, 2017). Opportunities and Antisemitism. Housing in Paris, 1943–1944. *Politika, le politique à l'épreuve des sciences sociales,* 1–15.

Balibar, É. (2004). *We, the people of Europe? Reflection on transnational citizenship*. Princeton/Oxford: Princeton University Press.

Balibar, É. (2016). *Europe: crise et fin?*. Lormont: Édition le Bord de l'eau.

Banning, E. B. (2011). So Fair a House: Göbleki Tepe and the Identification of Temples in the Pre-Pottery Neolithic of the Near East. *Current Anthropology, 52*(5), 619–660.

Bourdieu, P. (1986). The forms of capital. In Richardson,J. (Ed.), *Handbook of theory and research for the sociology of education* (pp. 241–258). Westport, CT: Greenwood.

Braidotti, R. (2002). *Nuovi soggetti nomadi*. Roma: Luca Sossella Editore.

Braidotti, R., & Dolphijn, R. (Eds.). (2014). *This Deleuzian Century. Art, Actism, Life*. Leiden: Brill.

Bunker, E. (2002). *Nomadic art of the Eastern Eurasian Steppes: The Eugene V. Thaw and Other New York collections*. New Haven: Yale University Press.

Childe, V. G. (1950). The urban revolution. *Town Planning Review, 21,* 3–17.

Chugunov, K. V., Parzinger, H., & Nagler, A. (2004). Chronology and cultural affinity of the Kurgan Arzhan-2 complex according to archaeological data. In E. M., Scott, A. Y. Alekseev, & G. Zaitseva (Eds.), *Impact of the environment on human migration in Eurasia. Proceedings of the NATO Advanced Research Workshop, held in St. Petersburg, 15–18 November 2003. Nato Science Series* (vol. 42, pp. 1–8). Dordrecht: Kluwer.

Croucher, S. K., & Weiss, L. (Eds.). (2011). *The archaeology of capitalism in colonial contexts. Postcolonial historical archaeologies*. New York: Springer.

Cunliff, B. (2015). *By Steppe, desert, and ocean*. Oxford: Oxford University Press.

Davis-Kimball, J., Bashilov, V. A., & Yablonski, L. T. (Eds.). (1995). *Nomads of the Eurasian Steppes in the early iron age*. Berkely, CA: Zinat Press.

Davis-Kimball, J., Murphy, E. M., Koryakova, L., & Yablonsky, L. (Eds.). (2000). *Kurgans, ritual sites, and settlements: Eurasian Bronze and Iron Age. BAR International Series 890*. Oxford: Archaeopress.

Dean, K., & Massumi, B. (1992). *First & last emperors. The absolute state and the body of the despot*. New York: Aunotomedia.

Deleuze, G., & Guattari, F. (1987). *A thousand plateaus. Capitalism and Schizophrenia*. Minneapolis/London: University of Minnesota Press.

Di Cosmo, N. (2002). *Ancient China and its enemies. The rise of nomadic power in East Asian history*. Cambridge: Cambridge University Press.

Dockx, N., & Gielen, P. (Eds.). (2018). *Commonism. A new aesthetics of the real*. Amsterdam: Valiz.

Eliade, M. (1964). *Shamanism. Archaic techniques of ecstasy*. New York: Pantheon Books.

Faegre, T. (1979). *Tents. Architecture of the Nomads*. New York: Anchor Books.

Foster, B. R. (1996). *Before the muses. An anthology of Akkadian Literature I-II*. Bethesda: CDL Press.

Foucault, M. (1971). *L'ordre du discours*. Paris: Gallimard.

Frachetti, M. D. (2012). Multiregional emergence of mobile Pastoralism and nonuniform institutional complexity across Eurasia. *Current Anthropology, 53*(1), 2–38.

Francfort, H. P., & Hamayon, R. N. (Eds.) (2001). *The concept of Shamanism: Uses and abuses*, Bibliotheca Shamanistica 10. Budapest: Akadémiai Kiadó.

Gardiner-Garden, J. (1987a). Apollodoros of Artemita and the Central Asian Skythians. *Papers on Inner Asia 3*. Bloomington: Research Institute for Inner Asian Studies.

Gardiner-Garden, J. (1987b). Greek Conceptions on Inner Asian Geography and Ethnography from Ephoros to Eratosthenes. *Papers on Inner Asia 9*. Bloomington: Research Institute for Inner Asian Studies.

Gardiner-Garden, J. (1987c). Herodotos' Contemporaries on Skythian Geography and Ethnography. *Papers on Inner Asia 10*. Bloomington: Research Institute for Inner Asian Studies.

Gardiner-Garden, J. (1987d). Ktesias on Central Asian History and Ethnography. *Papers on Inner Asia 6*. Bloomington: Research Institute for Inner Asian Studies.

Gelb, I., Steinkeller, P., & Whiting, R. M. (1991). *Earliest land tenure systems in the near east: Ancient Kudurrus*. OIP 104. Chicago, IL: The Oriental Institute of the University of Chicago.

Giddens, A. (1991). *Modernity and self-identity. Self and society in the late modern age*. Cambridge: Polity Press.

Gignoux, P. (2001). *Man and Cosmos in Ancient Iran*. Serie Orientale 91. Roma: Is.I.A.O.

Goody, J. (2000). Technologies of the Intellect. Writing and the written world. In J. Goody (Ed.), *The power of the written tradition* (pp. 132–151). Washington, DC: Smithsonian Institute Press.

Gorshenina, S., Bornet, P., Fuchs, M. E., & Rapin, C. (Eds.). (2019). *"Masters" and "Natives". Digging the Others' Past. Worlds of South and Inner Asia 8*. Berlin/Boston: De Gruyter.

Gramsci, A. (1976). *Letters from prison*. Translated by L. Lawner. New York: Harper & Row.

Graves-Brown, P., Harrison, R., & Piccini, A. (Eds.). (2013). *The Oxford handbook of the archaeology of the contemporary world*. Oxford: Oxford University Press.

Grjaznov, M. P. (1984). *Der Großkurgan von Aržan in Tuva, Südsibirien*. München: Verlag.

Haraway, D. J. (2016). *Staying with trouble. Making kin in the Chthulucene*. Durham/London: Duke University Press.

Hardt, M., & Negri, A. (2017). *Assembly*. Oxford: Oxford University Press.

Ishay, M. (2008). *The history of human rights: From ancient times to globalization era*. New York: Norton and Co.

Ivantchik, A. I. (2005). Early Eurasian Nomads and the civilizations of the ancient near east (Eight-Seventh Century BCE). In R., Amitai, & M. Biran (Eds.), *Mongols, Turks, and Others. Eurasian Nomads and the Sedentary World* (pp. 103–126). Leiden/Boston: Brill.

Jacobson, E., Kubarev, V., & Tseevendorj, D. (2001). *Répertoire Des Pétroglyphs d'Asie Centrale. Sous la direction de Henri-Paul Francfort et Jakov A. Sher. Fascicule N. 6: Mongolie du Nord-Ouest Tsagaan Salaa/Baga Oigor*, Mémoires de la Mission Archéologique Française en Asie Centrale Tome V.6, (2 voll.). Paris.

Jacobson-Tepfer, E., Kubarev, V., & Tseevendorj, D. (2006). *Répertoire Des Pétroglyphs d'Asie Centrale. Sous la direction de Henri-Paul Francfort et Jakov A. Sher. Fascicule N. 7: Mongolie du Nord-Ouest Haut Tsagaan Gol*, Mémoires de la Mission Archéologique Française en Asie Centrale V.7, (2 voll.). Paris.

Jettmar, K. (1967). *Art of the steppes*. New York: Greystone.

Khazanov, A. M. (1994). *Nomads and the outside world*. Madison: The University of Wisconsin Press.

Khazanov, A. M., & Schlee, G. (Eds.). (2012). *Who Owns the Stock? Collective and multiple property rights in animals*. New York: Berghahn Books.

Klejn, L. (2017). Archaeology in Soviet Russia. In L. R., Lozny (Ed.), *Archaeology of the communist era. A political history of archaeology of the 20th century* (pp. 59–99). Berlin: Springer Nature.

Koryakova, L., & Epimakhov, A. (2007). *The Urals and Western Siberia in the bronze and iron ages*. Cambridge: Cambridge University Press.

Kradin, N. N. (2011). A panorama of social archaeology in Russia. In L. R. Lozny (Ed.), *Comparative archaeologies. A sociological view of the science of the past* (pp. 243–271). Berlin: Springer Nature.

Kubarev, V. D., & Jacobson, E. (1996). *Répertoire Des Pétroglyphs d'Asie Centrale. Fascicule N. 3: Sibérie du Sud 3: Kalbak-Tash I (République de l'Altai)*, Mémoires de la Mission Archéologique Française en Asie Centrale V.3. Paris.

Kuzmina, E. E. (2008). *The prehistory of the silk road.* Philadelphia: University of Pennsylvania Press.

Lacan, J. (1982). Le symbolique, l'imaginaire et le réel. In *Bulletin de l'Association Freudienne I*: 4–13.

Lash, S. (1999). *another modernity: A different rationality*. Oxford: Blackwell.

Leone, M. P., & Knauf, J. E. (Eds.). (2015). *Historical archaeologies of capitalism*. New York: Springer.

Levis, C., Costa, F. R., Bongers, F., Peña-Claros, M., Clement, C. R., Junqueira, A. B., et al. (2017). Persistent effects of pre-columbian plant domestication on Amazonian forest composition. *Science, 355*, 925–931.

Liebmann, M., & Rizvi, U. Z. (Eds.). (2008). *Archaeology and postcolonial critique*. Lanham: Altamira Press.

Liverani, M. (2006). *Uruk: The first city*. London: Equinox.

Lorblanchet, M., & Bahn, P. G. (2017). *The FIRST ARTIST. In search of the world's oldest art*. London: Thames & Hudson.

Lydon, J., & Rizvi, U. Z. (Eds.). (2010). *Handbook of postcolonial archaeology, world archaeological Congress research handbooks in archaeology 3*. Walnut Creek: Left Coast Press.

Maffesoli, M. (1991). The ethics of aesthetics. *Theory, Culture and Society, 8*(1), 7–20.

Mar'jašev, A. N., Gorjaèev, S. S., & Potapov, S. A. (1998). *Répertoire Des Pétroglyphs d'Asie Centrale. Sous la direction de Jakov A. Sher et Henri-Paul Francfort. Fascicule N. 5: Kazakhstan 1: Choix de Petroglyphes du Semirech'e (Felsbilder im Siebenstromland)*, Mémoires de la Mission Archéologique Francaise en Asie Centrale V.5. Paris.

Mazar, A. (1992). *Archaeology of the land of the Bible. Volume I: 10,000–586 B.C.E.* New Haven: Yale University Press.

Michalowski, P. (1986). Mental maps and ideology: Reflections on Subartu. In H. Weiss (ed.), *The origins of cities in dry farming Syria and Mesopotamia in the Third Millennium*. Guilford, CN: Four Quarters Publishing.

Nissen, H. J. (1988). *The early history of the ancient near east*. Chicago: University of Chicago Press.

Nomeda & Gediminas Urbonas. (2018). Organizational Aesthetics and emotional infrastructure. In N., Dockx, & P., Gielen (Eds.). *Commonism. A new aesthetics of the real*. Amsterdam: Valiz.

Notroff, J., Dietrich, O., & Schmidt, K. (2016). Gathering of the dead? The early neolithic sanctuaries of Göbleki Tepe, Southeastern Turkey. In C. Renfrew, M. J. Boyd, & I. Morley (Eds.), *Death rituals, social order and the archaeology of immortality in the ancient world "death shall have no dominion"* (pp. 65–81). Cambridge: Cambridge University Press.

Nussbaum, M., & Sen, A. (1993). *The quality of life*. Oxford: Oxford University Press.

Piotrovski, B. (1973–1974). From the Lands of Scythians: Ancient Treasures from the Museums of the U.S.S.R., 3000 B.C.–100 B.C. *The Metropolitan Museum of Art Bulletin* 32.5. New York: Arno Press.

Potts, D. T. (2014). *Nomadism in Iran. From antiquity to modern era*. New York: Oxford University Press.

Rose, C. M. (1985). Possession as the origin of property. *The University of Chicago Law Reviews, 52*(1), 73–88.

Roth, M. T. (1997). *Law collections from Mesopotamia and Asia Minor*. Atlanta: Scholars Press.

Said, E. (1978). *Orientalism*. New York: Pantheon Books.

Schmidt, K. (2000). Göbekli Tepe, Southeastern Turkey. A Preliminary Report on the 1995–1999 Excavations. *Paléorient, 26*(1), 45–54.

Schmidt, K. (2001). Göbekli Tepe and the Early Neolithic Sites of the Urfa Region: A Synopsis of New Results and Current Views. *Neo-Lithics, 1*(1), 9–11.

Schmidt, K. (2011) Göbekli Tepe: a Neolithic site in southeastern Anatolia. In S. R., Steadman, & G., McMahon (Eds.), *Oxford handbook of ancient Anatolia. 10,000–323 B.C.E.*: 918-33. Oxford: Oxford University Press.

Scott, E. M., Alekseev, A. Y., & Zaitseva, G. (Eds.). (2004). *Impact of the Environment on Human Migration in Eurasia. Proceedings of the NATO Advanced Research Workshop, Held in St. Petersburg, 15–18 November 2003. Nato Science Series, vol. 42*. Dordrecht: Kluwer.

Sher, J. A. (1994). *Répertoire Des Pétroglyphs d'Asie Centrale. Fascicule N. 1: Sibérie du Sud 1: Oglakhty I-III (Russie, Khakassie)*, Mémoires de la Mission Archéologique Française en Asie Centrale V.1. Paris.

Sher, J. A. (1995). *Répertoire Des Pétroglyphs d'Asie Centrale. Sous la direction de Henri-Paul Francfort et Jakov A. Sher. Fascicule N. 2: Sibérie du Sud: Tepsej I-III, Ust'-Tuba I-VI (Russie, Khakassie)*, Mémoires de la Mission Archéologique Française en Asie Centrale 2. Paris.

Sher, J. A., Savinov, D, Legchilo, N., & Sher, M. (1999). *Répertoire Des Pétroglyphs d'Asie Centrale. Sous la direction de Jakov A. Sher et Henri-Paul Francfort et. Fascicule N. 4: Sibérie du Sud: Cheremushny Log, Ust'-Kulog,,Stèles de Khakassie*, Mémoires de la Mission Archéologique Francaise en Asie Centrale V.4. Paris.

Simmel, G. (1911). *Die Geselligkeit. Beispiel der Reinen oder Formalen Soziologie*, in *Grundfragen der Soziologie (Individuum und Gesellschaft)*. Translation Donaggio, E. (1997). *La socievolezza*. Roma: Armando.

Toshio, H. (2013). The Beginning and the Maturity of Nomadic Powers in the Eurasian Steppes: Growing and Downsizing of Elite Tumuli. *Ancient Civilizations from Scythia to Siberia* 19: 105–141. Leiden/New York:Brill.

Tönnies, F. (1963/1887). *Community and Society*. New York: Harper & Row.

Verderame, L. (2018). Slavery in third millennium Mesopotamia: An overview of sources and studies. *Journal of Global Slavery, 3,* 13–40.

Vinogradov, N. B, & Epimakhov, A. V. (2000). From a Settled Way of Life to Nomadism: Variants in Models of Transition. In J., Davis-Kimball, E. M., Murphy, L., Koryakova, & L. T. Yablonsky (Eds.), *Ritual sites, and settlements: Eurasian bronze and iron age. BAR International Series* (vol 890, pp. 240–246). Oxford: Archaeopress.

Viveiros de Castro, E. (2012). *Cosmological Perspectivism in Amazonia and Elsewhere. Four Lectures Given in the Department of Social Anthropology, Cambridge University, February-March 1998*. Hau Masterclass Series Vol. 1. Manchester: HAU-N.E.T.

Viveiros de Castro, E. (2019). *Politique des multiplicités: Pierre Clastre face à l'État*. Bellevaux: Édition Dehors.

Volk, T. (1998). *Gaia's body. Towards a physiology of earth*. New York: Springer.

Weber, M. (1966). *The city*. New York: Free Press.

Westbrook, R. (Ed.). (2003). *A history of ancient near eastern law. Handbook of oriental studies*. Leiden: Brill.

Over There: The Mediterranean Surface and the Archetype of the Island as Contemporary Paradigms for Accessing Cultural Commons

Novella Oliana

Abstract

This chapter focuses on the role of contemporary visual artists and on their contribution to the complex discourse of transforming cultural commons. By analyzing the composite space of the Mediterranean, the author's investigation aims at clarifying the perspective of an operational approach in art as a perceptual experience in which research, methodology and theory are connected. Here, the image of the sea surface becomes a *habitus,* a mental disposition, a space to inhabit and a membrane between the intimate and *extimate* dimensions of the body which observes, represents and perceives. The image of the Mediterranean Sea is thus considered as a contemporary *templum*, an interface where it is possible to outline and decode the trajectories of current crossings and exiles. The process of artistic creation dismantles the complexity of places: research practice becomes both trace and compass in the sea of contradictions and complexities characterizing our contemporary world.

1 Introduction

What is the role of contemporary artists in the framework of an operational perspective involving social innovation? How can contemporary art contribute to a discourse on transforming cultural commons? Those are the questions that moved me to reconsider my research. As Cindy Foley, Executive Deputy Director for Learning and Experience at the Columbus Museum of Art, points out in her well known TED Talk, nothing can actually be perceived as vague and sometimes

N. Oliana (✉)
Department of Visual Arts, Aix Marseille Université, Marseille, France
e-mail: novella.oliana@gmail.com

E. Macrì et al. (eds.), *Cultural Commons and Urban Dynamics*,
https://doi.org/10.1007/978-3-030-54418-8_18

undefined as art: unwilling to adhere to the logic of standardization, art is generally associated with creativity, imagination and the freedom from a pre-established framework. However, how can something apparently so indeterminate be also so tangible? Art possesses nonetheless the faculty of producing an output that affects reality, and is related to the materiality of the body which feels, moves and perceives in the space. Therefore, what does thinking like an artist mean and how this functional thought can provoke change in the framework of transforming urban and social contexts, as well as in their perception and representation? My contribution as a visual artist and researcher is an attempt to answer this question by focusing on a complex space such as the Mediterranean, particularly its sea surface. I consider this territory not only as a symbolic and allegorical space, but also as a social context with its shared heritage and emerging commons. I investigate its complexity through artistic research which I consider a tool for redefining its ever-transforming space that constantly destroys and rebuilds itself. I also explore the relationship between urban sites, the sea and coastlines as natural borders and as metaphorical emplacements for perceptual experiences leading to the understanding of the essence of this territory.

2 Methodological Considerations

I would firstly like to introduce a methodological consideration by drawing attention to the "operational perspective" of an artistic approach: what is *operational* in art involves the creative process itself. To give an example, let's think about the self-explicative photographic work by John Hilliard, *Camera recording its own condition* (*7 Apertures, 10 Speeds, 2 Mirrors*) [Tate collection]: within the very limit of this image it is possible to reckon the process of creation of the image itself and of the medium which is, at the same time, a path of investigation and of representation. In a very eloquent way, this image gives shape to what Gilles Deleuze and Félix Guattari claimed, i.e. each work of art is a "bloc of sensation, that is to say a compound of percepts and affects" (Deleuze and Guattari 1996: 163). Artworks look for the creation of experiences within reality and generates sensations: similarly, Hilliard's image merges both the process and the operational approach by creating a cluster of visual and emotional information. These artistic gestures create an image which corresponds to an experimental space becoming, on the one hand, the place of the process for the artist, and on the other, the place of reception and perception for the viewer. In this way, visual creation and theoretical research are entangled within the same framework defining an interdependent, common and practicable field. This experimental space, welcoming both the viewer and involving the perspective of the artist, is a liminal performative area connecting different moments and allowing an exchange between body and perception, as well as between internal and external worlds.

The creation of a space for observation delimiting the field of vision recalls the construction of the *templum* (from the latin *temno*, i.e. *I cut*) in the ancient Roman period, which was the field of observation for the augurs. This portion of space allowed reading and interpreting the traces left from the passage of birds in the sky and to decrypt these signs (Charbonnier 2018: 31). Then, through metonymy, the *templum* gave also its name to the building the emplacement of which was defined by this practice. This concluded space recalls also Leon Battista Alberti's *window* who, in his essay *De Pictura,* dated 1435, claims: "*First, where I have to paint, I trace a quadrangle of right angles, as large as I like, and which I consider to be an open window through where I see that which there I will paint.*" In our contemporary world, this window opening on a visual representation is the *image*, both as a physical object revealing a fragment of space, and as a conceptual framework, inside which histories and common imaginaries are projected. This framework owns the characteristic of the device, i.e. the one showing and depicting at the same time, by connecting different spaces, worlds and histories. Photography and contemporary images function like this: they constitute our first contact and knowledge of the world and condense in their layers of meaning the comprehension of reality. One must also consider that contemporary images, accessible through interfaces and screens, are able to compact in their limited and defined space both the device and the message, giving shape to what we can call the stratified visual text of reality in its ever-transforming complexity. This perspective amplifies what Louis Marin calls "sign and process", by defining three spaces for representation: the space of visibility (i.e. what shows the representation), the represented space (i.e. what we see) and the space of representation (i.e. the frame, the screen or the image itself) (Marin 1988: 62). Particularly, contemporary images are no longer seen, but are enjoyed through gestures—*swiping, scrolling, zooming*, etc.—by which it is possible to navigate from one image to the other; our visual perception is therefore incredibly stimulated by the redundancy, heterogeneity and the rapidity in which visual material is proposed. The image as a space of creation, observation and interaction is, therefore, a defined area where common imaginaries and perceptions are projected: as in a map—the earliest representation of a concluded space where something happens—it is possible to contact a rendition of reality, observe itineraries, imagine paths and recall personal and shared histories.

3 Theoretical and Practical Analysis

So, let's start looking at a map of the Mediterranean which is part of my visual work (Fig. 1): by inverting the image to its photographic negative, geographical and perceptual references are subverted.

Fig. 1 Universi complementari #1 (Oliana 2018)

Visual codes and colors commonly employed to depict the land and the water (i.e. yellow and blue) are reversed: what was blue becomes yellow and vice versa, for the complementarity of colors. Therefore, the Mediterranean Sea surface reveals itself like an emerged land or an island in the center of the map. It is possible to observe how the elements of water and land alternate constantly, creating a complementary territory which is contained and containing at the same time. According to Alfred Korzybski, founder of the general semantics, "the map is not the territory" (Korzibsky 1933: 747): a map, depicting an abstraction of what we perceive to be the reality becomes a tool for comprehending, rearranging and experimenting the world. This abstraction conveys what we glimpse through our senses and therefore is nourished by our imaginaries, beliefs and projections. The idea of interrelated dimensions conveyed by this map as well as the patterns of separation and connection that the Mediterranean territory itself bears characterize this changing space where common symbols and myths are shared. Among them, the paradigm of displacement is something that recalls the tradition referring all the way back to the Odyssey and to Ulysses' journey until contemporary migrations. On the one hand, creative displacement results in a perceptual experience, and on the other, imagination reshapes itineraries and geographies, by defining a universe of common cultural references and local specificities. In the Mediterranean, personal stories and iconic journeys are entangled to chronicled events throughout history: let's think about the recent film by the Italian director Gianfranco Rosi, *Fuocoammare,* in which, while chanting the story of its own journey from the mountain to the Mediterranean—ideally imagined as a way of escaping—a migrant claims that "the sea is not a road". Not only are we called to reflect on the personal narration of this man which is entangled to the contemporary chronicle witnessed by this territory, but we are also invited to focus on the geographical configuration of this space and on its metaphorical outcome. The natural formation of this aquatic surface, originally generated by the collapsing of the Gibraltar strait, creates a particular territory which becomes a pivotal space of passage and crossing.

This is very clear in the work *Méditerranée sans frontières* by the French artist Sabine Réthoré who reverses the map of the Mediterranean in order to rethink our relationship with this territory, our perception and representation of it. In this map, it is possible to remark the centrality of the Messina sea strait which, like the center of an hourglass, connects two different areas. The image of the strait as a funnel is also outlined by La Cecla and Zanini (2004) who comment how this particular space is "*strictly* necessary", by playing with the Italian assonance of the same word "stretto" used to design both the geographical *strait* and what is *closely* indispensable. According to their perspective, the strait becomes a crucial space of transition and a metaphor of transformation for the human condition.

This same approach is visible in my work in which this particular space coincides with the Mediterranean Sea surface itself and with its visual representation: I investigate a relational dimension of a physical and mental space that "cannot but be", i.e. that I consider *necessary* for comprehending a complex universe. I also refer to the definition of "necessary space" given by the French designer and architect Charlotte Perriand by putting in relation body and perception: according to her point of view, there is a space for our actions which claim places and emplacements. "*[...] L'espace ça se crée. Il y a l'espace nécessaire et puis il y a l'espace créé, c'est- à-dire visuellement on peut créer de l'espace sans qu'il y est beaucoup de mètres carrés pour autant. Par contre, c'est absolument nécessaire de trouver au bout de nos doigts précisément tout ce dont nous avons besoin. C'est ce que j'appelle la fonction, la fonction d'une part et la création d'espace d'autre part*". It's not only about considering the visibility of a space but also its function in order to inhabit it. In fact, inhabiting (from the latin *habitus)* not only defines the habit, the behavior and the way of establishing a relation, but also refers to the clothes enclosing the body which, in turn, moves and acts in the space. I consider the image of the sea surface as a *habitus,* a mental disposition, a surface to inhabit and a membrane between the intimate and *extimate* dimension of the body which observes, represents and perceives. This image I download from the Internet by typing the word *sea* in different languages, is the focus of my visual research: it is both the mock-up I use and also the conceptual framework on which I build my discourse (Figs. 2, 3, 4 and 5). As a cluster of space and time, this image I

Fig. 2 Idea di mare (Oliana 2017)

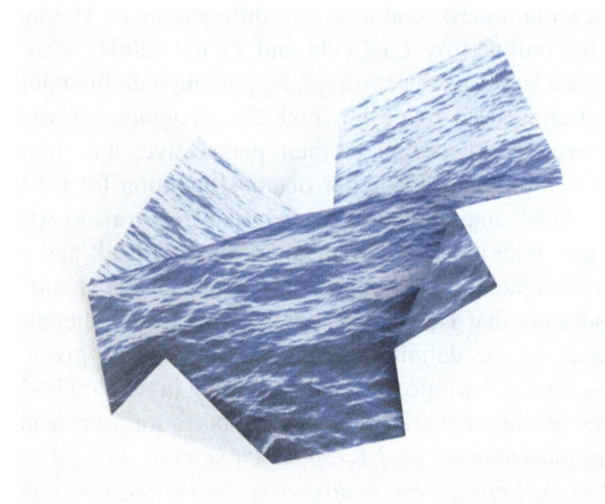

Fig. 3 Porzione di mare piegata 7 volte (Oliana 2018)

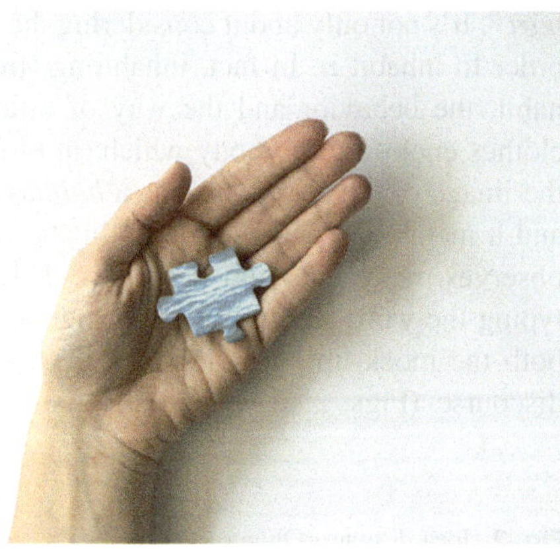

Fig. 4 Le casse-tête (Oliana 2018)

manipulate is a definite portion of aquatic territory functioning as an abstraction, where it is possible to reckon all sorts of projections and imaginaries.

The surface, both as a membrane and as a space connecting other spaces, recalls the concept of *heterotopia* (Foucault 1984: 45) which, according to Michel Foucault, defines all transforming contexts and that can be considered as one of the main characteristics of contemporary cultures, affected by the outbreak of new media and technologies. For instance, the screen as a contemporary device functions as a *heterotopia*—by connecting distant representations, places and spaces—and at the same time a haptic space (from the ancient Greek *haptesthai,* meaning *to touch*), i.e. connecting visual perception through touch (Bruno 2016: 194). The Mediterranean aquatic surface as a huge space of transition, where pressing social and geopolitical issues are observed, can be considered as a contemporary

Fig. 5 Possibili idee di mare #2 (Oliana 2017)

heterotopia: by becoming a sort of device itself, it contains projections and common heritages and, at the same time, it shows complexities and transformations.

Like a window open on history, it is a place to inhabit and a place inhabited by images, signs, gestures, habits which both contribute to create it and to change it. As a mentally and geographically defined territory, it is a place where it is possible to experience the paradigms of transition and displacement which, in turn, end up being the same operational perspectives of investigation and representation of its transforming essence.

The process of creation of images and representations, as well as of construction and deconstruction embraced by the gestures characterizing the artistic creation, dismantle the complexity of places, thus leading to the comprehension of the spatial and social contexts where it occurs. Contemporary visual practices that stem from those assumptions are conceived to raise attention to the transformations happening in the spaces where they come to take action; they also aim at offering perceptual experiences for the audience in order to redefine transformations and rethinking the relationship with the space. For instance, in the Southern coastline of the Mediterranean and particularly in the city of Beirut, the performative action "This sea is mine" (2012), by the Lebanese artist Tania El Khoury together with the Dictaphone Group, aimed at denouncing the inaccessibility of the sea from the Beirut seafront, brutally privatized since the 1970s. By inviting people to a journey on a fishing boat —made usually impossible due to the lack of free access to the sea—the performative gesture of the artist was meant to redefine paths in the city, to overcome physical obstacles and borders preventing the access to the coastline, and finally to reclaim the connection to the sea as a crucial element, representing both the spirit of the city and of its inhabitants. The sea, conveying the opposing paradigms of the here and there, is the theater of this displacement in the space that traces a shared itinerary through a new architecture involving emotions, perceptions and memory. Moving in the space becomes an operational approach for defining experimental spaces where it is possible to rethink and understand the transformations of the territory and the way in which they affect social contexts and identities.

In the short film *Dream of Sea* (2006), shot both in the village of Biddu and in the city of Ramallah in Palestine, the Italian directors Sara Zavarise and Stefano Collizzolli with their colleagues from Zalab association describe a particular sea, shaped through the reveries of the people they interview in the street: "What is the sea?", they ask. In a land fragmented by the Israeli occupation and separated by borders, walls and barriers, the sea becomes "a memory" or something seen on television because it is impossible to reach it. "*Al-baḥr sci kebīr*", the sea is something big, sang the Lebanese Fairouz: if the sea is an unspeakable dream for the adults, for the kids who have never seen it, it is shaped into the confined space of small swimming pools called "Saffa Sea" or "Birzeit Sea". This three-minute documentary sketches a life which is dreamed not to be regretted, in order to overcome the walls limiting the space of the territory and of the soul.

Thanks to the exploration of these paths, the sea surface turns into an entangled place: here, it is possible to experiment a new gaze, aiming at crushing superimposed limitations. In this way, such artistic interventions encourage to regain access to a conscious vision: this one represents a model for the acquisition of a new self-insight, in order to rethink one's social identity in a transforming world. This kind of "(senti)mental paths" or "performative cartographies" reorient perception and merge the inner journey of the self with the exploration of changing social contexts and territories. The operations meant to modify the spatial configuration of the world around us and that are filtered by imagination result in sensible alternatives that are able to disrupt perception.

This is the case in my installation *8 infiniti circa* (2019, Figs. 6 and 7) exhibited during the open-air and site-specific international art and photography festival Gibellina PhotoRoad (directed and curated by Arianna Catania with On Image association, Gibellina municipality, Fondazione Orestiadi, Festival Images Vevey). By covering a wall of the city in Piazza Beuys with images, I recreated a counter-narrative of the sea in the city. This action of displacing a distant element, which takes the shape of a poster on the wall, modifies both the aesthetics of the wall itself and of the urban context, by transforming the geographical space that this element conveys. This intervention aims at designing a place in which shape and content are changed, thus generating areas of contact and separation. The installation *8 infiniti circa* is a cartography of a mental and visible territory: it transforms the urban site by becoming a poster, a text rich of information and a map for inhabiting a space. My images printed on a large scale not only define new emplacements, but they also seem to tear up the wall and to reshape it at the same time. The connection between the figure of the sea and the idea of destruction is very much present both in the history of the city itself—which was destroyed by the Belice earthquake in 1968 and rebuilt far away from its original site—and in the frayed edges of the wall where my works are installed. My images turn into a material itinerary that encourages the viewer to start a journey within the city and the space, so as to retrace a new path for memory.

Besides, in the well-known legend of the "memory palace", Simonides, Greek poet of the fifth century B.C, is said to dine in the company of dignitaries and other personalities of that time. During the dinner, he walks away from the table for a

Fig. 6 8 infiniti circa (Oliana, 2019, reproduced thanks to Gibellina Photo Road 2019)

Fig. 7 8 infiniti circa (Oliana, 2019, reproduced thanks to Gibellina Photo Road 2019)

moment when suddenly an earthquake destroys the palace and crushes its roof that falls onto the guests, killing them all. The only way Simonides, the only survivor, can recognize the victims is to remember the place where everyone was seated. Similarly, by facing the tragedy of the Belice earthquake, one can reconnect fragments of its personal identity through the emplacements where my images are installed. They offer a sentimental cartography as well as a material and mental itinerary through the tragedy.

As we have seen, a metaphorical displacement can also convey the materiality of a work of art, by connecting the space of its narrative with the one of his reception. *Lo spazio necessario* (Fig. 8), a research workshop I conducted with the Italian artist Michela Palermo at the Ecomuseo Mare Memoria Viva in Palermo (Sicily), is an artistic intervention aiming at connecting personal memories with the quest for identity associated with a transformed territory.

Fig. 8 Lo spazio necessario, Cartolina (reproduced thanks to Ecomuseo Mare Memoria Viva and Minimum 2019). Lo spazio necessario has been possible thanks to the collaboration of Minimum Palermo, Ecomuseo Mare Memoria Viva and thanks to all the participants: Pierluigi Bizzini, Anna D'Elia, Annamaria Fricano, Gerlando Giaccone, Gloria Guglielmo, Maria Concetta Immè, Giuseppe Iannello, Giuseppe Scafidi, Valentina Sestieri e Laura Tellini

The Ecomuseo Mare Memoria Viva, with the coordination of Cristina Alga, has assembled a collection of family photos in the past few years, with the objective of rebuilding the collective memory of the Southern coastline of Palermo which was brutally modified by urban demolitions and reconstructions in the 1950s and 1960s. One of the most evident consequences of this aggressive action is the increased distance between the sea and the city: the debris caused by the demolition of buildings and Art Nouveau Bathhouse were discharged on the coast determining violent modifications of the seabed as well as of the landscape. The sea, once part of the life of the inhabitants, has become now mostly invisible and inaccessible. By reshaping the relation between memory, image and place, the workshop has explored this physical and metaphorical distance by designing a narrative path meant to inhabit this gap between the sea and the urban center. Several bi-dimensional and tri-dimensional paper devices have been prepared for the participants who have been able to create new "loci" (places, clusters) where images have been installed. These emplacements have functioned as clusters of space and memory, thus reshaping new ideal frontiers through the manipulation and the bending of the images. In this new mental architecture, archive materials (images, stories, videos and screenshots) have been rescued and restored to collective and private history. Plain paper sheets or *bombonnière* boxes, which are part of the cultural tradition of Palermo, have changed their semantic function to become receptacles for new rearranged and imagined "souvenirs" (Fig. 9–12). These compositions, result of the workshop, have been exhibited at Fondazione Orestiadi in July 2019 during the Gibellina PhotoRoad festival. The city itself, like the sea, is a moving entity which, in this way, is restored to a new dimension including common narrations, traditions and cultural heritages.

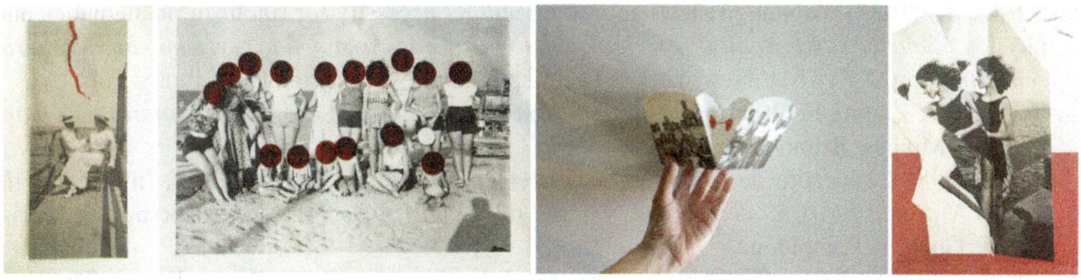

Fig. 9–12 Lo spazio necessario, compositions (reproduced thanks to Ecomuseo Mare Memoria Viva and Minimum 2019)

Observing the Mediterranean space through the fabrication of abstractions in an interdisciplinary perspective allows investigating the complexity of this territory. By revealing the process underlying the photographic gesture, the image itself becomes a condensed cluster and an open surface where space and time are connected. In this way, it is possible to outline the impact of an artistic intervention as a perceptual experience in which research, methodology and theory are connected. The image of the Mediterranean becomes thus a contemporary *templum*, or an interface where it is possible to outline and decode the trajectories of contemporary crossings and exiles; it conveys also the same space where research can be developed, in order to create the possibility for an embodied knowledge.

Eventually, my contribution aims at suggesting a possible redefinition of the role of contemporary art research and the political posture of the artists in order to recreate an adjustable framework for the pressing changes we are witnessing as far as cultural commons and social contexts are concerned. Contemporary artists are invested by the big responsibility of generating tools for understanding reality: they become catalysts of perception and knowledge in ever-transforming contexts. Therefore, an operational perspective in art implies the interdependence of theory and practice which shape an artistic thought prompted to interdisciplinarity and dialog. Research practice becomes a possible path that nourishes an artistic intervention meant to rethink, reshape and access emerging commons, by being both trace and compass in the sea of contradictions and complexities characterizing our contemporary world.

References

Bruno, G. (2016). *Superfici. A proposito di estetica, materialità e media.* Monza: Johan&Levi.

Charbonnier, L. (2018). Cadre et regard, décontractions d'un dispositive. In B. Mario & J. Carbone (Eds.), *Voir selon les écrans, penser selon les écrans.* Sesto San Giovanni: Ed. Mimesis.

Deleuze, G., & Guattari, F. (1996). *What is philosophy?* New York: Columbia University Press.

Foucault, M. (1984). Des espaces autres. In Conférence au Cercle d'études architecturales, 14 mars 1967, Architecture, Mouvement, Continuité, n°5, October 1984, pp. 46–49, *Dits et écrits II.* Paris: Gallimard, «Quarto».

Korzibsky, A. (1933). A Non-Aristotelian system and its necessity for rigour in mathematics and physics. *Science and Sanity: An introduction to non-Aristotelian systems and general semantics* (pp. 747–761). New York: The International Non-Aristotelian Library Pub. Co.

La Cecla, F., & Zanini, P. (2004). *Lo stretto indispensabile. Storie e geografie di un tratto di mare limitato*. Milano: Bruno Mondadori.

Marin, L. (1988). Le cadre de la représentation et quelques-unes de ces figures. In *Cahiers du Musée National d'Art Moderne* (Vol. 24, pp. 62–81). "Art de voir, art de décrire", II. Paris: Centre Georges Pompidou.

Sinisgalli, R. (Ed.). (2006). *Il nuovo De Pictura di Leon Battista Alberti*. Roma, Kappa: The New De Pictura of Leon Battista Alberti.

Web References

Dream of sea. https://vimeo.com/22309536.

Eco-museo Mare Memoria Viva. https://www.marememoriaviva.it/.

Fondazione Orestiadi. https://www.fondazioneorestiadi.it/.

Gibellina Photo Road. https://www.gibellinaphotoroad.it/.

Minimum studio, Lo spazio necessario. https://www.minimumstudio.it/Lo-Spazio-Necessario-workshop-by-Novella-Oliana-and-Michela-Palermo.

Perriand, C. *France culture*. https://www.franceculture.fr/design/charlotte-perriand-lespace-ca-se-cree.

Qalandia International. https://www.qalandiyainternational.org/.

Sabine Réthoré. http://sabine-rethore.net/fr/cartes/mediterraneesans.html.

Teaching art or teaching to think like an artist? Cindy Foley' TED talk. https://www.youtube.com/watch?v=ZcFRfJb2ONk.

This sea is mine. https://www.e-flux.com/announcements/66002/qalandiya-international-iiithis-sea-is-mine/.

Zalab. http://www.zalab.org/projects/immagini-oltre-il-muro/.

Tate Gallery, John Hilliard. https://www.tate.org.uk/art/artists/john-hilliard-1287.

The Design for a Welcoming City: Urban Space and Visitor Flow

Ilaria Bollati and Luisa Collina

Abstract

This chapter explores the new ways of living and moving through and across urban spaces, inside an information and technology society. It introduces a design perspective, presenting a real case history: the new Visitor Space in Milan, crafted thanks to a scientific agreement between the *Politecnico di Milano* and the *Chamber of Commerce of Milano, Monza Brianza and Lodi*. It is an accurate design project to welcome people in an environment where private and public dimensions, as well as analog and digital components, come together creating a multisensory experience, favoring different ways to perceive and live a city.

1 Brief Introduction

Cities can be interpreted as a complex environment characterised by a deep and tangled stratification of tangible and intangible levels (Lupi 2013; Decandia 2014). A survey, commissioned by Domus in 2018, besides showing Milan as one of the most vibrant and desired metropolitan areas, emphasizes the presence of new current visitor fluxes toward the city not only for touristic reasons (Domus Forum 2018).

I. Bollati (✉) · L. Collina
Department of Design, Politecnico di Milano, Milan, Italy
e-mail: ilaria.bollati@polimi.it

L. Collina
e-mail: luisa.collina@polimi.it

E. Macrì et al. (eds.), *Cultural Commons and Urban Dynamics*,
https://doi.org/10.1007/978-3-030-54418-8_19

Symmetrically, cities, integrated with new enabling technologies, multiply their knowledge possibilities in terms of reading, interpreting, and the participation of the cultural asset.

In such a theoretical framework, the new *Visitor Space* in Milan has been crafted thanks to a scientific agreement between the *Politecnico di Milano* and the *Chamber of Commerce of Milano, Monza Brianza and Lodi.* As a real case history, it offers an accurate design project to welcome people in an environment where analog and digital components come together creating a multisensory experience. An informative place was born to favor knowledge, to share enjoyment and urban experiences, generating cultural values and different ways to perceive and live a city.

The central aspect of this essay is the design of a place of encounter among people. It puts in the field both urban and cultural commons, not limiting them to the physical reality of the space. It understands them as actions and not as objects, while private and public dimensions are blurring away (Borch and Kornberger 2015).

2 New Ways of Living and Moving Through and Across Vibrant Urban Spaces

Cities can be seen as vibrant, living, and dense urban compositions that are always different. "Cities are complex systems, with emerging qualities that cannot be reduced to static understandings or representations" (Lupi 2013). They are being intensively reshaped by unexpected dynamics. Taking on articulated connotations, their urban spaces are "more mixed than pure, not so smooth and homogeneous as changing, harlequin, zebra-striped and in multiple, connected networks" (Serres 1993, p. 270).

A lot of disciplines argue that the idea of a city—and its urban spaces above all—is undergoing deep, irreversible changes. In the past, the city itself was considered the pivot around which the entire territory was organised. It was a clear, delimited, and circumscribed entity. Today, however, it has expanded into a myriad of spaces, difficult to enclose within a limit or a boundary (Decandia 2014). The ancient physical hierarchies and dichotomies—center/edge, inside/outside, city/country, real/virtual, public/private—are less definite and seem to overlap, and blend with each other, becoming more and more difficult to understand and map out.

Increasingly fragmented and heterogeneous spatialities are emerging inside cities, activating several new fields of dialog and occasions of encounter. They take into account not only their urban morphology and architectures, but all their vibrant and ever-changing networks of human and social flows (Bollati 2014). Today, in particular, cities compete for liveliness and quality of life (Hall 1998; Richards and Palmer 2007; Morea 2019).

In this regard, *The Future of Cities* was discussed during the first *Domusforum* that took place in Milan in 2018, emphasizing the complexity of cities in terms of architecture, economy, social sciences, and citizen emotions. The proposed analysis was based on a survey commissioned by *Domus* and executed by Nielsen, gathering and measuring consumer data. Besides showing Milan as one of the liveliest and most creative metropolitan areas, with high-quality urban life and urban atmosphere, the research highlights the presence of four main current tourist migratory fluxes toward the city: A range of new Metropolis actors called *newcomer, traveler, globe trotter*, or *city user* (Domus Forum 2018).

A smooth, permeable, versatile, and flexible urban backbone allows metropolises like Milan to encourage new flows of ideas, content, and experiences that fuel and feed off each other, reciprocally. "A great variety of new ways of living and inhabiting, of moving through and across space, often transcending administrative and political borders" (Decandia 2014, p. 3) is outlining new, less-defined multiple city geographies (Serres 1993; Foucault 1994; Amin and Thrift 2002; Sassen 2004).

As Branzi put it, "A sort of invisible city is progressively replacing or putting into second place the physical, figurative one" (Branzi 2006, p. 12), and our visual viewpoint of the same city breaks into personal fragments and dynamic human grids. Relations between men and urban places are ever-changing. A polymorphous reality and a polyphonic interpretation of the city, with an extraordinary number of simultaneous dimensions, no longer takes shape based on points or objects, but rather on social relations, meanings, times, and ways of use. The multiplicity of the involved social interactions, information, people, and emotions holds an intense exchange with the surrounding architecture, drafting the tangible urban morphology.

The city is not a text that can be subjected to a single point of view, and our culture must grasp the sense of this new, absurd, elusive geography. Many interpretations of urban dynamics come to configure the urban place primarily as a relational field, describing the movement and life in a contemporary city as an entering-and-exiting of arbitrary juxtapositions of "urban interiors" that generate situations: Interactions between places, information, and people, gradually moving the focus from the single space, from the single moment to the process of living in a public city (Bourriaud 2002; Branzi 2006).

It should, therefore, be noted that the relationships at play and the processes that take shape in urban spaces (despite appearing as uniform flows) are not easily interpretable. Related behaviors often reveal heterogeneous purposes and multiple reasons. Those who move in the urban fabric do so moved by different reasons.

3 An Authentic Exploration of the Urban Space Belongs to Us

We can no longer be satisfied with seeing only what can be seen, by gazing at a distance, but we need to get closer to things again; enter inside the territory; re-discover its variegated density and range of populations. A density that cannot be understood from afar, remaining

> in those towers from which we once believed we could learn about the world, but one that can only be grasped if we manage to immerse ourselves in the living body of its flesh so as to begin an authentic exploration of the urban landscape that belongs to us. (Decandia 2014, p. 3)

An urban landscape is not only the physical result of different human interventions of remote or recent pasts that continue to last today. Factually, it consists of the methods of use, the meanings, or the symbolic appropriation created by people who live, work, and visit that same urban space (Dal Pozzolo 2001). It is simultaneously both a built environment and a social setting.

Urban space is the element that identifies the story of a community, whether it is seen as a place of permanence (for locals or city users) or of transient nomadic presence (for visitors such as newcomers, travelers, and globe trotters). It is an area that hosts a history—either a general one or many specific—that interacts with the actual daily life of that same area, creating a present synthesis of possible relationships between the past and future. Urban spaces are not isolated entities but a complex system of places, activities, events, initiatives, and actions that occur at the edges between ephemeral—all that has a short life—and provisional—all that moves into the medium-long term (Fassi 2012; De Rosa and Mazzarello 2019).

Adapting the definition of the concept of Place—as proposed by *Studio Azzurro*—to the urban context, we could assert that an urban space "is also the appreciation of individual aspects that are each equally able to develop a dialogue with the complex forces of the global world. […] Involvement with a place means vitalizing and caring about its landscape and culture but also generating an approach toward the place itself, a concept of public good that rekindles love, concern and respect" (Cirifino et al. 2011, p. 25). Urban spaces form a mosaic of dynamics that reflects the roots and cultural orientations of the resident community, its new members, and the visitors who explore the city, extracting its identity and understanding both its memory and imagination (Trimarchi 2019).

Therefore, a key question emerges: How can we facilitate and gradually bring out virtuous circles of cultural development and knowledge of the metropolitan territory and urban context we live in or are about to visit?

On the one hand, as locals, we would like to further explore the urban context we live in, letting ourselves be surprised by secret city spots or places we take for granted too often. On the other hand, as visitors, we have recently become more aware and sensitive to environmental sustainability, heterogeneous contexts, and to the cultural and socioeconomic conditions of our destinations. A new desire to "see"—even thanks to new technologies—poses further questions about the sense of the places we live and visit, increasingly mixing the real and imaginary knowledge of a destination—the tangible and intangible experiences—looking for the spontaneity and authenticity of places.

Following this logic, the city and its urban spaces become a "place of the mind" and not just a roster of places and attractions that are structured by tourist guides imposing a limited amount of "must-see"—buildings, artworks, specific environments—and forgetting about many others. The city is a personal collage of a multitude of tips, information, and suggestions offered by different sources such as book guides, websites, blogs, friends, locals, spontaneous encounters, and other tourist experiences. Although travel and culture professionals often tend to propose targeted and studied itineraries and formats of the visitor experience, the role of the visitor has changed, as visitors now have the opportunity to be active protagonists and planners of their own experience. A personalized experience and the possibility of "feeling part of a place" become components that are worthy of consideration when designing experiences (Bollati et al., forthcoming).

4 Exploring Urban Space Inside an Information and Technology Society

According to Gartner (2010), people today access the Internet mainly through mobile technology, since today's visitors "are now in large percentage digital natives, born and bred in virtual worlds" (Amaro and Tornatora 2019, p. 144). Whether we like it or not, technologies are becoming ever-present in our everyday life and they are gradually causing changes in daily habits. Mobile devices are changing the way people access information, city knowledge, urban contexts and events, habits, and culture. They enable visitors to connect with others, search for data, and create personal and shareable content. Technological advances and digital transformations are deeply influencing our lives, impacting our habits, and how we perceive our surroundings (Castells 2000).

Moreover, the boundary between virtual and physical space is thinning and becoming more invisible. We live in different spaces and times simultaneously, and digital access to services is increasingly transforming into something more physical in order to allow a real exchange of experience and knowledge (Piccinno 2019). For instance, today's mobile technology and location-based services—apart from providing additional information and directions—are an excellent new opportunity for cities and their cultural institutions to reach a wider audience (Proctor 2011), enhancing traditional cultural consumption and supporting the visitor's tangible experience (Ceconello 2012).

The first web-conveyed approach to and knowledge of a city has a greater impact on visitors' choices, and social networks allow direct easy access to useful information for their visit. However, travelers tend to rely more on information received from other visitors rather than that supplied by tour operators, given that direct experiences are considered as a guarantee of neutrality and truth of judgment, unconditioned by any particular interests. The experience of our peers and the word-of-mouth is perceived as more reliable than the professional advice given by those who provide the cultural offer (Caves 2000).

Therefore, technological and mobile devices are able to support visitors during all the stages of their journey: Organisation, arrival, activity planning, and return home, with regards to their demands, needs, or wishes. "Technology is therefore an inevitable challenge, but it also offers an extraordinary opportunity. It offers effective instruments that make it possible to gather, order, and display data in ways that were hitherto unknown" (Cirifino et al. 2011, p. 24).

5 The Specific Case: A Multimedia Living Room for Visitors

Thanks to an interdisciplinary scientific agreement between the *Politecnico di Milano* and the *Chamber of Commerce of Milano, Monza Brianza and Lodi*, the new *Visitor Space* in Milan—a project designed to welcome people in an environment where analog and digital technologies come together creating a multisensory experience—was crafted.

In July 2018, the *Chamber of Commerce of Milano Monza Brianza Lodi*—owner of the venue in which the project is based—together with *Yes Milano*—the new Milan City Council brand dedicated to the promotion of the city and to the organisation of events—asked *Politecnico di Milano* to help design a new space for visitors, as the previous urban center was closed that year.

The space—which opened in December 2018—is an emblematic and strategic space not only for the two involved Institutions but also for the city. It is located in a historical building in the city center, *Camera dei Notari* in *Palazzo Giureconsulti.* It is a welcoming and highly technological place, created by a team of experts inside the University, in collaboration with *Camer Anebbia*—a multimedia visual artist collective, operating in the field of interactive and sensitive spaces.

The project development and the *Action Research* process (Muratovski 2010) included a meta-design work structured through data collection (both qualitative and quantitative), desk research, benchmarking, meetings, and co-design sessions through round tables. The project takes on a set of questions deriving from a trivial yet crucial assumption: At least once in our lives, each of us has been and will be a visitor. Hence, what needs do we have in a city we know nothing about yet? Which services do we use? Are there any aids that can promote our experience and increase our connection with the living spaces, usually taken for granted?

The first stage of the project identified one key need. Every time we move around a city for a while, we feel the need to stop and take a break. We need to take a breather along the way. That break, which is propaedeutic to the visit, allows us to recharge ourselves mentally, instrumentally, and physically. As visitors, we are continually invited to collect useful information to outline a personal experience of the city or use our personal devices to find our way in new contexts. Moreover, after long journeys, we feel the need of unwinding our tired bodies. These are the reasons that triggered our concept: An urban "Living Room" to welcome visitors and citizens in an environment where analog and digital technologies come together, creating a multisensory and cross-media experience. A place that favors knowledge, not in the sense of accumulated information but rather as one that presents a great cognitive and atmospheric kaleidoscope. It is an informative, engaging, and unexpected space designed to help discover Milan and the region of *Lombardia*,

Fig. 1 An image of the space in the daytime. © Samuele Baruzzi, Politecnico di Milano

which have two different souls: one that fully expresses itself in the daytime, and one in the nighttime (Fig. 1).

During the day, visitors learn and release information in a mutual relationship of exchange with the domestic atmosphere and space. A warm environment with a strong visual character—equipped with tapestries and custom-made wooden furniture and design objects—welcomes the city guest.

Once inside, two touch screens—similar to big mirrors—can be activated by the presence and touch of visitors, giving access to a hothouse of ideas and events in the city. On the left side of the room, there is a stylized map of Milan, suggesting frequently asked information and itineraries to follow. This map welcomes an analogical interaction through which visitors can propose their own sightseeing and cultural tours of the city. Underneath, lockers with appropriate technical equipment allow charging of personal devices. On the opposite side, there is a *stream machine*, which is a large interactive monitor. It looks like a hanging picture that welcomes the visitor with colorful changing patterns (Fig. 2).

Every visitor is invited to create endless personal combinations: After a brief questionnaire, visitors can send the created image directly to their own inbox, transforming it into a gift, a souvenir. This method allows the *Visitor Space* to track and develop the knowledge of people and their motivations and desires. Finally, this urban Living Room becomes a place that displays the world of Design. Independent publishing houses or *Design Magazines* offer books to read here. Design furniture gives character to the space in cyclically changing collaborations. The furnishing elements and their oversized narrative labels become a vehicle for the discovery of the world of Italian Design.

Moreover, the *Chamber of Commerce*, one of the main stakeholders, expressed a clear need from the start, from the very first meetings: The space should be experienced all day, 24 h, even when the doors are closed and no staff is inside. This way, the space is able to show both its day and its night souls. Hidden

Fig. 2 An image of the interactive installation called *stream machine*. © Politecnico di Milano

projectors, to be activated solely during the night, transform the big windows into transparent walls: A real multimedia magic lantern. The projections are interactive. On the inner walls of the *Camera dei Notari*, the projections change simply with one touch. All one has to do is choose and touch the "theme" on the glass window. By doing so, never-before-seen multimedia content is activated (Fig. 3).

By touching these words, the visitor changes the projection and, after a few minutes of video, can move on to the choice of a different theme. The narration begins. Decorations and videos come to life on the ceiling and vertical surfaces. For a first experimental experience, it was decided to offer a sensory immersion in three other places of interest inside the territory of Milan, Monza Brianza, and Lodi as well: One that can be easily visited—*Tempio dell'Incoronata in Lodi*—one that is inaccessible—*inside Villa Reale in Monza*—and one that is easily accessible but that is little known not only to tourists but to locals as well—*interior frescoes of Palazzo Giureconsulti*.

The windows and the perimeter of the space become access membranes. They attract passersby. Once again, they invite them to stop and want to "see", investigate further, raising their eyes both physically and conceptually. The accessibility denoting this tiny space and its openness to the urban community should be understood as permeability: As the ability to "*enter a space*" without hesitation and effort (Poot et al. 2015) (Fig. 4).

Content comes out of the physical perimeters and meets the visitor with emotion. In this project, *Design* enhances *Technology*: It helps make it accessible and increases the value of the learning and emotional experience. It combines *Technology* (tools) with *Art* (language) and *Territory* (substance).

Fig. 3 A concept visualisation of the space in the nighttime. © Ilaria Bollati, Politecnico di Milano

Fig. 4 An image of the use of an interactive window as a content access membrane. © Samuele Baruzzi, Politecnico di Milano

6 Perforating the Skin of Things

The presented project suggests how *Design* can be a trigger of cultural city experiences, becoming a know-how provider and social engager. It also shows how *Digital technology* has become a strong support of the tourist experience, activating fields of dialog with growing heterogeneous connotations. Digital reagent devices react to the visitor presence and elicit the reaction. They create dialog, combine differences, and trigger memories, multiplying the levels of narrative urban space content.

The *Visitor Space* guides people toward the discovery of the city from a new point of view, multiplying the diopters. The area of the city of Milan presents itself —offering essential information for general orientation—through various events and activities. It aims at stimulating both the resident community and outside visitors toward the discovery of unknown approaches and views of the city. The *Visitor Space* suggests new relations between the different points, attractions, and cultural places of the city map, rearranged in a great variety of possible ways, via reciprocal, nonsymmetrical correlations.

Therefore, it invites to move beyond the apparent conventional picture of the city, widening the boundaries of our gaze: "Perforating the skin of things, to see how things become things and the world becomes world" (Merleau Ponty 1964, p. 49); "leave aside everything that prevents us from seeing, all the passed-on ideas, the pre-constituted images that continue to encumber our visual field and capacity for understanding" (quoted by Barenghi 1992, p. 346). This space enables us to have a more complete, authentic, and spontaneous knowledge of the urban context, fostering mutual exchanges between citizens and visitors. By sharing common values, residents are preparing to share spaces and spend time together, overcoming the distinction between city host and guest.

The *Visitor Space* helps increase knowledge of the city and keeps it alive, triggering lively and meaningful processes of learning. Its multimedia and analogic content is not made of "*finished stories*", but relational and interactive ones. Visitors are offered the possibility to combine them according to personal preferences, creating their own expressive and urban adventures, using their own sensibilities, needs, tastes, and imagination within an environment that is not ready-made but offers a "series of possibilities for action" (Diodato 2005, p. 57). During the experience, multimedia and analog interfaces appeal not only to the intellect but also to the senses, "to open up affective, vital relations with city places once more, and produce, energize, put into circulation, and socialize a collective intelligence to which the capacity to cultivate and take care of the different qualities of territories could once again be entrusted" (Decandia 2014, p. 4).

The multimedia language tells an urban story "in a smooth, coherent, and absorbing way; but above all, it is the language through which we communicate today, capturing our imagination and expressing itself in new forms of behavior. It has led to the inevitable influence that the medium has exerted over us for years but, if inverted, allows us to potentially reconnect with a shared feeling, a vehicle for dialogue between different people from far and wide, in a way that has not happened for centuries. Its language has a certain similarity to the oral culture on which the characteristics of discursive thought were based on: Indeterminacy, repeatability, immediacy, simultaneousness, fragmentation, and connectivity" (Cirifino et al. 2011, p. 24).

7 Conclusions

The *Visitor Spac*e is characterised by an overlap and commixture of what we used to consider polarities: The boundaries between tangible and intangible, hardware and software, private and public are indeed thinning and blurring away (Borch and Kornberger 2015). The case here analysed occurs in an institutional—although private—space used for shared enjoyment, generating cultural values and different ways to perceive and live a city; a place of encounter between people. While the *Chamber of Commerce* is the owner of the space, the visitor is the owner of the personal cultural experience he brings inside it. However, the space consumption is public, open to all: Citizens and external visitors without any discrimination.

We could, therefore, conclude that the *Visitor Space* taken into account is neither private nor public: It is the *Chamber of Commerce*'s answer to a will to create a space with a cognitive advantage, while interacting with the territorial government.

The importance of public city spaces is increasingly recognised as a crucial feature by many different scholars. The theory of the commons, as this edited volume demonstrates, is aimed at rethinking some urban practices, especially where a failure on part of the market or state is found (Borch and Kornberger 2015). The case study this chapter focuses on is, conversely, an exemplary case in which public value is provided by a partnership of public and private institutions. The project here presented and analyzed outlines a clear sharing of urban experiences; a case study in which the contexts of state and market learn from the teachings of experiences of urban commons, and implement a virtuous process of coproduction and co-appropriation, while maintaining a clear distinction from the notions of urban and cultural commons.

These urban and cultural commons are not limited to the physical reality of the space, but rather take on their meaning from practice. They are actions, not objects. The *Visitor Spac*e generates an exchange of cognitive flows with the local community and territory. These flows are directed toward specific cultural sites; they bring together and coagulate virtuous explorations that are "softer" than congested mass experiences. This brings to us different urban touchpoints where people can relate at different levels and at different times when experiencing the city.

Visitor Space Credits—*Yes Milano Tourism Space*

Project
Camera di Commercio di Milano, Monza Brianza e Lodi
Supported by
Comune di Milano e YESMILANO
Designed by
Politecnico di Milano
In collaboration with
La Triennale di Milano
Curators
Luisa Collina | Politecnico di Milano
Project coordination and executive production
Ilaria Bollati, Claudia Mastrantoni | Politecnico di Milano
With Samuele Baruzzi | Politecnico di Milano
Visual identity and graphic design
Umberto Tolino | Politecnico di Milano with Agnese Bartolucci, Riccardo Fuccelli, Eleonora Rossetti, Marco Valli | Politecnico di Milano
Exhibit design
Ilaria Bollati, Claudia Mastrantoni | Politecnico di Milano
Michela Fenoli | EXPLORA S.C.p.A
Multimedia project
CamerAnebbia, StreamColors and Politecnico di Milano
Special thanks to
Ethimo

References

Amaro, O., & Tornatora, M. (2019). In C. Benincasa, G. Neri, & M. Trimarchi, *New maps for the desires of an emerging world* (pp. 101–126). New York: Columbia University Press.

Amin, A., & Thrift, N. (2002). *Cities: Reimaging the Urban*. Cambrige: Polity Press.

Bollati, I. (2014). *VOICES: an urban map of sentiment. Tratto da Tafter Journal, 73*. https://www.tafterjournal.it/2014/07/04/voices-an-urban-map-of-sentiment/.

Bollati, I., Mastrantoni, C., Tolino, U., & Collina, L. (forthcoming). New technological space for tourists. Design as a trigger of experience, osmotic-membrane interface, know-how provider and social engager. *Design Culture(s): Cumulus 2020*. Rome.

Borch, C., & Kornberger, M. (2015). *Urban commons. Rethinking the city*. Oxon: Space, materiality and the normative. Abingdon: Routledge.

Bourriaud, N. (2002). *Relational Aesthetics*. Les presses du réel.

Branzi, A. (2006). *Modernità debole e diffusa. Il mondo del progetto all'inizio del XXI secolo*. Milano: Skirà.

Castells, M. (2000). *The rise of the network society*. Cambrige: Blackwell Publishers.

Caves, R. E. (2000). *Creative industries: Contracts between art and commerce*. Cambridge: Harvard University Press.

Ceconello, M. (2012). *Tafter Journal*. Tratto da Mobile technologies: new ways to access tourism, culture and cities. https://www.tafterjournal.it/2012/10/01/mobile-technologies-new-ways-to-access-tourism-culture-and-cities/.

Cirifino, F., Giardina Papa, E., & Rosa, P. (2011). *Musei di narrazione. Percorsi interattivi e affreschi multimediali*. Milano: Silvana Editoriale.

Dal Pozzolo, L. (2001). *Fuori città senza campagna: paesaggio e progetto nella città diffusa*. Milano: Franco Angeli.

De Rosa, A., & Mazzarello, M. (2019). Italianway: An entrepreneurial innovation for hospitality in contemporary. In M. Brugleri, *Multidisciplinary design of sharing services* (pp. 229–239). Berlin: Springer.

Decandia, L. (2014). Towards a polyphonic urban score. *City, territory and architecture*. Springer Open.

Diodato, R. (2005). *Estetica del virtuale*. Milano: Bruno Mondadori.

Domus Forum, (2018). The future of cities. Retrieved from https://www.domusweb.it/en/events/forum-2018/2018/newcomers-travellers-and-city-users-who-are-the-actors-of-the-new-metropolis.html.

Fassi, D. (2012). *Temporary urban solution*. Maggioli Editore.

Foucault, M. (1994). *Eterotropia. Luoghi e non-luoghi metropolitani*. Milano: Mimesis. Millepiani.

Gartner. (January 13, 2010). *Gartner highlights key predictions for IT organizations and users in 2010 and beyond*. Retrieved May 18, 2011, from Gartner http://www.gartner.com/it/page.jsp?id=1278413.

Hall, P. G. (1998). *Cities in civilization: Culture. Technology and urban order*. London: Weidenfeld and Nicolson.

Lupi, G. (2013). *Intercettare il futuro. Mappe del possibile*. Retrieved from *Tafter Journal, 55*. http://www.tafterjournal.com.

Merleau Ponty, M. (1964). *L'Oeil et l'Esprit*. Paris: Gallimard.

Morea, V. (2019). Art and territorial changes in the Italian experience. In C. Benincasa, G. Neri, & M. Trimarchi, *Art and economics in the city. New cultural maps* (pp. 38–47). New York: Columbia University Press.

Muratovski, G. (2010). Design and design research: The conflict between the principles in design education and practices in industry. *Design Principles and Practices, 4*(2), 377–386.

Piccinno, G. (2019). Between the digital and the physical: Reinventing the spaces to accommodate sharing services. In M. Bruglieri, *Multidisciplinary design of sharing services*. (pp. 183–206). Berlin: Springer.

Poot, T., Van Acker, M., & De Vos, E. (2015). The public interior: The meeting place for the urban and the interior. *IDEA Journal, 2015*, 44–55.

Proctor, N. (2011). *From headphones to microphones: mobile social media in the Museum as distributed network*. Tratto da Smithsonian Institution. https://cdn.shopify.com/s/files/1/0062/7112/files/FromHeadphonesToMicrophonesExtract.pdf.

Richards, G., & Palmer, R. (2007). *Eventful cities: Cultural management and urban revitalisation*. Amsterdam: Elsevier.

Sassen, S. (2004). Local actors in global politics. *Current Sociology, 52*(4), 649–670.

Serres, M. (1993). *Les origines de la géométrie. Tiers livre des fondations*. Paris: Flammarion.

Trimarchi, M. (2019). *Conference urban common and cultural value. Cultural commons and urban dynamics*. Tratto da innovativeheritage.net.

The Vicissitudes of Digital Dissent

Arthur Clay

Abstract

The paper is inspired by diverse levels of agency in the arts. It covers present uses of communication technologies in the arts and how these intersect with social activism, offering a basis of understanding of content and method of the process of social protest using virtual space. The artworks and the scenarios, in which they are presented, are used to establish "a guide", or a repertoire of common practice. More sophisticated levels of agency are approached through coupling common electronic marketing practices to the use of new technologies such as Augmented Reality, in order to point out subversive ways of protesting in areas where either physical presence is impossible or where public assembly is repressed. Being controversial in nature, the paper acts as a guide on how to make protesting in virtual domains real and how to be socially disruptive using communication technologies. The paper concludes with the coming to the understanding that a need for change is key to innovation and social renewal, and to conceive possible scenarios for (art) works that use art as an agency to advocate change.

A. Clay (✉)
Virtuale Switzerland, Basel, Switzerland
e-mail: arthur@virtuale-switzerland.org

'Digital Art Weeks' International, Zurich, Switzerland

E. Macrì et al. (eds.), *Cultural Commons and Urban Dynamics*,
https://doi.org/10.1007/978-3-030-54418-8_20

1 Looking Glass Culture

With the ever-increasing use of new communication tools and Internet-based media, a new era of art practice and art experience has opened up to us through the simple understanding that our smartphones are now the looking glass into the virtual worlds that the twenty-first century has authored. The new communication tools that we carry with us in our pockets are steadily increasing in power and are now allowing us to do more with each coming day. The culture of today is one built around mobility to the point of establishing a society of nomads, who wander from virtual space to virtual space by simply substituting physical movement with the movement of data. We login, and we are there, and we are at the same time everywhere. Our identities become a mix between what we are and how we want to be perceived: multifarious, omnipresent, and perpetually updating.

Of course, along with our new electronic identity and all of the newly found powers of transformation that correspond with it are the transgressions and infractions that come about through the different ways in which our security can be compromised and our privacy infringed upon through such practices as hacking, phishing, spamming, cyberstalking, and of course, through information theft. For the sake of keeping equilibrium between what has been gained and what has been lost, we might pose the following question: Are the infractions mentioned solely the tools of cybercrime, or could they be part of a movement that promotes social change through agency?

As an example, the term "iJacking" refers in actuality to the theft and use of third-party electronic data, or simply termed as information theft. However, when the concept of iJacking is extended and applied to the appropriation of space for the presentation of arts, it can be described as something that is not causing infraction but allowing intervention to take place, which is in actuality aesthetically charged social agency. Proof of this is the advent of the "invisible arts", or art that is created in such a way that it can only be viewed by the use of a smartphone. When a device is required to view an artwork, the setup is called a "looking glass" situation, because the artwork is out of plain sight and the eye needs some form of technical assistance to view it.

The invisible arts use new technologies such as Augmented and Virtual Reality and the artworks created with those technologies are made much more powerful when they are linked to emerging technologies such as computer vision, ubiquitous sensing, and artificial intelligence. Further, invisible artworks can be effortlessly put in the hands of anyone owning a mobile phone through innovations in the field of applications for smart devices, whose advent and wide use have established an unprecedented moment in which art can be presented outside of the established venues of the art world and to an audience that goes far beyond the confines of the art world (Fig. 1).

When technology moves forward and puts new tools in the hands of the artist, innovation often takes place as well on the conceptual level. By flipping the concept of ijacking data to ijacking space, a conceptual "retooling" results, and ijacking the

Fig. 1 Public monuments are often the best meeting points in a city and were perfect targets for use as AR gateways. The Kropcke Uhr, for example, is located in the city centre of Hanover and was ijacked by masking its windows with dedicated graphics which made four of the works available to the public through simply scanning in the given QR codes

electronic appropriation of space for the presentation of works of invisible art is made possible. This came about as an innovation brought forward through the mass use of new communication tools and the widespread influence of hacker culture. Basically, it can be said that from the use of the smartphone in sync with the new global navigation satellite system, an entire genre of new art form has been put in the palm of our hands.

Although diverse in form, the invisible arts are slowly surmounting to a new wave of socially active artworks, which are capable of awakening discussion amongst the general public, because, outside of portraying a practice of savvy artistic intervention in public space, artists are tending to infuse their works with political messages addressing the present social agenda.

Exhibitions that focus on the presentation of invisible arts are, therefore, hidden and mysterious by their very nature. Ironically, those very qualities make it plausible to address a mass audience, because the artworks are already in the palm of the hand of everyone who has a smart device.

How such works are able to cross over from the invisible to the visible is made possible through combined use of new technologies, which include geotagging and image recognition. Geotagging involves providing latitude and longitude coordinates to where the works are to be placed. These coordinates are then used for linking media content to locations. The media simply downloads to the smart device and is then visible at a set location; image recognition is used to match up and overlay material from virtual space over an image in real space, offering the possibility of adding a second layer to mask out the images in real space. Regardless of which technology is used to make the invisible visible, when we view the results over a mobile device, the results are unique and the experience impressive.

The phenomena of iJacking spaces bring an era of new public art that spawned by technical innovation, and because technical innovation has taken place in electronic communication, it is obvious that art created by applying those innovations should be infused with social agency and be used to move public opinion through a process involving mass communication at the level of social networking.

Given that there are limited opportunities to exhibit in established art spaces and that a gatekeeping attitude prevails in many such spaces, it is hardly surprising that artists would be influenced by hacker culture and are now learning how to expand the possibilities of social engagement to overstep the gatekeepers. It is also then hardly a wonder that an exhibition dedicated to ijacking space would come to use anon culture as an integral part of its branding, in order to clearly designate that ijacking spaces takes place by occupying space for artistic intervention by digital means.

There are several parallels that can be drawn between the invisible arts and a few of the original goals of anons. One of these goals that could be considered as having something in common with anons is the intent to stage a retaliation against the aforementioned gatekeepers of established art spaces and their gatekeeping strategies, which set the limits and boundaries in terms of the scope of what art institutions bring and what type of dialogue is offered to the art community and the general public. Setting such limitations may serve the purpose of creating a hierarchy of artists, but at the same time, it drastically reduces the number of artists who are able to show their work and succeed at establishing themselves as professional artists (Fig. 2).

Acting against such gatekeeping practices in order to bring about a more encompassing and inclusive vision for the arts is parallel to how anons have often targeted groups who were responsible for enforcing copyright-focused campaigns. In a similar manner, exhibitions that make use of ijacking spaces to target cultural institutions, who create and enforce boundaries through the adoption of practices of commercial gallery spaces, are forced through virtual squatting to operate as true institutes of culture who are pushed to open up and act beyond trend.

2 Digital Dissent

The best presentations of artworks have always been those that unfold out of an all-embracing conceptual basis, which also determines how the content of the exhibition is to be experienced by those who view it. Along this line of thought and after several years of gaining experience in the production and presentation of invisible arts, I conceived and realized a far-reaching project in an act “digital dissent”, which explored the application of ijacking space with contrasting

Fig. 2 The use of a "Walk of Fame Stars" concept as gateways to AR artworks proved to be a very successful approach to getting the general public to view the works. By placing the stars exactly at the locations where the artworks can be viewed, no instructions outside of a "scan me!" were needed. After scanning the QR code, the artworks would appear in perfect positions for viewing

technologies and through a variety of media. The project took the term iJacking as its title and used it to portray the actual strategy for the presentation of invisible artworks using guerrilla-like tactics in both private and public spaces. Adding the name of the city to the title, it became clear that the approach had to do with ijacking space and not information and that the project was viral in nature and could move from city to city.

The complete title of the project was, therefore "iJacking Hannover" and it began as a forced monologue that moved into a dialogue with prominent art institutes in Hannover. I term the monologue "false" because it was carried out via email spamming targeting all possible staff members of the institutes under fire. The normal communications route would have been to write to those in authority who have the power to decide. However, as the project made use of the latest communication tools, I found it to be very appropriate to also adopt certain aspects of the digital culture from which the widespread use of those tools was spawned. A broader communication practice was therefore of paramount importance, in which transparency, being one of the key elements in today's digital culture, was its most obvious characteristic. So by sending the same emails directly to directors, board members, curators, educators, docents, attendants, staff members, and all the way down to temporary interns, the playing field was levelled and by doing so the established hierarchy and decision chain were ignored as well as undermined.

The mailings were, of course, a jest but one that was flavoured with the threat of an illegal occupation. Basically, the mails were used as the primary tool for announcing to the targeted institutes that their spaces would be "ijacked" and what the terms and conditions were to avoid it through participation. It was made clear to them that the consequence was that artworks that they did not select would be used, installed, and marketed as a standard exhibition taking place in their space. Although the works were not visible, they would still have the effect of physically occupying the space, because it would pull the attention of the visitors to the museum away from what was actually on display in real space for that which was on display in virtual space (Fig. 3).

Directly put, I designed the project so that the sacred realm of the museum would be transformed into a pirated art space, blurring the director's focus, the curators' choices, and distracting the public from the actual chosen content of the institute. Along with the virtual takeover of the space, the artworks which make up that takeover and which define the exhibition, as one taking place in a parallel virtual space, would be widely marketed as artworks selected by parasitic entities unwillingly hosted by the institute. This would, of course, be implemented to spark a conversation with the public that is quite distant from the one intended by the institute. So, the purpose of such an occupation was not only to appropriate space through because it could simply be done, or even to promote a completely new genre of artwork, but more so to ignite a discussion on the changes that are being brought through the drift away from the established practices and spaces.

Fig. 3 An application was used to swap contents out in the exhibition at the Kestner Gesellschaft during the iJacking Hannover project. Here, the work of the artist Nevin Aladag was digitally erased from view as a commentary on the exhibition itself and also to nurture a dialogue around such tactics when they are employed to critique an exhibition

In terms of how the institutes reacted to the spamming, the threat of being ijacked, and how the project team dealt with it, I can say that if a targeted institute was open to having a dialogue with me then they could participate as an equal partner in a discussion concerning the changes in arts organizations in light of today's increasing use of virtual space; if the targeted institute was not open to talking with me and taking part in the discussion, the emails would simply continue as before and in addition to the that personal visits would be made to the institute asking floor staff and visitors if they knew when the planned iJacking exhibition would begin or if they had already heard about the iJacking exhibition (Fig. 4).

The ensuing state of confusion brought about further opportunities. For example, when a staff member felt that something was not proper and felt obliged to report the incident to others. This guerrilla-like approach also placed a strong accent on the fact that there seemed to be a complete lack of awareness of the technological revolution in the institutes. This pointed out the apparent irony that institutes believe that they operate with the conviction that they are the leading force behind contemporary art and believe that they are the centre point of contemporary society.

When being overrun by technology that allows for the placing of an exhibition inside their own institute without their permission or ability to do anything about it, it becomes clear that they are not at the centre point for the arts nor are they

Fig. 4 An image of the tour map created for the iJacking Hannover project. Distributed throughout the city and easy available to the general public, the map offered a comprehensive overview of the artworks on display, where they were placed, and how they could be accessed via smart devices

participating in contemporary society as it participates in itself: i.e. through the rise of the virtual. Although the project was certainly in the form of a disinformation campaign, the efforts made to disrupt the establishment helped to establish a branding of the project and aided greatly in spreading the existence of the project by word of mouth.

3 Adopting the Lutz

The process described above where space is virtually occupied is in line with the anon concept of the "lutz", because it embraces the practice of pranking and entertainment to approach issues that are actually serious conflicts. For the iJacking Hannover project and its approach to digital occupation, the adoption of the lutz can be understood as an attempt in experimenting with new ways of partaking in the art world without asking for institutional consent and to force a dialogue with it that is of mutual benefit to a more varied selection of artists and to a wider audience. Although the spamming of emails and the ad hoc visits were a jesting undertaking, the content of the artworks as well as the strategy that put them into the public eye were not, because both pointed out serious issues in regard to the arts in society and did so by pointing out problems that we all share such as decaying environment, the problems of consumerism, and issues of social decay.

Although the motivations and the methods used to present artworks for such invisible art projects are almost one and the same as those of the anon, the efforts made in presenting art are not in retaliation against copyright-focused campaigns or copyright protection agencies. In a similar manner, however, they do make a strong statement against institutional censorship that is consequential to present-day policies in curation, which are more often than less created through influencers stemming from the marketing offices of art schools and from institutes that focus on art sales.

Another good example of this from another perspective is the widespread problems created by ageism, which are centre to a widespread trend of institutions solely interested in selecting the "young and promising". This becomes apparent in that curatorial practices which repeatedly totter between the up and promising and the truly established. Raising a voice against this through including artists outside of these poles is a move towards establishing a wider participatory basis in the arts by acknowledging its role in transforming society by the inclusive and not the exclusive (Fig. 5).

By operating with a high degree of mediating ability at the interface between the individual and the masses, invisible art exhibition projects are able to take the needed opportunity to reflect on and open up a potentially controversial discourse surrounding the arts and their political and social nature. The process brings these into dialogue with institutions that strive to structure and shape society but who seem to remain partial to extending a wider notion of art by acknowledging the need for inclusion.

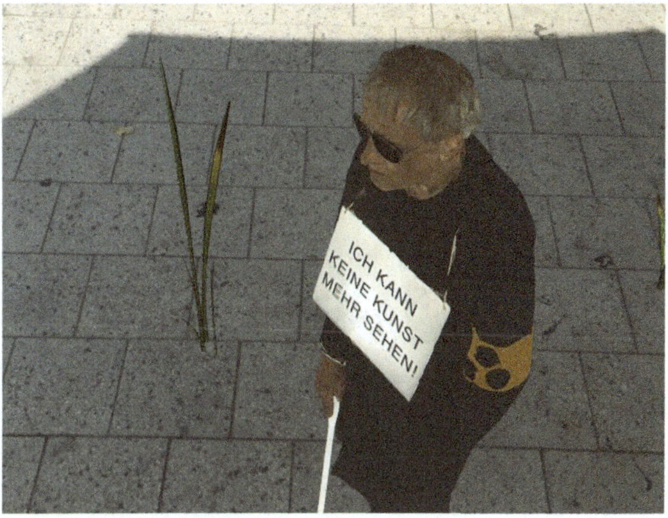

Fig. 5 The image depicts a new virtual version of the acclaimed artwork "Ich kann keine Kunst mehr sehen!" by Tim Ulrichs. Created as part of the Virtuale Switzerland bootstrapping program, this work is a good example of how an artwork can take on new dimensions when it is revived through re-creating it using modern media such as AR

Of course, changing attitudes requires that exhibitions involving a wider circle of artists still require a certain amount of success that is all too often measured through the quantitative response of the media and the enthusiasm of the public, which is reflected solely through the amount of media obtained and the number of visitors to the exhibition. Fortunately, what exists in virtual space can spread virtually, and all of the tools that are used in social media to evaluate activity can be used in a creative manner to provide the needed key performance factors to measure the response at the quantitative level.

This is, of course, accomplished in part by having prominent institutes take part, increasing the number of artists participating, and by paying close attention to where the "hot spots" in a city are and how these can be used to catch the attention of pedestrians who willingly engage as visitors to the exhibition (Fig. 6).

So the key factor in engaging members of what can be termed a random public is inherent in carefully pairing the artworks with the locations at which they are going to be seen. So, it is the relationship between the artwork and the surroundings that sparks a dialogue between the artwork and the place it is viewed in. It is the dialogue itself that inspires longer engagements by viewers, which in turn allows participation to be extended to those who are curious as to what others are doing and to be propelled through social networks as experiences summed up in images and Selfies go viral through clicks and shares.

Fig. 6 The image shows a moment of the AR Performance of "iLife in iLand" with the artist Regina Frank. Here, a wide range of plants that have the ability to heal environmental misdeeds slowly grow out of the climate change dress she is wearing. The occupation of the performance by digital means became obvious as the performer vanished behind a wall of overgrowth in an act against human-centric behaviour

4 Towards the Viral

Although the use of AR to create art has spread since around 2005, the technology was only being used by the selected few, who were in the position to make use of it through their skills as artists and their ability to code. However, if the prerequisite to create such artworks is the ability to code, then the selection of artists as well as the number of artworks available is limited. So one aspect in curating the iJacking Hannover project was the need to address these limitations, because if the social impact was to be the result of the exhibition, a strategy that goes beyond offering opportunities only to those who are technologically versed was conceptually fundamental to the project (Fig. 7).

So, in addition to working with artists who were native to the field of AR, I used a strategy of bootstrapping in the iJacking project, which allowed artists to participate who were not in the position to take advantage of the new technologies due to lack of technical knowledge. The approach I took was to team them up with technically adept collaborators, so that the artists could create artworks using AR technologies. This allowed them to extend what they were already voicing in their work with materials and dimensions that were not yet known to them. The project, therefore, engaged established and not so established local artists with the opportunity to create invisible artworks and integrated them into the iJacking Hannover program. The effort resulted in putting innovations that were in the hands of a few into the hands of the many (Fig. 8).

Fig. 7 The "Portal Gardens" artwork by the Japanese artist, Yasayuki Saegusa, is an interactive artwork that pays homage to a pioneer Butoh Dancer. By focusing the camera of the smart device, viewers are able to accompany the lantern into the heavens in an act of homage, sympathising with the loss of a great artist while acknowledging an art form that has caused much disruption in Japan

Fig. 8 The "Coming of a New Dimension" by the Swiss-American artist, Arthur Clay, is an example of an artwork in which the viewer becomes completely immersed in a 3D construct. Here, as witnesses to an invasion of earth from alien beings, who on seeing the large print on the sidewalk from above, felt invited to visit earth to impart a concept of living beyond time

Fig. 9 The "FahrBar ArtBar" was built by XYZ Cargo of Hamburg and had multiple functions during the iJacking Hannover project, which included acting as a mobile minibar, as a Wi-Fi station, and as a meeting point for those interested in the project and wanting to find out more about the artworks on exhibit. The FahrBar proved to be an essential item for running the tours and providing visitors with the needed physical contact point

The bootstrapped works became an integral part of the program and were placed in public space, introducing the artists to the process of how a work is placed according to its ability to blend the virtual with the real with the goal of bringing about a clear relationship between the artwork and the place at which it is viewed so that a dialogue between the placed work and those who view it results.

With this approach, the selection of artists became more inclusive and the use of the technologies was infused with virality that quickly spread to others. This allowed us not only to put powerful tools into the hands of others, but also to be able to witness how the gesture of doing so contributed to artists' development and how their participation echoed outward and helped in developing an audience for the project in general. The ramifications of the project became then clear to local artists, who as the primary actors of the local cultural environment were enabled to "voice" their opinions concerning issues at hand within their community and to do so to a larger public (Fig. 9).

5 Categories of Immersion

How effective an artwork is in making the connection to the place at which it is viewed and how well the dialogue can be comprehended depend largely on how the artist has used the diverse possibilities of what is available for creating the artwork.

Audio, for example, aids greatly in creating a feeling of immersion, which will have some effect on how long a visitor will stay engaged with an artwork. Also, whether the artwork uses moving or static images or whether it is passive or interactive can determine if the viewers are actually able to follow the artist's intentions. Moving images, interactivity, and participation allow for greater depths of communication and clearly weigh in on an artwork's quality and on its ability to communicate to the viewer. Both the quality of the artwork and the degree to which it "speaks" to its audience determine whether the artwork will be promoted by word of mouth and whether it gets picked up by the media, which in the long rung determine whether it will have an impact on society.

If the invisible arts could be divided into categories, they would be separated by those works which are passive or active in terms of interactivity and those that are immersive or not in terms of experience. Amongst the artworks in the iJacking Hannover, one could find extremely diverse uses and combinations of media. For example, interactive works that were part of the iJacking Hannover project included "Portal Gardens" by Yasayuki Saegusa, "Ich kann keine Kunst mehr sehen!" by Timm Ulrichs, "We AR Butterflies" by the author, Arthur Clay, and Ingo Lie's "Ecce Homo". A few examples from the same festival of passive works, or those that are not interactive, would be "Visitors" by the Swiss arts group "Studer/van den Berg", "This is not Clay" by Jake Hempson, "Ascensions of Cod" by Will Pappenheimer, and Virtuale Nature by Andrew Burrell (Fig. 10).

Fig. 10 Four of the many butterfly assets from the work "We AR Butterflies", which was produced during workshops with children in various countries around the world. The work was appropriately installed in front of the Hannover Opera at the site of the Memorial to the Murdered Jews of Hannover. The intervention using digital means is a unique way to re-engage existing monuments and to create a dialogue with the public

Many of the works involved moving images (animations) and very few of them were static. The "Crystal Coffin" by Lilly & Honglei is the only completely static work that was shown. However, it was extremely effective as a work, because it acted as a virtual prop for Selfies which were then shared in social media. Whether works involved interactivity or movement or not is less important than if they were immersive in their design. A few of the artworks that have a high level of immersion in the exhibition were "Ascensions of Cod" by Will Pappenheimer and "The Coming of a New Dimension" by the author, Arthur Clay (Fig. 11).

The experience of immersion by the viewer is one of the most powerful features of this type of artwork, because the viewer feels that they are viewing the work from within it, and because they are able to move through the work and watch it change with each step they take, they feel that they are actually part of that work itself. In my work "The Coming of a New Dimension", hybrid objects that look like a mix of aliens and machines fall from space while the viewer experiences the passing of time as the scenery changes from space-like to earth-like. In the work "The Ascension of Cod", a school of cod fish spiral around and slowly ascend into the heavens, and although the movement of the fish is colourful and brilliant, the work makes it obvious to the viewer that they are witnessing the coming extinction of this species.

Fig. 11 The "Ecce Homo" artwork created by Ingo Lie and Arthur Clay is a modern interpretation of a subject that has occupied artists for centuries. In the form of a 3D cross, the work explores and at the same time it raises a critical voice about the church dogma

6 Happiness Is the Way

Crowned by the press as the premier AR project in Germany, the iJacking project infused art into the urban space of Hannover city in a subtle and poetic manner, exploring the use of new and established technologies to occupy public and private spaces with art, doing so to nurture a dialogue about the role of art and institutions in regard to art in society. Although conceived, curated, and realised solely by the author, Arthur Clay and Virtuale Switzerland, the guerilla tactics used to propel the project forward won over important cultural partners in Hanover, who in turn made it possible that the project and the artworks being presented found their way into very professional circles, which were previously unavailable to those outside the sacred "gates" of the art establishment (Fig. 12).

For making what was invisible truly visible, much was dependent on those participating institutes. These included Kestner Gesellschaft, Städtische Galerie KUBUS, Kunsthalle Faust, Kunstverein Hanover, Sprengel Museum, and the diverse governmental department such as City Marketing. Together, they all made it possible for the general public to access the works by allowing QR codes that served as gates to artworks to be present in museum lobbies, integrated into monuments, placed on store windows, and plastered down on sidewalks.

Of course, after I was able to get certain partnerships on board, it became much easier for me to further integrate what the project had to offer into the standard cultural agenda. So for those interested, a series of guided tours were offered

Fig. 12 The artwork "Ascensions of Cod" by Will Pappenheimer depicts the disappearance of a species of cod fish once so plentiful that they were known as the hallmark of New England fisheries. In 2014, a scientific survey revealed that up to 80% of this species of cod have been either fished or suffered from the effects of warming oceans

throughout the duration of the exhibition. The tours entailed more than just guiding a group of persons around to view artworks: Each of the tours was accompanied by an arts professional, who was able to demonstrate how to use a mobile device to view the artworks, explain the artist's true intentions, and even entertain them with information on artists and the sights where the works were installed. All of this is accomplished underway, while the group makes its way through diverse points in the city. With the viewing of each of the works, the visitors experienced not only the place at which it was installed anew, but also how the work virtually augments the space.

The approach to taking a tour was to provide a viewing experience that was very diverse and included a wide range of artworks, representative of the possibilities that the technology had to offer. Through participation, the possibilities of invisible art became apparent as visitors experienced the variety of the works, i.e. those that were interactive and those that were not, those that used a variety of media such as sound and video, and those that were purely static.

Further, comparisons between artists native to the technologies and those who were bootstrapped offered the visitors the opportunity to see what was accomplished by local artists and what the leading works were by internationals. Artworks that were part of the bootstrapping program included works by renowned artists such as Regina Frank, Ingo Lie, Yasayuki Saegusa, and Timm Ulrichs. Two of the listed artists were local to Hannover while Regina Frank and Yasayuki Saegusa came from outside of the cultural climate of Hannover.

7 Drawing Conclusions

Any event that is implemented in a similar way as iJacking Hannover reflects the changing uses of public and private spaces that are the result of the advent of new communication technologies. Empowered with new tools, spaces can be occupied by the virtual and new voices which are able to ring out and create impact by the fact that although the occupation is purely virtual, it is made very real through public participation.

As mentioned, the project made invisible artworks accessible to general public and did so without the permission of those who reign over and administer those spaces, bringing artists notoriety through notorious but highly effective practices of marketing using digital tools. In this way, meta-protests concerning the environment in such works as "The Ascension of Cod" by Will Pappenheimer and "iLife in iLand" by Regina Frank were brought directly to a powerful faction of the society who are tech savvy and communicate over networks and do so beyond local boundaries by simply connecting the outside world with real-time experiences.

Many of the dialogues that were created through the placement of the artworks dealt with cultural identity and inheritance, which can be reconstructed through reimagining the past prompted by new perspectives embedded in the artworks. This process was experienced in such works as "Portal Garden" by Yasayuki Saegusa and "Ecce Homo" by Ingo Lie. In his work, Saegusa acknowledges a rather politically charged art form and crowns it as the most innovative dance movement of modern Japan by offering homage to it. Here, visitors can participate in the homage by guiding the lanterns in the project into the heavens. Ingo Lie's artwork, created in collaboration with the author, connects the traditions and reinterprets the biblical phrase "behold the man" in a provocative way at a place, where it can only provoke a dialogue about the church, its role in society, and the artist's power to critic both.

Political statements are made in several works. My work "We AR Butterflies" proposes a more harmonious society by reminding everyone who view the work that the future lies in what we choose to place emphasis on. Here, as countless butterflies mapped with the faces of children of diverse nations flock around the Memorial to the Murdered Jews of Hannover, the viewer combines the real and the virtual with the beautiful and the horrible. This combination raises questions in the mind of the viewer: How is it possible that such events actually take place and what consequences of such are for future generations if they should be allowed to happen?

The concept of ijacking space that was inspired by the ideas of the anon and as applied in the project iJacking Hannover clearly proves that art can and must go beyond providing beauty and awe, so that pertinent questions concerning society can be raised in public and made known to those who might bring about needed change. Clearly, through the digital transformation that is currently influencing all aspects of our society, many critical issues can now be raised and discussed more openly, with broad engagement, and with a high level of transparency. As suggested by the artists through the artworks that they presented in the iJacking project, it is crucial that dialogues take place before we are once again censored, subject to repression, and socially defeated, and the future arrives in a cascade of loss.

References

Clay, A. (2013). *Augmented reality and social reality meet*. http://www.virtuale-switzerland.org/?p=1130

Clay, A. (2015). *iJacking Hanover: Tour Guide*. Basel: Verein Virtuale Switzerland.

Beuys, J. (1992). *Kunst = Kapital*. Wangen/Allgäu: FIU-Verlag.

Heibach, F., Heibach, C., & Wenz, K. (2004). *The aesthetics of digital poetry*. Ostfildern-Ruit: Hatje Cantz Verlag.

Burroughs, W. (2001). *Die elektronische Revolution*. Bonn: Expanded Media Editions.

Brotschie, A. (1995). *A book of surrealist games*. Boston & London: Shambhala Redstone Editions.

Chomsky, N. (2012). *Occupy!*. Münster: UNRAST-Verlag.

Clay, A. Senior, T. (2015). *On science, on art on, society*. Aalborg, Denmark & Delft, Netherlands: River Publishers.

Coleman, G. (2014). *Hacker, Hoaxer, whistleblower, spy: The many faces of anonymous*. Online: Verso.

Critical Art Ensemble. (1997). *The electronic disturbance*. Cambridge, MA: Semiotext/MIT Press.

Critical Art Ensemble. (1998). *Electronic civil disobedience & other unpopular ideas*. New York: Autonomedia.
Ford, S. (2006). *Die Situationistische Internationale, Eine Gebrauchsanleitung*. Hamburg: Verlag Lutz Schulenburg.
Gell, A. (1998). *Art and agency, an anthropological theory*. Oxford: Clarendon Press.
Hass, P., & Holzinger, S. (2006). *Weizenbaum, Rebel at Work*. Berlin: Il Mare Film.
Hofmann, A. (1971). *Steal this book*. New York: Pirate Editions.
Kaczynski, T. J. (2008). *The unabomber manifesto: industrial society and its future*. Wingspan Classics.
Nezvanova, N. (2010). *Selected writings*. Online: Greyscale Press.
Sadler, S. (1998). *The situationist city*. Cambridge, Massachusetts & London: MIT Press.

Berlin, a Repurposed Ruin, and Constant Change as the Fixed Condition: A Photo-Comic

Pablo Arboleda and Pawel Jankiewicz

Abstract

Located at a former train depot, today ZK/U (Centre for Arts and Urbanistics) is progressively becoming a creative catalyst in Berlin. The goal of this chapter is to explore the processes by which derelict sites are repurposed as new cultural landmarks though minimal, DIY architectural interventions, retaining ruined materiality as an aesthetic value. To bridge the gap between scholarship and the arts, the authors opted for elaborating a photo-comic, and thus, methodology relied on fieldnotes, photos and interviews to grasp the motivations and commitments enabling life within ZK/U and the surrounding Moabit City Garden. Framed by architecture, urban studies, human geography and critical heritage, this chapter builds on ZK/U's collaborative and open-minded spirit.

P. Arboleda (✉)
School of Geographical and Earth Sciences, University of Glasgow, Glasgow, UK
e-mail: Pablo.Arboleda@glasgow.ac.uk

P. Jankiewicz
Independent Writer, Berlin, Germany
e-mail: pj44@wp.pl

E. Macrì et al. (eds.), *Cultural Commons and Urban Dynamics*,
https://doi.org/10.1007/978-3-030-54418-8_21

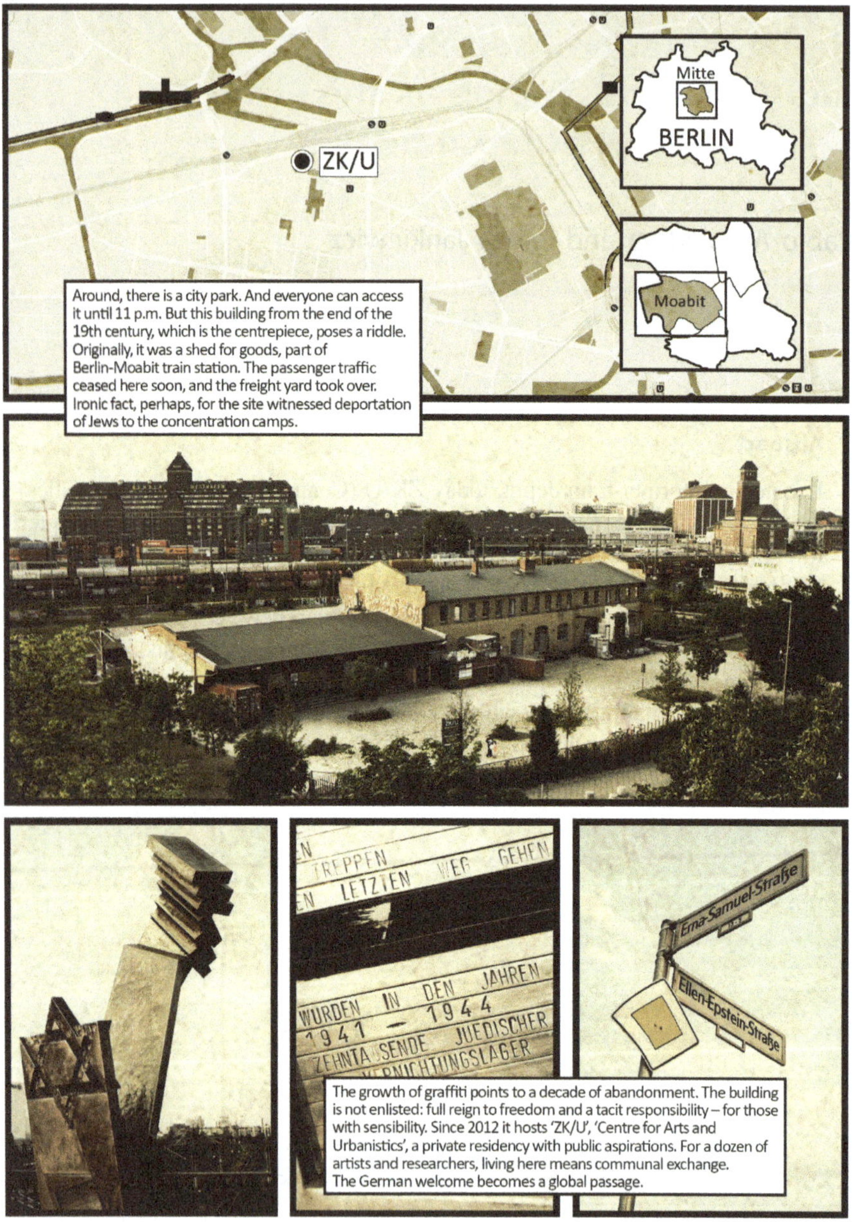
ZK/U
Mitte
BERLIN
Moabit
Around, there is a city park. And everyone can access it until 11 p.m. But this building from the end of the 19th century, which is the centrepiece, poses a riddle. Originally, it was a shed for goods, part of Berlin-Moabit train station. The passenger traffic ceased here soon, and the freight yard took over. Ironic fact, perhaps, for the site witnessed deportation of Jews to the concentration camps.
TREPPEN
LETZTEN WEG GEHEN
WURDEN IN DEN JAHREN
1941 — 1944
JUEDISCHER
Erna-Samuel-Straße
Ellen-Epstein-Straße
The growth of graffiti points to a decade of abandonment. The building is not enlisted: full reign to freedom and a tacit responsibility – for those with sensibility. Since 2012 it hosts 'ZK/U', 'Centre for Arts and Urbanistics', a private residency with public aspirations. For a dozen of artists and researchers, living here means communal exchange. The German welcome becomes a global passage.

ZK/U
Zentrum für Kunst und Urbanistik
ZK/U INFO
Willkommen!
Welcome!
WWW.ZKU-BERLIN.ORG//////
The opening of the Centre was a result of a 3-year process of reflection, community meetings and a public contest with 70 proposals on the table. KUNSTrePUBLIK, a registered association with a non-profit status, won – thanks to an economically feasible idea that respected the character of the place.
They bought the building for 1€. A substantial sum, since it presented a 'minus value', as states one of the founders, Matthias Einhoff. The renovation costed 1.2 million euro.
Plus: 1€ includes the park's caretaking: cleaning, watering, cutting the grass. And the land stays with the Municipality. It's a 40-year lease for 1,100€ a month. After that, if the district wants the building back, they are to pay its revalued cost. Once again, creation of value boils down to desire. Poor-but-sexy Berlin, where honey-traps turn money-traps too[1].

'I still have a luggage in Berlin', sang the great Marlene Dietrich. We might repurpose it: 'Berlin, the leftover capital'.
And further: what's left and what's capital here? The town is a mecca of DIY; of participative, minimal, re-appropriation projects. Beyond ZK/U, the traces of abandonment are also a strong card. Ruin aesthetics is no longer conceived as a stigma but as a purposeful cultural and identity value[2]. A sign of resistance to the neoliberal city or a selling point? Lo and behold: both[3].
There's the effect of scale: one tag is dirt, a hundred is Berlin. Tags, cracking paint, stickers. The Berlin walls are still claiming freedom and social inclusion, constantly rewriting the private and the public: 'WE were here'.

ZK/U has three main sources of income: residents, events and occasional funding from institutions. We were the residents.
As it happens, we met in the communal kitchen – that radiant scene of daily life, a pump for ZK/U's arteries. Art was visible, though we were both interested in the 'U' part of the thing. We took as a premise that the content of the notion 'ZK/U' was fluid, inhabited the ongoing projects. For us, the 'Urban' in question was that porous[4], shifting tissue which made our 'Centre'. And we both valued interdisciplinarity. An architect and a writer.
Who is who?
ZK/U's 10 house commands
Treat each other with respect
Any form of violence, vandalism and intolerance is prohibited. We cannot
sexism and intimidating behaviour towards each other.
Please tell us if something happens that makes you feel threatened in any
'(...) not a fixed set of ideas and principles (...) continuous formation', reads ZK/U's website. Ours was an attempt to use the residency program to investigate its formula.

Sometimes it's a forced choice, this opening for the 'continuous formation'. Ruination is not only a trait of the buildings.
Living among others poses a challenge. Yet the commonplace offers the answers. The range of options in ZK/U was admirable; sprouting from grassroot incentives, through dinner conversations, up to bike tours and curator visits. Here a methodology awaited. It allowed for on-site verification, 5 interviews conducted, 1,800 photos taken. A total of 8 months of in- and cohabitation. The path that leads from the fieldwork to the output was to be collaborative, we concluded, or wasn't to be at all.
And we found a form that could capture and communicate this flux of different speeds and intensities: photo-comic. *La Grieta* by Carlos Spottorno and Guillermo Abril gave us the hint.

Schultheiss
PILSENER
Zum Stammtisch
Like the earhquake-proof constructions, Moabit retains built-in cracks. It has no slick image to stick to. Identity politics didn't come with one-liner on 'what it is about'. Other cool-and-shabby districts can point at 'the thing'. Kreuzberg – graffiti; Friedrichshain – techno; Neukölln – startups. Moabit is just a hood. To be sure, it feels like a city.
DÖNER
KEBAP
Bar
0,99
Over half of Moabiters have a migration background. Many are descendants of Turkish workers arriving in the 1970s. Arabic cuisine flourishes too. But newcomers aren't inscribed into an overtly 'global' frame, akin to the clean-cut international style in architecture. It is Germanness that welcomes them – one from under the sign of the 'Kneipe', a pub where everyone asks for your name. Even the English speech picks here a local, kitschy warmth. The hip is held at bay. Still...
CAFE
LET'S RULE THE WORLD! BUT FIRST LET'S HAVE COFFEE!

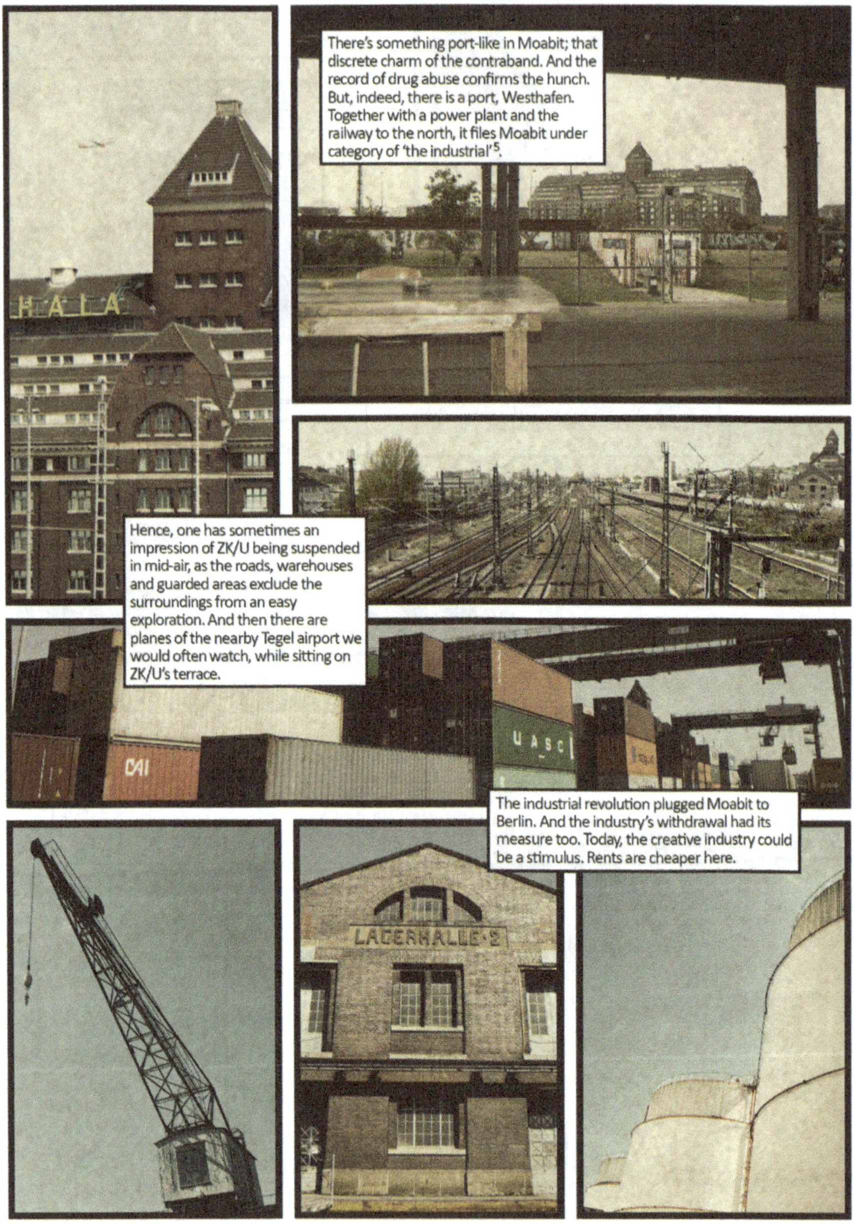
There's something port-like in Moabit; that discrete charm of the contraband. And the record of drug abuse confirms the hunch. But, indeed, there is a port, Westhafen. Together with a power plant and the railway to the north, it files Moabit under category of 'the industrial'[5].
Hence, one has sometimes an impression of ZK/U being suspended in mid-air, as the roads, warehouses and guarded areas exclude the surroundings from an easy exploration. And then there are planes of the nearby Tegel airport we would often watch, while sitting on ZK/U's terrace.
The industrial revolution plugged Moabit to Berlin. And the industry's withdrawal had its measure too. Today, the creative industry could be a stimulus. Rents are cheaper here.
LAGERHALLE 2

A trope of Arabic poetry, 'wuquf 'ala al-atlal' – or 'stopping by the ruins' – tells of a wandering Bedouin chancing upon an ancient rubble, becoming lost in a meditation that breaks the ruins' time-space pattern. Thus, cul-de-sac-led, ZK/U has an entrance that is also an exit, a problem which is its own solution. The park is receptive. Turkish grilling, hipster shining, motherly caring, elderly rolling. Intercultural, intergenerational. Inter-class.
Form follows function: 'a bank looks like a bank, neat and secured, because it wants you to think that your money is safe' – says Matthias. He is aware that ZK/U provides a different image. It's not a museum, but rather a site of 'desacralization' – of architecture, precisely, and of social relations. Yet, when the users' function comes first, a re-sacralisation occurs. The faithful become here the priests.

Ruins, admitting flows, tides of inside and outside, have their pulse. And this results in vitality[6].
The urban beehive project 'Moabees', located at ZK/U's front, and the community garden just across the path by the eastern wing of the building, are co-ventures: sharing the same philosophy, while keeping their own institutional standing, history of activity and online presence. They are examples of ruins' seductive power to host and coexist with new uses. Parasites? Not at all. Rather symbiotic relations. Completing by not completing. In ZK/U, there is no such a thing as a finalised space[7].
kontakt: buergergarten@stephankiez.de
Community garden next to ZK/U
organized by Bürste e.V.
If you have any questions, please ask to the gardeners.
Let's join us!
contact: buergergarten@stephankiez.de
Here's a formula for value production. And it's in the order of nothing less than materialization of a vision. Participative effort at the root / Pervaded by lightness: artistic invention and local affection[8].

SILO HOUSE
Self-built works of Jan Körbes concern resources and re-use. This questions the architecture that lends itself too easily to the profiteering scheme[9]. Still, he deems his approach 'not ecological, but logical'. His Silo House next to ZK/U's entrance is a mobile structure, a repurposed grain silo. A former resident, Ali Reza, found there his temporary and informal refuge. Ali benefits from ZK/U and ZK/U benefits from Silo, which became a local attraction. It has even postcards for the visitors.
Using blackboards found in a nearby school that shut down, Jan also built the so-called ZK/U's 'spaceship'. As if some percolating chalk-sketches, ideas of the spectators projected thereon can turn it into their lab. From podcast recordings to video installations, from a conference room to a reading-oasis – a true charmer.

Jan – the author also of the park's furniture, made of old tyres – starts his recycling with looking for a thing's potential, but in the end he retains visible the traces of its original function. DIY would not be a movement had it shielded its manual from view.
The shared insight of ZK/U dwellers and its satellites is that a new desire, stemming from the immanence of life, always arrives in a context. Exchangeability of parts is thus a prerequisite and an effect of a collective vigour[10]. And in ZK/U this finds concrete, material instances. Everyone can intervene on the building, after discussing with KUNSTreREPUBLIK. The bird-shaped decorations on the roof will be eventually removed. Just as that gypsy wagon has been, folded and taken further.

Ella Ponizovsky doesn't like referring to her work as street art. It has alternative connotations for her. What she's aiming at is rather art-in-the-street. And her calligraphies – intertwining Yiddish, German and Arabic – straddle that liquid border between migration and integration.
In April 2019 she painted both sides of ZK/U. Now, one is asking 'Where from?' and the other 'Where to?' Written with limepaint, the mural is intended to stay there for years, but eventually disappear. 'Leaving footprints, but not carrying a luggage' – as Ella says. Thereby, these in-and-outscriptions affirm the constant change that gives to this place its character.[11]
Not unlike a migrant, ZK/U is subject to regular, transient modifications according to punctual uses. Living here requires flexing and relaxing. And these swings in the park, made from old railway tracks, literally testify to this.

The experience of change can inspire a special relation to things. For an object preserves the lost time; fertilizes the now, giving it a meaningful foundation. Care for the original materiality is the very soul of the place. We asked where was it inscribed in ZK/U's dailiness, and presence of a new breed of architect quickly became palpable to us.
ZEPPELIN
hier mieten!
Gustavo Sanromán has a background in history studies. And as the janitor, or 'Hausmeister', he works by hands, touches and feels. This combination predestines him for the 'constant struggle against entropy' he declares, 'keeping it in reasonable levels'. Thus balancing the aesthetics of juxtaposition[12]. Twice per year the office people gather to throw stuff away. His is the sentimental relation to it. But this means curating its objecthood, retaining it ready-to-hand. And with reutilization, storage becomes a rationale.

Change breeds complaints. Noise, emotional strain due to attachment, dirt in the sink. ZK/U didn't establish strong physical boundaries between the residency, with its privacy, and the public. Indeed, sometimes people tend to use the residential part. The residents need to find a modus vivendi, to negotiate the borders. But in Art/Urbanistics permeability offers more positives than negatives[13].
Yet again, the building appears here as a blueprint of the apt savoir-faire. Take the terrace. Formally speaking, it belongs to ZK/U. It was decided, however, to split it in two halves by a shifting wall. The part with the studios is for residents, the other side has a public use calculated therein. Thus one can socialize with the visitors, or suggest them an alternative.

ZK/U
It's all about cooperation. ZK/U thrives on its audience, and so do the residents' portfolios. Moabit without the Centre would also be less itself.
Many public events, like the monthly flea-market, are held onsite and they are widely advertised in the neighbourhood. The incentive is found on the both sides of the gate. And it brings food stalls, crafts and music. And every two months, the door is open for people to visit the latest resident production. At times individual residents stage their own public events too.
The Main Hall is also a source of income. It is a space for ethical rent where not everything goes. The proposed activities cannot counter ZK/U's ideological profile. Community, diversity, integration, participation, culture and sustainability are welcome. Refrained is the opposite.

Every morning an archaeology of few empty bottles and butts appears without digging the ground. Youngsters chilled out in this corner the night before. Take it easy.
Gelaal Zaher is a son of a Palestinian refugee, and from his association 'Karame' ('dignity' in Arabic) coordinates this or that bunch of immigrant kids in Moabit. The neighbourhood gives him a sense of familiarity which now he extends to ZK/U. He finds here a spot to integrate kids in their activities, like graffiti.
– 'THANKS FOR THIS PLACE', says one of the tags.
DANKE
FUR
DIESE ORT
And VIP BOX, one of the Centre's experimental architectures, is where Karame grown-ups meet to play cards. Its accordion unfolding gives an instant feeling of being 'in'. For those who have found 'it'. The 'je ne sais quoi' of the social.

The place incites in people a mindful behaviour. In Matthias' assessment, ZK/U offers an informal control of the area, for the mere presence of grassroot caretakers prevents from anything-goes.
And Moabit is not a fairy tale. Low rates of education, poverty, unemployment. Drugs. Yet ZK/U is not merely a cultural spot – it conveys an inclusive dimension. Social coherence implies social peace. Of course that entropy is always around the corner. The plan? A progressive sense of communal belonging. ZK/U needs to show growth.
Vanishing of the public space is a stigmatizing factor, it reads 'losers'. In May 2019, an art collective organized a symbolic burial to mourn the very loss. Us no-longer-in-place were the coffin. The park by ZK/U received it – cemetery-like. People gave their speeches. Both a funeral service and a political demonstration.

Self-criticism concerns 'bridging'. The Arab community, however vital for the park, doesn't fully map onto ZK/U's cultural program. Not all the residents take part in the collective life either. And a satisfying formula of engaging them with the locality is still pending. Points taken.
An aporia is looming: isn't ZK/U the first step in gentrification? Matthias assumes this, one of his goals is to navigate the tension. But he doesn't give in to the blackmail of equating culture and exclusion, though resistance requires a broader political consensus. Sadly, not all the needs can be catered in here. Another point taken – the perfect is lacking.
In the meantime, KUNSTrePUBLIK is engaging in further projects across the city, like that of 'Haus der Statistik'. Also a ruin to be curated, though in Berlin's strict centre.

Thus far the uniqueness of ZK/U rested in its remarkable capacity to attract and integrate various cultural motivations. It was the very ruination that allowed for this. Unlike the majority of the new constructions, too slick to engage without bouncing off, the ruin's porous connectivity in only few years created a cultural landmark.
But future is always near these days. The building is scheduled for expansion. The visuals, copyright by 'Peter Grundmann Architekten', show a panoptic viewpoint: an open rooftop with trees. Matthias claims this won't be a revolution, but an evolution to enhance ZK/U's values. He deems the heterogeneity crucial for accommodating technicalities and to increase participation.
Gustavo, though regretting the loss of the original wooden ceiling, accepts the fate as a collective desire. So far, he's the only one who can access the roof. And sunsets over the port are breath-taking.

Paralleled by its disorderly aesthetics, exchange and experimentation go on in ZK/U. We saw how cultural entrepreneurs are instrumental in reimagining a building that would have possibly disappeared otherwise. Yet preservation takes multiple forms; and for once, public institutions are not in charge. But the 'public' is there, not necessarily at odds with the private. Ethics are the third term. Only with their wiring one can intuit, and cultivate, a ruin as an expansion of a conventional cultural space. Expansion of the urban. Expansion of heritage. A room for making a change.
easyJet
ZK/U
'A room for making a change' is a non-trivial way of understanding the 'constant change'. Whilst the identity of a place is forged through static, repetitive patterns, in ZK/U each element needs to give way, make room, allow. The repetition of non-repetition makes a charged paradox. Constant change is the fixed condition of a new kind of identity, and the repurposed ruin lends us a metaphor to think it. Orienting, though in a temporal 'dérive' – it is not unlike this vanishing point, seen from the leaving plane. Someone must be watching us from the terrace.

Acknowledgements We would like to thank all the people who participated in this research as interviewees: Matthias Einhoff, Ella Ponizovsky, Jan Körbers, Gelaal Zaher and Ali Reza. Our gratitude is extended to every single fellow resident and office worker at ZK/U, who made our stay truly interesting and enjoyable—and to the architecture studio 'Peter Grundmann Architekten' for granting permission to reproduce two of their images advancing the future of the building. We owe a great debt to Hayden Lorimer, Lazaros Karaliotas and Alfredo González-Ruibal for their insights. Shout out to the 'Distinct Inside' team, Ivana Dilova and Michael Hazell, for the common explorations of Moabit and the critical edge by our 'what's cool, what not' considerations. Last but not least, special thanks to the organizers of the conference 'Cutural Commons and Urban Dynamics: a new economic paradigm for a complex social map', held in October 2019 in Catanzaro Lido (Italy), where a first draft of this paper was presented.

Funding

This work has been possible due to the funding granted by the Urban Studies Foundation in the form of a Post-doctoral Research Fellowship awarded to Pablo Arboleda.

Reference Notes

Bille, M., & Sørensen, T. F. (2016). Architecture becoming new spaces. In M. Bille & T. F. Sørensen (Eds.), *Elements of architecture: Assembling archaeology, atmosphere and the performance of building spaces* (pp. 343–347). London: Routledge.

Cairns, S., & Jacobs, J. M. (2014). *Buildings must die: A perverse view of architecture.* Cambridge: MIT Press.

Cirugeda, S. (2014). Self-build as a strategy for participatory construction processes. Recetas Urbanas. *Architecture & Environment, 2*(2), 21–27. https://doi.org/10.12966/ae.05.02.2014.

Cresswell, T. (2011). Value, gleaning and the archive at Maxwell Street, Chicago. *Transactions of the Institute of British Geographers, 37*(1), 164–76. https://doi.org/10.1111/j.1475-5661.2011.00453.x.

Deslandes, A. (2013). Exemplary amateurism: Thoughts on DIY urbanism. *Cultural Studies Review, 19*(1), 216–227. https://doi.org/10.5130/csr.v19i1.2481.

Edensor, T. (2005). *Industrial ruins: Space, aesthetics and materiality.* Oxford: Berg Publishers.

Göbel, H. K. (2015). *The re-use of urban ruins: Atmospheric inquiries of the city.* London: Routledge.

Hausdorf, N., & Goller, A. (2015). *Superstructural Berlin: A superstructural tourist guide to Berlin for the visitor and the new resident.* Whichester: Zero Books.

Jenkins, L. (2002). Geography and architecture: 11, Rue du Conservatoire and the permeability of buildings. *Space and Culture, 5*(3), 222–236. https://doi.org/10.1177/1206331202005003003.

Nawratek, K. (2011). *City as a political idea.* Plymouth: University of Plymouth Press.

Nawratek, K. (2012). *Holes in the whole: Introduction to the urban revolutions.* Winchester: Zero Books.

Pyzik, A. (2014). *Poor but sexy: Culture clashes in Europe East and West.* Winchester: Zero Books.

Sandler, D. (2016). *Counterpreservation: Architectural decay in Berlin since 1989.* Ithaca: Cornell University Press.

The manufacturer's authorised representative in the EU is Springer Nature Customer Service Centre GmbH, Europaplatz 3, 69115 Heidelberg, Germany. If you have any concerns regarding our products, please contact ProductSafety@springernature.com

Printed and bound by CPI Group (UK) Ltd, Croydon, CR0 4YY
28/09/2026
02224090-0019